Neoliberalism and Culture in China and Hong Kong

This book examines the period leading up to the Hong Kong handover in 1997—the "countdown of time"—and by using iconic cultural symbols such as the countdown clock, the Hong Kong Museum exhibitions and cultural heritage sites, argues that China has undergone a transition to neoliberal state, in part through its reunification with Hong Kong.

The problem of synchronization with the world, a Chinese phrase that epitomizes China's engagement with modern capitalism since the first Opium War, was characterized throughout the 20th century as a "humiliation," "weakness," "tragedy" and "disaster," with China in the role of the victim of capitalist globalization. During the reunification with Hong Kong, these conventional expressions were replaced by new ones such as "de-humiliation," "return," "self-esteem" and "revival." Hai Ren gives an ethnographic and historical analysis of this cultural and political transformation of China's globalization experience by looking closely at public history practices in mainland China and Hong Kong and how the reconfiguration of everyday life and cultural norms led to the development of this neoliberal China.

As a book that straddles Chinese and Hong Kong, history, politics, cultural heritage and museum studies more generally, it can be regarded as a work of cultural political economy that will appeal to students and scholars of all of the above.

Hai Ren is Assistant Professor of East Asian Studies and Anthropology at the University of Arizona, USA.

Routledge Contemporary China Series

1 **Nationalism, Democracy and National Integration in China**
Leong Liew and Wang Shaoguang

2 **Hong Kong's Tortuous Democratization**
A comparative analysis
Ming Sing

3 **China's Business Reforms**
Institutional challenges in a globalised economy
Edited by Russell Smyth and Cherrie Zhu

4 **Challenges for China's Development**
An enterprise perspective
Edited by David H. Brown and Alasdair MacBean

5 **New Crime in China**
Public order and human rights
Ron Keith and Zhiqiu Lin

6 **Non-Governmental Organizations in Contemporary China**
Paving the way to civil society?
Qiusha Ma

7 **Globalization and the Chinese City**
Fulong Wu

8 **The Politics of China's Accession to the World Trade Organization**
The dragon goes global
Hui Feng

9 **Narrating China**
Jia Pingwa and his fictional world
Yiyan Wang

10 **Sex, Science and Morality in China**
Joanne McMillan

11 **Politics in China Since 1949**
Legitimizing authoritarian rule
Robert Weatherley

12 **International Human Resource Management in Chinese Multinationals**
Jie Shen and Vincent Edwards

13 **Unemployment in China**
Economy, human resources and labour markets
Edited by Grace Lee and Malcolm Warner

14 **China and Africa**
Engagement and compromise
Ian Taylor

15 **Gender and Education in China**
Gender discourses and women's schooling in the early twentieth century
Paul J. Bailey

16 **SARS**
Reception and interpretation in three Chinese cities
Edited by Deborah Davis and Helen Siu

17 **Human Security and the Chinese State**
Historical transformations and the modern quest for sovereignty
Robert E. Bedeski

18 **Gender and Work in Urban China**
Women workers of the unlucky generation
Liu Jieyu

19 **China's State Enterprise Reform**
From Marx to the market
John Hassard, Jackie Sheehan, Meixiang Zhou, Jane Terpstra-Tong and Jonathan Morris

20 **Cultural Heritage Management in China**
Preserving the cities of the Pearl River Delta
Edited by Hilary du Cros and Yok-shiu F. Lee

21 **Paying for Progress**
Public finance, human welfare and inequality in China
Edited by Vivienne Shue and Christine Wong

22 **China's Foreign Trade Policy**
The new constituencies
Edited by Ka Zeng

23 **Hong Kong, China**
Learning to belong to a nation
Gordon Mathews, Tai-lok Lui, and Eric Kit-wai Ma

24 **China Turns to Multilateralism**
Foreign policy and regional security
Edited by Guoguang Wu and Helen Lansdowne

25 **Tourism and Tibetan Culture in Transition**
A place called Shangrila
Åshild Kolås

26 **China's Emerging Cities**
The making of new urbanism
Edited by Fulong Wu

27 **China–US Relations Transformed**
Perceptions and strategic interactions
Edited by Suisheng Zhao

28 **The Chinese Party-State in the 21st Century**
Adaptation and the reinvention of legitimacy
Edited by André Laliberté and Marc Lanteigne

29 **Political Change in Macao**
Sonny Shiu-Hing Lo

30 **China's Energy Geopolitics**
The Shanghai Cooperation Organization and Central Asia
Thrassy N. Marketos

31 **Regime Legitimacy in Contemporary China**
Institutional change and stability
Edited by Thomas Heberer and Gunter Schubert

32 **U.S.–China Relations**
China policy on Capitol Hill
Tao Xie

33 **Chinese Kinship**
Contemporary anthropological perspectives
Edited by Susanne Brandtstädter and Gonçalo D. Santos

34 **Politics and Government in Hong Kong**
Crisis under Chinese sovereignty
Edited by Ming Sing

35 **Rethinking Chinese Popular Culture**
Cannibalizations of the canon
Edited by Carlos Rojas and Eileen Cheng-yin Chow

36 **Institutional Balancing in the Asia Pacific**
Economic interdependence and China's rise
Kai He

37 **Rent Seeking in China**
Edited by Tak-Wing Ngo and Yongping Wu

38 **China, Xinjiang and Central Asia**
History, transition and crossborder interaction into the 21st century
Edited by Colin Mackerras and Michael Clarke

39 **Intellectual Property Rights in China**
Politics of piracy, trade and protection
Gordon Cheung

40 **Developing China**
Land, politics and social conditions
George C.S. Lin

41 **State and Society Responses to Social Welfare Needs in China**
Serving the people
Edited by Jonathan Schwartz and Shawn Shieh

42 **Gay and Lesbian Subculture in Urban China**
Loretta Wing Wah Ho

43 **The Politics of Heritage Tourism in China**
A view from Lijiang
Xiaobo Su and Peggy Teo

44 **Suicide and Justice**
A Chinese perspective
Wu Fei

45 **Management Training and Development in China**
Educating managers in a globalized economy
Edited by Malcolm Warner and Keith Goodall

46 **Patron–Client Politics and Elections in Hong Kong**
Bruce Kam-kwan Kwong

47 **Chinese Family Business and the Equal Inheritance System**
Unravelling the myth
Victor Zheng

48 **Reconciling State, Market and Civil Society in China**
The long march towards prosperity
Paolo Urio

49 **Innovation in China**
The Chinese software industry
Shang-Ling Jui

50 **Mobility, Migration and the Chinese Scientific Research System**
Koen Jonkers

51 **Chinese Film Stars**
Edited by Mary Farquhar and Yingjin Zhang

52 **Chinese Male Homosexualities**
Memba, Tongzhi and Golden Boy
Travis S.K. Kong

53 **Industrialisation and Rural Livelihoods in China**
Agricultural processing in Sichuan
Susanne Lingohr-Wolf

54 **Law, Policy and Practice on China's Periphery**
Selective adaptation and institutional capacity
Pitman B. Potter

55 **China–Africa Development Relations**
Edited by Christopher M. Dent

56 **Neoliberalism and Culture in China and Hong Kong**
The countdown of time
Hai Ren

Neoliberalism and Culture in China and Hong Kong

The countdown of time

Hai Ren

Routledge
Taylor & Francis Group
LONDON AND NEW YORK

First published 2010
by Routledge
2 Park Square, Milton Park, Abingdon, Oxon OX14 4RN

Simultaneously published in the USA and Canada
by Routledge
270 Madison Avenue, New York, NY 10016

Routledge is an imprint of the Taylor & Francis Group, an informa business

Typeset in Times New Roman by
RefineCatch Limited, Bungay, Suffolk
Printed and bound in Great Britain by
CPI Antony Rowe, Chippenham, Wiltshire

British Library Cataloguing in Publication Data
A catalogue record for this book is available from the British Library

Library of Congress Cataloging in Publication Data
A catalog record for this book has been requested

ISBN: 978-0-415-58262-9 (hbk)
ISBN: 978-0-203-84493-9 (ebk)

Contents

List of figures and tables

Figures

Tables

Preface

This book analyzes the historical transformation of China from a socialist country to a neoliberal state during the process of its reunification with Hong Kong from the late 1970s to the late 1990s. Underpinning a whole spectrum of changes ranging from sovereignty and government to everyday experiences is the reconstitution of the Chinese nation state, not only through the Chinese government's resumption of sovereignty over Hong Kong, a territory lost in the nineteenth century, but also through a remaking of socialist (mainland) China to be *synchronic* with the contemporary capitalist world. *Synchronization* is the term the Chinese use to describe an ongoing process of making that country's economic system more compatible with global capitalist practices while maintaining a socialist government. In this book, I describe the same process as one of neoliberal globalization.

Globalization emerges as an important concept in this synchronization with the capitalist world. Instead of treating globalization as a homogenizing process of Westernization spreading relentlessly across the world since the 1970s, I examine globalization as a general process that interfaces with a variety of governmental organizations and institutions, communities, and individuals. More specifically, I argue that the emergence of neoliberalism as the predominant logic of the late twentieth century is closely tied to the systemic social, political, and cultural changes in this period. The international rise of neoliberalism was inseparable not only from internal conflicts between neoliberals and Keynesians within capitalist welfare states such as Britain and the United States, but also from external battles between capitalist and communist countries during the Cold War. In the Chinese context, as this book shows, neoliberalism is inseparable from problems of national reunification, rejection of Maoist socialist politics in the period from 1978 to 1989, changes to the constitutions of the Chinese Communist Party and of China, and modifications of citizens' behaviors.

I argue that unification with Hong Kong created a critical historical condition that enabled China to become a neoliberal state. Previous scholars have typically examined China's neoliberal process in relation to such aspects as the development of special economic zones, the proliferation of non-state-owned enterprises, and China's entry into the World Trade Organization. It has been investigated in terms of the rapidly increasing income gaps between the rich and the poor, and of new protests against globalization by workers in the Sunbelt and Rustbelt, by property owners, and by farmers who have lost their land across the country. These however are specific aspects of neoliberal practices and their consequences. What I offer in this book is a critical understanding of the dominant role Hong Kong's return played in China's neoliberalization, as shown by radical reconfigurations of the mainland's sovereignty, government, and everyday life. The successful negotiation of the 1984 Sino–British Joint Declaration that set in motion Hong Kong's return entailed a change of national sovereignty. This international agreement also dovetailed with the government's political decision in the period from 1978 to 1989 to completely reject Maoist socialism that attempted to realize the dream of communism. The Hong Kong countdown clock, erected in Tiananmen Square in 1994, synchronized these concrete political and social transformations by orchestrating a shift in the national mindset from feelings of national humiliation (deriving from China's first engagement with the world in the nineteenth century, which resulted in its loss of the Hong Kong and Macao territories) to pride in China's national revival and success (arising from its contemporary globalization experience). The problem of rewriting history was addressed through spectacle, media, and the transformation of cultural organizations into cultural enterprises. Eventually, the co-presence of Hong Kong and (mainland) China became equated with the coexistence of capitalism and socialism. In discussing these changes, my analysis of China's neoliberalization synthesizes the macro level of systemic and structural changes with the micro level of individual and everyday practices and experiences.

My purpose in this book is to extend critical inquiry into neoliberalism. Here, I would like to discuss how my use of the concept of neoliberalism relates to existing scholarship. Readers who are more interested in the historical process of China's transformation may skip this theoretical section and go to the next chapter. Currently, neoliberalism is commonly understood as a policy approach to globalization. One of the most frequently cited examples of neoliberalism is the "Washington Consensus," a list of concrete policies agreed among Washington-based international economic organizations such as the International Monetary Fund (IMF) and the World Bank. Its main elements include fiscal policy discipline, redirection of public spending, tax reform, market-determined interest rates, competitive exchange rates, trade liberalization, privatization of state enterprises, deregulation, legal security for property rights, and the financialization of capital.[1] Going beyond this narrow understanding, I argue that the Washington Consensus and the Chinese neoliberalism discussed in this book are just two examples of broader neoliberal manifestations, and so, I treat neoliberalism as a political theory of political economy with associated practices that became dominant in contemporary globalization.

Neoliberalism refers to the political philosophy of such theorists as Milton Friedman, Friedrich A. Hayek, and Robert Nozick. It is by no means a homogeneous philosophy. As Anna-Maria Blomgren points out, "It ranges over a wide expanse in regard to ethical foundations as well as to normative conclusions. At the one end of the line is 'anarcho-liberalism,' arguing for a complete *laissez-faire*, and the abolishment of all government. At the other end is 'classical liberalism,' demanding a government with functions exceeding those of the so-called night-watchman state."[2] Despite this heterogeneity, neoliberal philosophy is founded on the principal of placing individual freedom and private property rights above all else. In this book, you will read some of the ways this principle has become incorporated into Chinese neoliberalism. It is well known that writings of these philosophers have become very popular among Chinese neoliberals. Less well known are the direct contacts between Chinese leaders and neoliberal theorists like Friedman, who considers Hong Kong's model of neoliberal development as the freest in the world. This book's analysis of the historical event of Hong Kong's return to China sheds light on these connections in addition to providing an understanding of neoliberal practices in China and Hong Kong.

On being put into practice, neoliberalism takes various political economic forms. Existing scholarship addresses the political economy of neoliberalism by examining structural changes of capitalism and of the state. In *A Brief History of Neoliberalism*, one of the most influential such studies, David Harvey explains that neoliberalism is "a theory of political economic practices that proposes that human well-being can best be advanced by liberating individual entrepreneurial freedoms and skills within an institutional framework characterized by strong private property rights, free markets and free trades."[3] The state plays a critical role in the creation and preservation of an institutional framework appropriate to neoliberal practices.[4] This in-depth study of China's neoliberal transformation extends Harvey's important work by showing that China's neoliberal practices are inseparable from Cold War politics as well as recent globalization experiences around the world.

Other scholars examine neoliberalism as a set of governmental technologies. In their "Introduction" to *Privatizing China*, Aihwa Ong and Li Zhang advocate analyzing neoliberalism as "a mobile set of calculative practices that articulate diverse political environments in a contingent manner."[5] Accordingly, "Any political regime can adopt a neoliberal technology of governing and self-governing without changing its entire state apparatus or character."[6] This important conception helps to explain the coexistence of antagonist practices such as those between neoliberal practices and "illiberal forms of industrial and state controls."[7] Nevertheless, other critical questions are yet to be answered. For example, how do we define "calculation?" Is it related to economic rationalism as well as social norms, rules and laws? If some individuals in a state like China become self-governing neoliberal subjects while others do not, how do we draw the lines between neoliberal and "illiberal" practices? How is the generic state category of "the people" reconfigured in neoliberal practices? How do the state and its ruling party or parties reconstitute their relations to the people they claim to represent? This book addresses some of these questions.

My exploration of the relationship between neoliberalism and sovereignty contributes to the debate about the constitutional relationship between the state and its people, an important issue underdeveloped in the scholarship on neoliberalism. Building on Ong's work,[8] I propose to use the concept of neoliberal sovereignty to refer to the transference of the supreme power of the sovereign (or part of it) to the economic individual. My survey of the scholarship has recognized certain evolving intersections between modern economic and political theories. One of them is the emergence of what I call the neoliberal state, in which the figure of the political sovereign (the sovereign in the conventional sense) is displaced by the figure of the economic sovereign, which is derived from the figure of the "economic man" (*homo economicus*). That is, it is in the neoliberal state where the economic individual takes on the role of the sovereign. Consequently, the rule of exception applies in the economic realm, which increasingly overrides the relevance of other realms of human lives. This is a neoliberal human condition.

To understand the evolving neoliberal politics of the state, it is necessary to pay attention to the operations of the sovereign power to decide what elements and parts might be counted as one within the state.[9] Alain Badiou makes a distinction between the state as a situation in which elements are grouped into parts (or sets) and the state as the meta-structure of that situation.[10] This distinction enables us to consider a special characteristic of the state. The state functions as the government that rules a country through juridical means. Simultaneously, it also operates as something above or beyond the government, in that the state's meta-structure enables state sovereignty through the legal constitutional framework of the nation state.[11] As Giorgio Agamben points out, a sovereign state becomes possible only when the state establishes legal rules and norms while paradoxically placing itself outside them as an exception.[12] Since the state is tied to the category of the people, how does the state vest its sovereignty in a strategic relation to its people?

Philosophers of state sovereignty tend to treat the people either as the collective body (i.e. the people) or the individual body (i.e. the citizen). Historically, there are two major lines of modern thought on sovereignty. One asserts that sovereignty is vested directly in the sovereign by divine or natural right, while the other maintains that it is vested in the people. In the latter case, there is a further division. For Thomas Hobbes and his followers, the people transfer their sovereignty to the sovereign. By comparison, for Jean Bodin and Jean-Jacques Rousseau and their followers, the people retain their sovereignty. In his 1576 *Six Books of the Republic*, Jean Bodin argues that natural law and divine law confer upon the sovereign the right to rule. And, the sovereign is not above divine law or natural law; he is above (i.e. not bound by) only positive law—laws formally made by humans. That is, the sovereign is bound by ethics, not by human-made laws. The sovereign's legitimate power to disregard human-made laws is commonly understood as the sovereign's supreme quality. For Carl Schmitt, the formal qualities of the modern state (legal normativeness, rational regularity and evenness, and objective and technical refinements) are less important to sovereignty than its human quality of making decisions. Thus, Schmitt declares: "sovereign is he who decides on the exceptional case."[13]

Democracy is a strategic expression of the relationship between sovereignty and the people. In a representative democracy, which permits a transfer of the exercise of sovereignty from the people to the parliament (or the congress), the parliament (not the executive power) is, ultimately, the source of sovereignty. By comparison, the republican form of government acknowledges that the sovereign power is founded in the people, individually, rather than in the whole body of free citizens, as in a democratic form. Thus, no majority can deprive a minority of their exercises of sovereignty. These two forms of government are ideal. In practice, they are often mixed to fit in an appropriate national context. This is true in many Western countries such as those in Europe and North America. If sovereignty is perpetually vested somewhere between the collective body of the people and the individual body of the citizen, the supreme power of sovereignty—that is, its absolute privilege of disregarding and even violating the human-made laws—is also located somewhere between these two bodies.

It is in the context of the development of neoliberal political and economical practices through the globalization since the 1970s that I speak of the neoliberal state and neoliberal sovereignty as well as neoliberal manifestations of the sovereignty–people relationship. For neoliberal political theorists such as Friedman and Hayek, the kind of social life associated with the spontaneous order or governed by natural law is treated as supreme, above the kind of social life that is regulated by positive law, or human-made laws. The former is supreme as far as it enables the individual's freedom to choose and it secures individual liberty and well-being. In light of the above relationship between sovereignty and the people, neoliberal theorists vest sovereignty in the individual whose life is governed by natural law. This individual becomes sovereign when he or she exercises his or her freedom to choose by following natural law or being ethical on the one hand and by disregarding positive law on the other hand. Moreover, this sovereign individual further becomes neoliberal under the condition that the natural law and its derived ethics, which constrain the sovereign individual, are expressed in the form of the market. Thus, Friedman believes that economic freedom is the precondition of political freedom.[14] Gary Becker, another important economist and theorist, argues that transgression of laws and norms in the form of delinquency is an important characteristic of the sovereign neoliberal individual. Through economic rationalism and its mundane practices in everyday life, the neoliberal individual exercises his sovereign power by rejecting the normal functions of laws in order to secure his liberty. For example, a driver may disregard parking rules by parking in a red zone reserved by a fire truck if he calculates that the benefits of legal transgression exceed the fines of a parking violation.[15] This situation applies to other acts of law- or rule-transgression such as drug trafficking, human-smuggling, international migration, corruption, and financial market manipulation. While calculation follows economic rationalism, transgression exercises the sovereign power of individual liberty. According to this line of neoliberal reasoning, the real problem in the neoliberal practice of everyday life is not whether the neoliberal individual conducts the act of transgressing rules or laws; rather, it is whether the neoliberal individual has the capacity to do so in pursuit of individual liberty and well-being.

The issue of capacity in the individual's life-building process is about making appropriate choices. For influential behavior economists such as Richard H. Thaler, Cass R. Sunstein, and Dan Ariely,[16] no human fits in the ideal model of the "economic man." Instead, she or he is an ordinary human being who has flaws, behaves in irrational ways, and is always inclined to follow her or his inertias. Consequently, she or he often makes bad choices in life or does not have an adequate capacity to make good choices. Based on this line of reasoning, behavior economists argue that government can formulate policies, which include mobilizing private means, to design and create various kinds of strategies and apparatuses to shape subject formation toward improving the capacity of making better choices. Thus, the state does play an important role in the creation and improvement of an institutional framework appropriate to the practice of neoliberalism in everyday life. For example, as soon as Barack Obama replaced George W. Bush as the president of the United States in 2009, his administration employed the above-mentioned behavior economists as architects to design new government policies to shape subject formation of American citizens, especially their ways of managing personal finances, a major problem of the economic crisis.[17]

In this book, as I show, the ways in which the Chinese government deployed culture (broadly defined to include history, aesthetics, and everyday life) as an important means to address public feelings of pride, patriotism, and nationalism during the countdown to Hong Kong's return aimed at shaping Chinese citizens to develop and improve their capacities of making right choices, becoming neoliberal sovereign individuals.[18] One important characteristic of Chinese neoliberalism, which derives from Deng Xiaoping's "one country, two systems" framework, is its valuation of patriotism. In the context of discussing who might be appropriate future Hong Kong leaders, for example, Deng states that the Chinese government requires them to be "patriotic" (i.e. "to love the Motherland and Hong Kong").[19] They may "believe in capitalism, feudalism, or even the slavery system;" that is, they don't need to "agree with China's socialist system."[20] To reframe Deng's argument in terms of the neoliberal philosophy, development-oriented patriotism functions more like a nature law or an ethic that constrains the sovereign; by contrast, socialism, capitalism, feudalism, or the slavery system is merely artificial and thus does not constrain the sovereign.

Therefore, I argue that Chinese neoliberalism is a strategic experimentation of the political philosophy regarding the neoliberal state, neoliberal sovereignty, and neoliberal citizenship. China's neoliberal transformation in the context of globalization since the 1970s shows four major characteristics of neoliberalism.[21] First, in theory it extends economic rationality to all aspects of human life, and thus, is in practice a constructivist project. Second, the transition to a neoliberal state (in both theory and practice) requires political intervention and orchestration by the state. Simultaneously, the state itself becomes an enterprise organized by market rationality, and its legitimacy is dependent on the health and growth of the economy. Third, citizenship takes the moral form of an entrepreneurial subject: neoliberalism measures every citizen's conduct as economic behavior. The neoliberal citizen calculates rather than obeys rules. Moreover, the success of an individual's life is judged by "making it on one's own" and taking responsibility for one's own life, in contrast to the concept of a government safety net to catch the disadvantaged. Fourth, governmental and social policies are formulated according to these criteria.

Acknowledgements

My research on the book would not be possible without the generous support of many institutions and individuals. My field trips to Hong Kong and (mainland) China from 1995 to 2007 were funded by the China Times Cultural Foundation, the Washington State China Relations Council, the Wenner-Gren Foundation for Anthropological Research, a faculty development grant from Bowling Green State University, a visiting scholar fellowship from the Institute for Collaborative Research and Public Humanities at the Ohio State University, and an international travel grant from the University of Arizona. In Hong Kong, the Centre of Asian Studies at the University of Hong Kong and the Universities Service Centre at the Chinese University of Hong Kong sponsored my trips to Hong Kong. Supports from the Institute for the Study of Culture and Society at Bowling Green State University, the Institute for Collaborative Research and Public Humanities at the Ohio State University, and the College of Humanities at the University of Arizona made possible to relieve me from teaching responsibilities to complete and revise the book manuscript. I am grateful to these institutions for their generous support.

Over the years, I have had many conversations with the audiences of my lectures and seminars in Hong Kong, the United States, and Europe, which have greatly enriched the development of this project. I would like to thank the following institutions for those opportunities: the University of Hong Kong, the Chinese University of Hong Kong, the University of California at Berkeley, the Ohio State University, the University of Michigan, Bowling Green State University, the University of Oregon, Harvard University, the University of Washington, the University of Wisconsin, Leiden University, the University of Pittsburgh, and the University of Arizona.

It would be impossible to name all those who have helped me in the research and writing of this book. Elizabeth Sinn, S. L. Wong, Coonoor Kripalani, Jean Hung, and Michelle H. W. Fong offered assistance when I first began my research in Hong Kong. Both Rubie Watson and Woody Watson offered helpful advices on my research in Hong Kong. Kristi Heim, Lisa Hoffman, Bill Driscoll, and Siu-woo Cheung made me feel at home during my trips to Hong Kong. Chris Zacher, Rick Livingston, Xiaomei Chen, and Kirk Denton at the Ohio State University offered their insightful suggestions. Xin Liu, Andrew Jones, and Aihwa Ong at UC Berkeley kindly provided their ideas. Lydia Liu and Li Tuo shared critical and constructive suggestions for improving the first draft. I acknowledge the encouragement and support of my former colleagues at Bowling Green State University: Vicki Patraka, Don McQuarrie, Rob Buffington, Joe Austin, Ellen Berry, Jack Santino, Susana Peña, Marilyn F. Motz, Jeremy Wallach, Jeff Brown, and Bernice Aguilar. At various stages, I benefited greatly from conversations and discussions with Ann Anagnost, Stevan Harrell, Li Zhang, Ralph Litzinger, Lisa Hoffman, Yongming Zhou, Yue Dong, Hairong Yan, Pun Ngai, Tze-lan Sang, David Brent, Lorri Hagman, Kristi Heim, Haiyan Lee, Andrea Arai, Hillel Schwartz, Davin Heckman, Jesook Song, Gabi Lukacs, Fabio Lanza, Eithne Luibhéid, Elizabeth Kennedy, Spike Peterson, Susan Shaw, Adam Geary, Miranda Joseph, Laura Briggs, Laura Gutierrez, Sandy Soto, Sallie Marston, Brian Silverstein, Steve Lansing, Ted Park, Jane Hill, Helen Siu, Ming K. Chan, and Stephen Chan. I would like to thank my editor, Stephanie Rogers, for her enthusiasm and helpful guidance. Thanks to Leanne Hinves for editorial assistance and good work. My appreciation to the anonymous readers who offered constructive and thoughtful suggestions. I am grateful to Eithne Luibhéid, who not only shared comments and suggestions to improve the work almost at every stage but also provided enduring intellectual encouragement and inspiration. I dedicate this book to her.

Introduction

The role of reunification with Hong Kong in the neoliberalization of the Chinese state

The deep symbolic meaning for the Chinese government of the July 1, 1997, reunification of Hong Kong with the People's Republic of China, is clearly illustrated through a comparison of two cultural representations of historical artifacts, one an exhibition in a shopping mall, the other contained in an internationally released film. Both address the Treaty of Nanjing, the 1842 agreement between China and Great Britain that ended the first Opium War (1840–1842) and ceded Hong Kong to Britain. On September 2, 1997, I visited "The Treaty of Nanjing," an exhibition inside Plaza Hollywood, a new shopping mall in Hong Kong's Kowloon District. The exhibition, organized by two youth organizations (one in Hong Kong and the other in Nanjing), lasted a week (from August 29 to September 3) and contained about one hundred illustrations and artifacts portraying the main events associated with the treaty, including British military invasion, signing of the treaty, national catastrophes, resistance to foreign aggression, and development of China. The stated aim of the exhibition was to educate Hong Kong's youth to "keep national humiliation in mind, [and] develop China vigorously (*wuwang guochi, zhenxing zhonghua*)" (both English and Chinese text original). Although the mall was bustling, very few people looked at the exhibit, and those who did seemed to scan it quickly, as if it were a commercial advertisement. On the one hand, an exhibition inside a shopping center (rather than a museum or a government institution) seemed out of place; on the other hand, the very presence of a patriotic exhibition from Nanjing in post-1997 Hong Kong was an event more significant than the reception of its content.[1]

In contrast with this shopping mall exhibition, the 1997 film *The Opium War* (*yapian zhanzheng*, directed by Xie Jin) used a series of artifacts to great effect in portraying the British case for declaring war. This fictionalized scene represents how major British opium traders such as Lancelot Dent and William Jardine—driven by self-interest and determined to gain reparation for goods confiscated and burned by Lin Zexu, the commissioner of Emperor Daoguang—influenced the British government. In the following scene, the invented character of a British businessman named only Danton, who has just returned from southern China, addresses the British Parliament to make the case for war against China and the ease of defeating the current, decadent emperor, playing off the dual meaning of *china* as porcelain and the country's name:[2]

> Mr. Speaker, Honoured Gentlemen, I come before you to present the plight of a group of defenseless British subjects blockaded in an attempt to starve them into submission. Made to surrender their property in trade which was then destroyed, who were then driven from their quarters in Guangzhou to be confined aboard our ship without food, without water, without medicine. There to float under the pestilent heat of the sun [dramatic pause]. Before I set out on my journey to England, I was obligated to take even my daughter who, being sick, was unable to travel with me. I may never see her alive again. And yet our glorious Union Jack still flaps high on our mast.

After establishing his grievance, not without a touch of personal self-interest, and noting some members in the chamber nodding their heads in agreement, Danton proceeded to play the dual role of gift giver and interpreter: "Gentlemen, your countrymen and your sovereign have been grievously wronged. They look to you for reparation. To that end, your representative living in China, Captain Charles Elliot, gave me letters, which I have delivered to the Prime Minister. There are also gifts to be delivered to the house." Two men then enter the chamber carrying a heavy chest, which they place in front of the Speaker. Danton removes the first artifact from it and continues:

> This is a piece of Chinese bronzeware made over 2,000 years ago. This is adorned with figures of sacred spirits, representing their highest ideals [pointing out the figures]. Bronze was the strongest metal then known to the world. [Danton taps the vessel with a stick, producing a magnificent sound that resonates with the positive responses of the audience.] Ever since that time the Chinese have called themselves the Hans.

Danton then takes out the second artifact, a jade vase with two rings hanging just below its neck. He raises the rings with his hands and gently releases them, producing a crisp ping that again greatly impresses his audience. Observing their responses, Danton continues, "This vase is carved from a single piece of jade. It dates from the Tang Dynasty, the golden age of China. Not only was this the most prosperous period in the history of China, the Tang was also the most civilized and cultured people in the world."

Finally, Danton takes out the third artifact, a yellow-colored royal porcelain vase with engraved decorations, which many members of Parliament visibly admire. Placing it between the first two artifacts, he makes his point clear:[3]

> This is a work of art from the China of the day. Like the great Qing Dynasty it represents, it appears sumptuously rich, plump and proud; it looks down on all around it, including the bronze and the jade. And yet it is filled with nothing but self-importance. One touch and it will shatter into pieces. [Danton knocks it to the ground, and it smashes. Noticing the shocked responses of the representatives, Danton points down to the shards.] This is the China I offer you.

Both this cinematic scene and the exhibition at a Hong Kong shopping center are situated within historical contexts. The film uses a display of important artifacts to personify the political decision to declare war against China, whereas the exhibition reminds Hong Kong residents of an unequal treaty that precipitated what the Chinese interpret as a national tragedy: the loss of Hong Kong. *The Opium War* is the first contemporary film produced by a major Chinese director to intentionally follow Hollywood's blockbuster film model exemplified by Steven Spielberg's films. It was privately financed by the company formed by Xie Jin, the film's director. In contrast, the shopping mall exhibition was a government effort to instill its version of patriotic education within the context of everyday life in post-1997 Hong Kong.

In China, the term commonly used to describe the ongoing process of making its economic system more compatible with global capitalist practices while maintaining a "socialist" government is "synchronization" (*yu shijie jiegui*).[4] While the film raises the issue of China's synchronization with the world, the exhibition is an example of its actual practice. In other words, Xie sought to raise the question of how the Chinese might engage in the global expansion of capitalism. According to Guo Weicheng (a writer who documented the making of *The Opium War* and journalist with the *People's Daily*, an official Chinese government newspaper), nineteenth-century British capitalism was so expansive that it operated on a global scale, not merely in terms of its production, which extracted resources from all over the world, but also in terms of its consumption. The Chinese worldview lagged so far behind the rest of the world that this imperial state at the time was not even aware of Britain's claim that the nineteenth century belonged to it, and thus was not prepared to respond to British colonial expansion. The tragedy of the Opium War—China's loss not only of the war but also of sovereignty over part of its territory—must be viewed in the context of the lessons it learned about synchronization. If the first Opium War marked the first serious engagement between China and global capitalism, the country's reforms since the late 1970s mark the second engagement, and the lessons learned in the 1840s are still pertinent. Guo writes, "All of a sudden, we realize that we still face the same question raised in the Opium War one hundred and fifty years ago: How do we confront constant changes outside our country and engage with foreign civilizations?" His answer: "If we still do not have a civilization *synchronic with* [*bingjia qiqu*] Western civilization, we cannot stand up in this world" (my emphasis).[5]

In Guo's view, in the times of "sinkage" (*chenlun*) and "humiliation" (*chiru*), that is, the entire modern era of China (1840–1978), the country was not synchronized with the capitalist world. By contrast, in the new era of "reforms and opening" (*gaige kaifang*), a time of "awakening" (*juexing*) and "revitalization" (*zhenxing*), the country has consciously become synchronic with the capitalist world. The patriotic exhibition in a Hong Kong shopping mall is just one of many attempts at synchronization.

In this book, I describe what Guo calls China's synchronization with the world as an economic and sociocultural neoliberalization of the Chinese nation state that has occurred since it began taking steps toward active participation in global capitalism in the 1970s, a process conditioned by the pivotal historical event of reunifying *socialist* China with *capitalist* Hong Kong. Outside China the Chinese government's resumption of sovereignty over Hong Kong has commonly been characterized from the British perspective as the "Hong Kong handover." In contrast, mainland Chinese and Hong Kong residents call it "Hong Kong's return" (*Xianggang huigui*), which encompasses a whole spectrum of changes from sovereignty and government to everyday experiences. What underpins all the changes is the reconstitution of the Chinese nation state, not simply in the Chinese government's resumption of sovereignty over a territory lost in the nineteenth century, but more important, in a remaking of Chinese civilization to be synchronic with contemporary Western civilization.

China's neoliberal transformation has occurred largely through establishing a relationship between "reforms and opening" and national reunification, two seemingly parallel historical agendas of the socialist state since the late 1970s.[6] The former basically entails various national development projects addressing the "modernization" (*xiandaihua*) of four major areas: economy, culture, technology, and administration. The reunification issue revolves around the status of Taiwan, Hong Kong, and Macau. The Chinese government's reforms and opening project has allowed the development of new kinds of productive enterprises that are not state controlled and collectively owned. This policy change contradicts both the policies of Mao Zedong's socialist government, which had eliminated all forms of private ownership and their associated productive relations, and the constitution of the Chinese Communist Party (CCP), the ruling party of China founded on commitment to the causes and interests of the working class. To resolve these two contradictions, Deng Xiaoping's government first made a political decision to declare the Cultural Revolution (1966–1976), a complete failure that caused chaos in the Chinese state, thereby opening up possibilities for rejecting Maoist practices (including the prohibition of private ownership). Building on this decision, Deng and his successors gradually modified the Communist Party constitution and incorporated key changes as amendments to the national constitution, as I describe later.

The reincorporation of capitalist Hong Kong into socialist China has, I argue, done what no other contemporary event could have done: It provided both the historical precondition for and the primary process of China's radical neoliberal transformation.[7] Under British rule, Hong Kong was recognized not simply as a capitalist economy, but as one of the freest market economies in the world.[8] The Sino–British Joint Declaration of 1984 that set out the conditions for Hong Kong's return to China called for Hong Kong to retain its capitalist system and a measure of political autonomy for a period of fifty years, a provision commonly referred to as "one country, two systems" (*yiguo, liangzhi*) and viewed by the Chinese as a potentially long-term arrangement. This framework was first proposed by Deng Xiaoping during the Sino–British negotiation process (for details, see Chapter 1). It was extended to create various types of special economic and political zones, enabling the practical coexistence between socialist and capitalist spaces. Thus, the legal framework of "one country, two systems," upon being translated into political and economic practices in China, shaped the transformation of the Chinese state into a neoliberal state. By casting reunification as an issue of national sovereignty that was not open to compromise, the Chinese government made this a default justification for all political, economic, social, and cultural changes. That is, reunification with Hong Kong demanded the supreme power of sovereignty to act ethically by not abiding by existing (Maoist) socialist norms and laws. Thus, anything incompatible with regaining sovereignty over Hong Kong was to be modified, changed, or rejected—including Maoist practices of mobilizing and empowering ordinary people, political representation of the working class, socialist productive relations, economic policies, and nationalism.

China's neoliberal transformation witnessed a shift in the way in which the supreme power of sovereignty constructed the relationship between the state and the people. In Maoist China, the sovereign power was founded on the collective body of the people (deemed the working class and excluding other classes such as the capitalists). In the neoliberal transformation, the sovereignty of the people gradually shifted to the individual body of the citizen. This transference of sovereignty can be seen in the realm of cultural transformation during Hong Kong's return. The December 19, 1994, installation in Tiananmen Square of a giant clock counting down to the reunification date provided a unique public relations tool around which to coordinate economic reforms and frame collective and individual nationalistic expressions about the recovery of a lost object (Hong Kong). Spectacles of the countdown, as staged in museums, the mass media, theme parks, and historical sites, expressed themes of regaining face after humiliation, the joy of a mother (the PRC) reuniting with a long-lost child (Hong Kong), and the pleasure of seeking revenge at a site of national humiliation. Ultimately, Hong Kong's return became a dual problem of the state (the legitimate neoliberal transformation) and government (the normalization of entrepreneurial citizenship keyed to specific times in the countdown).

According to a common belief expressed by Guo Weicheng, the imperial Chinese state lost the Opium War because the Qing government was not prepared for it and responded passively to the initial wave of global capitalism. This defeat and the signing of the Treaty of Nanjing fundamentally shaped the modern Chinese historical experience. Hong Kong's return presents an opportunity to learn a lesson from the past and take advantage of the global expansion of capitalism. In its successful, voluntary, and affirmative synchronization with the West, the Chinese government has pursued a series of strategies, one of the most significant being the Sino–British Joint Declaration. China's neoliberalization has taken place without the external pressures of the Washington Consensus (unlike in Latin America and Eastern Europe),[9] without the invasion of foreign military forces (unlike in many countries in the Middle East and Africa), and best of all, without China renouncing its commitment to "socialism with Chinese characteristics." Prior to discussing the ways in which this process manifests a Chinese experience of neoliberalism, I would like to place it within the global context of neoliberal political and economic practices. In contrast to the majority of scholars of neoliberalism, who essentially place China outside the global neoliberal process, I argue that China has played an important and active role in shaping the global process.

Neoliberalism and globalization

Neoliberalism emerged first in Western Europe and North America after World War I, and its influence gradually expanded in the Cold War period. Not until the 1970s did neoliberalism begin to assume a dominant role in the global expansion of capitalism. However, the expansion of neoliberal politics to the whole world was not possible until influential communist countries retreated from their socialist policies. This began with China's rejection of Maoist practices in the late 1970s and was furthered by the collapse of state socialism as an alternative to capitalism in 1989–1990. In this historical context, I use the phrase "neoliberal globalization" to describe a global process that imposed neoliberalism as a fundamental legitimizing principle in developing, shaping, and reconstructing nation states, including Western capitalist states such as the United States and Britain; former communist countries in Eastern Europe; and developing countries like China, Mexico, and Chile.

Before the age of neoliberal globalization, neoliberalism was indeed a Western phenomenon. As a set of economic policies opposed to the interventionism of the welfare state, neoliberalism encompassed three major schools. The first one, the Freiburg or Ordo–Liberal School, was formed at the University of Freiburg in Germany in the 1930s and played an important role in shaping the principles of economic policy in West Germany in the late 1940s and the 1950s.[10] Its primary concern was the constitutional foundations of a free economy and society. The second school was developed by the economist and political philosopher Friedrich August von Hayek. His 1944 publication *The Road to Serfdom* was a key text of neoliberalism, and his establishment of the Society of Mont-Pèlerin in 1947 organized a group of scholars (including George Joseph Stigler, Milton Friedman, Michael Polanyi, and Karl Popper) to combat Keynesianism—an economic theory named after the British economist John Maynard Keynes, which promotes a mixed economy in which both the state and the private sector play important roles—and the social solidarity that prevailed after World War II, and to prepare the theoretical foundations for a new kind of capitalist order liberated from any regulation.[11] Finally, the Monetarist School, led by Milton Friedman, was formed in the United States in the 1950s to reject macro-measurements and macro-models of the economy (that is, Keynesianism). This school embraced treating the entire economy as having a supply-and-demand equilibrium. Inflation was regarded as being caused solely by variations in the money supply, in contrast to Keynesian economics, which largely ignored monetary policy. Friedman's neoliberalism had a practical appeal because regulating the money supply does not, at least on the surface, imply much government intervention in the economy. This critique pushed Keynesians toward a more "balanced" view of monetary policy and inspired revisions to Keynesian economics. Although Friedman was relatively more successful in shaping government policies than Hayek was, both schools were relatively marginal to the dominant paradigm of Keynesianism until the economic crisis precipitated by the 1974 oil embargo.

Keynesian economics arose in the late 1920s when the world economic system began to break down after its shaky recovery following World War I. With the global drop in production, critics of the gold standard, market self-correction, and production-driven paradigms of economics became vocal. Some pointed to the Soviet Union as an ostensibly successful planned economy that had avoided the disasters of the capitalist world and argued for a move toward socialism. Others pointed to the success of fascism in Mussolini's Italy. Into this atmosphere stepped Keynes, promising not to institute revolution but to save capitalism. He circulated a simple thesis: the economic problems were on the demand side. There were more factories and transportation networks than individuals could use given their current ability to pay. Keynes asserted that the aggregate demand for goods was the driving factor of the economy, especially in periods of downturn. From this he argued that the government was responsible for helping to pull a country out of a depression by instituting policies to promote demand at a *macro* level, in order to fight high unemployment and deflation of the sort seen during the 1930s. Keynes believed that if the government increased its spending, then the citizens would be encouraged to spend more because more money would be in circulation. People would start to invest more, and the economy would climb back up to normal.

The domination of Keynesianism was largely sustained by the Cold War. Political and military competition with the communist bloc ensured that Western capitalist countries, supported by their citizens, prioritized the role of the state. From the end of World War II to the 1970s, capitalist governments sought to demonstrate that capitalism was better than communism for the average citizen, and the development of the welfare state in this period was tied to Cold War ideologies. The U.S. government used many international opportunities to show off the superiority of the American way of life—"rising productivity, higher wages, lower prices, and the importation of American-made goods"[12]—to the Soviet system. This, for example, was the emphasis of "The True Face of the United States," a 1952 traveling exhibition in France.[13] At the American Trade Exhibition in Moscow in 1959, Vice President Richard Nixon went so far as to tell the Russian people that all the homes, televisions, and radios owned by Americans had brought them closer than the Soviets to the Marxist ideal of an egalitarian society.[14] After the People's Republic of China was founded in 1949, a key aspect of U.S. Cold War policy in Asia became fostering Japan into a leading member of the Western bloc to block the spread of communism in Asia. According to some scholars, this necessitated a U.S. strategy that separated the Japanese mainland from Okinawa, South Korea, and Taiwan: Japan focused on American-style economic development while the latter areas became militarized.[15]

By the early 1970s, the interventionist approach of the Keynesian welfare state faced strong challenges not from the outside but from within. The energy crisis triggered by the 1974 oil embargo deepened the internal crisis of capitalist productivity. The average annual real growth rate of the gross domestic product (GDP) of the six leading developed capitalist countries dropped significantly after 1973.[16] This meant that further growth required an expanded global extraction of resources and raw materials. Meanwhile, corporate interests decided that the Keynesian regulationist approach no longer worked to their advantage. Looking for an alternative, they found neoliberalism, which called for free movement of goods, services, capital, and money across national boundaries. The economic instability of the decade also pushed the Chicago School of Economics, the leading institutional base of neoliberal economics, from the margins into the mainstream. Hayek was a co-recipient of the 1974 Nobel Prize in Economics; two yeas later, Friedman was the sole winner, and by 2007, Chicago School economists dominated the list of Nobel Prize recipients in economics.[17]

In the early stage of neoliberal globalization, a systematic experiment with neoliberalism was implemented in Latin America, especially by economists trained at the University of Chicago in the 1970s.[18] Under the Pinochet dictatorship after the coup of September 11, 1973, Chile carried out radical neoliberal programs, including deregulation, massive unemployment, repression of labor unions, redistribution of wealth in favor of the rich, and privatization of the public sector.[19] In 1979, Margaret Thatcher in Britain, and in 1980, Ronald Reagan in the United States, officially adopted neoliberalism. Throughout the Thatcher and Reagan administrations, a variety of neoliberal policies were systematically implemented, leading to privatization, reduction of social welfare, tax reduction for the rich, and increased public and individual debt.[20]

The Cold War came to an end with the collapse of state socialism in Eastern Europe in 1989–1990, a historical condition that enabled the further expansion of neoliberalism.[21] Neoliberal experiments first tried in Latin America were applied to such countries as Poland and Russia.[22] By the end of the twentieth century, under external pressure from the Washington Consensus, neoliberalization had spread widely throughout Latin America, not just in Chile and Bolivia, but also in Mexico, Argentina, Peru, and Brazil. It may be summarized as a series of practices that include privatization of state-owned enterprises, liberalization of pricing, liberalization of the capital market, loosening of restraints on financial policies, and trade liberalization.[23] Confronting the 1997–1998 financial crisis, which seriously affected many Asian countries such as Hong Kong, Taiwan, Thailand, Indonesia, and Korea, Asian governments began to take an active role in creating and improving the institutional framework appropriate to neoliberal practices. In South Korea, for example, the Korean state took the financial crisis as an invaluable opportunity to reposition its relationship to its people by addressing a range of key policy areas, including momentary policy, financial regulation, corporate governance, regulatory reform, industrial policy, the organization of public services, and labor market regulation.[24]

China's neoliberalization

In recent years, Chinese economists have initiated heated debates about the status of neoliberalism in China, especially about whether China as a "socialist country" should adopt neoliberalism.[25] They differentiate between Washington Consensus neoliberal policies and neoliberalism as an economic theory. Based on this distinction, some argue for the adoption of neoliberal policies while others argue for an evaluation of neoliberal policies in other countries to study whether they are applicable to the Chinese experience.[26] Chinese economists, especially those who take Marxist political economy seriously, are skeptical about neoliberalism when they consider the negative consequences of neoliberalization in Latin America and Russia, as well as anti-globalization movements around the world.[27] However, they have not publicly acknowledged China as a neoliberal state and have yet to consider whether China's economic reforms were fundamentally part of the process of neoliberal globalization. Although China was not pressured by any other country to undertake any neoliberal programs, I argue it did develop its own neoliberal path from the late 1970s on, within the process of Hong Kong's return.

In fact, China's neoliberalization began with what Wang Hui calls a "radical negation" of the Cultural Revolution, or of the Chinese sixties.[28] In the history of worldwide revolutionary politics, the Cultural Revolution was a key political event that triggered many worldwide anti-system movements in and after 1968.[29] Thus, its rejection in China may be regarded as the first significant event leading to the revival of neoliberalism in the late Cold War period.[30] The radical negation of the Cultural Revolution is part of a broader process of depoliticizing the political in China. From this perspective, the rejection of socialist politics and practices in China began in the late 1970s, when the Cultural Revolution was rejected, and was completed by the end of the Cold War in 1989, which was marked by the military repression of social movements in Beijing.[31]

The rejection of the Cultural Revolution was a governmental decision codified through passage of the Communiqué of the Third Plenum of the Eleventh Central Committee of the Communist Party of China. This decision excluded any possibility of a positive evaluation of any aspect of the Cultural Revolution. Once the Cultural Revolution was completely rejected, a whole sequence of political practices associated with Mao as a political leader, Maoism, and Mao's socialist experiment were reevaluated. Because of this depoliticized decision, political subjectivity associated with the Cultural Revolution was rejected. Those who participated in activities of the Cultural Revolution were evaluated to determine whether they should be held responsible for specific actions.[32]

While rejecting the Cultural Revolution and Maoist practices, Deng Xiaoping's government underwent reforms and opening in the second half of the 1970s. In this process, the Communist Party engaged in heated debates addressing important theoretical issues about the market, labor compensation, and civil rights—issues relevant to economic reforms. Subsequently, there was much widespread discussion about the problems of socialism, humanism, alienation, the market economy, and the question of ownership.[33] Many of the important questions raised were addressed gradually in two ways: (1) through a series of senior-level party meetings that institutionalized important policies of "economic reform" through the principle of "development as the undisputable truth" (*fazhan jiushi ying daoli*); and (2) through the project of "national reunification" (*guojia tongyi*) with Hong Kong.

Neoliberal reforms

Deng Xiaoping's "economic reforms" effectively turned the "socialist planned economy" (*shehuzhuyi jihua jingji*) into a "socialist market economy" (*shehuizhuyi shichang jingji*). The transformation, the gradual institutionalization of neoliberal policies, was achieved through a series of party meetings. The Third Plenum of the Eleventh Central Committee of the Communist Party of China in 1978 decided to begin economic reforms. Around the same time, many scholars and officials were debating whether a market economy, in contrast to a planned economy, was a characteristic of capitalism. Deng Xiaoping suggested that a market economy could be used to further socialism. This assessment was supported by the analysis of Steven N. S. Cheung (Zhang Wuchang), an influential Hong Kong-based neoliberal economist and a faithful follower of the Chicago School of Economics.[34] Cheung argued that such concepts as socialism, capitalism, market economy, and the market were elusive in China at the end of the 1970s and in the early 1980s. For this reason, the nature of the ownership of productive material was also hard to define. He suggested that a demarcation of productive resources as *private property* was a necessary step in clarifying these concepts and should consider three important conditions: (1) the right of property ownership is established through the right to refuse others the use of the property; (2) the owner has the right to use the productive material as a resource to earn profits for his or her own purposes; and (3) the owner has the right to give or sell the material to others.[35] According to his view, private property did not exist in China in the late 1970s and early 1980s. For example, in a situation where a farmer was allowed to lease agricultural land in this period, he (rarely she) might have both the right to refuse others the use of his contracted land and the right to earn profit. However, he did not have the right to sell the land to others. In this sense, the farmer was not a private landowner but merely a renter of land from the commune. Thus, according to Cheung's reasoning, market-oriented reforms initiated by Deng's government in this period did not really contradict state socialism.

Further enlarging the scale of economic reforms, the Third Plenum of the Twelfth Central Committee of the Communist Party of China in 1984 passed a decision on "the reform of the economic system" (*jingji tizhi*). A few years later, in 1988, Milton Friedman had a two-hour meeting with Zhao Ziyang, the general secretary of the Communist Party, in which he presented Zhao with a memo he had prepared with his friend Steven Cheung, who accompanied Friedman on this trip. The memo contained four suggestions: ending price control, ending inflation, decontrolling individual prices and wages, and decentralizing government controls of the economy and privatizing state enterprises.[36] The clear separation between state property ownership and the rights of enterprises that managed and used resources owned by the state seemed to be a concern shared by Zhao and Friedman, despite the fact that Zhao was a communist official and Friedman a neoliberal economist.[37]

After the 1989 social movements in China, many observers inside and outside of China wondered where China would go. Deng's visit to the special economic zones in southeastern China in 1992 reaffirmed the government's institutionalization of neoliberal economic policies. The Third Plenum of the Fourteenth Central Committee of the Communist Party of China in 1993 addressed issues of "the establishment of the socialist market economic system" (*shehuizhuyi shichang jingji tizhi*). Since then, China's neoliberalization has accelerated: some of Friedman's suggestions have been systematically adopted (for example, decentralization of government controls on the economy and privatization of state enterprises). In October 2003, the Third Plenum of the Sixteenth Central Committee of the Communist Party of China decided to "improve" (*gaishan*) "the socialist market economic system." At this time, the concept of "property right" (*chanquan*) was formally institutionalized and "three represents" (*sange daibiao*) were written into the revised party constitution.

Since 1978, the CCP has consistently maintained that China remains a fundamentally socialist system, and that this is not contradictory to implementing certain practical capitalist measures (including private ownership and market economy). Despite this claim, the process of China's economic development, as many scholars have documented, is inseparable from the economic globalization of capitalism, rather than an alternative to or outside it.[38] As the Communist Party meetings address constitutional problems of the CCP and the Chinese state, national reunification projects create practices to make China's transformation possible. This is the second means Chinese officials have used to clarify confusions about such important concepts as socialism, capitalism, and market economy and thus to accelerate the country's neoliberalization process.

Reunification with Hong Kong

Hong Kong's return to China, in process from the late 1970s to the late 1990s, was undisputedly the most important project of national reunification since 1842. The process of Hong Kong's return coincided with the neoliberalization of China, even though the particular historical trajectory followed by the Chinese state was different from other models of state neoliberalization around the world.[39] The state is a critical element in neoliberalization. Its political intervention and orchestration are necessary for the normalization of economic rationality as a purview of government. Meanwhile, the state itself becomes an enterprise organized by market rationality, and as such, the state focuses its legitimacy on the health and growth of the economy. To elaborate this point, I first discuss the narratives of neoliberals who have been influential in China over the past three decades, and then I examine China's reunification with Hong Kong.

In his 1988 memo to Zhao Ziyang, Friedman argued that only a state that relies primarily on "free private markets" to coordinate economic activities can achieve a high level of prosperity: markets and privatization alone are not enough. "What is needed is *free private markets*, where 'free' means open to competition, from both abroad and domestic sources" (emphasis in the original).[40] Under the condition of free private markets, Steven Cheung further argues, China's neoliberalization (economic reforms) needs to address the symbiotic relationship between the formation and transformation of an economic institution like the market and the change to the existing property structure of collective ownership. The development and operation of a market economy have to minimize the costs of this institutional change, which Cheung calls "transaction costs."[41] As long as the condition of free private markets exists, a firm that effectively minimizes transaction costs is a competitive enterprise.

Extending the theory of Ronald H. Coase, another Chicago School economist and 1991 Nobel Prize winner who argues for a broader understanding of the firm in relation to social cost,[42] Cheung argues that the state can be seen as an economic enterprise. The Chinese state may act in the market economy by becoming a "super firm," analogous to but more powerful than an ordinary firm: "Different industries, factories, communes, stores, and other agencies can be treated, in effect, as different divisions, departments, sub-departments, and so forth of that overall entity."[43] Whether socialist or capitalist, this super firm needs to operate within a free private ownership structure. Only in this way can the state become economically prosperous through minimizing the transaction costs incurred in the operation of an institutional arrangement and in adopting or changing an institution.[44]

Moreover, this theory of the state as a super firm also argues that the state transforms its governmental functions through economic rationality. Unlike an ordinary company, the state also operates as a government institution and thus possesses a kind of power an ordinary company does not have.[45] It may not be possible for the state to participate in the market in order to minimize its transaction costs. An option for the state in this situation is to pass laws that might help to reduce the transaction costs—for example, to impose safety standards on products made for export, as has been done in dealing with problems in foods and toys exported to the United States in the past several years.[46] Thus, the neoliberal theory of the state as a super firm considers the neoliberal state's dual role as both an economic enterprise and legislative institution. In other words, the neoliberal state's legislative and administrative functions should aim at promoting economic health.

Hong Kong's return to China entailed the development of a new Chinese state that was capable of accommodating the social, economic, and political differences between the mainland and Hong Kong. In particular, from the perspective of the mainland, the transformed Chinese state must be able to embrace the people of Hong Kong as part of the people of the People's Republic of China. This required a radical reconfiguration of the sovereign relationship between the state and the people, as well as modifications of economic, social, and political relations constrained by this new state–people configuration. The Chinese government's rejection of Maoist practices in the late 1970s reflected a concern for the new state–people relationship. Anything that was not socialist could only be treated as an exception. The restoration of the normative order of the state could not be completed without planting something as an exception to Maoist socialism. Once the project of national reunification (that is, the negotiations with Britain over the future of Hong Kong) created a historical condition enabling an exception, Deng Xiaoping's idea of "one country, two systems" was used to transform the sovereignty bound to Maoist political representation.

When considering unification of the capitalist Hong Kong and the socialist Chinese mainland, the Maoist state's representation of the proletariat (via revolution and proletariat dictatorship) had to be displaced to accommodate the state's representation of the capitalists (especially those from Hong Kong). In the history of the CCP, Mao Zedong played the key role in theoretically articulating the CCP's role within the framework of the modern socialist state.[47] During the war against Japanese invasion, Mao published a long essay entitled "New Democratic Theory" (1940), in which he considered the Chinese revolution as part of a worldwide revolution. Compared with the bourgeoisie revolutions in Europe and the Bolshevik Revolution in Russia, Mao argued, the Chinese revolution was unique because it took place in "a semi-colonial, semi-feudal state" (*ban zhimindi, ban fengjian guojia*), which had formed since the first Opium War in 1840. The CCP gradually emerged as the leader in this revolution after a series of failures by other groups, including the Nationalist Party under the leadership of Sun Yat-sen. For Mao, it was the CCP's historical responsibility to take the lead in radically revolutionizing the "semi-colonial, semi-feudal state." A key to the success of this revolution was to build a new state that completely replaced the old one. On the eve of the establishment of the People's Republic, Mao wrote another important essay, "On the People's Democratic Dictatorship"[48] (June 30, 1949), to commemorate the twenty-eighth anniversary of the CCP. This article outlined two fundamental principles of the new socialist state: (1) it was organized under "the leadership of the working class;" and (2) it would ally itself with the world proletariat of the socialist countries. These two principles permeated the government policies of socialist China until Hong Kong's return to China, when the state representation of the capitalists began to displace the state representation of the proletariat. Thus, in 1998, less than a year after Hong Kong's return, Jiang Zemin, the secretary general of the CCP and the president of China, asked the party members to propose new theories to account for the new political representation. In May 2000, he proclaimed "three represents" as the new theory of political representation. According to it, the CCP represents "the developmental requirement of the advanced productive forces in China" (*zhongguo xianjin shengchanli de fazhan yaoqiu*), "the progressive direction of advanced culture in China" (*zhongguo xianjin wenhua de qianjin fangxiang*), and "the fundamental interest of the vast majority of the people" (*zhongguo zui guangda renmin de genben liyi*).[49] In 2003, the Third Plenum of the Sixteenth Central Committee of the Communist Party of China formally incorporated this theory into the revised party constitution. This change made it possible for the post-1997 state to legitimately represent the people of Hong Kong as well as capitalists, whether from Hong Kong, the mainland, or other places such as Macau and Taiwan.

In addition to justifying the rejection of the Maoist political representation of the working classes, Deng's theory of "one country, two systems" was used to legitimize the creation of a series of four special economic zones (beginning in 1980) in Guangdong and Fujian provinces, where nonsocialist systems—not only private markets but also private controls of the economy and the population[50]—were developed. In 1984, the year of the signing of the Sino–British Joint Declaration, the government expanded the special economic zone concept to another fourteen coastal cities and to Hainan Island. In the 1990s, many priority development regions and export processing zones were established across the country. In 1997, Hong Kong became the first special administrative region of the People's Republic of China, and two years later, Macau became the second. Each region is supposed to operate for fifty years according to its own mini-constitution.

Within these special zones of private markets, the Chinese government operates effectively through state enterprises. Major state-owned companies, such as the Bank of China, China Travel Service, and China Resources, appropriated Hong Kong's free market system to enhance their status as super firms exactly as neoliberals expected them to. Chinese Travel Service, for example, leveraged its status as both a transnational company and a state-owned firm to advance the government's objective of realizing the "one country, two systems" framework (see Chapter 5). In recent years, the state firms that have operated effectively under the free private market system have expanded into areas in western China to develop free private markets there. For example, the real estate divisions of both China Resources and China Travel Service are major players in the development of private housing markets in the city of Chengdu in Sichuan Province. China Resource Land, Ltd. acquired via auction in 2005 a large piece of land (slightly more than fifty-six hectares) from a major state-owned manufacturing company that relocated to a suburban area outside the city. The real estate development project, entitled Twenty-Four City, is transforming the poor working-class residential area into a major middle-class community.[51]

Therefore, both the displacement of the socialist political paradigm and the establishment of economic zones have had huge impacts on Chinese society. In 2003 when "three represents" and property rights became formally institutionalized, the neoliberal transformation of the Communist Party-led state from a state of the working classes to one of the capitalist class (including the nouveaux riches) was completed. Around the same time, some Chinese scholars used the idea of the "relatively comfortable society" (*xiaokang shehui*) to elaborate Jiang's "three represents." Others have begun to consider how the embracement of neoliberalization may present serious challenges to Chinese socialism. Chinese economist Yu Wenlie, for example, mentioned four major problems in 2004:

1 The increasing gap between the rich and the poor presents a challenge to the socialist distribution system (*fenpei zhidu*).
2 The privatization of state-owned enterprises and "state-owned assets" (*guoyou zichan*) damages the socialist "collective ownership system" (*gongyouzhi*).
3 The government's "malfunctions," or "misbehaviors" (*shiwei*), in the market damage the socialist market economic system.
4 "The urban-rural twofold economic structure" (*cheng xiang eryuan jingji jiegou*) and the increasing economic gaps among regions damage the balanced development of the national economy.[52]

In 2005, President Hu Jintao proposed the idea of the "harmonious society" (*hexie shehui*) as the emphasis of the government. It covers six aspects:

democracy and rule of law, fairness and justice, sincerity and friendliness, full-scale vitality, stability and orderliness, and harmony between humans and nature.[53] Scholars and policymakers use this framework in debating the proper way to address the problems of increasing socioeconomic inequality. Neoliberal economists argue that the current state of inequality, despite being a problem of social harmony, should be maintained for the sake of developing a more "efficient" society, even if this means that some must be sacrificed. Scholars on the left, by contrast, argue for the elimination or amelioration of the effects of inequality to pursue the ideal of the harmonious society.[54] Despite holding different views on the problem of social inequality, both sides generally share a common concern; that is, how to address inequality, an issue that may create social risks that affect the state's normative order.[55]

Neoliberal synchronization: History, aesthetics, and everyday life

Treating Hong Kong's return as a sovereignty issue allowed the Chinese state to create a necessary historical condition for incorporating capitalism into the Chinese system. To deal with the incompatibilities between two systems, however, the state had to transform Hong Kong's return into a governmental process, thereby putting neoliberalism into practice. The political and economic implementation of the "one country, two systems" framework needed to address the problem of national attitudes developed since the first Opium War. One set of attitudes relates to China's historical experience as a victim of capitalist globalization in the nineteenth century: for example, "humiliation" (*chiru*), "weakness" (*ruanruo*), "tragedy" (*beiju*), "pains" (*tongku*), and "disasters" (*zhainan*). These public feelings were treated as ingredients essential to the dominant story about how the CCP emerged as the party that led the Chinese people in establishing an independent, revolutionary modern nation state. Meanwhile, a second set of attitudes addresses China's contemporary experience of decolonization: "revival" (*zhenxing*), "return" (*huigui*), "self-esteem" (*zihao*), and "self-confidence" (*zixin*). The development of these new national feelings reworked the former set of attitudes, which were closely associated with Western imperialism and colonialism. In China, this process is commonly referred to by the media as "the erasure of national shame and the revitalization of the Chinese nation" (*xuexi guochi, zhenxing zhonghua*). For the purpose of this book, I call it an affective economy of neoliberal synchronization,[56] a necessary step toward making China's socialist system compatible with Hong Kong's capitalist system. This affective economy employs communication as the means to generate economic growth as consumption and promotes a citizen's moral conduct as an economic behavior. Neoliberal synchronization as part of Hong Kong's return transformed all the important dimensions that the concept of "culture" (*wenhua*) usually designates: history, aesthetics, and everyday life.[57]

The historical dimension of culture deals with the problem of modern historical time and its narration during Hong Kong's return to China.[58] Hong Kong's return, in a way, effectively addressed the dialectics of narrating the story of building a modern Chinese nation state: the rhetoric of the inexorable reunification of the motherland on the one hand, and of overcoming national shame on the other. Between the two historical international agreements—from the Treaty of Nanjing (1842) to the Sino–British Joint Declaration (1984)—official narratives of modern Chinese history have shifted significantly. In the context of nineteenth-century Western colonialism and imperialism, the dominant state discourse of modern China focused on revolutionary modernity, linking the struggles of the Chinese people in resisting Western colonialism and imperialism in China to the emergence of the CCP as their leader. With Hong Kong's impending return, the conventional discourse was modified to emphasize neoliberal modernity, celebrating the successes of economic reforms and the state's prosperity and strength.[59]

This modification of the dominant state narratives about modern Chinese history was made possible by effective displays of historical and cultural artifacts. No museums were more important in doing this than the National Museum of Chinese Revolution, focusing on modern Chinese history, and the National Museum of Chinese History. During Hong Kong's return, regular exhibitions were staged on the topic of modern historical time, especially with regard to the relationship between China and Hong Kong (for details, see Chapter 3). The two museums merged in 2003 to form the new National Museum of China which, significantly, dropped "revolution" (*geming*) from its name. This development of a mega-museum—reportedly following the mainstream path of reforming Chinese museums to make them economically accountable[60]—definitely contributes to the depoliticizing process of rejecting the Maoist past.

The deployment of artifacts to promote China's neoliberal synchronization was so common that it went far beyond the confines of museums, extending into shopping malls, theme parks, films, and the Internet. The First Chinese Communist Party Congress Meeting Hall, a museum in Shanghai devoted to the historical representation of the birth of the CCP, is a good example of this change. By the 1920s, the treaty-port of Shanghai became a premier offshore site for foreign companies. Working conditions there were among the worst in the world. Worker resistance to them helped give birth to the CCP in 1921.[61] The museum's exhibition begins with important figures and events related to this early and the later history of the CCP and ends with a celebration of modern China under the leadership of the Communist Party of China. As one visitor writes, "When I visited the museum in July 2004, there was also a special Deng Xiaoping exhibition. Viewing the museum in the prescribed order, the Deng exhibit was the final thing to see before leaving. The museum as a whole reinforces this idea of a lineage from Shanghai 1921 to the present economic reforms instituted by Deng."[62]

This emphasis on contemporary successes dovetails with the general atmosphere of the museum's "supremely bourgeois surroundings," a more than 30,000-square-meter area called Xintiandi (New Universe), a trendy, upscale shopping district redeveloped by the Shui On Group (a Hong Kong-based real estate development company headed by Vincent Hong Sui Lo) in the late 1990s. This area contains an array of boutiques, restaurants, pubs, galleries, and clubs, including Starbucks, the Ye Shanghai nightclub, and the Che Guevara restaurant. Xintiandi itself has become a landmark marking the area as a tourist destination. Xintiandi brands of French wine and other products are for sale in a district shop.[63] The museum's historical representation cannot be separated from this commercial urban environment that has turned into a theme-park-like space. This was reinforced by a museum staff member, who claimed that the surrounding environment effectively helped visitors to reflect on the contemporary significance of the museum's historical exhibition.[64]

The changing relationship between historical representation and exhibition, a crucial issue for the state's neoliberal transformation, is a problem of spectacle, of linking the aesthetic dimension of culture to history. On December 19, 1994, a giant clock was installed in Beijing's Tiananmen Square to count down to Hong Kong's return to China on July 1, 1997. The clock motif was widely promoted by mass media ranging from newspapers and magazines to television stations. Countdown clocks were adopted by CCTV, China's largest television network owned by the Chinese government, and by many newspapers across the country. A countdown clock played a dual role for media companies. Not only did it indicate the time remaining until July 1, 1997, but it also attracted many commercial sponsors. The Tiananmen clock's designer also set up another clock beside the Luohu Bridge, a busy border crossing between Hong Kong and the Shenzhen Special Economic Zone.

This device of the Tiananmen clock accelerated the process of Hong Kong's return and declared the historical event a spectacle. Numerous Chinese and foreign visitors had their photos taken in front of it. Some Chinese citizens were married in front of it. On June 30–July 1, 1997, a large-scale national celebration, broadcast live by both Chinese and foreign media, was staged in front of the clock. In sum, the Hong Kong countdown became one of the most successful and influential international marketing campaigns in contemporary China,[65] effectively establishing a new mode of mass campaign called the "public relations campaign" (*gongguan chehua*), an alternative to the conventional ideological campaigns controlled by the Communist Party's "propaganda" (*xuanchuan*) division.

From the ideological state apparatus to the public relations state apparatus, the spectacle of the Hong Kong countdown legitimized the appearance of the neoliberal state.[66] This is accomplished both through encoding the neoliberal presence of the Chinese state, including the reorganization of its government along lines of economic rationality and its promotion of the norm of the citizen as an entrepreneurial subject, and by means of regulating the order and legislation of differences and identities according to the "one country, two systems" principle. The neoliberal state's spectacular appearance in the countdown was primarily economic.[67]

As an economic process, the Hong Kong countdown did not involve the conventional production of material goods, as in the case of manufacturing industries. Instead, communication was the means of production, and thus, the countdown became part of the informational economy (that is, the accumulation, extension, and circulation of information).[68] Chinese museums, for example, were transformed from "work units of the state cultural enterprises" (*guojia wenhua shiye danwei*) to units of the "culture industry" (*wenhua chanye*).[69] Being state apparatuses of public relations, they played an active and important role in the spectacle of the countdown. The First Chinese Communist Party Congress Meeting Hall has become part of its surrounding theme-park-like built environment. The National Museum of Chinese Revolution, a sponsor of the Tiananmen countdown clock, was incorporated into the media culture brought about by the clock and later became a new museum organization anchoring the process of economic reforms within China's museums (see Chapter 3).

The spectacle of the Hong Kong countdown primarily involved a combination of symbolic and affective activities. The former type produced all kinds of media products and symbols about Hong Kong's return (in such forms as commercial information and merchandise, souvenirs, historical artifacts, museum objects, and stories), while the latter type focused on the elicitation of such feelings as awakening, excitement, national pride, and even statehood (for details, see Chapter 2). The production of symbolic products and affects relied on a particular kind of communications media. As represented by the countdown clock, it was a convergent form of media—a nonlinear media, or multimedia—that integrates mechanical, electronic, and digital forms. Multimedia communication is aesthetic: it not only has a raw, material presence, but it is also a discourse encoding the representation of the state's history.[70] In the age of the "videosphere,"[71] moreover, multimedia communication uses new media technologies to enhance the encoding of history's differences and identities through a sense of acceleration that constructs a culture of disappearance: not a culture of absence, but one of replacement and substitution.[72] In the spectacle of the Hong Kong countdown, the official historical time switched from the socialist to the neoliberal timeline, which the Chinese media recently begin to call "China's time" (*Zhongguo shijian*) (see Conclusion, this volume). This switch was possible precisely because the spectacle itself deployed the technology of multimedia to enable a culture of disappearance.

As the multiplicity-based time constructed by the countdown clock was incorporated into individuals' everyday lives, it promoted the development of neoliberal citizenship, that is, the embodiment of economic rationalism in citizen's conduct. The incorporation of multiplicity-based time in daily life has two related consequences. First, the practice of everyday life is organized as a technical process of ordering, calculating, and coordinating. Under neoliberal conditions, the technical process is reoriented toward economic calculations (of costs, benefits, and efficiency), characteristics of the entrepreneurial subject. Second, regular uses of multiplicity-based time enable a process of reducing the impact of (or accommodating) different kinds of temporalities, especially seemingly contradictory ones such as those between being a patriotic citizen (linked to public feeling for the state) and being a self-serving calculative individual (focused on the interests of the private self) (see Chapters 2–4).

Hong Kong's neoliberal timeline: New identity and historical memory

The spectacle of the Hong Kong countdown was also crucially important to both the creation of a new Hong Kong cultural identity and the preservation of Hong Kong's historical past. Under British rule, Hong Kong had developed into a neoliberal economy that combined liberal–colonial–imperial government with ethnic entrepreneurialism. Compared with major capitalist countries such as the United States and Britain, Hong Kong is always singled out as an excellent example of how neoliberalism can work effectively and competitively. Friedman even argues that while many countries have tried neoliberalism since World War II, only Hong Kong's "experiment" has been successful and produced an authentic "free economy." By contrast, the United States is a mixed economy, and Britain and Israel are "socialist" economies.[73] International observers, who felt pessimistic about whether Hong Kong could survive after becoming China's Special Administrative Region, may be pleased by the apparent vitality of Hong Kong's neoliberalism. According to the American Heritage Foundation's influential annual global economic freedom index, which rates more than 160 countries in the world, Hong Kong has consistently ranked first since 1996, the year the Foundation began its index.[74] The Hong Kong Special Administrative Region has apparently retained its status as a free economy since 1997.

If we compare the speeds of economic and political developments after Hong Kong's return to China, it is not difficult to see that neoliberal economy maintains its vitality, while the development of representative democracy seems to slow down. The Democratic Party, for example, has lost seats to other political parties.[75] This situation suggests that Hong Kong's political reforms, including the development of a democratic political system, are conditioned by neoliberalism, which prioritizes economic freedom and rights over other types of freedoms and rights. Historically, the Hong Kong government's policies and laws have always focused on business, not on politics. Especially in the post-World War II period, the government was committed to *laissez-faire* practices. For example, John Cowperthwaite, the Financial Secretary (1961–1971) and a disciple of Adam Smith, lowered taxes and refused to impose tariffs.[76] Since Cowperthwaite, the Hong Kong government's economic policies have changed their labels including "positive non-intervention" (1971–1981), "consensus capitalism" (1991–1995), and "proactive market enabler" (2001–2003), but have remained faithful to "free market philosophy," as pointed out by Donald Tsang,[77] the Chief Executive of the Hong Kong Special Administrative Region (2005–present).

Under the government's neoliberal policies, economics and trade dominated almost every aspect of everyday life. Some have tried to describe the ideal figure of the Hong Kong individual that consequently emerged in the post-World War II period. Andrew Scobell, for example, calls this figure the "Hong Kong Man:"

> The Hong Kong Man . . . is a curious if not unique breed—extremely sophisticated; Western, yet Chinese; ambitious, but tempered with realism; self-seeking and yet proud of the territory he has created, as well as patriotic in many ways to China; flexible but steady . . . Hong Kong Man also has a taste for luxury items, both material and nonmaterial . . . Hong Kong Man also likes his freedoms, but not so much in the political sense. Hong Kong has never been a democracy . . . the majority of people do not seem particularly enthusiastic about democracy.[78]

Lee Yee, a Hong Kong-based writer, shares and supports Scobell's view:

> Hong Kong society is . . . law-abiding and stable; it is widely praised for its efficiency and the quality of its service industry. The territory's capitalists, professionals, and managers are enterprising, daring, inventive, and adaptable. Hong Kong workers are famed for their industriousness, professionalism, and level of education.[79]

Extending these views, I argue that this ideal Hong Kong individual is neoliberal because he or she pursues individual liberty through entrepreneurism and economic freedom. The laws this ideal Hong Kong individual follows are more economic than political. Consequently, the order and stability established and improved by the laws serve the purpose of the economy rather than of politics. However, the historical event of Hong Kong's return to China profoundly affects those who live according to this ideal neoliberal norm.

Between the signing of the Sino–British Joint Declaration in 1984 and the handover in 1997, Hong Kong developed a new epochal consciousness characterized by the idea that Hong Kong's return was not only a beginning or an end, but also a period of transition. July 1, 1997, was a temporal impasse prescribing a state of exigency for Hong Kong, as it did for China. The relationship between present and future became imminently unstable and thus called for immediate action.

In the 1984–1997 period, "China" or "the mainland" emerged to stand for the dreadful specter of the authoritarian state, an impression that was reinforced by the Chinese government's crackdown on social movements in 1989. On the other side, the socialist state had never represented Hong Kong residents as being included among "the people of China." Thus, many Hong Kong residents perceived that incorporation into the socialist state signaled the end of Hong Kong's system. In everyday life, Hong Kong residents commonly assumed that the replacement of Hong Kong's government would cause the disappearance of "Hong Kong's way of life," a phenomenon Ackbar Abbas calls a "culture of disappearance."[80]

In this culture of substitution and replacement during the transition period, many Hong Kong residents came "to view democratization of the territory's political system as one of the most viable safeguards against excessive interference by Beijing."[81] The Sino–British Joint Declaration and the subsequent Hong Kong laws (especially the Basic Law) called for administrative reforms of the Hong Kong government, but prohibited any changes of political representation through the Hong Kong government (see Chapter 1). Democracy in this context might be incorporated into administration to promote and maintain economic prosperity, but could not be established explicitly as a new political system that reordered the state–people relationship in the same way as the Chinese government does.[82] During the countdown, therefore, Hong Kong residents were told to be responsible for themselves in their daily lives.[83] In its award-winning 1995 fisherman television commercial, for example, the Hong Kong and Shanghai Bank Corporation (HSBC), the territory's largest bank, told the Hong Kong residents: "Your future is our future." Meanwhile, the story of the fisherman portrayed in the ad repeatedly emphasized one message: "In Hong Kong, whether you make a living all depends on you." This seemingly contradictory message affirmed a symbiosis between the corporation and the individual in confronting Hong Kong's future uncertainty,[84] including the difficulties of developing a democratic political system.

While many residents have emigrated (see Chapter 1), those in Hong Kong have developed a new Hong Kong "popular culture," one that encompasses architecture, cinema, television, literature, performance, and consumer culture.[85] Being diverse and fragmentary, Hong Kong's new (popular) culture has gone beyond the established discourses of Hong Kong as "a city for business," "a shopping heaven," and a "meeting place between the East and the West."[86] Filmmakers such as Wong Kar-wai, Ann Hui, Stanley Kwan, and Fruit Chan used cinema as a visual medium to reflect on the colony's temporal and spatial status and construct a new identity for Hong Kong.

Exemplified by such popular films as *Rouge* (1988, Stanley Kwan), the series *Once upon a Time in China* (1991–1993, directed by Tsui Hark), *Chungking Express* (1994, directed by Wong Kar-wai), and *Ashes of Time* (1994, directed by Wong Kar-wai), Hong Kong cinema in the transitional period problematized the visual by constructing "a sense of the elusiveness, the slipperiness, the ambivalences of Hong Kong's cultural space."[87] Action in daily life, as portrayed in these films, unfolded as a deployment of temporal strategies such as speeding up or slowing down a change, fixing a deadline, promising, waiting or letting the other wait, and acting at the right moment. The active deployment of temporal strategies allowed the development of the relationship between self-time and other-time.[88] What is remarkable about these films is the way in which the problem of the deadline saturates all aspects of everyday life. As the films show, everything in daily life has an ending or expiration date, whether it be a can of pineapple, a date with a friend, or a fight with an enemy. The obsession with a particular deadline attached the handover date to only one stream of time in everyday life, while it intentionally ignored or misrecognized the other streams of time in everyday life. These films represented one way in which the idea of the temporal break constituted by Hong Kong's "return" to China was used both aesthetically and technologically to construct a qualitatively new time for Hong Kong.

In the formulation of Hong Kong's culture, the search for Hong Kong's future primarily took the form of finding the right path to the past. The transition period witnessed a stunning growth of museums and historical preservation programs. To construct and represent Hong Kong's collective memories, museums and historical preservation projects developed a new notion of Hong Kong, which I call "Hongkong." As shown by the first permanent history exhibition, "The Story of Hong Kong" (1991–1998) at the Hong Kong Museum of History, and by the first heritage tourist project, the "Pingshan Heritage Trail" (opened in 1993) in the New Territories, Hongkong was constructed through the representation of Hong Kong in terms of a city–village relationship, that is, the historical relationship between the "City" (the urbanized area developed after the coming of the Europeans) and the "Village" (the rural area of southern Guangdong Province in the nineteenth century). This mode of historical representation of Hong Kong displaced an important element of Hong Kong's historical time—the historical time of southern China (particularly associated with the nineteenth century)—by incorporating the historical time of China into the self-time of Hong Kong. The deployment of this historical time enabled Hong Kong to address the problem of communal identity by linking it to Hong Kong's role in the global economy and transnational capitalism.

Organization of the book

As I have outlined, the neoliberalization of the Chinese nation state since the 1970s has been part of the process of neoliberal globalization. Both China's economic reforms and its national unification projects worked towards not only the rejection of Maoist socialist principles and practices but also the affirmation of economic rationality in a wide spectrum of fields, including national sovereignty, government policies and procedures, citizenship, and everyday life. Hong Kong's return to China was a pivotal event in China's neoliberalization. As soon as China and Britain had agreed that the Chinese government would regain sovereignty over Hong Kong, the sovereignty issue became a problem of the Chinese government. The process of the countdown to Hong Kong's return effectively expressed the way in which the Hong Kong question became linked to both national sovereignty and the governance of society. As the decisive technology of the state that forces the rule of exception, sovereignty made it imperative for the Chinese nation state to co-present and co-represent the mainland (a space embedded within the Maoist socialist historical time) and Hong Kong (a space rooted within the British liberal–colonial–imperial historical time). The sovereign technology itself could not resolve the actual incompatibilities between the two spaces and their historical times, however, even though it temporarily enabled the Chinese government to create special capitalist zones (special economic zones) within the Chinese mainland. To make the mainland and Hong Kong compatible, the Hong Kong countdown developed an affective economy that transformed the governmental problem of Hong Kong's return into a series of public relations campaigns. The entire sector of the culture industry was mobilized. Mass media, museums, and theme parks all played major roles in the affective economy of the countdown. Based on interviews, participant observations, archival research, and media analysis, this book details how Hong Kong's return enabled China's neoliberalization and created a historical condition for Hong Kong to develop a collective cultural identity inseparable from its own historical experience.[89]

Chapter 1 examines how the Chinese government addressed the Hong Kong question as a problem of national unification. Tracking the important steps in the negotiations between the Chinese and British governments over Hong Kong's return, this chapter shows that the Hong Kong question was not just a historical problem of getting Hong Kong back, but more important, it changed how the entire historical experience of the modern Chinese nation state was registered. The solutions to the Hong Kong question gradually moved beyond the diplomatic arrangements between China and Britain, signaling a change in the status of the Hong Kong question from a national sovereignty issue to a governmental problem. Thereby, Hong Kong's return could draw on the widespread participation of ordinary people in both China and Hong Kong.

The countdown to Hong Kong's return, as Chapter 2 shows, was a crucial process for expanding and disseminating the governmental problem of Hong Kong's return into Chinese society and economy. The Hong Kong countdown clock enabled an affective economy that addressed collective and individual feelings toward a past associated with the appearance of Hong Kong (as the object of the Chinese nation state lost in the nineteenth century). A cultural transformation closely tied to the development of this affective economy broke down the general governmental problem of Hong Kong's return to China into two specific issues: media aesthetic and media spectacle. Drawing on Rancière's work on the politics of aesthetics, I consider the countdown clock as a problem of media dialectic.[90] The countdown clock itself involved the material development of a new technology, or a new medium, that encoded the discourse of the countdown, the narration of the feelings about the reappearance of Hong Kong in the Chinese nation state. Meanwhile, through media spectacle, consumption practices incorporated the clock time embodied by the countdown device into the transformation of everyday life. My discussion of the first question focuses on a media aesthetic of neoliberalism, and my analysis of the second question addresses the construction of neoliberal subjects in everyday life.

Chapter 3 continues the theme of Hong Kong's return as a governmental problem, but focuses on examining history (one dimension of the concept of culture) as a governmental problem.[91] During the Hong Kong countdown, what emerged on the horizon was not merely the end of British colonial rule in Hong Kong but also the completion of what colonialism symbolized in historical representations of modern Chinese history. Under this condition, a new culture of substitution was formed. The revolutionary or socialist historical discourse about the feelings of humiliation, weakness, tragedy, pain, and disaster associated with the British occupation of Hong Kong in the nineteenth century was displaced by a new historical discourse of a civilization synchronic with contemporary western civilizations, a neoliberal discourse about decolonization, revival, national pride, and self-confidence. This discursive change is illustrated by a detailed discussion of two major exhibitions at the National Museum of Chinese Revolution, a "permanent" exhibition on the history of modern China and a large-scale temporal exhibition of the history of Hong Kong.

Shifting from the National Museum of Chinese Revolution to Yuanming Yuan (the Old Summer Palace), a cultural heritage site in Beijing, Chapter 4 further investigates the problem of history as individualized and everyday experiences shaped by the collective historical experience of the British occupation of Hong Kong. A number of theme parks have been developed at Yuanming Yuan since the end of the 1980s. I compare two of them. The Ruins Park of Yuanming Yuan (*yuanming yuan yizhi gongyuan*) was established at a major site of patriotic education. It constituted a kind of formal education designed to shape the moral character of Chinese citizens, in light of the fact that the original buildings on the site were burned and destroyed by the British and French in the second Opium War in 1860, a war that led to the British occupation of Kowloon (now a major section of the Hong Kong territory). In the context of Hong Kong's return, as the chapter shows, the site's operation as a theme park reoriented the expression of "national humiliation" toward an expression of national "revival." Meanwhile, Yuanming Yuan was increasingly becoming a pleasure garden or a site of consumption in leisure-oriented everyday life. This is illustrated by the development and operation of another theme park, the World Primitive Totems Garden (*shijie yuanshi tuteng huicui yuan*), which staged totem poles and masks to represent "remote," "primitive," and "ancient" cultures from outside China. Unlike the Ruins Park, the Totems Garden was explicitly tied to the process of neoliberal globalization, or to the active synchronization of China with the capitalist world. Because the garden was operated as a for-profit enterprise rather than a nonprofit organization, it exemplifies how museums and related organizations were transformed in the development of the "culture industry" (*wenhua chanye*). From a tourist perspective, both parks show that the individual experience of pleasure consumption was just as important as the collective experience of national humiliation. It was at the intersection between the historical experience and the quotidian experience that the spectacle of consumption became a force of time in redefining the meanings of Chinese history. Thus, in this chapter I demonstrate how Yuanming Yuan as an important site of memory was used to address the tension between patriotic education as part of the affective economy and pleasure consumption as a means for the neoliberal "synchronization with the world" (*yu shijie jiegui*).

The transformation of cultural institutions into a culture industry was part of the process of reorganizing the government according to economic principles of calculation and efficiency. The Hong Kong countdown process rendered this reorganization in a particular way so that it was compatible with the "one country, two systems" framework. Hong Kong-based Chinese state-owned organizations and companies played critical roles not only in facilitating the transformation of governmental organizations and enterprises but also in creating a co-presence between capitalism and socialism, in both Hong Kong and the mainland. To illustrate this point, Chapter 5 focuses on the business practices of a Hong Kong-based Chinese state-owned transnational corporation, China Travel Service (Holdings) Hong Kong, Ltd. (CTS).[92] The company regularly sponsored cultural and arts events in Hong Kong and, through sponsorship, educated Hong Kong residents about a "Chineseness" closely associated with socialist China, as shown by its participation in Hong Kong's Chinese Dance Festival in 1995. Thereby, CTS represented socialist China in capitalist Hong Kong prior to Hong Kong's return. Meanwhile, CTS deployed Hong Kong as a base for actively participating in transnational capitalism, especially in developing Shenzhen as China's first special economic zone, a capitalist space that existed in parallel with socialist spaces in China. The simultaneous spatial representations of capitalism and socialism, I argue, were possible only when the company operated as a super firm in the neoliberal sense.

While the countdown allowed China to reconfigure its historical time by incorporating Hong Kong into its national time, it also gave Hong Kong an opportunity to construct its own time. Based on historical research and ethnographic fieldwork,[93] Chapter 6 examines Hong Kong's stunning development of museums and historical preservation during the transition process, which constructed a Hongkong culture for the Hong Kong self that was projected to face extinction. The Hong Kong Museum of History was established in the mid-1970s, but it did not expand significantly until the 1990s.

The museum's "The Story of Hong Kong," which opened in 1991, was the first permanent exhibition on Hong Kong history. The Pingshan Heritage Trail in the New Territories, opened in 1993, was Hong Kong's first heritage trail, representing a significant development of monuments and historical buildings in the transition period. The development of museums and monuments functioned to build historical archives on Hong Kong that would last after 1997. Historical representations in the transition period encoded Hong Kong's history in a particular way that addressed a range of public feelings about China's resumption of sovereignty over Hong Kong, including the historical roles of Britain and China in the colony and the future uncertainty about Hong Kong's way of life.

Although Hong Kong and China seem to have constructed different narratives of the future, they have developed a shared neoliberal path. After all, Hong Kong has maintained one of the world's freest market economies, and China's economic success has recently emerged as an alternative model for world development. The countdown to the 2008 Beijing Olympics promotes the compelling idea of "one world, one dream" as a way of linking the world's future to China's economic development. In the context of the current popular and scholarly debates about the role of the rising China in the world, I conclude the book by asking readers to reflect critically on the relationship between globalization, neoliberalism, and democratic politics.

1 The Hong Kong question

From sovereignty to government

What the Chinese government called the "Hong Kong question" (*xianggang wenti*) was one of the most important national reunification problems in modern China. The Hong Kong question refers to a historical problem of British occupation of Hong Kong in the second half of the nineteenth century. The British gradually occupied the Hong Kong territories through three treaties. First, after the first Opium War (1840–1842), the Treaty of Nanjing (1842) ceded Britain Hong Kong Island. Next, after the second Opium War (1856–1860), Britain forced the Qing government to sign the Treaty of Beijing (1860), giving Britain the Kowloon Peninsula and Stonecutters Island. Finally, Britain leased the New Territories (the area north of Kowloon up to the Shenzhen River as well as 235 islands) through the Extension of the Colony treaty (1898), which granted a ninety-nine-year lease set to expire in 1997. The current geopolitical space called Hong Kong is a product of these three treaties.

The Hong Kong question permeates the entire historical experience of modern China. The Treaty of Nanjing marks the beginning of the modern era, when China moved out of an essentially isolated society and began joining an international system of nation states.[1] Through the nineteenth century the Qing government was forced to sign a series of "unequal treaties" (*bupingdeng tiaoyue*) with Western powers and Japan. By means of these treaties, a number of cities such as Shanghai and Guangzhou (Canton) became treaty ports, Hong Kong became a British colony and Macau a Portuguese colony,[2] and western imperial powers enjoyed the rights of extraterritoriality and most-favored nation trade status. Responding to the increasing foreign business, military, and religious presence in China, the Qing government gradually established the institutions of modern government. The first government office for dealing with foreign trade, the foreign-managed Inspectorate of Customs (later renamed the Qing Imperial Maritime Customs) was established in 1854. The first foreign affairs office, the Office for the Management of the Business of All Foreign Countries (*Zongli Yamen*) was established in 1861. Henry Wheaton's *Elements of International Law*, a text commonly used in international affairs, was translated into Chinese by W. A. P. Martin (an American missionary) for the government in 1862. In addition, beginning in the 1840s, large numbers of Chinese, especially those from southern and southeastern China, left the country in search of economic opportunities, immigrating to Southeast Asia, Australia, and South and North America.[3] According to one estimate, 2,355,000 Chinese lived and worked overseas between 1840 and 1900.[4] The numbers were so large that the category of "overseas Chinese" (*huaqiao*) was formed in the second half of the nineteenth century.

In addressing this historical legacy, the Chinese government faced three major challenges. The first was to recover the Hong Kong territories (especially the leased New Territories) through diplomatic negotiations with the British government. This could not be accomplished without simultaneously addressing the second challenge: how to deal with the entire experience of Western colonialism and imperialism in modern China, especially the problem of "sovereignty" (*zhuquan*) as marked by the loss of Hong Kong (more precisely, Hong Kong Island and the Kowloon Peninsula) and of Macau. The third challenge was to translate the solutions to the first two problems into the process of constructing a qualitatively new historical time for the Chinese nation state that incorporates places like Hong Kong and Macau. In this chapter I argue that in addressing the Hong Kong question, the Chinese government shifted the status of Hong Kong from a question of national sovereignty to a governmental problem. This shift was the important condition under which Hong Kong's return to China could become a process of cultural transformation.

In the Republican period (1911–1949), the Nationalist government addressed the Hong Kong question following the principle of "abolishing old treaties, signing new treaties" (*fei jiu yue, ding xing yue*). The Chinese government's negotiations with Britain in this period were always conditioned by the global expansion of Western imperialism, which divided the world into "spheres of influence." The Berlin Conference of 1884 parceled out Africa among the Western imperialist powers.[5] The Versailles Conference of 1919 epitomized the collusion of foreign powers in deciding the fate of China. As in Africa, China became a site of imperialist powers struggling over spheres of influence. Eighteen foreign powers, including Britain, Russia, Japan, Germany, France, and the United States, colonized various parts of China by force and enforced extraterritorial rights in some fifty treaty ports beginning in the 1840s.[6] At the Washington Conference of 1921, major Western powers formally recognized China as a sovereign nation state, giving it some increase in power. The Chinese delegation's request for the return of Hong Kong, however, was denied. In 1924, Sun Yat-sen, the leader of the Nationalist government, announced that the development of a modern, sovereign Chinese state had to be based on "abolishing all unequal treaties."[7] Over the following two decades, this became the guiding principle in negotiations with Britain over the future of Hong Kong. China's alliance with the Allied Forces in World War II presented a good opportunity for modifying existing treaties with the United States and Britain, and in 1942, China signed new treaties with both countries. The treaty with Britain, however, avoided the Hong Kong question despite China's efforts to address it.[8]

After the establishment of the People's Republic of China (PRC) in 1949, Mao Zedong declared that his communist government would not recognize any of the unequal treaties, including the three treaties regarding Hong Kong. In practice, however, the government's policy on Hong Kong followed the principle of "long-term consideration, gaining full benefit" (*changqi dasuan, chongfen liyong*). Until the end of the 1970s when Deng Xiaoping's government began to pressure Britain to return Hong Kong to China, this principle effectively preserved Hong Kong's status quo, including its capitalist system.[9] Occasionally, the Chinese government even actively avoided any interference in Hong Kong. In 1967, for example, Premier Zhou Enlai prohibited the People's Liberation Army from entering Hong Kong.

Several factors shaped the development of the long-term consideration, gaining full benefit policy. The communist government in the early years of the PRC needed international recognition and support, especially in light of the U.S.-led international embargo against the PRC. Britain, in contrast to the United States, not only did not actively support the Nationalist government in its fight against the communists during the civil war period, but it also was one of the first major Western powers to recognize the communist government in 1949. Thus, Mao's government wanted to take advantage of Britain's "neutral" position. Moreover, Chinese leaders believed that the new country, once it became stabilized, could use Hong Kong. Zhou Enlai's 1957 speech clearly laid out a strategy for addressing the Hong Kong question from the perspective economic development in China:

> We cannot treat Hong Kong like the inland. Our policy toward Hong Kong is different from that in the inland. Otherwise, the consequences will not be good. Because Hong Kong, under the British rule, is still a purely capitalist market, it cannot and should not become socialist. Hong Kong can survive and develop only if it fully follows the principles of capitalism. We can benefit from this . . . Hong Kong may become a useful harbor for our economy . . . Hong Kong's entrepreneurs are our friends; what they are doing is capitalist not imperialist. We have cooperated with the nationalist bourgeoisie in the past, and we should work with Hong Kong's entrepreneurs in the future . . . At present, to carry out socialist construction after the basic completion of socialist revolution, we may treat Hong Kong as the basis for establishing our economic ties with foreign countries, attracting foreign capital, and acquiring foreign currencies.[10]

Thus, Zhou explicitly made one major point: China's socialist system should not interfere with Hong Kong's capitalist system because the socialist economy in the Chinese "inland" (*neidi*) could use Hong Kong as a bridge to the capitalist market. During the Korean War, for example, goods from China were exported through Hong Kong for the sake of acquiring foreign currencies. Zhou's predominant economic view on the Hong Kong question, a perspective also containing a policy of nonintervention by the Chinese state, was inherited and further expanded by Deng Xiaoping during the economic reforms that began in the late 1970s.

A major reason that Mao's government paid special attention to the economic aspect of the Hong Kong question was a significant flow of laborers and capital from the mainland to the Hong Kong territories between the late 1940s and the beginning of the Cultural Revolution. Millions of these refugees and immigrants from China were unskilled laborers, but a few brought with them both capital and industrial-technological knowledge. According to one estimate, several billion Hong Kong dollars flowed into the territory in these two decades; between 1947 and 1949, some 228 Shanghai enterprises transferred their registration to Hong Kong. Hong Kong's textiles industry basically originated with the newly arrived settlers. Registered factories increased rapidly, from 2,384 in 1954 to 10,478 at the end of the 1960s.[11] Once Hong Kong's economic development absorbed the migrant laborers from China, the Hong Kong government began to control the territories' border with the PRC.[12] Meanwhile, the potential for the PRC to benefit from Hong Kong's rapid industrial development was the pragmatic basis for the Chinese government's policy toward Hong Kong.

As the PRC acquired more prominent international status in the early 1970s, the government began actively to address the Hong Kong question. In 1971, when the communist government of the mainland replaced the nationalist government of Taiwan at the United Nations, it also became the only legitimate government of China and the only one that could deal with the Hong Kong question on behalf of the Chinese people. In this political context, the government took two actions. The first concerned the relationship between national unification and the politics of the nation state. In establishing normal diplomatic relations with the United States through the Sino–American Joint Communiqué of February 28, 1972, the Chinese government opposed the principle of "one country, two governments" as a way to resolve the Taiwan question.[13] Although this principle related specifically to Taiwan, it also had implications for Hong Kong and Macau. The Chinese government's position was that the PRC could not unify with Taiwan, Hong Kong, and Macau if the governments in these territories had equal powers of national sovereignty, for example, to formulate national laws. Thus, the PRC would recognize the governments of Taiwan, Hong Kong, or Macau only if those governments had strictly administrative powers, reserving legislative and juridical powers for the Beijing government.[14]

The second action directly concerning Hong Kong and Macau was to have the United Nations exclude them from its list of territories that were considered colonies, to prevent them from following the route of many other former colonies and asserting their independence. On March 8, 1972, Huang Hua, the Chinese ambassador to the United Nations, sent a formal letter to the UN Special Committee on Colonization, stating China's position on Hong Kong and Macau:

> The settlement of the questions of Hong Kong and Macau is entirely within China's sovereign right and does not at all fall under the ordinary category of colonial territories. Consequently, they should not be included in the list of colonial territories covered by the declaration on the granting of independence to colonial countries and people (*South China Morning Post*, March 13, 1972).

Eventually, the UN General Assembly accepted the Special Committee on Colonization's recommendation to exclude Hong Kong and Macau from the list of colonial territories. By virtue of this resolution, the Chinese government effectively separated what they considered an issue of national sovereignty from the global context of colonialism, which in practice meant that international cooperative efforts would be entailed to resolve the territories' status. Consequently, the situation of these territories became merely a governmental problem of the Chinese state, a problem of the cultural formation of colonialism and imperialism—their historical, aesthetic, and everyday life aspects—all of which were to be resolved during the Hong Kong countdown period (1984–1997).

Once becoming one of the five permanent members of the United Nations, the PRC also formally established normal diplomatic relations with Britain (on March 13, 1972). This created a channel by which the Chinese government could directly engage the British government in negotiations over the Hong Kong problem. In the early 1970s, Chinese leaders such as Zhou Enlai and Mao Zedong mentioned several times in meetings with British officials that China and Britain had to address the future of Hong Kong because Britain's lease of the New Territories would expire within a few decades.[15] No substantial talks took place however until Deng Xiaoping succeeded Mao as leader of the Chinese government.

Entering the new era of reforms in 1978, the Chinese government expressed a strong desire to recover Hong Kong and developed a policy of treating Hong Kong as a problem of national reunification. In March 1979, Deng Xiaoping met Murray MacLehose, Hong Kong's twenty-fifth governor, and explicitly told him that the PRC would grant Hong Kong a special position and guarantee its special treatment, regardless of how the Hong Kong question were resolved. It was in this important meeting that Deng said, "In a relatively long period of time in this century and the next century, Hong Kong will maintain its capitalism, and China its socialism. Thus, the investors should have confidence."[16] The idea of allowing socialism and capitalism to coexist was formally incorporated into the "one country, two systems" principle.

The "one country, two systems" principle was formulated to solve the problem of national unification in a way that positively shaped economic reforms. Deng and other senior government officials who had personally experienced the chaos of the Cultural Revolution viewed the avoidance of both internal social unrest and international conflicts as necessary for China's successful economic development. The "one country, two systems" principle would accomplish this. In a meeting with an overseas Chinese scholar, Li Yaoji, in January 1982, Deng first used the phrase "one country, two systems," and explained that it applied to both Taiwan and Hong Kong: "Two systems are permissible, if they don't destroy our system, and we don't destroy theirs."[17]

The implementation of the "one country, two systems" principle in addressing Hong Kong's status enabled the Chinese government to take the lead in diplomatic negotiations with the British government. Three months before the first scheduled diplomatic meeting in September 1982, Deng Xiaoping announced the core values of the one country, two system principle with regard to Hong Kong: "regaining [China's] sovereignty; preserving [Hong Kong's] prosperity; maintaining [Hong Kong's] system; and Hong Kong's people ruling Hong Kong."

Between September 1982 and July 1984, the two countries held formal diplomatic negotiations over the future of Hong Kong. Deng Xiaoping laid out China's position clearly at his first meeting with British Prime Minister Margaret Thatcher. From the perspective of the Chinese government, three issues needed to be resolved. The first was the issue of sovereignty. When Britain's lease of the New Territories expired on July 1, 1997, China was determined to take all of the Hong Kong territories back—not just the New Territories, but also Hong Kong Island and Kowloon, which had been ceded to Britain by other, separate treaties. Second, Hong Kong would retain a local government to maintain the territory's prosperity after its return. Deng said:

> To preserve Hong Kong's prosperity, we hope to receive Britain's cooperation. This, however, doesn't mean that Hong Kong's continuous prosperity must be based on [maintaining] the British administration. Hong Kong's continuous prosperity essentially depends on how China, after taking Hong Kong back, administers Hong Kong by adopting policies appropriate for Hong Kong. Hong Kong's present political and economic system, and even most of Hong Kong's laws can be preserved. Of course, some reforms are needed. Hong Kong will continue its practice of capitalism; many currently effective institutions will be kept.[18]

Finally, it was vital to avoid any chaos or instability during the transition period. Deng told Thatcher that should a serious incident happen in this period, China would consider taking Hong Kong back earlier by whatever means were appropriate. Thus, China's position covered the issues of China's sovereignty, Hong Kong's government, and the transition.

From the British perspective, the three treaties relating to Hong Kong were still valid. Their position was that Britain had taken permanent possession of Hong Kong Island and Kowloon while temporarily leasing the New Territories. The British government wanted to extend its lease over the New Territories after 1997 and thus retain sovereignty over the entire Hong Kong territories. This proposal faced two practical difficulties. First, the Chinese government refused to consider extension of the New Territories lease. Second, from a practical standpoint, the New Territories not only accounted for most of Hong Kong's area, but also supplied necessary resources such as drinking water and food to Hong Kong Island and Kowloon. Thus, the latter could hardly survive without the New Territories. Knowing that the lease-extension proposal would be rejected by China, Britain's real objective was to seek continued governance of Hong Kong in the name of preserving its prosperity. However, Deng Xiaoping's anticipatory statement about China's plan to retain Hong Kong's capitalist system weakened Britain's argument. Even Margaret Thatcher considered Deng's "one country, two systems" a brilliant idea.[19] The two sides agreed quickly on the first two issues (sovereignty and government), then moved on to discuss cooperative arrangements for the transfer of sovereignty. On December 19, 1984, representatives of the Chinese and British governments officially signed the Sino–British Joint Declaration, under which the Chinese government would resume sovereignty over Hong Kong on July 1, 1997.

Between December 1984 and July 1997, the status of the Hong Kong question shifted significantly. Prior to the signing of the Joint Declaration, the Hong Kong question was conditioned by the three nineteenth-century treaties. Because the territories legally belonged to Britain, China could not legitimately formulate concrete policies and laws that would govern the daily lives of Hong Kong's residents. Once the Joint Declaration effectively replaced the old treaties, however, the Hong Kong question changed from being a matter of regaining national sovereignty to a problem of governance. In collaboration with the British government, the Chinese government actively planned how post-1997 Hong Kong was to be governed.

Diplomats from two countries formed the Joint Liaison Group to prepare for the transfer of sovereignty, while the Chinese government focused on developing the Basic Law for the future Hong Kong Special Administrative Region. In June 1985, the government appointed the Basic Law Drafting Committee, consisting of thirty-six members from the mainland and twenty-three from Hong Kong. Soon thereafter, the Hong Kong committee members formed the Basic Law Consultative Committee (consisting of 180 members, all from Hong Kong), whose job was to advise the Drafting Committee.

The drafting of the Basic Law followed the principle that Hong Kong's people would administer Hong Kong's affairs, but it also raised the question of selecting the future leadership of Hong Kong. According to Deng Xiaoping, "Hong Kong people can administer Hong Kong. I am confident of this. Hong Kong was able to achieve its prosperity because of the Hong Kong people, the majority of which are in fact Chinese." As to which of the "Hong Kong people" could govern the future Hong Kong, Deng emphasized that those selected should primarily be "patriots" (*aiguozhe*). Who is a patriot? Deng answered:

> A patriot respects his own nationality (*minzu*), sincerely supports the Motherland's resumption of sovereignty over Hong Kong, and does not cause any damage to Hong Kong's prosperity and stability. Anyone who possesses these qualities is a patriot, regardless whether [the person] believes in capitalism, feudalism, or even the slavery system. We do not require that Hong Kong patriots agree with China's socialist system, we only require them to love the Motherland and Hong Kong.[20]

In 1987, Deng met with the Drafting Committee to address two critical questions raised about Hong Kong's government. First, what would be the appropriate form of government in post-1997 Hong Kong? Would the Hong Kong people be able to vote for their representatives in direct elections? Deng answered:

> Hong Kong's [future] system should not become Westernized, completely duplicating the West. Hong Kong's present system, which is not the same as that in Britain and the United States, has been developed over the past one and a half centuries. If we change it completely by introducing three separate legislative, executive, and juridical branches as a measure of democracy's meaning, I am afraid this is inappropriate . . . Does a direct election system serve the interest of Hong Kong? I don't believe it does. As I have said previously, Hong Kong people will administer Hong Kong. Will this happen only by means of the direct election system? We said that those who govern Hong Kong's affairs should be Hong Kong people who love the Motherland and Hong Kong. Will a direct election select these kinds of people? . . . Even if we decide to adopt the direct election system, we still need a period of transition and to proceed step by step.[21]

Deng's speech pointed to three aspects of the central government's position on Hong Kong's governance. As a colony, Hong Kong's local government[22] had not had the same democratic structure as British government. It was not appropriate to change this situation in the final years of British rule. Second, if changes were necessary, they should not aim at Westernization or duplication of a Western system of government. Finally, the Chinese government explicitly opposed a direct election system because it could not guarantee the selection of patriots as Hong Kong's leaders. In sum, the Chinese government's position was that Hong Kong's government should change very little prior to the handover.

The Drafting Committee's second concern was whether the Chinese government would intervene for the purpose of maintaining Hong Kong's stability. Deng responded,

> The central government won't damage Hong Kong's interest. At the same time, we don't want to see incidents damaging to both national and Hong Kong's interests. For example, if some people [in Hong Kong] use swear words to curse the Chinese Communist Party or China, we would still tolerate them. However, if they began to act, in the name of "democracy," to use Hong Kong as a base for opposing the mainland, we have to do something. The first intervention would come from Hong Kong's administration, not from the mainland's army in Hong Kong. [However,] only in the situation of chaos, major social disorder, would the Hong Kong-based army get involved. Nevertheless, intervention is always [a necessary option].[23]

Beijing's major concern, understandable for historical reasons, was that Hong Kong could potentially be used as a base for opposing its government. After all, Hong Kong had been an important base of revolutionary activity that had contributed to the collapse of the Qing Dynasty and the establishment of the Republic of China in 1911. Hong Kong also became a safe haven for refugees from China, especially for the capitalists who escaped from the mainland at the end of the 1940s and for those labeled class enemies by the PRC before and during the Cultural Revolution. These former outcasts could use Hong Kong as a base for future dissident activity. The government's bottom line seemed to be that as long as anti-China activists did not create social disorder, they would be tolerated.

While no anti-China incidents in Hong Kong before 1997 created chaos either in the territories or on the Chinese mainland, the dissident movement in China in 1989, ironically, seriously affected the transitional Hong Kong. No longer willing to tolerate student and citizen demonstrations in Beijing's Tiananmen Square and in other cities, the Chinese government deployed the People's Liberation Army to repress the demonstrators, during which hundreds of protestors were killed at Tiananmen Square. More than one million Hong Kong residents (of a total population of 5.6 million) took part in demonstrations supporting the democratic movement in China and protesting the Chinese government's brutal repression. After the signing of the 1984 Joint Declaration, Hong Kong residents protested against Britain or China because some of them felt that they were victims of British colonialism, and yet, were not allowed to participate in the Sino–British negotiations over the future of the place they call home.[24] In 1989, their demonstrations against the Chinese government's repression marked a beginning of calling for meaningful changes of Hong Kong's political system. When asked about the effects of the dissident movement in China on her, for example, the popular film actress Deanie Ip said:

> Since June 4, I've felt that nothing is more important than the achievement of democracy . . . I don't know much about democracy or human rights, but since June 4, I've been going to the bookstores, thinking

> maybe it's not too late to learn. The events of June 4 made me want to learn more about democracy . . . become a person who respects other people, a person who knows about citizens' rights.[25]

While some Hong Kong residents like Ip consciously learned about democracy and struggled for its costs, large numbers of them began to emigrate overseas, Canada being a popular destination. Each year between 1990 and 1996, more than ten thousand Hong Kong immigrants settled there.[26] Hong Kong residents' response to the 1989 military crackdown expressed a shared anxiety about their post-1997 future, especially what life would be like under the sovereignty of the Chinese nation state. According to one observer

> Since the signing of the Joint Declaration, discontent had been simmering. Many felt betrayed by the British. Frustration turned into resentment of both the British and China. The majority of the people of Hong Kong were legally British but ethnically Chinese. Few, if any, thought of themselves as British, but neither did they identify with a China governed by the Communists.[27]

In Hong Kong cinema, one of the most important forms of popular culture in the territory, the future nationhood was expressed as distracted and disarticulated (Tsui Hark's films); utterly and permanently lost (Wong Kai-wai's films); displaced and relocated (films of Johnnie To and Ching Siu-tung); remembered and reconstructed (films of Jeff Lau and Corey Yuen); and destroyed and reinvented (Stephen Chiau's films).[28] Despite their different emphases, these expressions all pointed to the same underlying fears over the autonomy or lack thereof of post-1997 Hong Kong.

In July 1989, both to address Hong Kong residents' concerns for the future and to restore their confidence in Hong Kong, the British government announced a package of measures: the introduction of a bill of rights for Hong Kong, increasing the number of directly elected government officials to develop a democratic system of political representation, and creation of a nationality scheme that would give prominent Hong Kong residents British passports and thereby the confidence to remain until and beyond 1997.[29] On accepting appointment as Hong Kong's governor, Christopher Patten undertook a series of political reforms. He argued that legislators and civil servants could remain in office through the transfer of power, so that these reforms would survive the transfer of power. In his first annual policy speech in October 1992, Patten outlined his proposal for elections for the three tiers of government between then and 1997. In the next election (scheduled for 1995) the sixty-member Legislative Council would be reconstituted to eliminate the twenty-one seats historically appointed by the governor. These seats would be filled by increasing from eighteen to twenty the number of seats directly elected from geographic constituencies, and by increasing the number of indirectly elected members representing professional and other groups (functional constituencies) from twenty-one to thirty; simultaneously, the functional constituency electorate would expand from 110,000 to 2.7 million (almost the entire workforce). An election committee comprising elected members of the district boards would select the remaining ten members. In addition, Patten also proposed that the geographic constituencies become single-seat constituencies, that the voting age be lowered from twenty-one to eighteen, and that the appointed seats on the district boards be abolished.[30]

Patten's action marked a significant departure from longstanding British policy that between 1969 and 1995 had actively hindered the development of a representative government in Hong Kong. According to a recently declassified government report entitled *Hong Kong: Long Term Study* (written by a ministerial committee in 1969), the British government, in view of the possible return of Hong Kong to China, would "endeavor to avoid doing anything in Hong Kong to make the transfer more difficult, for example, by constitutional changes toward representative and more responsible government."[31] This secret report showed that the British government had neither the intention of nor a plan for developing a representative democracy in Hong Kong until shortly before the handover.[32]

Patten's reforms also encouraged the development of political parties, which had been discouraged by the colony's political structure and were illegal before 1990. Subsequently, three major types of parties emerged. First were "pro-democracy parties," of which the Democratic Party, established in 1994, quickly became the most influential in government by winning local popular elections. Second were "pro-business parties," which operated within the functional constituencies selecting the thirty indirectly elected Legislative Council members; of these the Liberal Party established in 1993 was most prominent. The third group, referred to as "pro-China parties," promoted Beijing's interests. Because the Chinese Communist Party had technically been illegal in Hong Kong since the 1920s, it had operated underground through trade unions and front organizations such as the Democratic Alliance for the Betterment of Hong Kong (DAB). In addition, the CCP had multiple nongovernmental channels of influence in pre-1997 Hong Kong, including pro-China newspapers (such as *Wen Hui Pao* and *Ta Kung Pao*), and major corporate groups, such as the Bank of China, China Resources, the China International Trust and Investment Corporation (CITIC), and China Travel Service.[33]

The Chinese government flatly rejected Patten's proposed political reforms, announcing in August 1994 that, regardless of what Patten did before 1997, the British Hong Kong government would be dissolved by July 1, 1997, and a new government formed in accordance with the Basic Law. Moreover, Beijing also challenged whether a democratic government would have the power to preserve Hong Kong's "free market" economy. In 1993, for example, Zhou Nan, director of the Hong Kong Bureau of China's Xinhua News Agency, reiterated the vital connection Deng Xiaoping had elaborated between

Hong Kong's economic prosperity and its political stability. As quoted by Zhou, Deng reportedly said:

> Hong Kong's achievement today cannot be separated from Hong Kong compatriots' hard-working wisdom and path-breaking creativity. However, it has been based on unique conditions: long-term stability, undisturbed by politics and with few political disputes throughout the whole society; excellent geographic and meteorological conditions; plus Britain's administration and China's support. Because of them, Hong Kong's development has been faster than that of most of the industrialized countries in Western Europe. We do not support radical political disputes in Hong Kong. If efforts and energies were focused on political disputes, Hong Kong would lose vitality, its investments would disappear, and large numbers of people would become unemployed. These circumstances have already happened in Europe, America, and Asia. Therefore, we must follow the Basic Law to maintain Hong Kong's system, making as little change as possible.[34]

As this speech shows, although Deng did not use the word neoliberalism, he was nevertheless aware of something special about Hong Kong's capitalism, that is, its spirit, that especially associated with Hong Kong people's entrepreneurialism. This capitalist spirit and economic development potential were independent of and separate from democracy; he believed that Hong Kong's economic prosperity had been based on the absence of social disorder associated with political disputes, a situation unique in the global context. Thus, in effect, Deng argued that there was no inherent connection between entrepreneurial capitalism and democracy, and political disputes should be kept separate from economic development. Both China and Britain, according to Deng, had contributed to Hong Kong's development.

The Basic Law was finalized in 1990,[35] and in the spring of 1992 Deng Xiaoping traveled to the Shenzhen Special Economic Zone to observe the achievements of China's economic reforms. His speeches during this trip set forth the principal guidelines for reorienting governmental logic toward economic measures rather than political ideologies. As the resolution to the Hong Kong question moved beyond the diplomatic arrangements between China and Britain, they began drawing widespread participation of ordinary people in both China and Hong Kong. The December 19, 1994, installation of the Hong Kong countdown clock transformed Hong Kong's return from diplomatic wrangling to impending fact. As an entirely new concept of time used in synchronizing Chinese society, the countdown became widely accepted in everyday life; appropriated in media advertisements; and implemented in official activities (see Chapter 2). By the time the Chinese government resumed its sovereignty over Hong Kong on July 1, 1997, and Hong Kong officially became a special administrative region of the People's Republic of China, the three temporal elements that had constituted the "historical time" of the Chinese nation state—colonialism, socialism, and capitalism—had been completely reordered to construct a qualitatively "new time" of modernity.

From the birth of the modern Chinese nation state in the first quarter of the twentieth century, when the Hong Kong question was first raised, Sino–British negotiations about the future of Hong Kong had taken about sixty years to reach a resolution. Many important factors contributed to the Chinese and British finally reaching an agreement. The expiration of Britain's lease of the New Territories from China was an obvious one. A more important reason, however, was that both countries agreed on maintaining Hong Kong's capitalist system, as expressed in the goal of preserving "Hong Kong's prosperity." This was not at all incidental. Deng Xiaoping and Margaret Thatcher, despite coming from different national and historical perspectives, arguably favored a similar ideology of neoliberal development. The two leaders were neoliberals in practice; that is, both took actions to separate the government from the market economy while retaining the prerogative of government to intervene when necessary to support the economy.[36] While Thatcher's government systematically implemented such neoliberal policies as privatization, reduction of social welfare, and tax reduction, Deng's government first rejected the politics of the Cultural Revolution, and then took advantage of Hong Kong's return to undertake a cultural transformation. The beginning of this transformation during the transition period is the topic of the next chapter.

2 The affective economy of the Hong Kong countdown

Media convergence, public feelings, and neoliberal subjectivity

On the tenth anniversary of the signing of the Sino–British Joint Declaration, a giant clock, mounted on a 16-meter-high, 9.6-meter-wide metal panel and overhung with Chinese national flags and emblems, was installed between two pillars in front of the building jointly occupied by the National Museum of Chinese History and the National Museum of Chinese Revolution (Figure 2.1). At the top of the panel were the five gold stars of the Chinese flag. Underneath them were four lines of Chinese characters:

> The Chinese Government (*Zhongguo zhengfu*)
> Resumes the exercise of sovereignty over Hong Kong (*dui Xianggang huifu xingshi zhuquan*)
> Counting down time (*daojishi*)
> to July 1, 1997 (*ju 1997 nian 7 yue 1 ri*).

Beneath that was a digital readout of the days (*tian*) and seconds (*miao*) remaining until the British withdrawal from Hong Kong. Near the bottom, in small characters, appeared the names of the clock's sponsors, including the magazine *China Brand-names*, China's Southern Aviation Engineering Company, Linghua Food-Flavoring Group, Ji'ning, Shangdong, and the National Museum of Chinese Revolution. Finally, below these sponsors, was the date on which the clock began its countdown: December 19, 1994. From 11:10 on that date until 0:00 on July 1, 1997, the Tiananmen countdown clock counted 925 days, or 79,879,800 seconds. A week after the handover, on July 8, 1997, the clock was moved from Tiananmen Square to a new permanent home at the Cultural Square (*wenhua guangchang*) under the Badaling section of the Great Wall. Meanwhile, a 1:16-scale replica was made for display at the National Museum of Chinese Revolution.[1]

During the process of Hong Kong's return to China, the iconography of the Hong Kong countdown clock enabled an affective economy that addressed collective and individual feelings toward the past loss of and impending reunification with Hong Kong. As described in the introduction, a cultural transformation in the development of this affective economy broke down the general governmental problem of Hong Kong's return into two specific

Figure 2.1 The Hong Kong countdown clock, Tiananmen Square, Beijing (photo by the author).

components: media aesthetic and media spectacle. As a problem of media dialectic, the countdown clock itself involved the development of new media technology and materials.[2] A multimedia device, it functioned as a timepiece telling multiplicity-based or nonlinear time, as I describe later in the chapter. The significance of this new temporality may be appreciated through a historical discussion of China's public time-telling. Meanwhile, the uses of the countdown device and its embodied temporality encoded the discourse of the countdown in such a way as to shape narratives about the public's feelings toward the reappearance of Hong Kong in the Chinese nation state. Departing from the conventional communication model of ideological campaigns by the Chinese Communist Party (CCP), the Hong Kong countdown took the form of a "public relations campaign" (*gongguan chehua*). To understand why it has been considered one of the most successful public relations campaigns in recent years, it is necessary to undertake a close examination of the way in which affective labor was involved in shaping discourses of the countdown. Meanwhile, a series of media spectacles incorporated the countdown clock into activities of everyday life.[3] As an ordinary timepiece is used in planning daily activities, the countdown clock became a time-telling tool for organizing everyday life during (and after) Hong Kong's return to China. The consumption of a media spectacle like the countdown clock, I will show, concretely shaped the Hong Kong countdown as a government project of circulating the neoliberal norm of the entrepreneurial subject in society.

Toward multiplicity-based time: A history of media convergence in public time-telling

The Tiananmen countdown clock is not a conventional mechanical timepiece; rather, it is a multimedia device that integrates mechanical, electric, and digital media. It supports a new notion of time that is qualitatively different than the kind of time recorded by a conventional mechanical clock. This new notion of time, which goes beyond the linear notion of clock time, regards time as not only objective and precise, but also subjective and reflective. The qualities of objectiveness and precision allow time to become practical and manageable, while the qualities of subjectivity and reflection, which are experiential and cultural, make possible the creative use of time in social action, including reconciling seemingly contradictory temporalities. This multiplicity-based time became the temporal structure of the Hong Kong countdown to coordinate the relationship between different temporal frames such as the political time of patriotism and the economic time of making money. A historical examination of public time-telling helps in understanding the changing relationship between media and time-telling, an important issue raised by the Hong Kong countdown clock.

Until recently sound, not sight, had been the most important aspect of time-telling in China. Drums and bells were widely used to broadcast the time in Chinese towns and cities until clocks were used at the beginning of the twentieth century. Available historical records have traced the use of drums in time-telling to the ninth century. As the *New History of the Tang Dynasty* (*Xin Tang shu*) tells us:

> At sunset, the [public] drums were beaten eight hundred times and the gates were closed . . . At the fifth watch [dawn], the drums within the palace were beaten, and then the drums in all the streets were beaten so that the noise would be heard everywhere; then all the gates of the wards and markets were opened.[4]

During the Tang Dynasty, some cities had as many as ten drum towers. Each tower functioned as a slave timepiece synchronized with the master timepiece (the drum in the palace). The drums over all the city gates relayed the sound of the official drum to the public. Other cities had only one drum tower (as Beijing did from the Yuan to the Qing dynasties). The drum tower in Beijing (constructed in 1272) had twenty-four drums (each with a leather-covered head 1.5 meters in diameter), and next to it was a bell tower housing a 5.5-meter-high bronze bell. Every day at the *yin* (about 5:00 a.m.) and the *wu* (about 7:00 p.m.) double-hours, the drums and bell were struck twice. In between these times the bell stayed silent and only the drums announced the changing of the nightly watches. Thus, a public drum tower in a traditional Chinese city had two functions: to announce the beginning and end of the day and to signal the nightly watches.[5]

In a city like Beijing, the sounds of the drums and bells regulated when residents worked, rested, opened the city gates, and retreated into individual courtyard compounds. The daily schedule of a farmer, in contrast, was to work in the field from sunrise to dark. His work was interrupted only by the noon meal that his family brought him in accordance with traditional custom. The farmer's wife might assist with field labor to a greater or lesser degree, depending on local practice. But she was always the spinner and weaver, and her work might last until midnight if she could afford the oil or share a light with another woman.[6] In some areas, a farm drum and a farm water clock were used to coordinate collective work. In Sichuan (or Szechwan) Province, for example, collective farming was practiced in the Song and Yuan dynasties. The *Book of Agriculture* (*Nongshu*) (written by Wang Zhen in the Yuan Dynasty) cites a poem:

> The weeding drum is seen when one enters Szechwan. It is used first to cause [the farmers] to assemble, then to give rhythm to their work and keep them from conversations which might hinder their work. The sound of the drum is powerful and brisk, varying in speed and pitch but having not melody. It is continuously heard from morning till evening.[7]

Thus, the weeding drum was an effective means for regulating farmwork and discouraging dalliance, rather than for measuring the passage of time per se.

Whereas the drum was used to coordinate large-scale activities in cities and rural areas, sundials, water clocks, and incense sticks were most often used to tell time for individuals and small groups, for example, within a family or temple. The widespread use of incense is preserved in a common expression: "the time of burning an incense stick" (*yi zhu xiang de shi hou*).[8] Although a more exact system for measuring and telling time was developed to coordinate the harmonious relationship between heavenly and human affairs, it was used primarily by emperors and officials, not by ordinary people, particularly in rural areas. For ordinary people, the passage of time was measured using specific experiences such as drinking hot tea, consuming a bowl of rice, traveling a specified distance, or burning a stick of incense.

The introduction of mechanical clocks was tied to the history of Jesuit missionaries in China. After Chen Rui (1513–1585), the viceroy of the two Guang provinces (Guangdong and Guangxi), approved their missions in

1583, Italian Jesuit Michele Ruggieri, head of the Jesuit mission in Macao, came to Zhaoqing, Guangdong, accompanied by a young Jesuit priest, Matteo Ricci (1552–1610). They made an iron clock for the viceroy by 1584.[9] This historical incident opened a new chapter in European–Chinese contacts, after which clocks became one of the most important gifts Europeans used to curry favor with the Chinese elite. The gradual progression of Jesuit missions across China was made possible, at least in part, by the presentation of these clocks as gifts. In 1793, the delegation of Lord Macartney also presented the Emperor Qianlong with a timepiece showing the lunar phases.[10]

In addition to the Jesuit missionaries and official visitors from Europe, private companies also traded clocks with the Chinese. From the seventeenth to the early nineteenth centuries, what the British referred to as "sing-songs" dominated Sino–European trade: clocks, watches, and mechanical toys, made for the East Asia market, such as snuffboxes containing jeweled birds that sang when the lid was opened. Cox & Beale (the predecessor of Jardine, Matheson & Co.) was an important dealer in English sing-songs.[11] Such objects were one of the very few classes of European offerings to interest the Chinese before the age of full industrial production. Joseph Needham and his collaborators made an interesting comment on the significance of the sing-song trade:

> The important points are that the trade in clocks was the first, and for a long time the only, provision of machinery from the Western European to the Eastern Asian area; and secondly that its volume was far too small to compensate in any degree for the great drain in silver bullion caused by the purchase of tea, silk and minor "China goods" for the demands of the English home market. It was to counter this drain that the importation of Indian opium, though prohibited by the Chinese authorities, was undertaken. The Opium Wars . . . were the results. The "sing-song" trade . . . fell off very much after 1815, partly because of the growth of the Chinese clock-making industry, which produced timepieces for half the cost.[12]

Clearly, the replacement of clocks by opium in Sino–European trade was a crucial factor in the Opium Wars, which resulted in a series of other historical incidents: the British colonization of Hong Kong (1842–1898), the burning and looting of the imperial Summer Palace Yuanming Yuan (1860 and 1900), and the opening of port cities to international trade (1842, 1860, and 1900). Hence, the making of historical time in modern China should be separated neither from the economy of clock time nor from the history of Sino–European relations, including Hong Kong and its return to China.

As for European clocks imported to China, those made or bought in Europe by the Jesuits were of the modern type, constructed of metal with spring or weight drives and striking mechanisms. The Chinese named them "self-sounding bells" (*zi ming zhong*), referring to an object that automatically gives voice to time. Soon after the establishment of the Mission House by

Ruggieri in 1583, Ricci set up a big clock facing the street. According to Ricci's diary, the clock told time not only for passersby but also for people at a distance, by sounding the hour on a large bell.[13] By about 1603, clocks made for the China trade began to adopt the Chinese twelve double-hours time system.[14] Both Wang Shizhen, in his *Occasional Discussions North of Chizhou* (*Chi bei ou tan*) (1691), and Wang Renjun, in his *Scientific Traces in Olden Times* (*Ge zhi gu wei*) (1896), described the clock tower of a Christian church dedicated to the Blessed Virgin, near Ningbo, Zhejiang, where there was also a wind-organ and a telescope:

> There is a Standard Time Tower (*ding shi tai*) which has a huge bell underneath it. On a platform with images of immortals at the corners there are jacks which strike the bell and which are operated by revolving machinery . . . It sounds according to the (double-) hours, striking once at the end of *tzu* [*zi*] (11 p.m.–1 a.m.) and twelve at the beginning of *wu* (11 a.m.–1 p.m.), then going on from the end of *wu* when it strikes one, to the beginning of *tzu* [*zi*] when it strikes twelve. Day and night follow each other on the ring without the slightest error, a pointer indicating the twelve signs on a round dial. At every hour the bell sounds, the figures of the toads, etc., move, and the pointer indicates a particular position.[15]

How do we assess the significance of the adaptation of European clocks to the Chinese double-hours system? David L. Landes argues that once Ricci "brought European clocks to China," the Chinese "dramatically" changed their old attitude of rejecting European objects. Their acceptance of European clocks was "progress" not in the sense of "the transformation of indigenous technology," but in "the adoption of an alien device."[16] One could argue that the Chinese missed the opportunity to use European time-keeping technology to renew and improve their indigenous technology. However, why should the Chinese be expected to do this? From the perspective of European missionaries like Ricci, whether the Chinese adopted European clocks was far less important than whether the Chinese interest in clocks facilitated their missionary work.[17] Thus, from 1583 to 1912, although the clocks on Christian churches and foreign banks might have influenced the temporal concepts of nearby residents, and the clocks presented to Chinese officials and emperors were favored gifts, overall, they had very little impact on the Chinese concept of time.

This situation began to change when the Chinese government decided to adopt the Western calendar system after the collapse of the Qing Dynasty in 1911. The Nationalist Republic of China (1911–1949) used two calendar systems.[18] The first counted from 1911 and was based on the time the Republic of China had been in existence: the First Year of the Republic was 1911; the Second Year of the Republic, 1912; the Third Year of the Republic, 1913, and so forth. The second system began with 1912 and counted upward according to the Western Gregorian calendar.

Although every regime in Chinese history had had a standardized calendar, and more than one hundred calendrical systems had been used before 1911, it was not until 1912 that China instituted a national standard time.[19] China's national standard time was related to the international standard time system established in 1884 and calculated from Greenwich Mean Time.[20] Four international time zones (the fifth through eighth zones east of the Greenwich Mean Time) cross the territories of China, but only the local time of the eighth time zone at 120§ east longitude was used as the national standard time.

In the Republic of China, astronomical observatories were responsible for monitoring the time in cities where they were located. The French established China's first astronomical observatory in 1872 and began to inform local merchants of the time in 1884 when international standard time was instituted. The Germans set up an astronomical observatory in Qingdao in 1899 and began to inform local merchants of the time in 1904.[21] In 1926, the local telegram station began sending time signals to the whole country and to ships at sea. Radio was a common medium for time-telling. Other means of time-telling included firing a cannon at noon, setting up clocks at major intersections, and sending telegrams. Although the National Astronomical Observatory was established in Beijing in 1912, it did not begin its time-telling service until two years after the observatory moved to the capital city, Nanjing. (Initially, a cannon was fired at noon.) Beginning on April 1, 1929, the city of Nanjing used a K.S. electric clock (made in Germany) to send a public time signal at 6:00 p.m. each day (later changed to noon each day). In addition, the observatory also answered telephone inquires about the time. Public time-telling was disrupted by the Anti-Japanese Invasion War (1937–1945), but resumed thereafter. From 1947 to 1949, the Central Radio Station announced clock time to the whole country. Although the international standard time of the eighth time zone at 120§ east longitude was designated as the national standard time in the 1910s, the implementation of the standard time was a long process. Not until March 1935 did the Ministry of Communications require all telegram bureaus across the nation to use the standard time, and the Shanghai Wireless Telegram Bureau and Nanjing Wired Telegram Bureau were responsible for sending time signals to other telegram bureaus.[22]

After the PRC was established in 1949, the government decided to continue use of the Western calendar system and the local time of 120§ east longitude as the national standard time, referred to as "Beijing time" (*Beijing shijian*). (Beijing Time is, in fact, 14 minutes, 30 seconds off from the actual local time of Beijing.) In the PRC, mass media, particularly radio and television, played important roles in disseminating the consciousness of clock time across the country, particularly to the rural areas. From 1949 to the 1980s, radio was the most important mass medium, consisting of a national radio network, the Central People's Broadcasting Station, composed of the existing government-owned stations and the commercial stations in Shanghai. Radio signals from Beijing were transmitted across the country via a series of repeater stations that fed the signals to loudspeakers hung in central locations of villages so that everyone could hear the new government's voice and be subject to its temporal regulation of the day. During the 1949–1959 decade, the number of stations at the county level exploded from eight to 11,124, with 4,570,000 loudspeakers.[23] In the 1970s, personal radios began to appear in homes. By 1981, 42 percent of rural households and 100 percent of urban households had at least one radio.[24]

Chinese television began in 1956 and remained experimental until the 1960s. Between 1967 and 1970, only a few thousand television sets were produced and sold domestically, and only a dozen cities had television stations. In the mid-1970s, a national network, China Central Television (CCTV), was gradually developed with the goal of unifying the country through presentation of official news and information, culturally appropriate entertainment, and use of the official language. By 1978, roughly half a million sets were sold per year, and in 1979, China's television industry expanded rapidly, with nearly two million sets sold. In the 1980s, China entered the television age as the United States had done in the 1950s. By 1986, 95 percent of all urban families owned at least one television set. By 1990, Chinese families owned some 150 million television sets—about one set for every eight people nationwide and one set for every three to four people in the cities. Home viewership was more than 600 million.[25]

The explosion of radio and television has shaped the Chinese people's temporal consciousness of clock time. The time is announced on the air every hour on the hour, and regular nationwide news broadcasts attract huge audiences. By the 1950s, a radio news broadcast was transmitted nationwide every evening at 8:30.[26] CCTV's Evening News at 7:00 p.m. has been the most watched news program in the country since the late 1970s. If up until the 1980s 8:30 p.m. was marked as a shared moment of national time as people all across the country turned on their radios, the 7:00 p.m. television news became more than a national moment. It has been marked as advertising time, one of the most expensive time slots in the broadcast day.

Sponsorship of the news broadcast is open for public bidding each year. In 1996, the then-unknown Qinchi Liquor Company from Shandong spent RMB¥ 60 million (about US$7.23 million, based on an exchange rate of US$1 = 8.3 RMB) to win the bid. That year it sold nearly RMB¥ 1 billion worth of liquor (about $120 million). In 1997, the newly famous company spent RMB¥ 320 million (about $38.55 million) to win that year's bid (I discuss this case further later in the chapter).[27] Now time is measured by money.

Television has also contributed to the development of a public sense of "real time," particularly through live broadcasts (*shikuang zhuanbo*) of sporting events (national and international) and of the annual Spring Festival Gala (*chunjie lianhuan wanhui*). The first "real time" television event was CCTV's live telecast of the Women's Volleyball World Cup in 1981.[28] Situating a televized event in real time makes it more meaningful, a fact that can be used for political ends. In the spring of 1989, a thawing of Sino–Soviet relations led Mikhail Gorbachev to plan a trip to Beijing. With China in the international spotlight, student activists occupied Tiananmen Square for an indefinite period, demanding democracy and civil rights. By the time of Gorbachev's arrival on May 14, the protesters numbered 300,000, and three days later, there were one million. Taking advantage of the fact that most international news agencies had sent cameras and reporters to cover the reconciliation of the two communist giants, the Chinese students demanded *live* coverage of the Tiananmen events on May 15. Although the Chinese authorities rejected the demand, many international news agencies did broadcast live images of Tiananmen Square. In Hong Kong, the images were displayed on a giant screen in the city stadium, linking viewers in Hong Kong with the students at Tiananmen Square. Paul Virilio calls this public use of real time, in which real-time continuity substitutes for real-space continuity "teletopia."[29]

With the establishment of the Hong Kong countdown clock in 1994, the relationship between media and public time-telling entered a new age. For the first time ever, a public clock displayed time to the second. Its technological precision, its use of a hybrid form of media (mechanical, electronic, and digital), and its important dual function of counting and telling time were all unprecedented, qualitative departures from the features of a conventional mechanical clock.

It is obvious that the change from a mechanical to a digital clock shifts the readout from the mechanical sweep of hour, minute, and second hands around a dial to a change of digits. Less obvious however is that this shift of time display also changes the way in which we perceive time. On a traditional clock, we can see the hands, their spatial positions, and the divisions on the clock face, but we cannot decode the time unless we already have an understanding of time and how it is represented on a clock face. Martin Heidegger points out:

> Looking at the clock is grounded in and guided by a taking-time-for-oneself . . . Looking at the clock and orienting oneself *toward time* is essentially a *now-saying*. Here the now is always already understood and *interpreted* in its complete structural content of datability, spannedness, publicness, and worldliness.[30]

The interpretation of time on a traditional clock (that is, one with hands) is situated in the context of spatial measurement. The movement of the clock hands appears visually as a spatial change, which provides a sense of the passage of time from one moment to the next. The ongoing movement of the hands represents a continuous series of moments in time—of linear time in motion.

In contrast to the traditional mechanical clock, the digital clock eliminates spatial measurement and thus eliminates the necessity of understanding linear time as a precondition for making sense of the readout. The digital clock translates each moment into a number; and the continuous cycling of numbers forms a series that is not merely an indication of time but is also an image. This image of time can be compared with a motion picture. As a sequence of photographic images on a reel of film forms a continuum of movement, so do the numbers and their display on a digital clock form an image continuum. The photographic–cinematic image continuum is based on the mechanical movement of images at a speed of twenty-four frames per second. The process of showing cinematic images is a mechanical one. As a result, the actual time the images are displayed may differ from the time frame in the cinematic narrative. As an example, Alfred Hitchcock's 1957 film *Four O'clock* contains a scene of a time bomb counting down. The last sixty seconds before the explosion (in cinematic narrative time) actually last for seventy-two seconds on the film (real time).[31] Hitchcock used motion pictures as a technology for representing time as fragmentary and contingent precisely because he recognized this discrepancy between narrative time and the actual time of narration.[32] The digital clock image continuum is however based on the movement of digits at the speed of real time, one digit per second.

The digital clock image continuum performs the function of time-telling in two ways. First, the continuous movement of digits forms a narrative time that coincides with clock time. In this way the narrative time of the rotation of numbers becomes the time of narration of the digital clock. A digital clock's representation of time, unlike that of a motion picture, has no temporal gap between narrative and real time. Second, the movement of digits also creates a predictability of time-telling based on the sequence of numbers (that is, in addition to the regular clock time). When number *1* appears on the screen, for example, the viewer knows that the next number must be *2*.

The countdown digital clock thus combines the time-telling function of a traditional mechanical clock with a counting, or measuring, function that the traditional mechanical clock lacks. The operation of a digital clock relies on a computer. The logic of digital display is the binary number system of 0s and 1s translated into either twelve or twenty-four hours, depending on the clock's readout.[33] This translation is usually carried out by a computer chip that integrates all the functions of the clock: It first counts accurately a frequency of the crystal oscillator, then generates that quantity as a binary number, and finally translates that binary number into a decimal number. The time 12:15:23, for example, is based on a translation of the three different numbers that indicate the hour, minute, and second. The binary number 1100 represents the hour of 12; the number 1111, the 15 minutes; and the number 10111, the 23 seconds. Whereas a typical digital clock tells time continuously in either twelve-hour or a twenty-four-hour cycles, a countdown digital clock has only one preset cycle, within which the clock functions as both a time-telling device and a counter. In the case of the Hong Kong countdown clock at Tiananmen Square, it displayed and counted a total of 925 days, or 79.8798 million seconds.

The Hong Kong countdown clock eliminated the movement of mechanical clock hands and thus required no knowledge of how to read a clock face as a condition for understanding the digital readout. In this way, time became an opportunity rather than a constraint. At the same time, the countdown clock incorporated the logic of numbers as a teleology of its operation such that the telling of time became more predictable and the counting of time more accountable.

The time told and counted by the countdown clock might appear to be fragmented or postmodern,[34] but it was actually a highly rationalized time, which was achieved through a new way of counting time in relation to infinity. Consider the sequence of natural numbers: 1, 2, 3, etc.; we could imagine counting this sequence indefinitely. However, one could never arrive at infinity at some point in the future, because for every point reached there is always an infinite distance between where one is and the destination of infinity. Natural numbers are ordinal; they denote rank only. Counting to infinity is a matter of pure repetition. Natural numbers exhibit the ultimate in stability.[35] When a traditional clock tells time on the basis of the sequence of natural numbers, it stabilizes the linear temporality of clock time via repetition. The counting undertaken by the Hong Kong countdown clock, in contrast, was an operation of setting limits on natural numbers (without giving up the notion of linear and continuous time). Instead of counting the infinite sequence of 1, 2, 3, etc., and sustaining stability, the Hong Kong countdown counted a finite sequence of numbers to the initiation of a change. Thus, the countdown itself as an operation did not merely keep the ordinal nature of numbers (that is, their ranking function), but it also assigned value relative to every number in the sequence. In this way, while order was maintained, the possibility of change was created within the counted period of time.

The Hong Kong countdown as a public relations campaign

By means of its highly rationalized temporality, the Hong Kong countdown clock played an important role in engineering the neoliberal transformation of Chinese society. On one level, the countdown clock counted time by annihilating a preset amount of time. In counting down 79.8798 million seconds, the clock reduced the temporal distance to a future event. When the countdown reached zero, China took Hong Kong back and the nation began a new temporality. Thus, the meaning of 0 was predetermined and was related both to the end of a present time and to the beginning of a future time. On another level, the temporality of the countdown was historical; it was inseparable from social uses of the evaporating time. The historical time in which the countdown clock operated was clearly indexed by the clock's relation to a range of social, historical, and economic factors. The clock's four sponsors—China's Southern Aviation Engineering Company; the Linghua Food-Flavoring Group, Ji'ning, Shangdong; the magazine *China Brandnames*; and the National Museum of Chinese Revolution—were illustrative of the range of interests invested in the countdown. The aviation company represented both the traditional manufacturing industry and technology-based national development. The food-flavoring company connoted consumption in daily life. The magazine represented capital accumulation in a nonindustrial sector. The museum ensured the countdown as a historical event relevant to the history of modern China. As was oft-repeated in the official media, the Hong Kong countdown clock was created "to express the longing of the Chinese people for Hong Kong's return, to stimulate the patriotic emotions of billions of the descendents of the Yan and Huang emperors both in China and overseas, to encourage Chinese citizens to be proud of and to believe in the nation, and to speed up economic development of our country."[36]

The Hong Kong countdown developed an affective economy that enabled China's synchronization with neoliberal globalization, as the countdown device and the temporality it represented were used as communicative tools in significant ways. The countdown deployed two major types of labor—affective and symbolic—each of which was associated with a particular type of product.[37] The affective labor focused on the production of discourses about such public feelings as "awakening," "excitement," "national pride," and even "country." Xi Guojin, the vice editor-in-chief of *China Brand-names* (*Zhongguo mingpai*), a magazine published by China News Agency, was responsible for developing the clock as "a form of concrete expression showing the strong desire of the Chinese people for the return of Hong Kong to the motherland."[38] On the evening of September 11, 1993, Xi picked up *Guangming Daily* (*Guangming ribao*, a major official newspaper of the CCP) to scan through the day's news. On page 7, he saw a photo taken by Chinese journalist Li Guoqing of the year 2000 countdown clock at the Pompidou Center (Center Beaubourg) in Paris. The photo caption read:

> If you come to take a photo in front of the entrance of the Pompidou Cultural Center before the year 2000, you are surely able to record accurately the time of the photo—a countdown clock located at the south end of the main entrance of the center will tell you how many seconds remain before the coming of the year 2000. The more than 200 million digits remaining on the countdown clock are diminishing second by second; eventually they will reach zero at 0:00 of the year 2000.

"The countdown clock, that's it!" Xi Guojin told himself. By early 1994, Xi Guojin had completed the design and received the final approval of the Chinese government. Zhengzhou-based Zhongyuan Display Technology Corporation (*Zhongyuan xianshi jishu gongsi*) manufactured the clock while Xi and other *China Brand-names* executives selected Tiananmen Square as the site for installing the clock because of the place's salient historical meaning: "On October 1, 1949, Mao Zedong declared at the Gate of Tiananmen that the Chinese people had stood up from then on. After forty years, the Chinese people who have stood up declare to the whole world that they will be sending the remains of colonialism to the museum of history by the end of the century!"[39]

As an artifact itself, the presence of the Hong Kong countdown clock at Tiananmen Square was of monumental significance. It contributed to a modification of the monumental space of Tiananmen Square as a public space. Hung Wu argues that the clock was a "soft monument" of the present (the 1990s) and was "deliberately shortsighted and goal-specific, created only for a particular, current event," and that "its temporary but extravagant existence reflect[ed] a more specific, practical, and fluid sense of time."[40] This sense of time of this "soft monument" was strikingly different from that of the "hard monuments" of the past (pre-1990s) in the square—such as the Monument to the People's Heroes, Mao's Memorial Hall, and the Gate of Heaven—that commemorated historical traditions and demanded faith in communism.[41] The temporality of the clock was indeed relatively temporary compared with the permanence of those monuments associated with Chinese socialism (e.g. Mao's Memorial Hall) and the premodern past (the Gate of Heaven or Tiananmen). However, the temporary status of the countdown clock did not diminish its significance in engineering social transformation, not only because of its instrumental purpose (counting down the seconds until the government's resumption of sovereignty over Hong Kong) but also its public evocation of an aesthetic of temporal disappearance, especially of accelerating disappearance as symbolized by digital technology.

The countdown clock initiated a mass culture of counting down. The Tiananmen clock established the national standard for making other countdown clocks before and after Hong Kong's return to China. By July 1, 1997, not only a large number, but also many different types of countdown clocks had been produced. Initially, the designer of the countdown clock had intended to set up two clocks, one in Beijing and the other in Hong Kong. But the Hong Kong site was dropped in consideration of the fact that Hong Kong was still under British control. In Beijing, before the final selection of the Tiananmen Square site, three other locations were considered for the clock: the Beijing Train Station, which is always full of people; the west gate of the Xinhua News Agency; and Qianmen, a busy commercial district just south of Tiananmen Square.[42] On July 1, 1995, the Tiananmen clock designer and the Shenzhen Branch of the Xinhua News Agency inaugurated another countdown clock following the same design but smaller (11 meters square) at the Luohu Bridge, a busy border crossing between Shenzhen and Hong Kong.[43] While the Tiananmen clock counted the days remaining until "the Chinese Government resumes sovereignty over Hong Kong" from 925 to 0,[44] other countdown clocks also predetermined 0 as the ending point of the countdown, but did not count the same period of time or for the same reason. In Shangshui, a northern district of the New Territories, for example, the district government inaugurated a countdown clock on June 30, 1996, to count the remaining 366 days before Hong Kong's "return to the motherland."[45]

In addition to affective labor, another type of communicative labor that the countdown deployed was symbolic labor, producing all kinds of media products and symbols about Hong Kong's return in such forms as commercial information and merchandise, souvenirs, historical artifacts, museum objects, and stories. In the final few months before July 1, 1997, a wide assortment of souvenirs was available in Hong Kong, some with a hefty price tag. For example, a twelve-inch-high crystal sculpture called "Back to the Motherland" (designed by the Shanghai sculptor Pan Xirou and made by Baccarat of Paris) was priced around $40,000. Many less-expensive objects had everyday utility: watches, T-shirts, calendars, insulated cup holders, pins, postcards, and alcoholic drinks. These Hong Kong souvenirs also encoded a range of meanings relative to the Hong Kong transition, from "handover" or "takeover" to "return to China" and "back to the motherland."[46]

The production of popular souvenirs was based on the practice of entrepreneurial capitalism. The canned "colonial air," for example, was a product of Congo Snappers, a company owned by American Jon Resnick (who had lived in Hong Kong for fifteen years) and his British partner Guy Nicholls (a Hong Kong resident for ten years). This metal can, priced around $7.50, looked no different from an ordinary food can on a supermarket shelf. The contents, "colonial air," reputedly came from the Peak and outside the Hong Kong Club, places where a majority of the British lived and socialized. The can's label itself incorporated two media forms: written words and visual imagery. The writing on the label marked the air as authentically "colonial" (see Figure 2.2). The six lines of text were differentiated by font size and ink color, from pale red to dark brown. The authenticity of the air as "colonial" was highlighted both by the words "colonial air" (in the largest type) and by the date "sealed before: 1st July 1997."

With respect to the souvenir's visual presentation, centered on the label is a black-and-white photograph of an Englishman with four Chinese men behind him, all facing the viewer. The Englishman, former Hong Kong Governor Frederick Lugard (July 1907–March 1912),[47] has a dark beard; wears a three-piece suit, tie, and hat; and is front and center in the image. The four Chinese men surrounding Lugard all wear Chinese-style long robes and hats, identifying them as mandarins or officials of the Qing Dynasty. The image evokes a colonial space in which the British dominated over the Chinese. Thus, along with the "colonial air," the image preserves a historical time of Hong Kong under British colonial rule.

By the time of the Hong Kong handover, more than four thousand cans had been sold. The souvenir received widespread international media attention: the *New York Times, Asian Wall Street Journal, South China Morning Post*, and *Newsweek* magazine, among others, ran stories about this object and showed an image of it. According to its creators, the product's consumption should focus on developing a sophisticated capacity to distinguish scents. They warned their customers that one whiff "could lead to extreme arrogance, stiffening of the upper lip or worse." "If you really have got a good nose for it,

Figure 2.2 Can of "colonial air," a souvenir produced by Congo Snappers, Hong Kong, 1997 (photo by the author).

you can pick up maybe the occasional cucumber sandwich or steak-and-kidney pies. Breathe deeply, there could be a chance of Smith's Best Bitter (beer)." And a sophisticated nose might detect "traces of linseed oil on cricket bats and fresh-cut grass from a bowling lawn in the colonial air."[48]

The canned "colonial air" souvenir was very creative, but it was by no means unique in marketing products through an association with the Hong Kong countdown. The Jiangsu-based Nantong Cigarette Company, for example, created a "1997" brand cigarette as early as 1995 to link its projects to the end of British rule in Hong Kong.[49] As July 1, 1997, approached the popular culture industry began many extraordinary efforts to identify, communicate, market, and sell "1997" (shorthand for Hong Kong's return to China) in the context of everyday life. The industry commonly used 1997 in three notable ways.

First, it was common practice for newspapers and television stations to designate regular and special 1997-related spaces or time slots as a way to attract commercial sponsors and increase profits. The date of Hong Kong's return, "1997," was often treated as a floating signifier for more specific themes for the purpose of differentiating sponsors. On July 1, 1996, for example, some popular signifiers included "1997," "Hong Kong's return to the motherland," "the first anniversary of the countdown of time," "the first preview of *Hong Kong's Vicissitudes*" (a twelve-episode television series about Hong Kong's history, produced by CCTV), and "the ceremony of enshrining Hong Kong's Basic Law at the Great Hall of Peoples in Beijing." All of them were seen as commercial "sales pitches" (*maidian*). The July 1, 1996, edition of the Hong Kong-based *Ta Kung Daily* (*Dagongbao*) published an eight-page advertising supplement to celebrate "the one-year anniversary of the countdown to Hong Kong's return to China" and to preview *Hong Kong's Vicissitudes*. The first page listed twelve holding companies and seventy-two member companies of "the Association of China's Enterprises in Hong Kong." Pages 2 to 8 listed an additional 127 companies and institutions in Hong Kong.[50] The June 28, 1996, edition of the Guangzhou-based weekly newspaper *Nanfang zhoumo* (*The Southern Weekend*), contained an advertisement for the IDALL Electronic Company in which the price tag of its DVD player, which read "1997," filled two-thirds of the advertisement. Above the number, a line of small Chinese characters reads: "The national standard sale price of IDALL DVD for only [. . .]"

Television stations frequently related their broadcasts to 1997, both by airing special programs and by seeking commercial sponsors for certain popular regularly scheduled programs. From 1995 to 1997, for example, a frequent advertisement on television stations across the country was one for the Sichuan Changhong Electronics Group Corporation,[51] one of the largest television makers in China. The company prominently identified its Changhong brand television on CCTV as a 1997 model before February 1996. After the handover, the model year was replaced with images of professionals (men and women in business suits) against a backdrop of Hong Kong's Central District (a symbol for transnational capitalism). The voiceover told viewers that the company "regards its own task as encompassing producing national prosperity (*minzu changsheng*) and repaying the nation through business (*chanye baoguo*)."[52]

The second common practice connected to 1997 was to "auction" (*paimai*) advertising spaces or time slots for selected dates. The Chinese media widely viewed this practice as a creative way to make profits. On July 1, 1996 (the "first anniversary of the countdown of time"), for example, the *Guangdong Hong Kong Information Daily* (*Yuegang xinxi ribao*, a Guangzhon-based newspaper) auctioned ten pages of space dedicated to the Hong Kong countdown to be included in the July 1, 1997 edition. More than thirty companies participated in the bidding for the "celebratory advertisements" (*qingdian guanggao*). The bid for the first space started at RMB¥ 123,000 and ended at RMB¥ 1.4 million, which was paid by a company based in Shunde, Guangdong.

The final bid for space on the first page was RMB¥ 2.1 million, paid by another Guangdong-based company, about thirteen times more than the RMB¥ 166,000 minimum bid. By the end of the day, the newspaper received a total of RMB¥ 6.41 million. The newspaper's sales pitch was that the special advertisements in the July 1, 1997, edition would accompany news stories about Hong Kong's return to China and thus would become archival material bearing witness to this important historical event.[53]

From the perspective of a sponsoring company, becoming part of the history of the Hong Kong countdown was an important marketing strategy for promoting a brand. This was the story of the Qinchi Liquor Company of Shandong, the biggest commercial sponsor of CCTV in 1996 and 1997. On November 8, 1995, the company was crowned "the king of the bidders" (*biaowang*) because it contracted for RMB¥ 66,666,988.80 worth of advertising on CCTV in the year 1996. This figure was shocking to many observers because it meant the company's total advertising expenditure in 1996 would be more than twice its total gross revenues in 1995.[54] Throughout 1996, Qinchi's commercials aired during a variety of CCTV's programs in both prime time and other time slots. They appeared daily during the national "Weather Forecast" (*tianqi yubao*), right after the "Evening News" (7:00–7:30 p.m.) (*xinwen lianbo*), the country's most watched news program. Qinchi also sponsored the 1996 New Year celebration held at and broadcasted live by CCTV. The company's promotional slogan, "Forever green, forever Qinchi" (*yongyuan de luse, yongyuan de Qinchi*), became well known across the country.

The 1996 advertising campaign generated explosive profits. In order to pay for the advertisements while making a profit, the company had set a goal of at least RMB¥ 400 million in sales for 1996. It reached that goal in the first five months.[55] By the year's end, the company had grossed RMB¥ 950 million. According to Wang Zhuosheng, the company's CEO, "Each day, we gave away a Santana, but we earned an Audi" (*meitian songchu yiliang sangtana, zuanhui yiliang aodi*).[56] In addition to fame, pride, and profits, the mass advertising campaign also caused changes in the company's organization. By July 1996, the company had expanded into a "group" (*jituan*). The new Qinchi Liquor Group encompassed twelve companies employing more than 10,000 people. In addition, more than one hundred companies in Linqu, where the company was based, also benefited from the company's growth.[57] Because of its phenomenal success, a year later, on November 8, 1996, the company was again crowned the "king of the bidders," but with a much higher price tag of RMB¥ 320 million in contracted advertising with CCTV in 1997.

Significantly, the success of Qinchi, which leapt from obscurity to national prominence in one year, was largely due to the company's marketing strategy of tying its products to Hong Kong's return to China. On July 1, 1996, Qinchi held a news conference and banquet in Hong Kong, billed as "Qinchi Liquor Invites All Hong Kong People to Drink."[58] Accompanied by Wang Qingde (the Communist Party secretary of Linqu County in Shandong Province) and Tong Nian (the company's general manager), CEO Wang announced that to celebrate Hong Kong's reunification with China, the company planed to donate a special vintage "Qinchi Liquor" worth more than RMB¥ 12 million to Hong Kong residents on July 1, 1997. It would also donate the same amount of liquor to residents in ten major cities in China (Beijing, Shanghai, Guangzhou, Tianjin, Jinan, Nanjing, Wuhan, Xi'an, Shenyang, and Shijiazhuang). In 1997, the company paid to sponsor "the countdown clock of Hong Kong's Return to the Motherland" on Hong Kong's Asia Television. Therefore, the story of Qinchi is not only about the company's massive spending on television advertising but also about its successful public relations campaign that tied the Qinchi brand to the historical event of the Hong Kong countdown. The company's experimentation with commercial marketing during the Hong Kong countdown became in the late 1990s a widely cited example of how to conduct a successful advertising campaign.

The third common mass media practice of producing symbolic products during the Hong Kong countdown was to manufacture news about 1997 for commercial purposes. Newspapers and television stations often disguised an advertisement in the form of a news story about the business success of a company (like Qinchi or Changhong) under remarkable leadership from its management. Mass media organizations also deliberately concocted stories to boost sales. Journalists from *Beijing Evening News* (*Beijing wanbao*) on July 1, 1997, for example, phoned individuals whose pager or phone numbers contained the digits 1–9–9–7. They informed readers that the pager number 3–1997–7–1 belonged to an airline executive, and that the telephone numbers 6542–1997, 6433–1997, and 6431–1997 belonged to ordinary residents in Beijing. The article also ostensibly quoted the owners describing how excited they were to own significant numbers.[59] In a sense, the journalists became telemarketers using 1–9–9–7 to generate human-interest stories for the paper. Meanwhile, the reported "excitement" of owning a number containing 1–9–9–7 was an extraordinary moment created out of the ordinary. Often, pollsters deliberately selected numbers containing 1–9–9–7 or 9–7. *Beijing Youth Daily*, for example, polled 104 Beijing residents who had 9–7 as the last two digits of their phone numbers about how they spent their time from 6:00 a.m. on June 30 to 12:00 p.m. on July 1, 1997.[60]

Unofficial media also capitalized on the significance of 1997. In Beijing, stalls selling newspapers, magazines, and paperbacks are located in every busy subway station. Some peddlers also hawk papers on the trains. One day in April 1996, a newspaper peddler caught the attention of passengers. He was selling a tabloid newspaper, usually referred to as a "small paper" (*xiaobao*).[61] Pushing through the crowd, the peddler announced in a loud voice, "China recovers Hong Kong!" (*Zhongguo shoufu Xianggang*) and "The Chinese Army attacks Taiwan!" (*Zhongguo jundui jingong Taiwan*). Even those passengers who didn't buy a paper heard the "startling voice that exaggerated facts" (*songren tingwen*). I could not resist buying a newspaper from him. It was a "weekly edition of the two-day weekend" (*shuangxiuri zhoukan*) published by the *Shanxi Science and Technology Daily* (*Shanxi keji ribao*) on

April 27, 1996. The front page was devoted to Hong Kong and contained three articles whose headlines were "The Great Attention in the World in 1997: Hong Kong's Return," "First Closing of the British Information Center Prior to 1997," and "The Last Colonial Army of the Great British Empire: The Upcoming Disappearance of the British Army in Hong Kong."[62] This example shows that tabloid papers (unofficial mass media) and their sellers actively exploited 1997 in the context of everyday life. In this case of selling the paper on a moving subway train, the peddler sold 1997 both through his language and by moving his body to contact with others.

In sum, through both affective and symbolic labor, the Hong Kong countdown operated as an affective economy, which not only guided expressions of public feelings toward Hong Kong's return, but also produced a whole sequence of informational products associated with the handover. Such feelings as excitement, success, and pride commonly substituted for feelings such as unhappiness, failure, and insecurity. Communication became the primary means of production not just for the mass media, but also for other industries, especially those producing consumer products. Departing from the passive, wait-and-see approach, one of the most celebrated business practices was entrepreneurialism.

Spectacular consumption and neoliberal subjectivity during the Hong Kong countdown

In the affective economy of the Hong Kong countdown, the consumption of a media spectacle like the Hong Kong countdown clock in everyday life had an important impact on citizens. As an ordinary clock would be used in planning daily activities, so was the countdown clock used as a tool for organizing everyday life during the transition period. As the multiplicity-based time constructed by the countdown clock was incorporated into everyday life activities, I argue it promoted the development of neoliberal citizenship, the integration of economic rationalism into the citizens' conduct. The use of multiplicity-based time in daily life means that organizing one's life becomes a technical process of ordering, calculating, and coordinating. More explicitly, under neoliberalism, the technical process is reoriented toward economic calculations (of costs, benefits, and efficiency), characteristics of the entrepreneurial subject.

The Tiananmen digital countdown clock itself was a spectacle, an image of remarkable clarity.[63] Its digital illumination enhanced both its role as an attraction and its function as a government document publicly announcing the government's resumption of sovereignty over Hong Kong. Chinese media even viewed the clock as a distinctive "cultural spectacle" (*renwen jingguan*). Tourists, both foreign and domestic, had their photos taken in front of it. One out of every four photos taken at Tiananmen Square was of the clock. At least eight couples held their wedding ceremonies in front of the clock.[64] In the final days before July 1, 1997, the clock emerged as the focus of public and mass media attention around the world. Celebrations took place around the operating clock. On June 30, 1997, the Beijing municipal government organized a seven-hour-long "evening celebration party" (*lianhuan wanhui*) called "Beijing Blesses You, Hong Kong" (*Beijing zhufu ni—Xianggang*) at Tiananmen Square. The center stage was placed directly below the clock. One hundred thousand people, including students, workers, peasants, cadres, journalists, and police, reportedly attended the celebration. They were selected from thousands of "work units" in the city of Beijing and its suburban counties and districts. The celebration officially began at 22:00 and lasted until 5:00 the next morning. During the final moments before midnight, everyone gathered in front of the clock and counted down the seconds from 10 to 0. Not only was the party televised live across the country, but it was also broadcast to audiences around the world.[65] The live CCTV worldwide broadcast via satellite was unprecedented; it included seventy-two hours of continuous broadcasting in Chinese and forty-one hours of programs in English.[66] Thousands of foreign journalists also covered the event. Under this condition, the clock's public image, as Paul Virilio might have put it, was on its way to substituting for a public space through the deployment of perceptible appearances by means of satellites, Hertzian networks, and fiber-optic cables.[67]

Although the Hong Kong countdown clock was a public time-telling device and was highly visible, it made no sound—unlike the ringing of a church bell, the announcing of the time during a radio or television broadcast, or the ticking of a mechanical clock—the forms of time-telling familiar in the past. The physical silence of the clock does not mean it was voiceless. In fact, the "silent" clock could be heard thousands of miles away, across the country, in Hong Kong, and around the world: the clock's audience was global. The Hong Kong art critic Oscar Ho said in 1993, "Time is running out: people in Hong Kong need to find their cultural heritage and to reassure their sense of identity, for in four years' time they might have lost it."[68] The Hong Kong-based scholar Li Siu-leung viewed the passing seconds of the countdown clock as a virtual clock time in Hong Kong that "controls from a distance the progressive steps of Hong Kong's history."[69] Thus, in Hong Kong, as Hung Wu pointed out, the countdown clock replicated the logic of an imperial drum tower by presenting an official schedule to "the people of Hong Kong as subjects of the People's Republic of China."[70]

The Hong Kong countdown effectively incorporated a multiplicity-based time into everyday life and the process of life-making and life-building. Some Beijing residents treated the Tiananmen clock as part of the everyday, and consequently, took for granted or accepted the clock as an unproblematic daily reality.[71] For example, a reporter quoted a young office worker who passed the clock each day on the way to and from work: "It has been there so long now, I hardly notice it any more . . . At first it was a novelty, a bit of fun, but now no one pays attention to it, except tourists."[72] The presence of the clock and the persistent passing of the seconds dictated by the computer inside it seemed to preclude any pause for reflection over the meaning of the transition.[73]

By July 1, 1997, many other countdown clock images had appeared. In Beijing, one could find countdown clocks on the streets (e.g. on neighborhood bulletin boards), and in schools and colleges (e.g. on chalkboards in classrooms), as well as in supermarkets and department stores (e.g. Yansha). Countdown clocks also appeared in newspaper columns and television programs. Newspapers such as *Beijing Youth Daily, Beijing Evening News, Dagong Daily*, and *Wenhui Daily* printed a countdown clock each day. *Beijing Youth Daily*, one of the most popular newspapers in Beijing, started its clock on March 23, 1997, one hundred days before July 1, 1997. Each countdown clock, published on the front page, announced "*x* days left before the Chinese government resumes its sovereignty over Hong Kong." *X*, a number from 100 to 1, lowered by one each day. Included with each countdown clock was the image of an important place related to Hong Kong, for example, Hong Kong's Victoria Harbor (one hundred days before the return), Tiananmen Square decorated for the return celebrations (two days before), or the Hong Kong Convention Center where the handover ceremony took place (one day before).

The mass production, transmission, and consumption of Hong Kong countdown clocks made it possible to use them as a time-sharing experience in organizing everyday life through purposeful, repetitive, programmable sequences of exchange and interaction among different social actors.[74] In Daliubukou in the Western District of Beijing, for example, Aunt Wang, the assistant director of the Daliubukou Neighborhood Committee, wrote the number of days left before "Hong Kong's Return" on a chalkboard every day. She changed the number of days in the evening, so that people in the neighborhood would see the correct count first thing in the morning.[75] The presence of the countdown clock connected the residents on a daily basis, regardless of whether or not a resident had an emotional connection with the handover.

Readers of *Beijing Youth Daily* even collected the set of clock illustrations published in the paper. For example, Li Jiming, a worker at an insurance company in Beijing, liked the fact that the countdown clocks pictured a series of historical places, so he collected the whole set of one hundred clocks.[76] Li was not alone. Hu Yufang, a parachuting coach, also collected all the newspaper's clocks. She said,

> As soon as I saw the first Hong Kong-return countdown clock published in *Beijing Youth Daily*, I was attracted by its creativity and began to collect them. During the ninety-nine days, I asked my child to go to buy the newspaper when I was out of town. A couple of times, I could not buy the paper from a newsstand, and I had to go to the printing factory to buy it. After I collect all one hundred clocks, I will use them to make a Chinese character *hui* (return) and keep them forever.[77]

The Chinese character *hui* in this instance was both a picture *and* a monument commemorating "Hong Kong's return." The artifact contextualized the one hundred images as a whole set, in which each image was connected to a date in the countdown period (one hundred days). Moreover, the making of this artifact was also a process of producing and managing a sense of self, not only because the production was based on collecting as a daily activity but also because the work's organization was disciplined by the countdown clock, which had been injected by the mass media into the realm of the everyday.

During the Hong Kong countdown, Chinese citizens treated the countdown as an economic rationale for making and building a successful life. This was the case of Wang Zheng, a resident and entrepreneur in Shenyang, who systematically incorporated "1997" into his own business and personal life.[78] Wang first conceived of the meaning of 1997 when he encountered a Hong Kong businessman while working in a hotel in Shenyang a few years after graduating from a vocational school specializing in tourism. He began to read books on Hong Kong history and decided to develop a business based on "1997." In September 1994, Wang established his company, named Ronglida-1997 Supermarket Chain" (*ronglida—1997 zixuan liansuo shangdian*) in Shenyang. Soon after its opening, many customers—sometimes, as many as one hundred each day—asked him about the meaning of "1997," and Wang explained that it referred to Hong Kong's return to China. In May 1995, Wang decided to explore other ways of using "1997." He brought a Dafa, a minivan made in Tianjin, and chose "LiaoA51997" as the license plate number because the reading of "51997" in Chinese sounds like "fortunate (*fu*) 1997." He also tried very hard to acquire a telephone number containing 1–9–9–7. In March 1997, he bought the number 482–1997 after a series of negotiations with a trading company, the number's previous owner. In addition to treating 1997 as a key to the success of his business, Wang also incorporated it into his personal life. In the summer of 1995, Wang met Li Yue, a graduate of the College of the Light Industries in Shenyang. When they became engaged, Wang and Li decided to drive to Hong Kong to be married there on July 1, 1997. Their plan had the full support of the Shenyang municipal government, which assisted them with getting the necessary permissions to enter Hong Kong. Meanwhile, the minivan maker, Tianjin Dafa, gave them a new van. To commemorate their wedding, the couple donated RMB¥ 1997.71 to the Hope Project (*xiwang gongcheng*)—a major nationwide philanthropic project supporting education in China's poor areas. Wang's story was remarkable because he actively appropriated 1997 not only as a marketing strategy for his business, which was related to daily consumption, but also as a rationale for structuring his own life. As this example shows, during the Hong Kong countdown, the temporality represented by the countdown clock regulated and regularized interactions among the market, government, and individual citizens through communication, or more specifically, storytelling.

From a post-1997 perspective, the effect of the Hong Kong countdown on the process of life-making and life-building may be evaluated by how memorable it was on a personal level. Many younger people remember Hong Kong's return because they fell in love for the first time in that year. In a blog dated June 7, 2005, the writer said that he would never forget Hong Kong's return because in 1997 he fell in love for the first time. That relationship, however, lasted only 6 years, 11 months, and 6 days (that is, it ended on May 5, 2005). The breakup clearly became a moment for reflection about time as a problem of life: "Only 26 days to seven years, how many seven-years can one have in life? If the passing of time will cure pain, how long will it take?"[79] In his blog, the young man's connection to Hong Kong's return involved neither an explicit relationship between Hong Kong and China nor other historical specificities like the Chinese government's resumption of sovereignty. Instead, it was all about his individual feelings, his love life and the pain it had caused. The breakup of the relationship elevated these feelings—expressed in the form of disappearance—to such a degree that he questioned the meaning of time in life.

Another personal memory of the Hong Kong countdown involved the experience of learning as a life-building practice. A college student who had just begun to learn about Internet-related technology decided to create an online exhibition about Hong Kong stamps as a way to learn web design. He first went to the library to study Hong Kong stamps and their history, then collected relevant information (both documents and images), classified them into relevant categories, and finally edited them into four sections and published them on the Internet. With the help of friends, he also created a Hong Kong countdown clock as part of the website. Because the creation of the site was his first work on the web, he always remembered that experience.[80] Thus, for this student, the memory of the Hong Kong countdown was tied to an apparently positive and successful learning experience.

Conclusion: Governing neoliberal time

In my historical discussion in the previous chapter, I outlined how the Chinese government's concern with the Hong Kong question in modern China shifted from diplomatic negotiations to practical preparations for the transfer of sovereignty. The Hong Kong countdown, which was marked by the installation of the Hong Kong countdown clock at Tiananmen Square, drew widespread attention from ordinary people in the Chinese mainland and Hong Kong. The development of multiplicity-based time as told by the multimedia countdown device (mechanical, electronic, and digital); the countdown as a public relations, rather than propaganda, campaign; and the consumption of media spectacles such as countdown clocks (in various media forms), souvenirs, consumer products, and commercial information all concretely shaped the Hong Kong countdown as a governmental project. This project encompassed new technologies of public time-telling; economic development through the communications and advertising industries;

and human development in the construction of a neoliberal norm of the entrepreneurial subject.

From the perspective of time as a socio-historical question, the management of the Hong Kong countdown was about governing neoliberal time—that is, making an exceptional time normative (both regular and regulative).[81] The Sino–British Joint Declaration created a specific governmental problem that was inseparable from time. First, the international agreement carved out a time period from the unfolding horizon of the future: specifically, the fifty years from 1997 to 2046 during which Hong Kong will operate as a special administrative region of China and thus enjoy a high degree of autonomy. Second, it also marked 1984–1997 as a transitional period during which Britain and China would work together to ensure the smooth transfer of power.

Both the 1984–1997 and the 1997–2046 time periods were closely linked to the treatment of the Hong Kong question as a governmental problem. In this context, the 1984–1997 period was normative, while the 1997–2046 period was exceptional. From 1984 to 1997, the countdown coded the process of Hong Kong's return to China in affective terms, through an affective economy in which communication was the means of production (as illustrated in this chapter). As a governmental project, the Hong Kong countdown was a normative, constructivist program that combined both technological and economic rationalities (of multiplicity-based time, calculability, efficiency, and technical automation). The presence of the 1997–2046 time frame was imperative in the transition period, because the preparation for a unified China could not possibly exclude this future time frame. However, this future time's presence during the transitional period was only virtual because it existed only in such subjective terms as confidence, expectation, hope, fear, and assurance. Thus, if its presence was real at all, it was in terms of the real uncertainty and anxiety over the impending changes from 1997 to 2046.[82]

Thus, from a governmental perspective, addressing the problem of time during the countdown meant regulating and regularizing a relationship between the two time frames. In terms of the embodiment of time,[83] the governmental problem actually took the form of shaping subjective formation. More specifically, it was about regulating and regularizing the relationship between two kinds of subjects: the citizen subject who acts in the normative situation in which he or she presents and is represented; and the sovereign subject who decides on the exceptional situation.[84] During the countdown, the future uncertainty of the 1997–2046 period became calculable both through technological means (via countdown devices) and through economic means (via entrepreneurial marketing practices). Meanwhile, through public consumption of the media spectacle, the calculation or management of the future uncertainty became tied to the process of life-making and life-building. That is, by treating the exceptional 1997–2046 time frame normatively in everyday life, the rule of exception became the norm.

3 History as a governmental discourse

In his poem "In Front of the Countdown Clock" published in *Renmin ribao* (June 27, 1997, p. 12), Li Yunpeng (a writer from Gansu Province) viewed the countdown clock not simply as a time-telling device but also as a "lesson book" that "must be read by every Chinese."[1] Its lessons were about "the history of humiliation and pride," about "how the nation humiliated in the past marches toward respect." Li stated, "Since the very moment when the weak and corrupt Qing court ceded Hong Kong in 1842, the countdown clock . . . has existed in the heart of the Chinese nation. Hundreds of millions of Chinese people had suffered hard to comprehend, placing their sights on national [redemption from] humiliation and defense." According to Li's reading, the countdown clock represented an animated book whose pages turned steadily to unfold a history of reconciliation. As a narrative device, the clock enabled the writer to imagine how the history of the nation could be reconstituted through reordering the relationship between the past and the future.

Li's individualized reading of the countdown clock in fact followed an established narrative of modern Chinese history during the Hong Kong countdown. In the process of reuniting with Hong Kong, the Chinese state reworked the relationships among colonialism, socialism, and capitalism to transform itself into a neoliberal state. The affective economy of the countdown established an effective politics of cultural disappearance by means of substituting existing national feelings with a set of new ones. The historical experience of China's nineteenth-century interactions with the imperial and colonial West—or the "first synchronization with the world" in the words of the official historian of the film *The Opium War* (see the introduction)—was conventionally used to provoke feelings of humiliation, tragedy, and pain. The absence of Hong Kong from China's territory was critical to the documentation and narration of this historical experience. During the countdown, almost all the imagery portraying feelings of humiliation, tragedy, and pain was replaced by spectacles of decolonizing celebrations, festivals, and exhibitions that encoded a new historical experience of revival, success, confidence, and pride. What Li's poem alluded to was precisely this historical trajectory of substitution.

How was this trajectory of substitution developed? How did it address the Hong Kong question as a problem of regulating and regularizing the affective economy of the countdown, that is, of reconciling feelings of national "revival" (*zhenxing*) with those of "national humiliation" (*guochi*)? To answer these questions, I analyze two important exhibitions of modern Chinese history that explicitly addressed the Hong Kong question as a historical problem: Modern China (*jindai zhongguo*) and Xianggang's (Hong Kong's) History and Development (*xianggang de lishi yu wenhua*). The former was a permanent exhibition, or "primary exhibition" (*jiben chenlie*) at Bejing's National Museum of Chinese Revolution (reorganized as part of the National Museum of China in February 2003). It was the country's largest and most comprehensive exhibition on modern China. The second exhibition, organized by the Ministry of Culture, the Hong Kong and Macao Offices of the State Council, and the Information Office of the State Council, was reportedly the country's first exhibition systematically showcasing Hong Kong's history and was a key event in celebrating Hong Kong's return.[2] This exhibition opened at the National Museum of Chinese Revolution in July 1996, then traveled to museums in Shanghai, Shenzhen, and Guangzhou. My comparison of the two exhibitions examines how they were produced under different historical and political conditions in order to highlight an important change in how the historical time of the Chinese nation state was represented during the Hong Kong countdown. This change, I argue, fundamentally supported the development of neoliberal citizenship.

Modern China on display

The Modern China exhibition at the National Museum of Chinese Revolution was the most comprehensive public display ever on modern Chinese history—and was viewed as the most authoritative, since its development was under the direct supervision of the Communist Party and the central government. In this way, it prescribed the standard for showcasing the historical period from 1840 (the beginning of the first Opium War) to 1949 (the establishment of the People's Republic). Moreover, among museum professionals, the museological techniques it used in representing modern history were also considered as setting a new national standard.

A discussion of the history of museology in China will help us to understand the exhibition's development and its techniques. This historical examination will also show the National Museum of Chinese Revolution's close ties to the politics of the CCP/Chinese state, especially how the museum's representations of modern Chinese history formulated and revised a knowledge that legitimized the rule of the CCP.

The National Museum of Chinese Revolution was one of a few museums under the direct supervision of the State Bureau of Cultural Relics (*guojia wenwuju*), a ministry-level branch of the State Council.[3] The Bureau of Cultural Relics has established four criteria for classifying the thousands of museums in China: by location (urban or rural), by administration (national, provincial, city, or county government), by the nature and contents of the collection, and by the museum's purpose (particular, commemorative, or general).[4] Among the four criteria, some are used more often and treated as more significant than others. The National Museum of Chinese Revolution, for example, was officially an urban, national, revolution, and particular-type museum, but it was always identified as a national and revolution-type rather than an urban and particular-type. The collection criterion, which is most commonly used by museum professionals, has three major categories: socio-history (*shehui lishi*), nature (*ziran*) or natural science (*ziran kexue*), and comprehensive (*zonghe*).[5] Moreover, each category contains subtypes. For the socio-history category the three subtypes are history, revolution, and art.

These three subtypes explicitly align with the way the Chinese government addresses history as a governmental discourse within the conventional Marxist framework of historical representation. This linear history narrates human development through a series of progressive stages from primitive to slave-owning, feudal, capitalist, and socialist societies, culminating in communist society.[6] The "history museum" (*lishi bowuguan*) subtype encompasses the historical span from the origin of humans in the Paleolithic Period to the beginning of the first Opium War in 1840, corresponding with the development from primitive to feudal society. The National Museum of Chinese History belongs to this subtype. The "revolution museum" (*geming bowuguan*) subtype continues the chronology of China's national history from 1840 to the present. Museums of this subtype, such as the National Museum of Chinese Revolution, are responsible for representing the modern and contemporary China, including the late Qing Dynasty (1840–1911), the Republic of China (1911–1949), and the People's Republic (1949–present). Every revolution museum is theoretically required to represent "the people's struggles against imperialism, feudalism and bureaucratic capitalism; the revolutionary movements; and famous figures" from 1840 on. The third subtype, "art museum" (*yishu bowuguan*) displays various types of arts, including pottery and porcelain, embroidery, painting, calligraphy, photography, folklore, literature, music, dance, sports, theater, and cinema.[7] Unlike the first two subtypes, an art museum does not need to display artifacts in chronological order.

Thus, both history and revolution subtypes of museums are critical to the representation of Chinese history, and they play different roles in shaping the historical narrative of the Chinese nation state. The history museum traces the history of the Chinese nation back to prehistoric times, representing it as having an origin in the mysterious past, whereas the revolution museum draws a clear temporal boundary for the beginning of the modern nation state. It is in the context of "revolution" that history is treated as a sign of the modern.[8] That is, the artifacts of revolution that designate the temporal space of the nation as modern also serve as temporal dividers for the modern nation state. The National Museum of Chinese Revolution exemplifies the way in which revolution artifacts are used to construct a historical discourse of modern China.

The museum's history is closely tied to that of the CCP within the context of Chinese socialism. The museum was established toward the end of the Great Leap Forward period (1958–1959). In August 1958, the Central Committee of the Chinese Communist Party met at Beidaihe to plan the establishment of two national museums in Beijing: the National Museum of Chinese History (*Zhongguo lishi bowuguan*) and the National Museum of Chinese Revolution (*Zhongguo geming bowuguan*). Around the same time, the Central Committee of the Military Affairs of the Chinese Communist Party also decided to establish the National Military Museum of the Chinese People's Revolution (*Zhongguo renmin geming junshi bowuguan*). Constructed within a year, these three museums opened to the public before the tenth anniversary of the founding of the People's Republic (October 1, 1959). The rapid development of these museums was possible for two reasons: their staffs were transferred from other museums (primarily from the Palace Museum) and universities, and the majority of their collections were acquired from other museums across the country, or were donated by government employees.[9] Whereas the National Museum of Chinese History functions as a representational space of the premodern nation, the National Museum of Chinese Revolution serves the same function for the modern nation state. Their division of labor in representing Chinese history is marked by a crucial distinction between two types of museum collections—*lishi wenwu* (historical artifacts) and *geming wenwu* (revolutionary artifacts)—based on the previously described socialist historical framework. *Lishi wenwu* refers to:

> . . . the remaining objects and sites made by humans ranging from the primitive to the slavery to the feudal society in our country, that is, all cultural remains which have historical, aesthetic, or scientific significance in the whole ancient time period from the origin of human beings in the Paleolithic Period to the period prior to the Opium War.[10]

Geming wenwu, then, represents the modern period from the beginning of the Opium War in 1840 to the present in the People's Republic.

Before it was merged into the National Museum of China in 2003, the National Museum of Chinese Revolution was charged with representing the national history of the Chinese revolution by developing the country's most comprehensive *geming wenwu* collections covering the entire modern period. The collections were supposed to illustrate the activities of anti-imperialism, anti-feudalism, and anti-bureaucratic capitalism, whether relative to revolutionary movements or prominent individuals.[11] How did the museum identify an artifact as a *geming wenwu?* According to Shen Qinglin, a senior staffer at the museum, "a jar, for example, may be used to contain rice, salt, or other materials and thus have a function in social life. It could be used to show a level of production and a lifestyle in a society. However, it is only when the jar's use played a role in revolutionary struggle that it can be treated and collected as a *geming wenwu*." The identification of a *geming wenwu* was usually possible after the activity associated with the artifact was recognized as revolutionary. The museum staff could not independently determine whether an activity associated with certain artifacts was revolutionary. Rather, they were required to follow the guidance of the CCP. The value of a *geming wenwu* might also correspond with its rarity. For example, hundreds of thousands of handmade wooden carts were used to assist the People's Liberation Army in fighting against the Nationalist Army during the civil war period (1946–1949). As these became fewer, they would become more valuable *geming wenwu*.[12]

The museum's primary (permanent) exhibitions were the most important because they established the national standard for representing revolutionary China, in terms of two aspects: the museological techniques of collection, preservation, research, exhibition, and education; and the historiography of Chinese revolutions.[13] From 1959 to 1996, the museum mounted exhibitions focusing on various "revolutions," including the Old Democratic Revolution (1840–1919), the New Democratic Revolution (1919–1949), and the Socialist Revolution and Construction in the People's Republic (after 1949).[14] In this period, the museum developed three permanent exhibitions: The Exhibition of the Old Democratic Revolutionary Period (1840–1919), The Exhibition of the New Democratic Revolutionary Period (entitled before the 1980s The Exhibition of the History of the Chinese Communist Party; 1919–1949), and The Exhibition of the Socialist Period (1949–present). In June 1996, the museum opened a new primary exhibition called Modern China (*jindai zhongguo*) (1840–1949) to replace the previous exhibitions for the first two periods. Notably, primary exhibitions on contemporary China since 1950 are very rare. One such exhibition was developed recently, but it is open to the public only on an irregular basis. Instead, exhibitions on contemporary China have tended to be temporary, and their contents usually focus on the country's achievements under the leadership of the CCP.

Public openings of primary exhibitions are scheduled to coincide with an important political event or significant date. The anniversary of the CCP (July 1) or Nation Day (October 1) are frequent choices, so that the exhibition's opening becomes part of the celebration of the Communist Party or the nation's founding. Other important dates are the anniversary of the founding of the People's Liberation Army (August 1), or birthdays of senior communist leaders such as Mao Zedong and Zhou Enlai. Thus, the opening of every major exhibition involved an official commemorative (*jinian*) or celebratory (*qingzhu*) ritual.

Since the exhibitions link the museum to the public, they are closely controlled and monitored by the Communist Party's Propaganda Department. Every exhibition must be approved prior to its public opening. Issues of who should be included in an exhibition, and which activities should be treated as revolutionary events are crucial to the finalization of an exhibition's storyline. If the supervising officials cannot reach consensus about these issues, they prohibit the opening of the exhibition until all necessary resolutions are reached. Therefore, the closure of all or part of an exhibition has been routine practice. Sometimes, senior communist officials have visited in person to approve or disapprove an exhibition.[15] The Exhibition of the History of the Chinese Communist Party, for example, was approved by the Central Committee and opened to the public on July 1, 1961, the fortieth anniversary of the Party. When the Cultural Revolution (1966–1976) began, the exhibition was closed. In spite of numerous revisions, some even under the explicit guidance of Zhou Enlai, the exhibition remained closed until the late 1970s.[16]

The opening of the Modern China primary exhibition in 1996 was a significant event. Its name, Modern China, shifted away from previous names, which had usually included "revolution" or "Chinese Communist Party." The removal of the word "revolution" was significant not because revolution was no longer a major focus in exhibitions, but because it was now clearly treated as part of the process of modern nation state building. The two thousand-square-meter exhibition used some 2,300 objects, documents, photos, charts, models, art works, and replicas of historical artifacts to showcase modern Chinese history. It included seven sections:

> [t]he invasion of imperialist countries and the reduction of China to a semi-colonial and semi-feudal society; the rescue of the dying country and the beginning of modernization; the 1911 revolution and the establishment of the Republic of China; the rule of northern warlords and the republican revolution on the basis of the cooperation between the Nationalist and the Communist Parties; the rule of the Nationalist Party Government and the Land Revolution; national resistance and the defeat of Japanese imperialism; and the Liberation War and the establishment of the People's Republic.

The main storyline of the exhibition was:

> [t]he reduction of China to a semi-feudal and semi-colonial society as a result of imperialist invasions and their alliances with the feudal forces, the Chinese people's brave fights against imperialism and feudalism, and the final achievement of the magnificent victory of the democratic revolution under the leadership of the Chinese Communist Party.[17]

Hence, the representation of China as a semi-feudal and semi-colonial society was a precondition for the representation of the leadership of the Communist Party. The purpose of the exhibition was to show that "the one-hundred-year modern Chinese history" (*zhongguo bainian de jindaishi*) was not only "a history of suffering" (*kunan shi*) under imperialism, feudalism, and colonialism, but also "a history of struggling" (*douzheng shi*) by the Chinese people.

The exhibition's narrative juxtaposition of "suffering" and "struggling" demonstrated why the emergence of the leadership of the Communist Party was necessary.[18] The Communist Party's legitimate rule of China was based on the representation of the presence of Western colonialism and imperialism in modern Chinese history. The exhibition's first section, entitled Big Powers Invaded China, China was Reduced to a Semi-Colonial Semi-Feudal Society (original text in English), addressed the Opium War and its consequences, clearly demonstrating how the exhibition carved out a temporal space for the modern Chinese nation state. The exhibit on the Opium War contained several artifacts: photographs contrasting the level of social development in China and the West prior to the Opium War; a cannon used by coastal troops at Humen; a statue of Lin Zexu (made in 1994);[19] Lin's letter to Emperor Daoguan regarding confiscating and destroying opium; weapons used in resisting the British at Sanyuanli, Guangzhou; a map of the war; and the ruins of Yuanmingyuan (the Old Summer Palace, burned in October 1860). These artifacts explicitly characterized the Opium War as a serious interruption, or temporal break, in Chinese history. According to the panel introducing this section:

> In 1840, Britain, the strongest capitalist power in the West, launched a war of aggression against China, knocking open China's door with opium and gunboats. Later, France, Russia, Japan, the United States, Germany and other imperialist powers came one after another to further spread the flames of aggressive war.
>
> The Chinese people fought a bloody battle and made great sacrifices. However, owing to the decadence of the Qing Government, the invasions ended up with the signing of unequal treaties of national betrayal and humiliation.
>
> Acting upon the unequal treaties, the imperialist powers forced China to cede its territories and pay indemnities. Besides, they seized a whole range of privileges including the station of troops, consular jurisdiction, control of commercial ports and customs, setting up factories, building railways and opening mines. They also supported the feudal forces of the Qing Dynasty and made them their instruments for the control of China.
>
> The aggression and oppression by the imperialist powers seriously harmed China's independence, sovereignty and territorial integrity, and accelerated the disintegration of the feudal economy and the emergence of capitalism in the country. China changed from an independent feudal state into a semi-colonial semi-feudal society.[20]

The narrative stated a clear link between the arrival of Western imperialism and colonialism and significant changes in Chinese historical time. The representation of the 1840 Opium War as an event that interrupted the continuity of Chinese historical time effectively constructed a historical boundary for a qualitatively new China, which was characterized as a "semi-colonial semi-feudal society" (*ban zhimindi ban fengjian shehui*). It was in this narrative space of a "semi-colonial semi-feudal society" that the representation of the emerging leadership of the Communist Party in modern China became possible. Thus, the narrative of modern China as a "semi-colonial semi-feudal society" established a symbiotic relationship between the legitimate rule of the Communist Party and the representation of Chinese modernity as conditioned by colonialism.

How did Modern China show this symbiotic relationship? Through a technique called *duibi* (comparison and contrast). The exhibition began with a small unit illustrating the contrasting social conditions in China and Europe prior to 1840. This unit, located before the text I quoted earlier, contained three black-and-white photos, a wooden plough, and a label. The photos highlighted the unit's comparative role: The first was captioned "the French people captured the Bastille, symbol of the feudal system" in 1789 (original text in English). The second showed a nineteenth-century steam locomotive made in Britain, representing the Industrial Revolution in Europe. The third photo displayed the Forbidden City, the "symbol of the feudality in China" (original text in English). In a clear contrast with the first two, this photo did not include any dates, but was twice as large as either of them, to emphasize the symbolic importance of the Forbidden City and, indeed, of China.

In this exhibit, pre-Opium War China was represented as not having experienced any revolutionary changes—neither a social revolution (exemplified by the French Revolution) nor industrial (exemplified by Britain's Industrial Revolution). This "backward" China was embodied by a wooden plough located in front of the photos to reinforce the perception of the absence of a revolution in "the mode of production" (*shengchan fangshi*). According to the conventional Marxist framework of social progression followed by the exhibit, a revolution in the mode of production determined changes in the "relations of production" (*shengchan guanxi*). The overall intent of this part of the exhibition was made explicit in the panel text: "On the eve of the Opium War, China was in the last stage of feudal society, characterized by political corruption, economic backwardness and seclusion. On the other hand, Britain, France, and other Western countries, having completed the bourgeois and the Industrial Revolution, were developing rapidly in economy, and therefore they badly needed a worldwide market" (original text in English).[21]

The technique of *duibi* used in this part of the exhibition was closely tied to a practice of dialectical materialism based on Mao's notion of "contradiction" (*maodun*). Chinese museums use many display techniques, including the combination of artifacts with supplemental materials, the use of space to highlight important artifacts, the display of a set of closely related artifacts as a unit, the symmetrical arrangement of artifacts in a display case, and the location of artifacts in their original setting.[22] Of these techniques, only *duibi* explicitly serves the purpose of revolutionary practices:[23] its comparison and contrast of artifacts materializes a dialectical relationship between two activities, classes, social systems, ideologies, or societies. It is through *duibi* that museums have applied the Maoist theory of *maodun* (contradiction) to construct a particular historical trajectory of change in Chinese society, which became possible only under the leadership of the CCP.

The connection between the Maoist theory of contradiction and the legitimacy of the rule of the CCP becomes clear if we understand an important distinction between the Maoist *jieji douzheng* (class struggle) and the Marxist class struggle. Both concepts refer to practices that resolve a problematic relationship, but a key difference between them lies in whether that relationship is based on commensurability or incommensurability. Marx carefully differentiates between contradiction and class struggle. For him, contradiction always refers to the conflict between productive forces and relations of production; and class struggle to that between the working class and the bourgeoisie. The former relationship is a *contradiction without antagonism*, which ultimately determines social change; whereas the latter relationship is an *antagonism without contradiction*, in which "denial does not originate from the 'inside' of identity itself but, in its most radical sense, *from outside*."[24] That is, class struggle is tied to antagonism rather than to contradiction. Moreover, in this class struggle, the worker derives his or her antagonism toward the management from the fact that a low salary denies his or her identity as a consumer. This antagonist practice is not inherent to the productive relations, but occurs between the productive relations and the identity of the worker, which exists outside the productive relations.

Similar to this Marxist notion of class struggle, the Maoist *jieji douzheng* also addresses the relationship between the working class and the bourgeoisie. However, it does not focus exclusively on this particular relationship. Moreover, *jieji douzheng* may deal with either a mutually dependent contradictory relationship or an inherently unequal oppositional contradiction.[25] In the case of the Modern China exhibition, the contrast and comparison between China and Europe prior to 1840 served to highlight a dual contradiction—not only the relationship between the feudal and the capitalist, but also that between the colonized and the colonizer. This contradictory relationship, according to Mao's theory of contradiction, was "oppositional" (*duikang de*) and incommensurable (rather than compatible). It would have to be resolved through revolutionary practices of advancing productive forces and establishing a new postcolonial nation state.[26] In the latter context, the new modern nation state needed to deal with the representation of the contradictory relationship between the "proletariat" (*wuchan jieji*) and the "bourgeoisie" (*zichan jieji*). The Modern China exhibition documented the emergence of the CCP as the leader of the proletarian struggle against the bourgeoisie, which was tied to feudalism, imperialism, and colonialism. This documentation was based on narrating the emergence of the modern period in a particular way—not as cosmopolitan or bourgeois, but as colonial—through references to a series of incidents following the Opium War.

In the historical narrative of colonial modernity, the loss of Hong Kong was a crucial incident. *Xianggang* (Hong Kong) in the exhibition designated either the whole Hong Kong region (*xianggang diqu*; that is, Hong Kong Island, Kowloon, and the New Territories) or just part of it. *Xianggang* became the key referent for characterizing Chinese society under feudalism, imperialism, and colonialism as a "semi-colonial semi-feudal society." From colonial modernity to the eventual establishment of the People's Republic, the exhibition highlighted the vitality of the people, of the country, and most importantly, of socialism under the leadership of the Communist Party. In this way, the exhibition developed a rationale under which the Communist Party legitimately ruled the new nation state.

If following Mao's theory of contradiction, the Communist Party's legitimacy depended on the arrival of Western colonialism and imperialism in China, as marked by the loss of Xianggang to Britain, this existential situation could change under certain historical conditions. Hong Kong's return to China in 1997 presented a problem for the portrayal of this mutually dependent contradictory relationship. The British occupation of Hong Kong made it possible for the Communist Party to take the lead in eliminating feudalism and colonialism from Chinese society. As long as Hong Kong's return was not in the picture, the presence of colonialism and imperialism there meant that the project of annihilating colonialism and imperialism was incomplete and the Communist Party could continue to claim leadership in state-building. The July 1, 1997, deadline, however, eliminated Xianggang as a sign for the presence of colonialism and imperialism and thus also imposed on the Communist Party a temporal limit for fulfilling its leadership role in state-building. To resolve this crisis in the Hong Kong countdown process, the Chinese government would have to address the changing historical condition of colonial modernity in order to reconfigure the legitimacy of the rule of the Communist Party. In this sense, the exhibition's use of the name Modern China in place of a name that included "revolution" was a sign of change.

Xianggang's history and development

A shift in museum representations of modern Chinese history took place during the Hong Kong countdown. "Revolutionary China" no longer occupied the central stage in modern Chinese history; rather, it was "modern China" that had become the leitmotif of Chinese history. Xianggang's status in modern Chinese history also began to change. In the previous historical narratives of "revolutionary China," Xianggang symbolized a loss, a tragedy of China in the global expansion of Western colonialism and imperialism. In historical representations during the countdown, Xianggang became a marker for a range of public feelings such as revival, success, and pride, all expressed through celebratory spectacles. The exhibition Xianggang's History and Development (hereafter, "the Xianggang exhibition"), opened to the public on July 1, 1996, at the National Museum of Chinese Revolution, was such a spectacle.

The main theme of the Xianggang exhibition was a detailed public display of Hong Kong's history from the official perspective of Hong Kong's return. Its main objective, as its introductory panel stated, was "to make audiences understand the historic processes of Xianggang's occupation by Britain and of its return to the Motherland, and to give them basic information about Xianggang's political, economic, cultural, and educational development." The exhibition contained four major sections. First, The Origin of the Xianggang Question showed that Xianggang had been part of China and how the British occupied Hong Kong Island and Kowloon and forced the Chinese government to lease the New Territories. The second section, Social Change of Xianggang, introduced the political system of the British Hong Kong government and showed Xianggang's economic development in finance, trade, shipping, tourism, and major educational and arts institutions. The next section, The Close Relationship of Xianggang to the Motherland, recognized the role of Xianggang in Chinese revolution over the past one hundred years, as well as Xianggang's economic investment in China since the late 1970s, Xianggang's donations to China's educational and natural disaster relief efforts, and the Chinese government's assistance to Xianggang in terms of natural resources such as fresh foods, drinking water, and industrial raw materials. The final section, The Resolution of the Xianggang Question, outlined the series of political negotiations between China and Britain over the Hong Kong question and summarized the main points of the Sino–British Joint Declaration. This section also showed how the Chinese government drafted and finalized the Basic Law of the Hong Kong Special Administrative Region and made efforts to ensure Xianggang's smooth transition.

As part of the Hong Kong countdown, the exhibition framed a historical discourse narrating a new set of affects about national revival. It contained a photo of the Hong Kong countdown clock and interpreted its significance in this way: "The sons and daughters of the Chinese nation, the people of every ethnic national group, were longing for the coming of Hong Kong's return in 1997." Liu Zhongde, minister of culture and head of the exhibition's organizing committee, delivered an opening speech in front of the actual countdown clock outside the museum building. He stated:

> The elimination of national humiliation through the recovery of Hong Kong has been a strong desire across several generations of the Chinese people. Only under the leadership of the Chinese Communist Party has China become strong enough to adopt the correct "one country, two systems" principle to realize that dream. Hong Kong's return marks a major step towards the magnificent goal of national unification.[27]

Liu's speech highlighted the language in the exhibition that described the significance of Hong Kong's return, expressing the link between Hong Kong's return and national feelings of recovery of national dignity, strength, and unity. Thus, to "greet [*yingjie*] the coming of the historical moment of our government's resuming sovereignty over Hong Kong" (introductory panel), the exhibition paralleled the "ticking" of the Hong Kong clock outside the museum in synchronizing historical representations of the countdown. The use of artifacts was critical in constructing a historical narrative about the postcolonial future of the modern Chinese nation state. In the exhibition, the establishment of a standard historical narrative about Xianggang worked closely with the redefinition of *geming wenwu* (revolutionary artifacts), the very category of collections upon which "revolution" museums depended to represent modern China as "revolutionary China."

By the time of the opening of the exhibition on July 1, 1996, Xianggang/Hong Kong had become one of the most popular topics covered by the Chinese media. As more publications and activities in China paid attention to Xianggang/Hong Kong, more diverse ways of describing the territory emerged. To correct inappropriate statements used in the media and to provide proper guidance to publications, the central government finally issued a national standard for representing Xianggang. This document was internally circulated among media organizations on the Chinese mainland by the beginning of 1997. As reported by a major Hong Kong newspaper,[28] the standard included a total of eleven categories concerning issues related to "one country, two systems", colonial rule, Xianggang history, and Sino–Hong Kong relations (see Table 3.1).

The Xianggang exhibition exemplified the government's intention and effort to establish a standard for describing Xianggang during the countdown. Regarding Hong Hong's relationship with China, for example, the exhibition's first section made an unequivocal statement:

> The Xianggang region has been an inseparable part of China's territory since ancient times and a place where the sons and daughters of the Chinese nation have lived and reproduced for generations. Prior to the British occupation, local socioeconomic and cultural education had reached a certain level; the place was not uninhabited and uncivilized. The Xianggang region was ruled by the Qin and Han dynasties according to historical records; the governments of the Yuan, Ming, and Qing dynasties had operated local offices in Tunmen, Guanfu, and Jiulong, had established a complete system of government, and had carried out an effective administration.

The most important aspect of this description was the designation of Hong Kong as the "Xianggang region." The term *Xianggang* or *Xianggang region* was used in conjunction with historical references and materials from Hong Kong, regardless of whether the context referred specifically to Hong Kong Island or to the entire region.[29] The exhibition standardized two elements in

Table 3.1 Standards for describing Hong Kong in Chinese publications

	Correct expressions	*Incorrect or wrong expressions*
British rule and Hong Kong's return	Britain has governed Xianggang according to colonial rules.	• Hong Kong is a British colony. • Hong Kong's return means a change in the colonizer. • China is the new colonizer of Hong Kong.
Sovereignty	• The Chinese government resumes sovereignty over Xianggang. • Xianggang returns to the motherland. • China takes back Xianggang. • Handover of government (*zhengquan jiaojie*)	• China takes back sovereignty of Hong Kong. • Return of sovereignty • Handover of sovereignty
Cooperative relations between Hong Kong and the mainland	• Xianggang is an inseparable part of China's territory. • "Guangdong and Xianggang joint venture" or "Beijing and Xianggang exchange" in reference to cooperation or joint ventures	Any statement that puts Hong Kong on the same level with China, such as "China and Hong Kong are two places," "Sino–Hong Kong joint venture," and "Sino–Hong Kong exchange."
How to name Hong Kong in conjunction with other countries	Refer to Hong Kong as a region: "countries and regions including Germany, France, and Xianggang participated in the conference."	Welcome Hong Kong compatriots to visit and invest in China.
The border between Shenzhen and Hong Kong	The administrative line (*guanlixian*)	The border (*bianjiexian*)
The reason for the "one country, two systems" principle	The idea of "one country, two systems" was originally proposed to solve the Taiwan question, but it was first applied to the Xianggang question.	The idea of "one country, two systems" was proposed to resolve the Hong Kong question.
The history of Hong Kong before the British occupation	Agriculture, fishing, ocean navigation, salt production, and education had been developed to a certain level in the Xianggang region prior to 1841. Historical documents show that more than 7,000 people lived on the island at the time and Chizhu had become a town of more than 2,000 residents.	• Before the British occupation, Hong Kong was merely an almost unpopulated island with uncultivated land. • Hong Kong has been developed from a tiny fishing village into a modern metropolis.

(Continued overleaf)

Table 3.1 Continued

	Correct expressions	*Incorrect or wrong expressions*
The Convention of Chuenpee, by which Britain first occupied Hong Kong Island	The Convention of Chuenpee did not take place. The British army invaded and took possession of Xianggang by force.	The Convention of Chuenpee was signed before the British army occupied Hong Kong.
The New Territories	Because "the New Territories" is a term used by the British and the territories are not new to China, the term must be placed in quotation marks.	The New Territories
Hong Kong-based anti-China political organizations	These names must appear in quotation marks: "the Democratic Party."	Portraying these organizations as legitimate
The three-tiered political structure of the British Hong Kong government	The three-tiered political structure of the British Hong Kong government expires on June 30, 1997.	The three-tiered political structure of the British Hong Kong government will be dissolved or abandoned on June 30, 1997.

Source: Ming Bao (Hong Kong), January 21, 1997, p. A11.

the conception of Xianggang: that Xianggang is an "inseparable part of China," and that the Chinese had inhabited Xianggang prior to the British occupation.

In addition to representing the politically correct relationship between Hong Kong and the Chinese inland, the Xianggang exhibition also demonstrated in significant ways how the formal historical representation of Xianggang made use of visual objects, especially what the organizer called "invaluable historical artifacts" (*zhengui de lishi wenwu*). This category of artifacts displaced the conventional category of *geming wenwu*, used by revolution museums since 1949. The 1,300-square-meter Xianggang exhibition was based almost entirely on about three hundred photographs, mainly from the Xinhua News Agency, the official news agency of the Chinese government. Thus, it was appropriate that the organizer called the exhibition a "large-scale pictorial exhibition" (*daxing tupian zhanlan*).

The use of graphic materials as the foundation of the display indeed marked the Xianggang exhibition as different from the Modern China exhibition. In Chinese museology, scholars regard the heavy use of graphic materials in an exhibition as a typical practice of a temporary (rather than primary) exhibition. Because primary exhibitions on the history of the CCP at the

National Museum of Chinese Revolution had used more historical documents (*wenxian*) than three-dimensional artifacts, they had been criticized as "unscientific" (from the perspective of museology). Critics argued that curators who focus on historical documents do not understand the distinction between a museum exhibition and a history book. "The visitor," a well-known museologist stated, "comes to a museum to view evidence of history rather than to read historical documents . . . Otherwise, the visitor could just buy a book that includes historical documents and read it at home without coming to the museum."[30] The Xianggang exhibition was designed as a temporary exhibition and thus retained the flexibility to use more graphic materials than physical artifacts. Moreover, the exhibition presented the many documents in a particular spatial order that could only be experienced through visiting. The exhibition presented a total of seventeen artifacts in fourteen cases:

1 Lin Zexu's report to Emperor Daoguang regarding the burning of opium (dated July 5, 1839);
2 letter of the British plenipotentiary Charles Elliot to the Chinese government (dated January 16, 1841);
3 letter of the Chinese official Deng Tingzhen to a friend about resisting the British in July 1840;
4 memo printed by a school in Guangdong regarding resistance to the British in the Opium War;
5 copy of the portion of the Treaty of Nanjing relating to Hong Kong;
6 copy of the portion of the Treaty of Beijing relating to Hong Kong;
7 copy of the Convention for the Extension of Hong Kong;
8–9 pair of Hero fountain pens used in signing the Sino–British Joint Declaration on December 19, 1984;
10–11 two badges commemorating the establishment of the Consulting Committee on the Basic Law of the Hong Kong Special Administrative Region;
12 booklet listing all the members of the Consulting Committee as of December 18, 1985;
13–14 consultative versions of the Basic Law (in both Chinese and English);
15 the book containing the Basic Law;
16 set of four commemorative stamps printed by the Ministry of Postal Services;
17 miniature topographic model of Hong Kong.

The organizer described and treated these artifacts as "invaluable historical artifacts" (*zhengui de lishi wenwu*).[31] This conceptualization of the displayed objects problematized the two conventional categories of "historical artifacts" (*lishi wenwu*) and "revolutionary artifacts" (*geming wenwu*). The "invaluable historical artifacts" designation fell outside the temporal space of historical artifacts ordinarily used in the history museum context, which normally covered the period prior to 1840. Moreover, these "invaluable historical artifacts" also displaced the category of "revolutionary artifacts" used in the revolution museum context. The first four items on the list, for example, would normally be collected and displayed as revolutionary artifacts, but now they were treated as historical artifacts. Such a displacement, a shift from revolutionary artifacts to historical artifacts, opened up the space of historical representation to encompass conventional revolutionary artifacts.

Once these artifacts were described and treated as historical artifacts, they no longer appeared in the exhibition simply to tell the story of Chinese revolution; instead, they were marked, placed, licensed, and authorized to construct a new representational space. Four historical artifacts, for example, were displayed in the section on Britain's Occupation of Xianggang. They were Elliot's letter requesting Hong Kong Island as a British business port, Deng Tingzhen's letter, the resistance memo circulated in the Opium War, and a copy of the Treaty of Nanjing (items 2–5). In Chinese museology, such a combination of artifacts to illustrate a particular topic is regarded as a practice of the "science of exhibition" (*chenlie xue*),[32] scientific organization of artifacts in a way that they join together to form a coherent space of signification. This section closely followed the "science of exhibition." Each artifact functioned as a reference for others within a hierarchical order. The most important piece in this artificial combination was the artifact of the Treaty of Nanjing, while other artifacts, though also meaningful, mainly played a supporting role in constructing a coherent atmosphere for the proper display of the treaty. As the exhibit's highlight, the Treaty of Nanjing itself was a carefully constructed artifact. Only the section regarding the cession of Xianggang was copied by hand onto a piece of pale yellow rice paper. It was placed and fixed by a transparent plastic thread on an opened book of the same size, which was made of white paper. This exhibit structure differentiated the key page from the rest of the book; and more important, it highlighted the most relevant section of the treaty. Finally, this artifact was carefully installed in a sealed display case (see Figure 3.1). Thus, the artifact was constructed and displayed in a way that marked it as a valuable and authentic historical artifact.

A photo on the wall behind the display case showed another handwritten copy of the cession of Xianggang in the Treaty of Nanjing. The juxtaposition of these two artifacts seemingly invited the visitor to compare the texts of the two artifacts. The key sentence of the photographed version was written according to the following format:

> The great emperor grants the cession of the Hong Kong Island to
> the great British monarch and his successors. [They] can permanently possess, manage as they wish, and administrate with laws.
> (大皇帝准將香港一島，給予
> 大英君主，暨嗣後世襲主位者，常遠據守，主掌任便，立法治理。)

Figure 3.1 A "valuable historical artifact" specially manufactured to represent the Treaty of Nanjing at the Xianggang's History and Development exhibition, National Museum of Chinese Revolution, Beijing, July 1, 1996 (photo by the author).

In contrast, the replicated treaty page read:

> The great emperor grants the cession of the Hong Kong Island to the British monarch. [She and her] successors can permanently manage and administrate with laws as they wish.
> (大皇帝准將香港一島給予英國
> 君主。暨嗣後世襲主位者，常遠主掌，任便立法治理。)

The two versions of the treaty contain subtle yet important differences in both the contents of these texts and their composition styles. The photographed version was written according to the format used by the Qing Dynasty for an official document. The style of the language showed respect for the British monarch. In contrast, the historical artifact version modified the writing style to show less respect for the British, in addition to deleting or changing the order of a few words: "The great British monarch" was replaced by "the British monarch"; and "permanently possess, manage as they wish, and administrate with laws" by "permanently manage and administrate with laws as they wish" (omitting "possess"). Clearly, the two versions of the treaty represent two different historical activities.

The textual and artificial reproduction of the Treaty of Nanjing modified the nature of the cession of Hong Kong Island. The deletion of the key word "possess" (*jushou*) delegitimized the British occupation of the island. The British "possession" of the island was reduced to mere "management" of it. This modification reflected the Chinese government's policy of not acknowledging Hong Kong as a British colony—as first indicated by Huang Hua's letter to the United Nations Special Committee on Colonization in 1972 (see Chapter 1). During the Sino–British negotiations over the future of Hong Kong, the British sought to treat Hong Kong as an independent entity, on the level of China and Britain. The Chinese government, however, rejected this elevation of Hong Kong's status. From the Chinese government's point of view, Hong Kong had always been part of China and was merely a territory temporarily occupied by a foreign power.[33] During the Hong Kong countdown, as shown by the approved language for describing British rule in Table 3.1 and this exhibit, the government wanted the public to perceive Xianggang not as a British colony but as a part of China governed by British colonial rules.

In addition to the style and content of the two treaty texts, the manner of their display also marked an important relationship between them. As mentioned, the artificial historical artifact was protected by a specially made display case, whereas the photo was merely one among a few hundred photos. In this way, the exhibition privileged the historical artifact representation over the photographic representation. Moreover, although the photo of the treaty testified to the existence of the original document, it contradicted the historical artifact's representation of the treaty. Was this instance merely an example of *duibi* (comparison and contrast), that is, the conventional museum technique tied closely to the representation of revolutionary China? No doubt, the juxtaposition of the photographic and artifactual representations was a demonstration of *duibi*, but it was not tied to the historical context of revolutionary China.

Instead, the practice shifted the historical context of the treaty from nineteenth-century colonialism and imperialism to neoliberalism in the Hong Kong countdown period. As a "reproduction" of the treaty, the historical artifact indeed removed the aura of the original treaty—the entire set of historical traditions and rituals previously associated with the treaty and with documents of that era.[34] No matter how formal its design was, the re-created artifact no longer represented the authentic treaty. Instead, it entered into a different circuit of history in which it bore witness to the Chinese government's reconfiguration of the historical time of the nation state during the Hong Kong countdown. In the new circuit of history, the reproduction and dissemiNation[35] of the treaty became an important way of creating a meaningful historical present.

The artificial re-representation of the treaty went beyond the Xianggang exhibition. At the National Military Museum of the Chinese People's Revolution in Beijing, for example, a similar representation of the treaty appeared in the Modern War Gallery. The artifact was just a page that appeared to be taken from a book. The section on Hong Kong was printed in complicated characters, and its content was exactly the same as in the historical artifact at the Xianggang exhibition. In July 1996, I had an opportunity to interview by telephone Mr. Huang, a curator of the Modern War Gallery. In our short conversation, Mr. Huang first appeared surprised when I asked him whether the contents of the printed page in the galley had been changed. Huang said that the text "should not be wrong" (*bu yinggai you cuowu*), but did not offer any explanation. I mentioned the photograph of the treaty in the Xianggang exhibition and explained how the photographed text was different from that in the printed page at this galley. In his response, he denied that the photographed version was "the official text" (*zhengshi wenzi*), nor did he think it was an unofficial "draft" (*caoqian wenzi*). Like me, wondered where the "original" document was. Eventually, he suggested that I look at Wang Tieya's collections of all the treaties signed between China and other countries prior to 1949.[36] The Treaty of Nanjing is contained in the first volume of Wang's book, and the text of the Hong Kong cession portion is almost identical to the photographed version.[37] The only difference is that the photographed text does not have the character "state" (*guo*) after the character "English" (*ying*). Thus, it conveys the meaning of "the British" whereas Wang's version conveys the idea of "Britain," a minor difference that has little effect on meaning.

The historical artifact version of the treaty also was displayed in the Hong Kong Special Administrative Region after 1997 at the Historical Facts of the Treaty of Nanjing exhibition held at Plaza Hollywood, a newly completed shopping mall at Diamond Hill, from August 29 to September 3, 1997. (I describe this exhibition in the introduction.) Like the Xianggang exhibition, this was a traveling exhibition designed to be assembled in a short period of time, use a wide range of display materials, and respond in a timely manner to a pressing political concern.[38] In this "pictorial exhibition" (*tupian zhan*), the Treaty of Nanjing was shown twice and in two different versions. In the section entitled Signing of the Treaty of Nanjing (original text in English) was a photo showing the full text of the treaty, with the portion on the cession of Hong Kong highlighted in red. The text itself was handwritten and the content was the same as in the photograph displayed at the Xianggang exhibition. Meanwhile, in the section called National Catastrophes (in English), the Hong Kong portion of the treaty was replicated. This version was not handwritten but printed in complicated Chinese characters. Its content matched that of the historical artifact version in the Xiangang exhibition.

Although the two exhibitions displayed two different versions of the treaty, they did not treat the relationship between them in the same way. In the Plaza Hollywood exhibition, the two versions of the treaty were shown as a sequence in the storyline. The full-text version appeared in the second section to recognize the treaty's signing, whereas the brief version appeared in the third section to portray the treaty as a cause of "national catastrophes." In the exhibition's storyline, the shortened-version artifact was to be viewed after the full-text artifact. Consequently, the act of recognizing the treaty's serious implications was structured discursively to succeed the act of recognizing its existence. This arrangement made sense given that Hong Kong had already become the Hong Kong Special Administrative Region.

In contrast with the sequence in the Plaza Hollywood exhibition, the two versions of the treaty in the Xianggang exhibition were placed so close together that they could be viewed simultaneously. This manner of display reflected the coexistence of two different historical presents during the Hong Kong countdown. As I discussed in the previous chapter, the first historical present referred to the post-1997 future of the Chinese nation state (specifically, the fifty years from 1997 to 2046) and the second to the transitional present (from 1984 to 1997). In light of this co-presence, the governmental problem during the countdown was how to make the first historical present become normative (regular and regulative) in the context of the second historical present.

Neoliberal subjectivity in historical representation

The Xianggang exhibition at the National Museum of Chinese Revolution provided visitors with both a space and an opportunity to fashion neoliberal subjectivity. On the opening day, a Beijing woman working for the Beijing Bureau of the British Broadcasting Corporation (BBC), after viewing the photographic and artifactual representations of the treaty, commented: "History, like women's fashions, is always selective" (*lishi xiang nuren de yifu yiyang, zongshi tiao lai tiao qu*). This short statement pointed out not only the materiality of a historical present but also the embodiment of that historical present. The woman was not the only one who used clothing as a metaphor for questioning historical representation. On the same day, a sixty-four-year-old man—a retired reporter from Hebei Province who introduced himself as Gebi ("desert")—was promoting the T-shirt he was wearing to the other visitors. On the front of the white T-shirt were Chinese characters written on a staff in the style of musical notes and reading, "We all have a home, its name is called China" (*women dou you yige jia, mingzi jiao zhongguo*); and the English words "HONG KONG TO BE RETURNED TO HOME LAND." On the back of the T-shirt, the large black Chinese character "return" (*gui*) was printed in a calligraphic style. Below the character were signatures. The relationship of the character to the signatures was carefully constructed to resemble a memorial. Hong Kong's "return" was the object to which the signatures paid tribute. The use of black ink for the character "return" contrasted sharply with the T-shirt's white color, evoking a feeling of mourning. Normally, a monument connotes remembrance (in the present), and mourning, the feeling toward the deceased's passing (in the past). In this case, however, the memorial function of the character "return" signified the future. The object of mourning was merely anticipated. The design of Gebi's T-shirt thus materialized the relationship between the post-1997 future and the transitional present.

Although the T-shirt functioned as a memorial to Xianggang's return to China, it was different from an ordinary monument placed permanently at a site. Since the man was wearing the T-shirt, his body became the site of the memorial, transforming the traditional site-sensitive memorial into a mobile one. Moreover, this mobile memorial was also expandable and circulative. As Gebi told his audience, new signatures would be added until the total number of signatures reached 1996, and he would be the 1997th person to sign it. In the process of getting the signatures, he would also collect the biographies of the signers. He planned eventually to donate the artifact to "the memorial hall of Hong Kong's return" (*Xianggang huigui ji'nian'guan*), which, he thought, ought to be built. With respect to whom he would invite to sign the T-shirt, he said he would ask only "famous people" (*mingren*), such as provincial party secretaries, mayors, county chiefs, and township heads, and would give them a T-shirt of the same design as a gift. Collecting the 1997 signatures, documenting the signers, and donating the final artifact to an imaginary museum would complete the whole process of making the 1997 T-shirt, and more important, build a Hong Kong's return memorial to extend the memory of Xianggang's return into the future. Thus, for him, the future of his T-shirt was inseparable from the post-1997 future of his country.

In the speech, Gebi referred to his Hong Kong memorial T-shirt as a "patriotic cultural T-shirt" (*aiguo wenhua shan*). Since his retirement, he said, he had wanted to do something meaningful. Taking advantage of the opportunity of Hong Kong's return, he and his friends designed the T-shirt to make some money. At the Xianggang exhibition, he told the audience that selling the T-shirts would be a practice of "earning patriotic money, earning money to be patriotic, being patriotic to earn money" (*zheng aiguo qian, zhengqian aiguo, aiguo zhengqian*). He was confident that his T-shirt project would make lots of money. He argued that his T-shirt was different from other "alternative" (*linglei*) cultural T-shirts sold by private entrepreneurs.[39] His targeted customers were government employees, members of the Communist Party and the Communist Youth League, and students. He claimed that his "cultural T-shirt" had a "patriotic social and cultural value;" and declared that he was the first person in China to link "cultural T-shirts" to "patriotic education." To evoke the importance of patriotic education, he said that people in Hong Kong had no such concepts as "*guojia*" (state or country) and "*minzu*" (nation). Almost everyone in his audience apparently agreed, because they were nodding their heads. Moved by his impassioned speech and attracted to his design, a factory manager took out his business card and handed it to Gebi, telling him that they should talk later. Two museum staff members also asked him to donate the T-shirt to the museum after he collected all 1997 signatures. These positive responses showed that Gebi's promotion of his T-shirt was initially successful.

Gebi's fashion show manipulated time in the same way as the Xianggang exhibition did. Like a ready-to-wear fashion show organized by the textile industry to promote mass awareness of the current fashions, his show also signaled a gesture, a readiness for mass production and thus consumption. However, ready-to-wear fashion shortens the duration of clothing as a product and always annihilates the present it captures. And its present time is measured in a forward direction. In contrast, the present time of Gebi's T-shirt was measured by the Hong Kong countdown clock. While his gesture of mass production was forward-looking, his memorialization of the future was a countdown practice. This way of organizing time was consistent with that of the exhibition.

Gebi could be viewed as an artifact, the "T-shirt man artifact," because he supplements the exhibition, performing the same function as the other artifacts on display. Both this artifact and the historical artifact that represented the Treaty of Nanjing referred to the same future time frame as a point of departure in the present. Moreover, they also materialized the future-present relationship in a monumental manner, whether they called it a "patriotic cultural T-shirt" or an "invaluable historical artifact." In both situations, the past did not enter into the domain of historical memory. Instead, it was the present substituting for the past that became the temporal material for the recollection and exhibition of the future. In this sense, either artifact could be called a "memorial of Hong Kong's return."

Through showing off his T-shirt, Gebi enacted the neoliberal norm of an entrepreneurial subject in his life-building process, just as the individuals I discussed in the previous chapter did. His story had two parts: One was the whole project of creating the T-shirt as a Hong Kong return memorial, which brought the future into a dialogue with the present. The temporality of the future was used as a tool in his life-building process. This part of the story was inseparable from its second part, which was the way in which he successfully promoted his T-shirt as a potentially profitable product. The connection between the cultural and the economic was effectively established by means of communication, especially by his mobilization of communicative labor in producing collective feelings about the moral conduct of making money in patriotic practices.

Reordering historical times

If the countdown clock were be used to signal changes, it would have to be used in connection with other media and other means of communication—such as Li Yunpeng's poem, Gebi's T-shirt, museum exhibitions, and mass media. In this affective economy of the countdown, historical representation was a pressing governmental problem. The historical discourse of modern China itself was decoded and recoded in the countdown, first by reordering the key temporal elements that constituted the historical time of the modern Chinese nation state, and then by asserting the superiority of one particular temporal element over the others.[40]

Three key temporal elements have constituted the historical time of modern China. The first is the colonial time associated with Western colonialism and imperialism in the nineteenth and first half of the twentieth centuries. Exemplified by the British occupation of Hong Kong, this was a time of national humiliation, loss, suffering, and pain. The second element is the revolutionary time when the CCP created an independent sovereign state representing the interests of the proletariat, or working class, and all those who were not represented by the Communist Party were excluded by the Maoist proletariat state. The third element is the neoliberal time associated with the economic reforms since the late 1970s. In this time, instead of reacting passively, the Chinese government has actively facilitated the neoliberal process of globalization (see Introduction to this volume).

As I discussed, until the Modern China exhibition at the National Museum of Chinese Revolution, all previous primary exhibitions on modern Chinese history at this important museum had focused on various practices of "revolution." The conventional historical representation (before the Hong Kong countdown) ordered the first two temporal elements by conferring superiority on the revolutionary time. Fundamentally, this historical representation encoded modern Chinese history as that of the CCP, whose leadership was critical to the process of state building. Paradoxically, its legitimacy was always confirmed by the colonial time, so that public feelings of national humiliation and disaster would be redirected toward feelings of loving the country and loving the party, as illustrated by the expression "No new China without the Chinese Communist Party" (*meiyou gongchandang jiu meiyou xinzhongguo*). In the context of economic reforms since the late 1970s, museums devoted to the representation of "revolutionary China" began to modify their exhibitions' main storylines. In the words of Kirk Denton, they "edged slowly away from standard narratives of class oppression and revolutionary struggle towards representations of the past that legitimize the contemporary ideology of commerce, entrepreneurship and market reform."[41] With respect to the Modern China exhibition—the country's most important museum exhibition on modern Chinese history because of its link to and direct approval by the central government—the use of "modern" in place of "revolution" in the title certainly reflected this change.

It was only under the historical condition of reunification with Hong Kong that the relationship between the three temporal elements was explicitly recoded to create a new historical time for the modern Chinese nation state. That very historical condition was tied to the logic of the Hong Kong countdown, of incorporating a specific future time (from 1997 to 2046) into a particular present time (the transitional period from 1984 to 1997). As the latter time was running out, the former shifted its status from an exception to a norm (see Chapter 2). This shifting process was expressed in various exhibitions devoted to Hong Kong's history or, rather, the history of Hong Kong's return to China. The name Xianggang's History and Development would suggest that this exhibition focused on Hong Kong. However, as shown by my analysis, it really addressed the way China reunited with Hong Kong. In the exhibition, Hong Kong was not viewed as a British colony; instead, it was merely administered by the British. Hong Kong also maintained a close relationship with the Chinese inland. Moreover, the exhibition also conveyed the superiority of the neoliberal time in the new historical timeline of the Chinese nation state, while the colonial time began to vanish within the period of the countdown. Consequently, the revolutionary time supported by the colonial time also began to disappear. What was portrayed as spectacular was the neoliberal time. Not only did the exhibition utilize the temporal logic of the countdown during which exception ruled, but it also celebrated the mobilization of the neoliberal norm of the entrepreneurial subject. Both were embodied by Gebi's promotion of his T-shirt.

4 Morality and pleasure in the synchronization with the world

In late June 1997, the Beijing municipal government held a lantern festival at the Park of Yuanming Yuan to celebrate Hong Kong's return.[1] Two 1997-meter-long dragon-shaped lanterns were lavishly displayed. The yellow-colored dragon guided visitors to move from the main entrance to the shores of the Sea of Happiness (*fuhai*), while the red-colored dragon highlighted the paths from the main entrance to the Great Fountains (*dashuifa*). In the Garden of Long Spring (*Changchuan yuan*), a miniaturized landscape of Hong Kong's Central District was staged on an island, illuminated by more than two thousand sets of lights (including special effects lights like neon lights and spotlights). Viewing the landscape from a distance, visitors could recognize the Bank of China Building, one of the most visible symbols of the Central District, and read a set of seven large Chinese characters placed in front of the diorama forming the slogan "Hong Kong's tomorrow will be better" (*Xianggang mingtian geng meihao*). This representation of Hong Kong focused narrowly on the Central District to the exclusion of other areas of Hong Kong. Not only did it highlight Hong Kong's urban and business dimensions, but it also spotlighted a major Chinese state-owned company in a prosperous and spectacular Hong Kong.

That Yuanming Yuan was chosen as a major site for celebrating Hong Kong's return was not incidental. The place is officially registered as an important "patriotic educational site" (*aiguozhuyi jiaoyu jidi*). During the second Opium War in 1860, the British and French looted and burned the imperial palace there. The Treaty of Beijing, signed in the same year, allowed Britain to annex Kowloon, a major part of the Hong Kong territory. Therefore, Yuanming Yuan was considered an important site for remembering "national humiliation" (*guochi*). The Chinese government's resumption of sovereignty over Hong Kong certainly meant regaining face from this humiliation. The celebration of Hong Kong's return served the purpose of patriotic education in a particular way. On June 21, 1997, the government placed a gift from Hong Kong, a ceremonial vessel, in front of the ruins of the Great Fountains. This *Shenghe baoding* ("treasure vessel of prosperity and peace") was a four-footed, two-handled, square vessel, weighing 1997 kilograms and measuring 2 meters in length, 1.5 meters in width, and 2.22 meters in height, and symbolizing the reappearance of Hong Kong in the Chinese nation state (Figure 4.1). In this context, patriotic education no longer focused on the criminal act of the British and the French and the loss of national sovereignty; rather, it emphasized both Hong Kong's spectacular urban prosperity and the reunion between Hong Kong and the Chinese mainland. Thus, the public expression of national humiliation was transformed into one of national revival in this new trajectory of patriotic education.

It is interesting to compare the lantern festival at Yuanming Yuan with the major celebrations held at Tiananmen Square. As described in chapter 2, the Beijing municipal government organized an extravagant "evening celebration party" (*lianhuan wanhui*) called Beijing Blesses You, Hong Kong (*Beijing zhufu ni, Xianggang*) in front of the countdown clock at Tiananmen Square on June 30, 1997. Reportedly, 100,000 people attended, selected from thousands of work units in the city of Beijing and its surroundings. The celebration officially began at 22:00 and lasted until 5:00 the next morning. During the final moments before midnight, everyone gathered in front of the clock and counted down the seconds from 10 to 0. The party was not only televised live across the country, but also broadcast to audiences around the world. Compared with this extravaganza, the lantern festival at Yuanming Yuan was much more mundane. For one, it did not prescreen its attendees. Anyone who paid the park admission was allowed to participate. The media did report on the festival, but did not give it the phenomenal publicity of the Tiananmen celebration. The festival at the

Figure 4.1 Visitors and the *Shenghe baoding* ("treasure vessel of prosperity and peace") at the ruins of the Great Fountains in 2000 (photo by the author).

park was more like a celebration of a public holiday than carefully coordinated political theater.

The festival's leisurely pace and atmosphere of relaxation and pleasure in fact continued the tradition of lantern festivals at the park. After all, the Yuanming Yuan imperial gardens had been Emperor Qianlong's favorite place to hold a lantern festival on every fifth day of the first month in the lunar calendar, when partygoers ate sweet dumplings made from glutinous rice flour (*yuanxiao*), viewed various colors and shapes of lanterns, and watched fireworks.[2] The nature garden was landscaped with terraced hillocks, a variety of lakes connected by bridges and meandering paths, and magnificent palace buildings. In such a garden, the colorful lanterns, lights, and magnificent fireworks created a series of spectacular scenes.[3] The atmosphere associated Yuanming Yuan with a garden of pleasure and happiness. Moreover, in the Qianlong period, Yuanming Yuan also contained a series of themed environments such as a replica of a market town outside the court, gardens evocative of southern China, and an open-air art gallery called Xianfa Tu (Perspective Picture), depicting European town life. Contemporary Yuanming Yuan continued this tradition with miniaturized models of Xiyang Lou (the European Buildings) as they had appeared pre-destruction, re-creation of all the landscaped gardens of Yuanming Yuan in its prime, and totem poles and masks representing primitive cultures of the (outside) world. The miniaturized Central District of Hong Kong fits perfectly within this context.

Thus, the lantern festival celebrating Hong Kong's return resonated with both the public expression of national revival and the spectacle of pleasure. This festival mirrored a seemingly paradoxical situation at the Park of Yuanming Yuan. On the one hand, it has been preserved and treated as a major site for formal patriotic education intended to shape the moral character of Chinese citizens. On the other, it is a park, a garden of pleasure, and a site of leisure and recreation in everyday life.[4] The original 350-hectare Yuanming Yuan imperial garden, located in what is now northwestern Beijing, contained several gardens, including the Garden of Perfect Brightness (*Yuanming yuan*), the Garden of Long Spring (*Changchun yuan*), the Garden of Variegated Spring (*Jichun yuan*), and the European Buildings (*Xiyang lou*). Five emperors of the Qing Dynasty—Yungzheng (1722–1735), Qianlong (1735–1796), Jiaqing (1796–1820), Daoguang (1820–1850), and Xianfeng (1850–1861)—had vacationed, given orders to government officials, and met foreign delegations there. Like the Forbidden City, it was also an imperial palace, known as the Old Summer Palace. The gardens were built over a period of more than 150 years. Construction on the Garden of Perfect Brightness began under Kangxi (1661–1722) in 1709 and was completed under Qianlong in 1774. The Garden of Long Spring, just east of the former garden, was built under Qianlong, beginning in 1751. The Garden of Variegated Spring was in existence by at least 1774.[5] Xiyang Lou was built during the period from 1747 to 1759. In 1860 British and French soldiers looted and burned the palace and gardens, which continued to decay until restoration began in 1976. Just as the imperial Yuanming Yuan was "a garden containing many smaller gardens" (*yuanzhongyuan*), the contemporary Yuanming Yuan consists of many small parks, each charging a separate entrance fee. Visitors might go to the Ruins Park of Yuanming Yuan (*Yuanming yuan yizhi gongyuan*), an exhibition hall displaying the "miniaturized landscape of Yuanming Yuan" (*Yuanming yuan weisuo jingguan*), the World Primitive Totems Garden (*Shijie yuanshi tuteng huicui yuan*), or an amusement park of paintball games.

In this chapter I examine how Yuanming Yuan became an important site articulating the relationship between neoliberal synchronization and the affective economy. More specifically, I investigate how spatial representations of the cultural other addressed the tension between patriotic education as part of the affective economy and pleasure consumption as a means of neoliberal "synchronization with the world" (*yu shijie jiegui*). At the Ruins Park of Yuanming Yuan, the representation of the cultural other focuses on the ruins of Xiyang Lou. The connection between the ruins of Xiyang Lou and the cultural other (Europe, in this case) is complicated. The buildings were originally designed by the Jesuits F. Ginssepe Castiglione (Italian, 1688–1766, aka Lang Shining), P. Michael Benoit (French, 1715–1774, aka Jiang Youren), and Jean Denis Attiret (French, 1702–1768, aka Wang Zhicheng) for Emperor Qianlong in the eighteenth century. The original buildings were regarded as a good example of China's learning from Europe and the ruins as evidence of Western imperialist aggression toward China. The display of the ruins encouraged expressions of patriotic feelings. Yet in the context of Hong Kong's return, the expression of national humiliation was reoriented toward one of national revival. This representation of the cultural other formed a landscape of power that disciplined its users to become morally awakened subjects.

Meanwhile, the World Primitive Totems Garden displayed another form of the cultural other—"remote" (*yaoyuan*), "primitive" (*yuanshi*), and "ancient" (*yuangu*) cultures—through a collection of totem poles and masks. Built on the Mind-Opening Isle (*haiyue kaijin*), an island in the Garden of Long Spring just south of Xiyang Lou, this spatial representation was explicitly tied to the process of neoliberal globalization, that is, the active synchronization of China with the capitalist, neoliberal world (see Introduction, this volume). Because the garden was operated as a for-profit rather than a nonprofit enterprise, it exemplified the reform of museums and their related organizations in the development of the "culture industry" (*wenhua chanye*). Meanwhile, the spatial representation of the cultural other formed a landscape of instrumental discipline where visitors practiced being proper consumers.

I regard these two forms of cultural representation and their relations to discipline at Yuanming Yuan as functioning similarly to the Tiananmen countdown clock. Because of its close material links to a series of important historical events and figures (to name a few, Qing rulers, European missionaries, foreign diplomats, and the second Opium War), Yuanming Yuan itself could be viewed as a public time-telling device that mobilized a multiplicity-based time to coordinate different kinds of temporalities, whether those associated with patriotism and nationalism or those tied to pleasure and consumption. In the context of Hong Kong's return to China, this treatment of Yuanming Yuan helps us to unfold and unpack the site's important relation to the governmental problem of historical narration.

A landscape of moral awakening: The Ruins Park of Yuanming Yuan

The name Ruins Park of Yuanming Yuan suggests that this park encompasses all material remains of the Old Summer Palace. In fact, however, "ruins" refers only to those of Xiyang Lou. Such a representation was a politics of disappearance in the sense that it displaced the official "scenes" (*jing*) of the Chinese-style buildings with European-style ones. That is, this representation of the Yuanming Yuan ruins encoded a discourse of collective memory.[6]

A shift of official "scenes"

Three sets of eighteenth-century images portrayed various parts of imperial Yuanming Yuan. The Garden of Perfect Brightness was designated as having "forty scenes" (*sishi jing*). A pictorial map of this garden was made in 1737.[7] In 1744, two court artists, Tang Tai and Shen Yuan, painted the "forty scenes;" and Qianlong himself wrote a series of poems on these sights. Around the same time, the Garden of Long Spring was determined to have "eight scenes" (*ba jing*), which were contained and described in the book *Ri xia jiu wen kao (A Study of What is Old in Beijing*) published in 1774.[8] In addition, Xiyang Lou was also portrayed by Castiglione, one of its three Jesuit designers, in a total of twenty copper engravings, each portraying a whole building or part of it.[9] Of these three sets of images, the first two had always been considered as the official representations of Yuanming Yuan.

Not only did the 1860 assault destroy the whole of Yuanming Yuan, but it also marked a shift in the official representation of Yuanming Yuan, adding images of the ruins to the three previous sets of images. The original wooden Chinese-style buildings in the Garden of Perfect Brightness and the Garden of Long Spring were completely destroyed in 1860. By contrast, the ruins of Xiyang Lou's stone buildings remained prominent, despite their gradual and persistent deterioration. Thus, the contemporary characterization of Yuanming Yuan as a ruins site is primarily based on the material visibility of Xiyang Lou.

From the inception of the Ruins Park of Yuanming Yuan in 1988, the symbolic importance of Xiyang Lou's ruins has always been the focus, yet the official representation of Yuanming Yuan has gone beyond the visible ruins.[10] According to *An Introduction to the History of Yuanming Yuan*, the official guidebook published by the park in 1994, the Xiyang Lou buildings exemplify "the successful construction of a large-scale European-style garden, an experiment that occupies an important place not only in the history of Chinese gardens but also in the history of East–West relations." Moreover, according to the author, Xiyang Lou's "construction:"

> . . . was well received in Europe. A missionary from Western Europe who witnessed it praised Xiyang Lou: Beautiful scenes and wonders join together. Whatever people could imagine, you will find there, for example, a variety of marvelous and wonderful fountains. The largest one could be compared with those at Versailles and Saint Claud. The missionary concluded, Yuanming Yuan was China's Versailles.[11]

The most widely circulated and quoted account was written by the French Jesuit Jean-Denis Attiret, another of the designers of Xiyang Lou. Attiret's description paid a great deal of attention to the Chinese buildings and the gardens themselves, not particularly to Xiyang Lou.[12] However, the park's appropriation of his writing reduces Attiret's overall impression of Yuanming Yuan to Xiyang Lou alone. In addition, there is no mention of eyewitness accounts of the Xiyang Lou buildings from Chinese writers. This is understandable because Chinese who visited European palaces like Versailles after 1860 could not possibly visit the original Yuanming Yuan and thus could hardly make such comparisons.[13]

Because the ruins park focuses on the achievements of Yuanming Yuan, it downplays Yuanming Yuan's "shortcomings" (*buzu*) by turning them into passive values of patriotism. The work *An Introduction to the History of Yuanming Yuan* states, "Of course, nothing is perfect. The large size of Yuanming Yuan, its constant expansion and reconstruction, the influence on feudal society of the decadence of several emperors, whatever angle we look at [Yuanming Yuan from], we can find shortcomings." Despite these "shortcomings," the guide continues:

> Back then, whoever witnessed the magnificent scene [of Yuanming Yuan] always recognized how wonderful it was. Some Westerners did not begin to view Chinese gardens with a clear vision until they looked at Yuanming Yuan. Anyway, Yuanming Yuan had earned honors for our ancient civilization and was the pride of our Chinese nation![14]

Thus, the appropriation of eighteenth-century European writings legitimizes such patriotic expressions as the "honor" (*rongyu*) of ancient Chinese civilization and the "pride" (*jiao'ao*) of the Chinese nation.[15]

The park's deployment of a comparative strategy reveals a specific politics of representation. European writings are used as a critical source of information validating the historical importance of the pre-1860 Yuanming Yuan. Europe is represented in a positive light because doing so enables the park to turn the criticism of feudal society into a celebration of patriotism. In this context, the park reduces the whole materiality of post-1860 Yuanming Yuan to that of Xiyang Lou. Even though Yuanming Yuan continued deteriorating and being looted between 1860 and the 1970s, the park only addresses the 1860–1900 period when the destruction was caused by Europeans, thereby representing Europe negatively through a politics of time.

The politics of time

The looting and burning of Yuanming Yuan by British and French soldiers in October 1860 was the most serious act of destruction, but Yuanming Yuan was further damaged in 1900 when the armies of eight foreign countries attacked Beijing.[16] After the collapse of the Qing Dynasty, the ruins were raided by local officials, warlords, soldiers, antique dealers, and peasants in search of construction materials such as bricks, marble, and decorative carvings. In the autumn of 1922, for example, Beijing Mayor Liu Menggeng took more than seven hundred carts of stones as construction material, and the building of the Beijing Library in 1929 also used stone from Xiyang Lou.[17] The destruction of Yuanming Yuan continued under the People's Republic. In 1970–1972, stones were taken from Xiyang Lou to construct a national underground defense facility. It was not until 1976 when the Management Office of Yuanming Yuan was established that the destruction of Xiyang Lou was halted.[18] Three images of the Great Fountains—a pre-destruction scene in the 1780s (Figure 4.2), a photograph from the 1920s (Figure 4.3), and another from 1996 (Figure 4.4)—clearly illustrate the ongoing deterioration of Xiyang Lou.

At the ruins park, the 1860–1900 period when the invading Europeans

Figure 4.2 The Great Fountains in the 1780s (from Osvald Sirén, *The Imperial Places of Peking*, vol. 3, plate 214).

Figure 4.3 The ruins of the Great Fountains in the 1920s (photo by Osvald Sirén, in *The Imperial Places of Peking*, vol. 3, plate 214).

Figure 4.4 Visitors at the ruins of the Great Fountains in 1996 (photo by the author).

destroyed Yuanming Yuan is treated as the tragic time in its history. Zhao Guanghua, the park's chief consultant, argues that Yuanming Yuan's 1860–1900 image was not only tragic, but also the most original, powerful, and thus beautiful one. The current ruins park, he argues, should:

> . . . protect the great historical significance of the "fire" and its vivid image. In building this "ruins garden," the exemplary scene should be that of before 1900 . . . The ruins garden was mostly covered by beautiful and intact hills, lakes, flowers, trees, bridges, and paths; the sites of remains and almost complete walls and doors; and fragments of decorative stone carvings and bronze statues.[19]

Thus, while Yuanming Yuan's tragic time was closely tied to the historical time of Western imperial presence in China, its tragic scene was also part of the nation's tragic engagement in nineteenth-century capitalist global expansion. From this perspective, the representation of Xiyang Lou's ruins is elevated to encode the historical discourse of the nation. In *An Introduction to the History of Yuanming Yuan*, the destruction of Yuanming Yuan in 1860 is characterized as "a page of the history of humiliation in modern Chinese history."[20]

> The history-making garden Yuanming Yuan was destroyed. It was destroyed by the British and French aggressors and by the decadency and weakness of the Qing government. Not only was its destruction evidence of Western invaders' barbaric destruction of a human culture, but it was also testimony to the fact that an ancient country of civilization, on becoming backward, was beaten. Our Chinese nation does not intend to oppress other nations, but we cannot tolerate others' oppression of us. Please try very hard, descendents of the Emperors Yan and Huang, to maintain the tragedy of Yuanming Yuan forever as an incident in the past![21]

The tragedy itself happened in the past, but the use of the ruins to tell a story of the tragedy remains a present project of constructing a historical discourse of collective memory that properly communicates national humiliation. Since the park's opening on June 29, 1988, Xiyang Lou's 1860 image has been used to shape the moral character of Chinese citizens. Visitors are encouraged to consider the present state of the ruins as the "original" one. This scene is linked both to the crime of looting and destruction by the British and the French in 1860 and to the war's historical consequences such as the signing of the Treaty of Beijing, the cession of Kowloon to Britain, and the circulation of looted artifacts around the world.

A landscape of moral awakening

The ruins park has four sections. From west to east, they are the Maze (*migong*), rebuilt as an amusement site; the Harmonious, Curious, and

Pleasant Building (*xieqiqu*); the Hall of Peaceful Sea (*haiyan tang*), located in the middle of the Xiyang Lou garden and formerly its largest structure; and the Great Fountains (*dashuifa*). In each section except the Maze, a miniature of the original building is displayed. Since the ruins of the Great Fountains are the most prominent, they are often treated as a special section. In 1996, for example, the section was walled off and managed as an independent park, requiring an additional admission fee.[22]

When I first visited the ruins of the Great Fountains as a college student in the summer of 1984, they were not walled off. College students from nearby universities (for example, Beijing and Qinghua universities) often went there, not primarily to see the ruins, which were largely hidden in overgrown vegetation. Instead, the site was a favorite picnicking or dating spot.[23] In the 1990s, the Great Fountains became a mini-sized theme park. Visitors could walk around the pool in front of the ruined building; climb the ruins (broken walls, foundation, and pillars); look at the miniature model of the original building; and read comments on the ruins.

The model, located at the eastern entrance to the site, is not merely an artifact illustrating the original Great Fountains, but is also a technology of representation, allowing the eye to perform a specific operation of manipulating and attending to the physical environment in certain ways, to construct an interior time and space within the viewing subject.[24] As an artifact representing the pre-1860 building, the miniature reconstructs the world of the imperial palace. Via reduction, the miniature compresses the pre-1860 everyday—associated with continuously evolving and expanding time and space—into a still, nostalgic world frozen in time and space. Thus, the miniature here is a device for arresting and removing a life from the realm of the everyday (albeit the everyday of the imperial family). The miniaturized palace may be seen as similar to the dollhouse in European and American contexts, as discussed by Susan Stewart; both represent a nostalgic world of wealth and emphasize the function of the object as a display item rather than a toy to be played with.[25] The display function of the miniaturized palace distances the viewer from the viewed object, and the separation of the viewer from the miniaturized palace is physically enforced. A cage of thick metal wires stands between the viewer and the transparent display case containing the palace miniature. The wire cage, intended to protect the artifact from damage, prevents any direct physical contact between the visitor and the model (see Figure 4.5).

The manner of display of the miniaturized palace, however, also allows it to discipline the way the visitor views the Great Fountains. The display case and wire cage physically reinforce the viewer's sense of distance, separation, or loss from the building that existed. The exhibit's discipline role is enhanced when the miniature and the ruins of the Great Fountains are viewed together. The placement of the miniature in proximity to the ruins creates a vista of time that supports a relationship between the narrative time of the miniaturized Great Fountains and the present time of the ruined Great Fountains.

Figure 4.5 A visitor viewing the miniature and the ruins of the Great Fountains, July 28, 1996 (photo by the author).

That is, against the backdrop of the ruins, the viewer may travel back in time not only to glimpse a glorious scene of the Great Fountains but also to revisit its brutal destruction.

The miniaturized palace, its display case and wire cage, and the ruins form a landscape of moral awakening. The association of these artifacts in the built environment animates, in a paradoxical way, the arrested life of the pre-1860 palace in a series of activities deliberately framed within a national story of humiliation. Viewers experience the pre-1860 palace in their mind's eye, while simultaneously viewing the ruins they have become imposes a reality on the mental image. The projected/protected/arrested pre-1860 perfect world can only be experienced as a deeply troubled world in the present built environment. Thus, the juxtaposition of the model and the ruins functions not only to represent the pre-1860 palace but also to evoke a sense of national tragedy.

I would like to discuss two popular tourist activities: photo-taking and graffiti-writing. Visitors, some dressed up in Qing-era costumes, pose themselves in the middle of fragmented pillars and broken walls and become part of the tragic scene.[26] While taking photos, visitors often comment on current affairs that may have nothing to do with the British and French looting and destruction in 1860. In the first half of 1996, for example, the Chinese media reported a series of incidents, including American military presence near Taiwan and trade disputes that were seen as the United States challenging China. The Chinese media repeatedly stated that the United States was exercising its hegemony (*baquan*) in these incidents. At the Great Fountains in July 1996, I overheard some visitors talking about bombing the United States and Japan. Apparently, the theme of the built environment encouraged visitors to recall a current international dispute.

Another common way of interacting with the ruins is to leave traces on them by writing or carving statements on them. The following inscriptions (my translations), which I collected in the summer of 1996, show certain ways of expressing public feelings about national humiliation:

- "Any history is a history of the present!" A person from Sichuan, July 18, 1990.
- "Never forget the national humiliation." September 5, 1995.
- "Never forget the national humiliation; revitalize the Chinese nation." November 7, 1993.
- "[We] hate the national humiliation after the visit; dedicate [ourselves] to the Chinese nation." Huang Hua and Sun Qifa, Hebei, July 20, 1995.
- "Desolate garden and national humiliation, hate, hate, and hate." May 20, 1996.
- "A backward country ought to be beaten."
- "I am proud of the revived country, never forget the national humiliation." May 1996.
- "History never forgets." July 1, 1996.
- "History won't happen again; the Chinese should strengthen themselves."
- "The humiliated history, unforgettable times, unforgettable!"
- "May the tragedy never happen again."
- "If there were no nation, there would be no people."
- "I don't want to come again!"
- "Transform anger into power, revive the Chinese nation." Han Yunqiao, Wuhan, Hubei, July 17, 1994.
- "The Chinese people transform anger into power to rebuild Yuanming Yuan." July 8, 1996.
- "The Chinese nation stands up, returns to our national majesty."
- "Look at ancient relics, sigh with deep feelings; inscribe the national humiliation, devote to strengthening." April 12, 1995.
- "The sin of the British and the French is unforgivable." February 3, 1994.
- "Down with the foreign devils." January 8, 1992.
- "Use the knife to cut out the national humiliation; use the sword to slice the national regret." July 8, 1996.
- "Yesterday, what a beautiful scene at Xiyang Lou; today, merely ruins for the tourists. Hate the British and the French who burned national treasures, what still awaits is the national revenge." July 20, 1995.
- "Yesterday [they] burned our garden, tomorrow [we] will burn their house." May 23, 1996.
- "Down with France and strike down Britain." 1993.
- "Burn L'Arc de Triomphe and bomb Buckingham Palace."

These writings may be grouped into three categories. Some statements explicitly express intense feelings of pain in terms such as "humiliation," "tragedy," and "sin." Other writings call for acts of revenge to ease the painful feelings, for example, burning, destroying, or bombing Britain or France. Still other inscriptions reflect on the historical relationship between the nation and the people. As a whole they demonstrate that the ruins work effectively as a site of memory for expressing patriotic feelings about building a stronger nation state.

To leave a trace of oneself at a famous religious, historical, political, or natural site is a traditional practice of Chinese travelers. The most common practice among ordinary people is to write "XXX [the person's name and sometimes also where the person comes from] has come to visit this place on XXX [date]." Literary or political figures usually write a phrase or even a whole poem or piece of prose.[27] In one sense, the inscriptions at the ruins of the Great Fountains resemble the tradition of leaving a trace of oneself during a visit. On the other hand, they depart from the tradition in that most of them are anonymous and thus leave no individual trace.

These inscriptions are in fact public expressions. Like the graffiti in a city like New York, they are intentionally anonymous and yet deliberately affect the meaning of a public space. Writing graffiti is a "wandering labor" of production.[28] That is, to produce graffiti, the writer has to stay on the move to avoid apprehension. At the same time, the authorities always intend to obliterate the writing with something else (for example, a coat of paint). The inscriptions at the ruins are significantly different from graffiti in two ways. First, the dates on the inscriptions I viewed, which ranged from 1990 to 1996, show that they were made after the formal establishment of the ruins park. The authorities do not appear to have any intention of obliterating any of the inscriptions, even though they ought to do so in order to protect the site, which has been officially registered as a "key national historical site" (*guojia zhongdian baohu danwei*). Thus, the accumulation of inscriptions over the years must function to support the official representation of the ruins as a site for patriotic education. Like labels in a museum exhibition, they interpret the meaning of the ruins. In writing or reading the inscriptions, visitors form a dialogical and interactive relationship with the ruins through which spatial discipline and subject formation are tied together.

Another important difference between these inscriptions and traditional graffiti is that the meaning of these inscriptions hardly diverges. All the writers attribute the destruction of Yuanming Yuan to a criminal act of the British and French in 1860. No matter how many inscriptions are produced, they express quite similar sentiments in a unified, patriotic voice. The ruins' association with Chinese nation-building has a long history beginning with China's encounter with Western powers in the late nineteenth century. The looting and destruction in 1860 first affected the Qing government. The Chinese ambassador to London, for example, wrote before 1887 that the incident awakened the nation:

> By the light of the burning palace which had been the pride and delight of her Emperor, she had commenced to see that she had been asleep while all the world was up and doing . . . The Summer Palace, with all its wealth of art, was a high price to pay for the lesson we there received, but not too high; it has taught us how to repair and triple fortify our battered armor; and it has done so.[29]

For this Chinese official, the fire of 1860 became a light illuminating the nation. Along with a series of other incidents, such as the signing of the Treaty of Beijing and the ceding of Kowloon to Britain, the light of the fire enabled the government to reform itself and join in the "family of nations." Prince Gong established a new foreign affairs office, the Zongli Yamen (the office of viceroy), in 1861.[30] He also authorized the publication of the third edition of Henry Wheaton's *Elements of International Law* in classical Chinese as *Wanguo Gongfa* (1864), translated by the American missionary W. A. P. Martin (aka Ding Weiliang) in collaboration with four Chinese scholars. This translation project explicitly provided a language of and about sovereignty to the Chinese government in the context of international relations.[31]

After the collapse of the Qing Dynasty in 1911, the ruins of Yuanming Yuan became a site that provoked nationalism, particularly among the intellectual elite such as professors and students of Beijing and Qinghua universities. Inscriptions could be seen on the ruins as early as 1915.[32] For example, a college student commented on the destruction of Yuanming Yuan in the early 1930s: "To destroy the collections of the finest art and architecture of a nation is the most serious punishment to the people of that nation at present and in the future."[33] Pioneers of the CCP like Li Dazhao also visited Yuanming Yuan to mourn the national loss.[34] Since the early twentieth century, as James Hevia points out, the "patriotic" Chinese subject has been constructed through the "pedagogy of the imperialism in nineteenth-century China:" In the process of "liberation" (*jiefang*) from the "national humiliation" caused by Western imperialism in China, the patriotic subject has been portrayed as "a muscular, pure, self-sacrificing anti-imperialist who could rise above historical shame and reclaim China's sovereign rights."[35]

This heroic and exemplary image of the ideal Chinese patriotic subject underwent a transformation in the 1990s. Since the formal establishment of the park, the ruins of Yuanming Yuan have become a site for mass consumption, and the number of inscriptions there has increased significantly. As a consumer spectacle, the ruins function as public relations material. The inscriptions are treated as "knowledge" or information, rather than propaganda.[36] In this way, patriotic education at the site is no longer simply a unidirectional transmission of patriotic messages; rather, it requires the user to play his or her part in acquiring patriotic information while interacting with the ruins. Therefore, the moral virtue of being a patriotic citizen cannot be separated from being a proper consumer.

The World Primitive Totems Garden

The cultivation of consumer citizenship at Yuanming Yuan actually goes beyond the ruins park. It is a major activity at the World Primitive Totems Garden, another built theme environment at Yuanming Yuan. Just south of the ruins park, the totem park is located on Mind-Opening Isle, one of the eight official "scenes" of the Garden of Long Spring. This small island was originally a terraced mound ascended by four flights of steps flanked by a white marble balustrade and accessible only by boat.[37] A floating bridge has since been built to provide visitors with easier access to the island. The three original buildings on the island, which were constructed for Qianlong's retreat, are no longer visible. Visitors can neither imagine the magnificence of these buildings, nor any longer see such royal objects as a throne, a desk with all kinds of stationery, and a pair of cloisonné crane and deer, which are listed in historical accounts as being inside one of the buildings.[38] Instead, they see "totems" (*tuteng*) and masks displayed throughout the garden and in two galleries, mainly representing indigenous peoples from North America, the South Pacific, and Africa (see Figure 4.6).

How is the meaning of *tuteng* explained to visitors? At the ticket booth, an information panel tells potential visitors:

Figure 4.6 The World Primitive Totems Garden, 1996 (photo by the author).

> For some [ordinary people], tuteng is a magic instrument.
> For some, tuteng is a spiritual foundation of the primitive people.
> For some, tuteng is an imaginary world of the human childhood.
> For some, tuteng is an immeasurably sacred object.
> For scholars and experts, tuteng is the origin of religion, the dawning of aesthetics, and the dawn of art.
> What is tuteng exactly?
> Tuteng is the translation of the English word "totem," derived from the word *ao tu te man* (ototeman)—in a dialect of the *A er gong jin*, a tribe of the *Ao ji bu wa* of the *Yin di an ren* in North America—meaning "the kinship between a brother and a sister."
> Is it really true that human ancestors had such a brother–sister kinship with such a strange image as a semi-human and semi-beast, a semi-human and semi-fish, or a semi-human and semi-plant? Whether the answer is yes or no, the greatly respected sacred tuteng objects greatly comforted human ancestors in barbaric ancient times. They also faithfully accompanied the humans passing through the long journey of their childhood.
> The World Primitive Totems Garden has collected and exhibited the primitive totems of peoples all over the world at the Mind-Opening Isle. It has provided visitors with an opportunity to wander in an imaginary human world that could be dated back to one million years ago.
> The Garden is a mysterious world of darkness. Everywhere is good for taking photos.
> The Garden is an artistic heaven where the high and the low meet, where you don't need to pay to take photos with primitive tuteng of various peoples.

This information introduces *tuteng* as being emblematic of human origins. And the park presents itself as both a wonderland (an "imaginary human world") and an opportunity for tourists to engage in such activities as photo taking.

Another information panel located at the entrance to the floating bridge describes more explicitly the function of *tuteng* objects for primitive peoples:

> The primitive people knew little either about the powerful and merciless world outside themselves or about their own world of giving birth, becoming old and ill, and approaching death. Under the pressure of nature, they must have experienced strong feelings of loneliness, insecurity, and fear. In search of spiritual supports, they needed to expel devils and to pray for protection. Thus, they created masks for repelling ghosts and avoiding the abnormal, and tuteng devices for protection.

The totems park characterizes the world of the primitive people as "dark," "primitive," "ancient," "magical," and "mysterious." This fantasy world is a frozen world absolutely separate from the everyday world of the represented primitive people. This world operates through the logic of "other" time, a type of transcendental time negating change and the flux of a lived reality.[39] The various shapes and styles of tuteng artifacts on display are different from totem poles and masks collected and displayed in museums. The masks of Native Americans (or First Peoples) in the Pacific Northwest, for example, were made to wear in rituals. And the pieces collected and displayed in museums like the Royal British Columbia Museum are authentic; they could again be used in rituals. By contrast, the "masks" at the totems park are created only for the purpose of exhibition and cannot be used in rituals and ceremonies. They are spectacles for tourist consumption.

Viewing the island from the mainland, the park seems to be a perfect, still universe, very much like the miniaturized palace in front of the ruins of the Great Fountains. Whereas the miniaturized palace is visually accessible but cannot be physically touched, the park on the island is visually inaccessible from the mainland but can be reached via the floating bridge. After paying an entrance fee (either ¥5 RMB yuan for a domestic visitor or ¥10 yuan for a foreign visitor), the visitor is permitted to enter the park. Stepping on the island, the visitor is immersed in the fantasy world and is enveloped by its shadows (dark, magic, mysterious, and dangerous). This process of visiting the garden corresponds with a transformation of experience,[40] a change made possible by the operation of the environment as a theme park, both a private business enterprise and a landscape for shadow plays.

The link between this park and its social engineering function can be understood through a discussion of "wandering"—a type of change that involves both the movement and the disciplining of the body—not only as an operation of the park, but also as a way to shape tourist behaviors in a particular way.[41] The establishment of this park was an experiment in profit-making practices at Yuanming Yuan. In the early 1990s, the Mentougou District Government of the City of Beijing allocated one million yuan to establish the park as an entity independent from the management of Yuanming Yuan. It leases the island from Yuanming Yuan for about ¥20,000 RMB yuan annually. Since its official opening in March 1995, the park has been profitable. According to a park manager, the park recovered two-thirds of the total investment in its first year of operation.[42]

The inclusion of this profit-oriented entity at Yuanming Yuan is significant because it represents a form of wandering, an experiment in transforming Yuanming Yuan from a cultural institution (*wenhua shiye*) to a cultural enterprise (*wenhua chanye*). In this context, the park's business operation of wandering moves forward into an uncertain future that is characterized both by a flexible organization of work and by dependence on the profitability of information and knowledge. In 1996, the company had fifteen employees, mostly migrant workers from outside Beijing. The young woman selling tickets at the gate, for example, was from Shandong. These migrant workers work full-time at the park, but the company's two managers work only part-time and have other regular jobs. Manager Wang Shuming, for example, worked two days a week in 1996; his primary job was with the Ministry of Domestic Trades (*Guonei maoyibu*). In his late thirties or early forties, Wang held an impressive list of positions, including as a consulting member of the Standing Committee of the Chinese Society for Commercial Economy (*Zhongguo shangye jingji xuehui*), an advisor to *Information Commerce* (*Xinxi chanye bao*) newspaper, a project director at the Institute of Cognitive Science (*Siwei kexue yanjiusuo*), a senior consultant for the Harbin Economic Zone, and a consultant for the Hong Kong-based Nanling Company.

The park's business management conforms to a form of economic entrepreneurialism. The park's profitability seems to result from the way in which the managers deploy their leisure time as work. They carve out work hours from their regular full-time jobs. In Mr. Wang's case, he simply took or "borrowed" some hours from his regular government job and made those hours productive for making profits. On a personal level, he gained an additional income to supplement his regular salary, which he considered insufficient to cover the rising cost of consumer goods. The practice of making borrowed time productive has been common, particularly among government employees, since the late 1980s. Many who work for nonprofit organizations such as museums, libraries, and research institutes take second jobs, which usually involve profit-making. In this way, business enterprises like this totems park have been developed through government subsidies in the form of work hours. Meanwhile, government employees who have second jobs also contribute to the efficiency of the government by diverting their extra energy—which would otherwise be spent on developing bureaucracy—to a productive purpose in the economy. This practice of time management is a form of exercising the neoliberal agency of sovereignty. That is, the treatment of an exceptional time (borrowed time) as a normal work time transgresses the nonprofit work rules through an economic rationale of efficiency.

This new way of managing work is in fact based on the use of information and knowledge in profit making. The company's operation depends upon expert knowledge and skills. The chief designer of the garden was Qiu Wanfu, a "cultural anthropologist" (*wenhua renleixuejia*) and an expert on totems.[43] Another scholar who participated in designing the totem garden was Zhang Yan, the author of the scholarly book *Totemism and the Primitive Culture* (*Tutengzhi yu yuanshi wenhua*). Ethnic and folk artists were also involved. The tuteng artifacts, for example, were carved by a folk artist from Guizhou who specialized in making masks used in local rituals.[44] In addition, the company has drawn on the knowledge system of museums, as it claims that the tuteng artifacts are based on museum collections around the world and represent 126 countries. Yet none of the displayed tuteng artifacts could be collected and displayed by a formal museum because they did not come from the actual cultures represented. Moreover, the tuteng artifacts are further removed from the already decontextualized setting of a museum collection and thus become further abstracted. It is through such an abstraction that the life of these artifacts is tied to consumer practices.

The park's creators present wandering as the proper way of visiting the fantasy world in "cultural tourism" (*wenhua luyou*). According to the information panel located at the entrance to the floating bridge, the purpose of cultural tourism is "to see the unseen and to hear the unheard." The information panel also suggests how a tourist might conduct his or her visit:

> By viewing tuteng with pleasure, a precious lifestyle in cultural tourism, you could acquire an elegant taste for spiritual enjoyment.
>
> Please come to the island to take photos with [objects from] the childhood of human beings.
>
> The Garden is located on Mind-Opening Isle in the middle of clusters of lotus flowers. Like a poem or a picture, the island is mysterious and absolutely peaceful. It is said that this is a "village within the city" or the "Eden for lovers."
>
> Are you tired of walking? Ten pavilions on the small island welcome you to take a break.
>
> Are you thirsty? Here you will find delicious tea and wonderful wine.
>
> Have you eaten? Here you will find picnic-style foods.
>
> On walking across the floating bridge, you will receive more than one surprise!!!

This information panel refers to wandering in the garden as a magical lifestyle leading to pleasure, good taste, and refinement. It suggests a series of activities available at the park, including viewing tuteng artifacts, taking photos, resting, eating, drinking, and dating. Thus, wandering is a discourse of consumption intended to shape tourist behavior in a particular way.

On crossing the bridge and stepping into the fantasy world, the tourist practices becoming an autonomous individual, a subject of instrumental discipline.[45] For the company that operates it, the theme park functions as a retail environment with a single purpose: to maximize profits. Thus, tourists are encouraged to tour the park in a way that maximizes their spending on food, drinks, film, and souvenirs. In such a carefully designed environment, the practice of wandering has two characteristics. First, wandering is an individualized practice of walking, a way of dealing with the unknown and the uncertain, as the tourist moves through an environment haunted by "primitive," "mysterious," "dangerous," and "magical" *tuteng* objects scattered throughout the garden. Second, wandering also requires that the tourist follow the road map of activities prescribed by the company to gain the most pleasure, taste, and fashion from the experience. It is through such activities as walking and taking photos that the tourist practices becoming an autonomous individual.

Photo taking, one of the most popular activities at the park, has two elements: the search for photographic scenes and the practice of understanding a dialectical relationship between light and shadow in the built environment. The tourist's engagement with photographic scenes at the garden is related not only to the company's marketing strategy, but also to the practice of searching for appropriate scenes and taking the photos. A panel of sample photos at the entrance suggests ideal spots for taking photos. Not only does the information function to introduce certain elements of the garden and its associated fantasy, but it is also a strategy by which the company suggests and thus directs the movement of tourists to consumption. Before taking a photo, the tourist has first to decide whether or not to follow the company's recommendation, then either to locate the suggested scene or to discover a new one in the garden. After reaching a scenic spot, the tourist has to know how to operate the camera properly in order to bring out the meaning of light, or to transform the scene into a visual representation.

The issue of light is especially important in the dim environment of the garden, which is filled with relatively tall trees and plants. Undoubtedly, the recording of a selected scene in the environment requires the tourist to know the technical procedure of using a flash or taking a long-exposure image. However, it also entails an intellectual process of commanding the dialectical relationship between light and shadow, between the known and the unknown, or between illumination and hallucination. Within this process, the sense of agency is enhanced and the tourist becomes an autonomous individual who relies on his or her entrepreneurial skills.

In sum, the movement onto the island garden corresponds with a change in the park's operation from presenting visitors with a mysterious world to disciplining them as consumers. Within the landscape, the wandering tourist's role changes from being a spectator (exterior to the represented fantasy world) to becoming a participant in the fantasy environment.

Alterity in the synchronization with the world

Both the Ruins Park of Xiyang Lou and the Primitive Totems Garden appropriate the theme of the cultural other (or of the non-Han and non-Chinese) in their operations as theme parks. The former utilizes Europe or "the West" (*xiyang*) as an object in patriotic education, whereas the latter treats "the primitive" as an object of pleasure. A comparison of the two representations of the cultural other reveals the way in which the uses of artifacts (both ruins and new artifacts) transform Yuanming Yuan as a site of historical memories. That is, what counts as moral virtues of an ideal, or normative, Chinese citizen is subject to negotiation (at least in the context of everyday life). The historical event of Hong Kong's return further legitimized the transformation of Yuanming Yuan in line with China's neoliberal synchronization with the world.

The two parks represent the cultural other in a particular way, highlighting its "negative" or undesirable dimensions: the evilness of the West at the ruins park and the underdevelopment of the primitive at the totems park. The former points to China as an injured civilization, and the latter to another China that is in the making. Through the spatial juxtaposition of the two representations within the Park of Yuanming Yuan, a sense of an orderly progression is established.[46] This order is related to the way in which the two parks treat the past as an important dimension in the communication-based economy—the communication of knowledge and information about the past as a means of production both for disciplining the moral character of the tourist and for accumulating capital. At the ruins park, the past explicitly refers to the period from 1860 to 1900. This emphasis seeks to cultivate a sense of an undesirable historical past and promote reflection on both Western colonial and imperial presences and their brutal effects on China. The park's operation as a built theme environment encourages visitors to express their feelings of moral awakening about China's failed synchronization with the world in the nineteenth century. Unlike the ruins park, the totems park does not tie the past to a particular historical time. Instead, it represents the past merely in the universal sense of underdevelopment associated with the primitive. The focus on associations with the primitive, such as underdevelopment and the unknown, encourages visitors to express a sense of success through consumption practices within the context of China's economic reforms, or what I call neoliberal synchronization with the world.

The juxtaposition of the two cultural representations at Yuanming Yuan points to a changing relationship between the use of artifacts and the narration of historical time, a change signaling the transformation of Yuanming Yuan as a site of historical memory. The way a cultural representation deploys artifacts is inseparable from the narration of time. At Xiyang Lou, ruins are key to the construction of a historical time because they offer material traces of the past. Xiyang Lou maintains two important temporal qualities of ruins: persistence and transience.[47] The persistent temporality of Xiyang Lou's ruins has three aspects. One aspect is the time of looting and destruction, which the park associated specifically with a British and French criminal act in 1860. Another refers to a time of national humiliation inseparable from the previous time. The second Opium War reinforced the tragedy of the first Opium War because the Treaty of Beijing further extended the repression of Western colonialism and imperialism in China: the cession of Kowloon to Britain in 1860 mirrored the cession of Hong Kong Island to Britain in 1842. Finally, however, the persistent temporality also has an aspect of immortality or survival. It is, after all, not the ruins that have survived the inexorable march of time; rather, it is the people who have survived the series of tragic incidents throughout history.[48] Because of their association with survival, the ruins may be used to cultivate a sense of achievement.

Transience is also an important characteristic of the ruins. The decay of Xiyang Lou's ruins is an inexorable process. Rather than being a natural process of the march of time, the decay has been mainly a result of human destruction, beginning with the 1860 fire and continuing through the salvage of building materials from the site. The ruins themselves have been disappearing. In their present form, they hardly suggest the original Xiyang Lou. The most elaborate building, the Hall of Peaceful Sea, has lost its authority to represent the whole garden. Instead, the best-preserved remains, those of the Great Fountains, have become the focus of the public's attention. The restored Maze is unconnected to the ruins nearby. The park's cultural representation of the 1860–1900 period certainly benefits from the ruins' incompleteness.

Whereas the Xiyang Lou ruins visually testify to the transient and persistent meanings of time, the original buildings on Mind-Opening Isle in the Garden of Long Spring are no longer visible. Their material traces are buried or covered by the new totem poles and masks. This material replacement is also a temporal displacement. The time associated with the built environment of Yuanming Yuan is replaced by the time of the built environment of the totems garden. This displacement testifies to the establishment of a regularizing relationship between time and money. The company that developed the gardens borrows time from other organizations to make a profit so that it can pay an annual lease fee to the Park of Yuanming Yuan. This signals a new trend in the operations of the Park of Yuanming Yuan. Venues of pleasure consumption—for eating, drinking, boating, fishing, mini-car racing, and playing paintball—provide regular sources of income for Yuanming Yuan. In this way, Yuanming Yuan itself as a site of historical memory has been transformed from a cultural institution that followed government-prescribed plans to a cultural enterprise that creates its own operational path based on market considerations.

Yuanming Yuan's transformation, however, has drawn criticism from many scholars and experts. Some critics consider the totems garden as in poor taste, and as a "greedy" and "irresponsible" act in the efforts to preserve Yuanming Yuan's ruins.[49] Others charge that the operation of the ruins park has made Xiyang Lou a place of "pleasure" or a "money tree" (*yaoqianshu*).[50] These critics argue that in the context of Yuanming Yuan's development as a cultural enterprise, the public no longer views the ruins site purely as a place of mourning for a national loss and of remembering the crime of Western imperialism. This situation has led to confusion about when Yuanming Yuan was looted and burned.[51]

The incorporation of capitalism into the Chinese system during Hong Kong's return simultaneously reinforced the transformation of Yuanming Yuan into a cultural enterprise and raised the public's attention to history as a governmental problem. In anticipation of Hong Kong's return to China, a series of educational "quiz shows" (*zhishi jingsai*) was broadcast on national television. Some of the questions addressed Yuanming Yuan. In one show, for example, the hostess asked, "Who burned Yuanming Yuan?" The contestant answered, "Yuanming Yuan was burned by the British invading army during the 1840 Opium War." Although the answer was not correct, the hostess responded, "Basically correct, add 10 points." In another show where the same question was asked, the answer was "It was burned in 1900." In spite of being incomplete and inaccurate, the answer was judged "completely correct."[52]

These confusions about Yuanming Yuan as a site of memory were part of the general problem of history as a governmental problem during the Hong Kong countdown. At such sites as Tiananmen Square and the National Museum of Chinese Revolution, the problem of history pertained to the collective historical experience associated with the British occupation of Hong Kong. At Yuanming Yuan, by comparison, the problem of history was more about contingent individual and everyday experiences shaped by the rationalized discourse of the collective historical experience. From the tourist perspective, the individual experience of pleasure consumption was just as important as the historical experience of national humiliation. It was at the intersection between the rational historical experience and the contingent quotidian experience that the spectacle of consumption became a force of time in redefining meanings of Chinese history. An article in the *Beijing Evening News* (an official paper of the Beijing Municipal Government) commented on the lantern festival held at Yuanming Yuan in late June 1997:

> The magnificent scene . . . deeply affects every visitor. Yes, only ten days left before the coming of the exciting moment. Looking at the ruins of the "Great Fountains" and of "Xiyang Lou"—which have been considered "shameful pillars" through which we could visualize the criminal fire set by the aggressors 137 years ago—this history should not be forgotten. However, it is more important to look forward to the future. Tomorrow will be ultimately brighter.[53]

From the tragic light of the fire (1860) to the festival light of the lanterns (1997), the problem of history was reoriented to address not only the pending incorporation of the capitalist Hong Kong into the Chinese nation state but also the present replacement of public feelings of national humiliation, tragedy, and shame with expressions of happiness, pleasure, and celebration.[54]

5 The super-firm in spatial representations of socialism and capitalism

For the Chinese state, ensuring that all information the public receives is consistent with its official propaganda is of paramount importance. Therefore, the state, through the CCP, used to control even minor details of "cultural organizations" (*wenhua jigou*) such as museums. In the case of the National Museum of Chinese Revolution, the approval of an exhibition was contingent on whether the exhibition portrayed positive representations of "revolution" such as, for example, the wise leadership of the Party and heroic resistance of the Chinese people against foreign repression. During the countdown to Hong Kong's return to China, the Chinese state gradually allowed state-owned and -operated organizations to evolve from cultural organizations to "cultural enterprises" (*wenhua chanye*) by incorporating economic principles into their operation and organization. At the First Chinese Communist Party Congress Meeting Hall, the National Museum of Chinese Revolution, Yuanming Yuan, and elsewhere, stories of economic success and prosperity replaced narratives of national humiliations and revolutionary practices. "Culture" (*wenhua*), the core of these organizations, was conceptualized in such market-oriented terms as "cultural products" (*wenhua chanpin*), "cultural market" (*wenhua shichang*), and "cultural public relations" (*wenhua gongguan*). And their "visitors" (*guanzhong*) became "consumers" (*xiaofeizhe*) or "tourists" (*youke*).

The integration of economic rationalism into the politics of the state by state-controlled organizations during the Hong Kong countdown was neither historically incidental nor merely a passive response to capitalist globalization. Rather, it was tied to the objective of realizing the "one country, two systems" framework for post-1997 China. That is, it was about developing the future Chinese state's capacity to accommodate both capitalism and socialism. The process of the Hong Kong countdown, as I show in this chapter, translated the ideological co-presence of socialism and capitalism into spatial coexistence through the spatial practice of developing special zones. Whether temporary or permanent, each zone maintained its sovereign appearance as a socialist or capitalist territory. In the process of developing these zones, the narrative of antagonism between socialism and capitalism shifted from an issue of propaganda (or ideology) to one of spatial representation. Thus, the development of built theme environments, such as theme parks, became a popular practice throughout the country precisely because "imagineering," or the spatial engineering of meanings tied to a particular built environment, was an important technology for treating socialism or capitalism as a theme of that environment.[1]

The Hong Kong-based Chinese state-owned transnational corporation China Travel Service (Holdings) Hong Kong Ltd. (CTS), for example, played a critical part in the spatial representations of socialism and capitalism. By performing a dual role as a Chinese state-owned company in Hong Kong and a Hong Kong-based company in China, CTS acted as a super firm. Just like any ordinary company, CTS applied economic principles of efficiency and calculation in its business operations to make profits. Unlike an ordinary company, however, CTS was a major state-owned company and thus enjoyed many privileges that an ordinary firm did not have. CTS drew on the government's juridical, administrative, and sovereign powers to expand its transnational operations, reduce its operational costs, and fulfill its responsibilities as an agent of the Chinese government. In pre-1997 Hong Kong, CTS created zones of socialist China within the colony. Through regular sponsorship of cultural and arts events in Hong Kong, the company's representation of socialist China shaped how Hong Kong residents viewed their everyday lives. Its participation in Hong Kong's Chinese Dance Festival in 1995, for example, explicitly aimed at cultivating a sense of socialist Chineseness among Hong Kong residents. Through this type of practice, the company inserted a time of the socialist nation into the historical time of Hong Kong, contributing to the development of a culture of disappearance in pre-1997 Hong Kong (see Chapter 6).

Meanwhile, CTS also used Hong Kong as a base for operating transnational capitalism, especially by facilitating highly mobile flows of Chinese state-owned capital and by creating special zones to shelter capitalism in pre-1997 China. The company played an important role in establishing the Shenzhen Special Economic Zone (Shenzhen SEZ), the country's first special economic zone aiming at normalizing the spatial representation of capitalism in China. More specifically, the company's establishment of three major theme parks—Splendid China, China Folk Culture Villages, and Window on the World—was closely tied to the spatial representation of capitalism in the Shenzhen SEZ. Therefore, as a super firm, CTS contributed not only to the smooth transition of Hong Kong from a British colony to a special administrative region of China through its representation of socialist China in capitalist Hong Kong, but also to the transformation of the Chinese mainland from a homogeneous socialist state to a heterogeneous neoliberal state through representing capitalist Hong Kong in socialist China.[2]

Spatial representation of socialist China in Hong Kong

Transnational capitalism, or the practice of transnational flows of goods, people, and information, assumed important governmental functions in the

Hong Kong countdown. Acting on behalf of the Chinese state, Hong Kong-based, Chinese state-owned transnational corporations played an important role in the social, cultural, and economic processes of Hong Kong during the countdown process, whether by investing capital, educating Hong Kong residents about China, or promoting pro-China politics in Hong Kong's public culture.

China has become an active player in the global economy since the early 1980s. During the Hong Kong countdown period (1984–1997),[3] China received more than US$204 billion of foreign direct investment (FDI) and invested US$21 billion overseas (see Figure 5.1). Along with Japan, Hong Kong, Taiwan, South Korea, and Singapore, China was a top East Asian investor in the global economy (see Figure 5.2). The United Nations Conference on Trade and Development annually lists the top fifty transnational corporations (TNCs) based in developing countries. In 1993 and 1994, 70 percent of these were based in East and Southeast Asia. In 1993, only one China-owned company, Citic Pacific Ltd. (based in Hong Kong), was among the top fifty (ranking nineteenth). In 1994, by contrast, China became one of only two developing countries to host eight of the top fifty TNCs, the other country being South Korea. By the end of 1995, at least nine hundred Chinese TNCs had established more than 4,600 foreign affiliates in over 130 countries.[4] China's foreign direct investment outflows averaged more than US$2.5 billion annually during the period 1990–1997.[5] During the countdown period, the Chinese state strategically increased its role in Hong Kong by investing about 60 percent of its total outflows there.[6]

To prepare its officials to engage in transnational capitalism, the Chinese government launched a series of training programs that included lessons

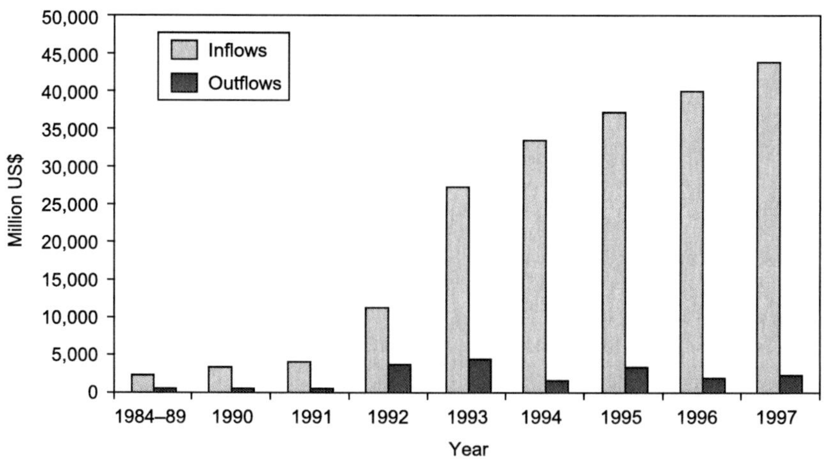

Figure 5.1 Inflows and outflows of foreign direct investment in China (1984–1997).

Source: United Nations Conference on Trade and Development, *World Investment Reports*, 1996 and 2000–2002.

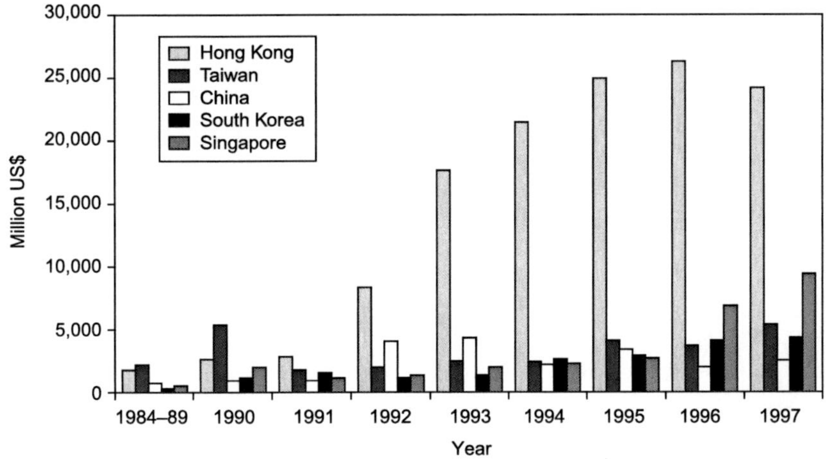

Figure 5.2 Outflows of foreign direct investment from five of the top six countries in East Asia (after Japan), 1984–1997.

Source: United Nations Conference on Trade and Development, *World Investment Reports*, 1996 and 2000–2002.

about Hong Kong's economic success. The Organization Department of the Central Committee of the Chinese Communist Party, for example, created a series of seminars just one year after Deng Xiaoping's famous trip to the special economic zones in southern China in 1992. In these seminars, government and party officials learned theoretical knowledge, useful information, and practical skills and strategies about the market economy. In the first two years of these seminars, 440 officials from all over the country and the central government were trained. As part of their learning, the trainees visited Japan, Germany, and Hong Kong. Because Hong Kong's economic success was of special interest, they were asked to write essays reflecting on how they might apply in China what they learned during their Hong Kong trips.[7]

The Chinese state has always participated in Hong Kong's economy through state-owned companies located there. Hong Kong-based Chinese TNCs were primarily owned by ministries of the central government or by provincial and municipal authorities. For example, the Ministry of Communication owned China Merchants Ltd. (involved in transportation, shipbuilding and repair, hotels, manufacturing and infrastructure investments, retailing, banking, and insurance). The Bank of China was the second largest bank in Hong Kong. One of the largest Chinese state-owned corporations in Hong Kong, CTS, was owned by the State Tourist Bureau. Its mission statement was "being based in Hong Kong, relying on the inland, and looking outward overseas."[8] In Hong Kong, the company acted as both a transnational corporation and an agency of the Chinese state. Meanwhile, in China, CTS was a principal developer of China's most important economic zone—the Shenzhen SEZ—by conducting business activities mainly related to the tourist and manufacturing industries. In the United States, CTS managed Splendid China, a theme park near Disney World in Orlando, Florida.

The company has been publicly listed in Hong Kong stock exchange as China Travel International Investment Hong Kong Ltd. (CTII) since July 1992. By 1996, CTII had incorporated eighteen principal subsidiaries and associated companies: ten in Hong Kong, five in China, two in the British Virgin Islands, and one in the Cayman Islands (see Table 5.1). Between 1989 and 1996, CTII diversified its business around its major operations. Starting in 1989 with two theme parks in China and a freight forwarding service between China and Hong Kong, CTII then acquired hotels in Hong Kong and became a tour operator arranging tours abroad (particularly to China); acquired a 51 percent interest in Tangshan Guofeng Steel, a joint venture with the Economic Development Corporation of Xugezhuang Fengnan County, Hebei; and expanded into property investment, industrial investment, and

Table 5.1 Principal subsidiaries and associated companies of China Travel International Investment Hong Kong Ltd., 1995

Hong Kong	*China*	*British Virgin Islands*	*Cayman Islands*
Freight Forwarding China Travel Service (Cargo) Hong Kong (100%) Wing Dah Hong (Hong Kong) (96.2%) Rida Co. (100%) Harbour Wide (40%) Storman (38%) *Tourism and Hotels* China Travel (HK & Macau Tour) Management Hong Kong (100%) Glading Development (100%) *Property Investment* Common Well (100%) Mart Harvest (100%) Triumph King (100%)	*Freight Forwarding* Chongqing Long Sight International Container Co. (25%) Sichuan Jieda Freight Transportation Co. (40%) *Theme Parks* Shenzhen Splendid China Development Co. (51%) Shenzhen The World Miniature Co. (51%) *Industrial Investment* Tangshan Guofeng Steel Co. (51%)	*Tourism and Hotels* Smart Concord Enterprises (100%) *Treasury Operations* Princess Capital (100%?)	*Treasury Operations* CTII Overseas Finance (100%)

Source: China Travel International Investment, Annual Report 1995, pp. 2, 47–49.

Note: Percentages refer to percentage of shares owned by CTII.

treasury operations. In the 1989–1997 period, CTII's annual turnover increased from US$20 million to about US$273.7 million, a thirteen-fold increase in nine years (see Figure 5.3). Most of the turnover originated from its Hong Kong business activities and from freight forwarding between China and Hong Kong. Not only did CTII become the biggest provider of freight services between Hong Kong and China, but it also owned the largest share of the 50 percent of the China-bound tourist market controlled by Hong Kong's China companies.

Throughout the countdown period, CTS regularly either sponsored or organized cultural and leisure-oriented activities in Hong Kong, thereby playing a pedagogical role in educating Hong Kong residents about China and promoting a sense of belonging to the Chinese nation. In typical CTS-sponsored or -organized events, ethnic minorities from China performed their dances and songs, demonstrated games, and displayed objects of their culture to Hong Kong residents. How these activities contributed to the incorporation of China's national time into everyday life in Hong Kong can be shown by a detailed discussion of the company's involvement in the Chinese Dance Parades, part of the Chinese Dance Festival presented by the Hong Kong Urban Council in October and November 1995.[9]

In the November 5, 1995, event held at the Hong Kong Cultural Center, forty professional ethnic minority performers from Shenzhen's China Folk Culture Villages represented CTS. Billed as the Ethnic Minority Arts Troupe, they were led by the vice general manger of Shenzhen Splendid China Development Company (a principal subsidiary of CTS).[10] Their trip to Hong Kong took full advantage of CTS's internal resources and facilities in Hong Kong. A tour bus owned and operated by a CTS subsidiary transported them to the

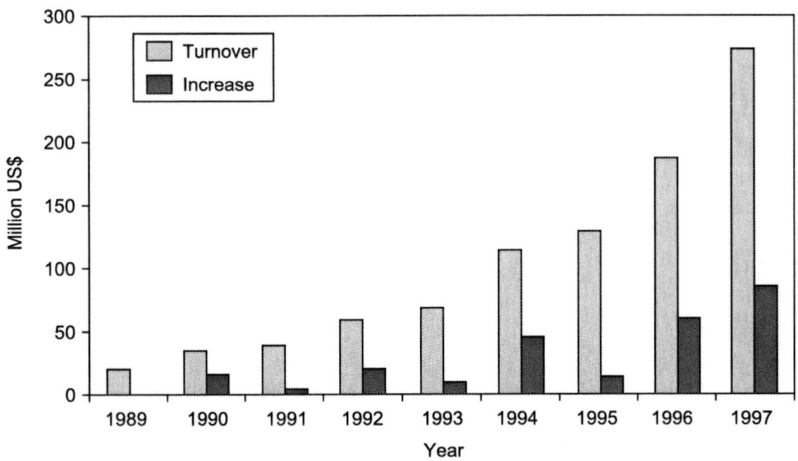

Figure 5.3 Annual turnover and increase over the previous year, China Travel International Investment Hong Kong Ltd., 1989–1997.

Source: China Travel International Investment, Annual Reports, 1992–1998.

location; and the Hotel New Harbour, also owned and managed by CTS, provided their accommodation.

The event included dances, songs, music, games, and displays of arts and crafts by "ethnic minorities" (*shaoshu minzu*). The distinctive ethnic clothing and "art" (songs and dances) of nine *shaoshu minzu*—the Uygur, Miao, Zang, Wa, Mongol, Bai, Dai, Yi, and Gaoshan—were introduced. The Gaoshan, for example, were introduced as the "mountain people" of Taiwan and represented by a spinning top game. A man and woman in their early twenties, both from Fujian Province in southeast China, performed the game dressed in Amis costumes. The man identified himself as a Gaoshan of Taiwan because his grandfather was an Amis from Taiwan's Hualien County. It should be noted that the designation Gaoshan is meaningful only in the context of China's ethnic classifications. In the late 1980s, after a series of successful political protests and struggles, these people adopted the name Aborigines (Yuanzhumin) as their official self-designation in Taiwan. "Aborigines" replaced the former Taiwanese name Shan-pao (*shanbao*), or "mountain compatriots," equivalent to the "mountain people" identifier used in China.[11] Thus, the use of the Gaoshan designation in China maintained the colonial name of Taiwan's aborigines while it served the purpose of integrating the classification of Taiwan's aborigines into the nation-building process in China.

CTS marked and marketed the notion of *minzu* (national ethnic group) as a spectacular "style." On the printed program, the Chinese phrase *duominzu wudao* (multiethnic dance) was juxtaposed with the English phrase "Chinese multi-national style dance." In light of China's classification of ethnic minority groups as a means of integrating them into the nation-building process, "multi-national" (or *duominzu*) could be read as "nationalized multiethnic," and "multi-national dance" as "nationalized multiethnic dance." Moreover, the use of "style" to refer to a nationalized ethnic dance (for example, the Gaoshan-style dance) was based on CTS's standard ways of representing ethnic minorities in its Shenzhen theme parks (discussed later). Thus, the combination of nation and style integrates two processes: nation-building and capital accumulation. Not only was an ethnic performance a spectacle ("style"), but it was also a representation of the Chinese nation.

In the CTS-sponsored performance, China was described as the "homeland" (*jiaxiang*) of Hong Kong residents. The moderator introduced the performance this way: "Respectful friends in the audience, how are you doing? We are the Ethnic Minority Arts Troupe of Shenzhen's China Folk Culture Villages. In this opportunity of the Hong Kong Dance Festival, we deliver to you, our friends, flowers from the *homeland*. We express to you our deepest *feelings*. Let the rich *customs of various ethnic groups* touch your heart!" (my translation and emphasis). This announcement of China as the homeland of Hong Kong residents tied in to a global project called "owning a piece of the homeland" (*yongyou yipian gutu*), in which ethnic Chinese overseas, Chinese nationals overseas, Hong Kong and Macau residents, and the Taiwanese were encouraged to invest. Approved by the State Tourist Bureau, the Ministry of Construction, and the State Bureau of Land Management, the project included the development of thirty-six parks in China and overseas to represent the "Homeland of the Chinese Nation." One park was located in each of China's thirty provinces. Three were built at the burial sites of the Yellow Emperor, Yan Emperor, and Fu Xi, respectively. And three more parks were planned for Taiwan, Hong Kong, and Macau. The total size of all the parks together would be 9.6 million square inches, symbolizing the size of the territories of China (9.6 million square kilometers). The Homeland project planned to sell a total of 9.6 million shares at a per-share price of US$100. Each share gave the buyer ownership of one square inch in each park (or thirty-six square inches all together). As the project's agent, CTS distributed brochures about this investment opportunity to the audience.

During the performance, China as the homeland was represented through ethnic songs and dances. The Wa performers, for example, performed "The Ah Wa People Sing a New Song" in standard Putonghua (Mandarin) Chinese, a popular song commonly performed in theme parks across the country.[12] Originally composed by a Han musician working for the Performance Troupe of the People's Liberation Army, the song's lyrics describe the conversion of Wa society to socialism in the late 1950s:

> Village to village, hamlet to hamlet, beating drums and striking gongs
> The Ah Wa sing a new song
> Chairman Mao enlightens the frontiers, mountains and rivers smile, and people celebrate
> Socialism is good, building a bridge to happiness
> The roads become wider and broader
> All rivers, mountains
> All peoples, closely united, marching forward
> Are ambitious to make mountains and rivers more beautiful
> No matter what Chairman Mao says to do, the Ah Wa people will do it
> Follow Chairman Mao, follow the Communist Party
> The Ah Wa people sing a new song, a new song [My translation]

Placing the Wa people in the historical time of socialist China (Mao's China), the song functioned to inscribe the Wa in the narrative of the Chinese nation.[13] This was not the only song at the festival closely linked to socialist China. Another well-known song, "A Golden Sun in Beijing" (*Beijing youge jin taiyang*), sung by the Zang, mentioned that the Tibetans, like the Wa, followed Chairman Mao "to march on the socialist golden avenue." Thus, these ethnic songs and dances transplanted vital signs of China—such as socialism, the Chinese government, and the CCP—to Hong Kong, and CTS's ethnic minority employees were deliberately deployed to represent socialist China in pre-1997 Hong Kong.

Through establishing a link between socialist China and capitalist Hong Kong, the ethnic performance temporarily transformed the festival site into a zone of socialist China. The performance took place in one of the most important public places in Hong Kong, the Hong Kong Cultural Center, located in the heart of Tsim Tsa Tsui, a popular tourist and shopping area. The center, which contains the Hong Kong Museum of Art and a major theater, regularly stages exhibitions and performances not only about Hong Kong but also about other countries. The CTS performance was unique in that it took place outdoors, in a plaza between the theater and the art museum against the backdrop of Victoria Harbour and Hong Kong Island (see Figure 5.4). The outdoor setting blended the performance into spectacles of everyday life in Hong Kong. The audience viewed the performance in the space of Hong Kong, a social space of commercial prosperity, intense competition, and fast-paced lifestyle. Victoria Harbour bustled with a relentless stream of ferries, cargo ships flying the flags of many nations, and junks loaded with tourists. Across the harbor, the Central District, Hong Kong's nerve center for flows and transactions of global capital, competed for the viewers' attention with spectacles of corporate logos, brand names, advertisements, and architecture. They reminded the audience that Hong Kong, a thriving capitalist economy, could exist in harmony with the theme of socialist China created by the ethnic performances at the Cultural Center.

In transforming the Cultural Center into a theme built environment,

Figure 5.4 A "multi-national-style dance" (*duominzu wudao*) performed by ethnic minority artists at the Hong Kong Cultural Center, November 5, 1995 (photo by the author).

CTS recoded the Cultural Center as a zone of socialist China by inserting China's national time into everyday life in Hong Kong. Simultaneously, CTS also appropriated the environment as a locale for promoting its products. The Splendid China Development Co. took advantage of all opportunities to advertise its two theme parks in Shenzhen, namely, the Splendid China and China Folk Culture Villages. On the back of the festival program was a carefully designed advertisement that appeared regularly in the company's promotional materials in 1995 (Figure 5.5). In the center of the ad was a Chinese pictographic character *yi* (art), its strokes composed of swaths of a photograph of the China Folk Culture Carnival Parade at the China Folk Culture Villages. To the left, right, and below were seven mini-scenes of the same performance. All of them were intended to lure the audience to the China Folk Culture Villages.

The advertisement produced a general image through synthesizing different modes of communication—handwriting (pictograph), printing, and photography. Because each mode of communication is linked to a particular form of media and associated with a particular means of time-telling (see Chapter 2), the combination of multiple modes seemingly generates a new kind of time constituted of discrete temporal rhythms. For this reason, the CTS image could be read only in a discrete or discontinuous manner. Every stroke of the character, every fragment of a scene, and every modification of color or texture was loaded with semantic potential and symbolic value.[14]

The ad used both Chinese and English text. It was entitled *Zhonghua Baiyi*

Figure 5.5 Advertisement for China Folk Culture Villages, 1995.

Shenghui in Chinese and "China Folk Culture Carnival Parade" in English. The Chinese words literarily translate as "Grand Performance of Chinese Arts," while the English title is reminiscent of a Disney performance. Although Walt Disney Company was not directly involved in designing the parade/ grand performance, it certainly influenced how Splendid China Development Co. conceived of it. In 1994, when Cao Xiaoning, the vice general manager of Splendid China, took a group of ethnic performers to work temporarily at Florida's Splendid China park, he visited Disney World and was inspired to produce his own Disney-style parade at China Folk Culture Villages. The company launched the parade in July 1995. Unlike Disney's parade, where the spectators line up along Main Street, the "parade" at the Chinese park is actually a stage performance in the square just inside the main entrance, which the audience watches sitting down.

The ad's use of Chinese and English opened up a social space of difference. On the right of the ad's title were both "zhongguo mei jianguo, shijie bukeneng" in Chinese ("never seen in China, absolutely impossible in the world") and "One of a Kind in China, Absolutely Impossible Outside China" in English. In the Chinese text, "zhongguo" (China) and "shijie" (the world) were contrasted as being mutually exclusive. The translingual practice of translating "zhongguo mei jianguo" (never seen in China) into English as "one of a kind in China," however, opens a semiotic gap between *zhongguo* and *China*.[15] The meaning of *zhongguo* as a spectacle in the world was juxtaposed with the meaning of *China* as a nation state.

Both the ethnic performance and the advertisement manifested the company's representation of China as a spectacle. The ethnic performance connected China to a particular kind of national feeling historically tied to the socialist nation state (that is, nationalized multiethnic "style"), whereas the advertisement presented China as a tourist attraction, a consumer spectacle. This treatment of China as a spectacle dovetailed with the spatial transformation of the built environment of the Hong Kong Cultural Center. Both the ethnic performance and the advertisement temporarily gave new meanings to the environment. In transforming the center into a built theme environment, CTS deployed the business technique of cross-promotion, or synergy, as a political strategy of representing socialist China in pre-1997 Hong Kong. It was through these entertaining yet educational, scattered yet assembled, efforts in Hong Kong that the co-presence of two parallel systems (that is, socialism and capitalism) became real during the countdown period.

Spatial representation of capitalism in socialist China

In the context of transnational capitalism, CTS also enjoyed its status as a Hong Kong-based company, because its revenues were treated as "foreign capital" in China. CTS represented a phenomenon of China's foreign direct investment called "round-tripping," a common practice of China's transnational corporations during the countdown period. The practice "involves the circular flow of capital out of China (in most cases to foreign affiliates of Chinese TNCs) and the subsequent 're-investment' of this 'foreign' capital in China for the purpose of benefiting from fiscal entitlements accorded to foreign investors."[16] Fiscal entitlements were the practical reason for round-tripping, but more important, this practice increased the mobility of China's capital in order to stimulate a change in China's economic structure. Funds that outflowed to a place like Hong Kong and inflowed back to China enjoyed a higher degree of mobility than funds that stayed in China. The practice of round-tripping converted Chinese funds into transnational capital. A Chinese state-owned TNC like CTS could perform the same role as a foreign TNC. Thus, both Chinese and foreign TNCs played important roles in transforming China's socioeconomic landscapes, but Chinese state-owned TNCs did much more to contribute to the state's plans for economic development.

During the Hong Kong countdown, CTS put into practice the government's "one country, two systems" framework in Hong Kong and also in China, playing an important role in making capitalism possible in socialist China. CTS's distinctive contribution was linking the practice of capitalism to the creation of particular, relatively isolated spaces. It produced two types of enclaves where mobilized state capital worked closely with foreign capital. One was the "special economic zone" (*jingji tequ*) and the other the "theme park" (*zhuti gongyuan*). Not only was the company a key developer of the Shenzhen SEZ, one of China's first special economic zones and the most successful one, but it also created the first three contemporary theme parks in China.

In 1985, the State Council approved a plan to develop the five hundred-hectare Overseas Chinese Town (OCT), a business park, as part of the Shenzhen SEZ. Ma Chi-man, CTS vice-chairman and general manager, was appointed director of OCT construction. Ma contracted the Singapore designer Meng Daqiang to design OCT as a Singapore-style town, in order to make it a window into China for attracting inflows of capital, technology, and professionals, particularly from overseas Chinese. By the mid-1990s, OCT itself housed more than one hundred transnational corporations. Among them, for example, Shenzhen Konka Electronics Group, China's first Sino–foreign joint consumer electronics enterprise, was capitalized by Kong Wah International, Hong Kong (www.konka.com.hk). Ranked first among China's industrial enterprises in 1993, the company produced US$246 million in that year. As the seventh largest joint venture in China in 1994, the company manufactured 30 percent of China's exported color televisions. Facing rapid increases in land and labor costs in Shenzhen SEZ, the company began to move its assembly operations to cheaper inland areas and to invest in or buy other state-owned enterprises in China.[17] The aggressive business expansion of OCT-based companies like Konka was further enhanced by the restructuring of OCT. On the eve of Hong Kong's return to China, the State Council approved OCT's reorganizing as the OCT Group, focusing on electronics, real estate, hotels, and tourism in China and overseas (www.chinaoct.com).

While developing OCT as a space for transnational capitalism, CTS also located the majority of its China-based business and its three theme park operations there: Splendid China (thirty hectares, opened in October 1989), China Folk Culture Villages (eighteen hectares, opened in October 1991), and Window on the World (forty-eight hectares, opened in the summer of 1994). These parks generated one hundred percent turnover in China alone over the 1989–1993 period. Although CTS's investment in steel production began to generate turnover in 1994, the theme parks' share of the company's total China-related turnover was still substantial and grew from 48.5 to 76.7 percent between 1994 and 1996. In 1997, the theme parks' share dropped to 49 percent after the government restricted the number of tourists to the Shenzhen SEZ and a uniform admission fee was adopted for domestic and foreign tourists on July 1, 1997.[18] In the same year, Changsha's Window on the World, a new CTS joint venture with OCT and Hunan Broadcasting and Television Center, opened to the public. For nine consecutive years (1989–1997), the combined theme park operations generated an average US$29.86 million annually.[19]

Both at OCT and at the three theme parks, the nationalized multiethnic was deployed as a major theme in giving cultural meanings to capital accumulation. The theme appeared in three forms: miniatures, life-sized buildings, and ethnic minorities. Integrated into a built environment, these forms of exhibition were more than displayed artifacts: they were also commodity spectacles. CTS used all three for reaching its objective of capital accumulation and for shaping the tourist's visit as an experience of consumption. The miniature took the form of "miniaturized scenic spots" (*weisuo jingguan*) at Splendid China, the first major commercial theme park built in the People's Republic of China.[20] The park showed about one hundred miniature models of scenic spots, including historical sites (such as the Great Wall, Dunhuang Mogao Grottoes, and Terra Cotta figures of soldiers and horses of the First Emperor), famous buildings (such as the Imperial Palace, and the Confucius Temple), and natural sites (such as Three Gorges of the Yangtze River, Huangshan Mountain, and the Stone Forest). Among them, eleven scenic spots were explicitly marked as being related to ethnic minority groups (*minzu*): the Daur fishing and hunting village, a Mongolian yurt, the Mausoleum of Genghis Khan, the Id Kah Mosque, the Potala Palace, the "wind and rain bridge, drum tower of the Dong," the Dong village, the Miao village, the Bouyei (Buyi) village, the Dai village, and the Manfeilong Pagoda.

The construction of these miniaturized ethnic scenic spots at Shenzhen SEZ served certain prescribed objectives. In a fascinating analysis of Splendid China, Anagnost rightly argues that the use of the miniature in compressing five thousand years of Chinese history into a tiny, thirty-hectare space was closely tied to the production of Shenzhen SEZ, whose history spans less than three decades.[21] That is, the miniature was a useful technology of representation in the production of a built theme environment because it could be used to capture and freeze time and space. At the Ruins Park of Yuanming Yuan, the miniaturized palaces brought back sights of the glorious past reduced to ruins in such way that the whole environment became a site for patriotic education. At Splendid China, by comparison, the miniaturized ethnic scenic spots contributed to a concentrated representation of China's ethnic minority groups, which are widely scattered around the country, in such a way that the whole built environment served to educate its visitors. Summarizing CTS's successful experience of managing the theme parks in Shenzhen, Ma Chi-man emphasized the importance of cultivating the tourist's sense of self. For him

> . . . management became strengthened when it paid attention to the cultivation of the tourist's self-respect (*zizun*), self-care (*ziai*), and self-discipline (*zilü*). This helped to create a cultural atmosphere conforming to the style (*gediao*) of the scenery, in which the tourist's experience became invisibly restrained to generate a self-consciousness about maintaining and following the order prescribed by the environment.[22]

Thus, the built theme environment was operated not merely as an instrumental space for capital accumulation but also a process for shaping its visitors to conduct themselves in specific ways.

Ethnic minorities were the third means used to display the nationalized multiethnic theme. China Folk Culture Villages contained twenty-four reconstructed life-sized villages representing twenty-one ethnic minority groups.[23] The park's brochure stated the guiding principle of the park's operation as "originating from real life but rising above it, and discarding the dross and selecting the essential."[24] A park manager explained to me how the park applied that principle to the representation of an ethnic minority group:

> Because of the limited space of each village, representation of an ethnic minority group had to be selective. For example, the cave house in northern Shaanxi represents a primitive dwelling custom. A bunch of hot peppers is usually hung outside a cave house. In the Folk Culture Villages, we hang many bunches of peppers and make the cave house appear more artistic. In doing this, we have created an environment to stimulate the interest of the tourists and to teach them [effectively] in a short period of time.[25]

The manager's use of "the cave house in northern Shaanxi"—commonly known as being inhabited by the Han people—as an example drew my attention to the way in which the park used "the folk" (*minsu*) to displace "the ethnic" (*minzu*).[26] Like the miniaturized representation of the ethnic, the folkloric representation of the ethnic (via life-size buildings and ethnic minority employees) produced the ethnic as something that was relatively independent of the historical time of socialist China. CTS could appropriate selected representations of national minority groups (in the name of "the folk") for the purpose of capital accumulation and yet still disseminate the idea of the nation state through a series of ethnic narratives.

The combined semiotic (linguistic) and meditative (spatial) process of displacing the ethnic as folk created a standard set of ethnic-themed commodities, including reconstructed, full-size villages complete with buildings, ethnic costumes, artifacts, performances, and festivals. The China Folk Culture Village became a standard for the commercial representation of the ethnic in China's theme park industry. Almost all theme parks representing national minorities hired ethnic minorities to serve as exhibits against backdrops of reconstructed ethnic buildings. Many managerial staff in other parks had worked in or with CTS theme parks.[27] Moreover, the company's labor organization also became a model. In 1995, the company had 1,450 employees, more than 500 of whom were ethnic minorities.[28] The average monthly salary for ethnic minority employees ranged from US$240 (2,000 RMB¥) to US$290 (2,400 RMB¥). Professional singers and dancers with at least four years of training were paid as much as US$435 (3,600 RMB¥) per month.

Each ethnic minority worker played a dual role in the company. Like all employees, he or she usually worked eight hours a day, six days a week. The worker was normally hired on a two-year contract, which might be renewed once.[29] This contract system allowed both flexibility for the company to dictate the length of employment and quick turnover of the ethnic minority employees. As a spectacle, the object of the tourist's gaze, an ethnic individual could not be displayed forever. The regular replacement of the ethnic minority employees was important for the sake of productivity. This labor organization facilitated the company's objective of using the built theme environment to speed up and intensify the transmission of information and values to the visitors.

Unlike a regular employee, however, an ethnic minority laborer possessed a special value marked by her or his body. To maximize the accumulation of capital from the display of ethnic bodies, the company established a series of procedures for selecting, training, and managing them. The criteria for selection of ethnic bodies included physical features (such as skin tone, hair color and texture, and face shape and color), gender, age, education, and skills. An appropriate candidate had to be young, attractive, and "typical of" an ethnic minority group. The face was the most crucial element of physical appearance in terms of making a body immediately recognizable as belonging to a particular ethnic group. Through both conversations with ethnic minority employees and observations of interactions between ethnic performers and tourists, I realized that the face of an ethnic minority functioned to mark a difference that was reassuring for the majority Han male visitors. Han visitors were attracted to the lure of the other in the ethnic faces presented to them. Several of the longer-term ethnic performers mentioned that Han visitors frequently said that the physical differences made the ethnic performers look like "foreigners." Moreover, the company deliberately maintained a sex ratio of 70 percent females and 30 percent males among the ethnic minority employees to enhance their attractiveness to the majority male visitors. Thus, both the exotic and the erotic were managed as two important elements of reassurance in realizing the company's objective of accumulation and the shaping of the tourist as consumer subject.

In addition to having the right physical characteristics, an ethnic minority laborer must also have certain talents—such as being able to sing, dance, make crafts, or weave—that could be shown in a staged setting. If physical characteristics were primarily markers of ethnic and gender differences, skills made it possible for an ethnic employee to interact with tourists in the built environment of a village. To ensure effective communication with the tourist and speedy transmission of information, the company trained the new hires to contextualize the histories and cultures of their own and other groups within the historical framework of socialist China. The conventional Marxist history ranks all ethnic minority groups according to the lineal continuum of time based on modes of production and social organizations, from the primitive (represented by the Jingpo, Wa, Gaoshan, and Naxi) to the most advanced (represented by the Han, Korean, Manchu, and Bai).[30] The company managers drew their knowledge of ethnic minorities entirely from ethnographic materials that supported the socialist linear continuum of historical time. As one manager claimed, they had read "many fieldwork materials."[31] Thus, the training was based on the premise that they, the managers, were more knowledgeable about ethnic cultures than the ethnic minority employees themselves.

As for the ethnic minority employees, they quickly learned during the training sessions what they were supposed to represent. A Jingpo performer, for example, told me how she learned about her own culture at the China Folk Culture Villages. At the age of seventeen, she was living at home without a job because she failed to pass the college entrance examination after graduating from high school. The company hired her during a recruiting trip to her home village. When she first arrived at the park and visited the "Jingpo village," she did not recognize the buildings and artifacts supposed to represent her people until she read the labels. "When I was at home in Yunnan, I lived as a Jingpo person of the 1980s. In the village here, these buildings are built based on old photos and investigative reports. I never saw [ones like] them at home." When I asked her to comment on these buildings, she said that the "bamboo buildings" on display in the village were "the most distinctive" because they were "primitive." This response showed her acceptance of the park's representation of the Jingpo as "primitive." At the same time, she acknowledged she was not happy about the implications of this representation. Park visitors generally came away with an impression of the Jingpo as being "poor" and "primitive." Sometimes she could not help telling visitors, "We no longer live like this!" Her comments showed that her personal experience as an ethnic employee was shaped by both the park's training and her daily interactions with visitors.

The park's representation of ethnic minorities addressed the displaced relationship between two streams of historical time: socialist and capitalist. Socialist historical time is linear in the sense that it incorporates the times of various ethnic minority groups into the historical time of the Chinese nation state by means of projecting the socialist time as the future horizon of the ethnic minorities. At the theme park, although socialist historical time constituted an epistemological condition for capital accumulation, capitalist historical time transformed that time into a national past-time. Ethnic minorities remained important only to the extent that they labored to represent capitalism. Ethnic minority performers and their associated artifacts and buildings, as well as mobilized Chinese state-owned capital, fabricated a spectacular image of China, a new Chinese nation state containing capitalist pockets.

The appearance of the neoliberal state: Super firm, affective labor, and built theme environments

The operations of CTS exemplified the process by which the Chinese government became an economic enterprise during the Hong Kong countdown. State-owned transnational companies like CTS helped the government to reorganize and operate Chinese society according to economic rationales of efficiency and calculation. Through transnational practices, state capital became much more mobile, and its accumulation followed the principle of flexibility. More important, transnational practices of state-owned capital were tied to the governmental objectives of the Chinese state. In the context of Hong Kong's return to China, they appeared to make possible the coexistence of capitalism and socialism, whether in Hong Kong or in China.

CTS's representation of socialism in Hong Kong and of capitalism in China operated through the communication-based economy; that is, the accumulation, extension, and circulation of information through communicative means. Socialism and capitalism were communicated as spectacles rather than political systems, which transformed the problem of representing them into one of managing them as an economic enterprise. In both Hong Kong and China, CTS's representation of socialism and capitalism was based not only on the labor of ethnic minorities but also on the medium of the built theme environment. Ethnic performers promoted and sold products (songs, dances, clothing, souvenirs, and architectures), signs, and symbols (their physical appearance, gender, and sex) associated with China's ethnic minorities. For the audiences and park visitors, this ethnic labor appeared to address their cosmopolitan feelings toward various types of the other (such as the past, the foreign, and the different). For the company, however, the purpose of the ethnic labor was to link these feelings to representations of socialism and capitalism. The company appropriated ethnic labor to address the Chinese government's objective of regulating and regularizing differences and identities according to the "one country, two systems" principle.

In addition, the company's representation of socialism and capitalism also relied on the medium of the built theme environment. As a particular medium of communication, the theme environment was used to influence the behaviors of its users (visitors, tourists, or consumers) through both its raw, material presence as a physical space and its encoded stories or themes about socialism and capitalism. In CTS operations, there were both conventional types of built theme environments (such as theme parks and theme hotels) and unconventional types (special economic zones, theme towns and streets), all of which were designed and operated through thematic narratives.[32] The communicative capacity of the built theme environment could be compared with that of narrative cinema. Early cinema (before 1907), as exemplified by the *cinématographe* of the lumières,[33] was used primarily as a device for indiscriminately recording all details of a happening. Despite its capacity for recording details beyond what the human eye could see, early cinema did not attach specific meanings to the recorded details.[34] The development of narrative cinema, by contrast, not only takes advantage of the medium's technical capacity for capturing details, but also relies on narration, or storytelling, to encode the meanings of a film through manipulating time. Like the early cinema, an ordinary built environment shelters all details of the happenings in the environment without discrimination. As a human environment, the space does not have a coherent meaning. Its users do not have a sense of place (that is, of identity). However, the development of a built theme environment inserts a narrative into the environment (medium) in the same way as narrative cinema does. While the raw material (the physical environment) mediates human activities, the designed and operated theme, or narrative, encodes their meanings through manipulating human movement. Whereas narrative cinema cultivates the visual attention, or capacity, of its users,[35] the built theme environment shapes its users' behaviors by normalizing their conduct.

In the historical context of Hong Kong's return, CTS produced and operated built theme environments as neoliberal zones in the sense of Ong's "zones of graduated sovereignty," exceptional spaces governed by their own rules that transgressed the normative rules applicable to the rest of the country. Consequently, during the dance festival the Hong Kong Cultural Center became a zone of the Chinese state, an exceptional space in pre-1997 Hong Kong, through an ethnic narrative of the Chinese nation. Similarly, such built theme environments as Splendid China, China Folk Culture Villages, Window on the World, Overseas Chinese Town, and Shenzhen SEZ were designed and planned as capitalist zones, exceptional spaces inside the still socialist China. The business operations of these built theme environments carried out the politics of the Chinese state in realizing the "one country, two systems" principle.

6 Memories of the future in Hong Kong

Between the signing of the Sino–British Joint Declaration on December 19, 1984, and the Chinese government's resumption of sovereignty over Hong Kong on July 1, 1997, Hong Kong developed a new epochal consciousness characterized by the idea that Hong Kong's own historical time had not only a beginning and an end, but also was a period of transition. The development of this time consciousness came about through the reconfiguration of Hong Kong's modernity. As on the Chinese mainland, Hong Kong's modern historical experience can be divided into three temporalities: the colonial time of British rule (1842–1997), the transitional time of the Hong Kong countdown (1984–1997), and the national time of the Hong Kong Special Administrative Region (HKSAR; 1997–2046). All three were shaped by international agreements. The Treaty of Nanjing (1842), the Treaty of Beijing (1860), and the Extension of the Colony treaty (1898) were the cornerstones of the first temporality. The Sino–British Joint Declaration (1984) authorized the appearance of the second temporality, and the Basic Law of the HKSAR (1990) prescribed the legitimacy of the third. During the countdown process, each temporality was tied to a particular dimension of historical time: the first to the past, the second to the present, and the third to the future. The perception of July 1, 1997, as an ultimate deadline reordered the relationship between the past, the present, and the future. It first made Hong Kong's past problematic and then encouraged the displacement of the past as a problem of the present. The development of a new Hong Kong cultural identity thus became inseparable from finding appropriate solutions to the problem of the present.

The historical meaning in Hong Kong of the Chinese government's resumption of sovereignty over the territory was never one-dimensional. In fact, many terms were used to refer to the historical event: *wuiguai* ("return" in Cantonese), *huigui* ("return" in Putonghua), handover, transition, decolonization, reinstatement, restoration, reversion, retrocession, reunification, "returnification," and even "fall" and "death."[1] July 1, 1997, was treated as a kind of due date: a "judgment day," a "deadline," or an "expiration date."[2] In almost every kind of cultural product in Hong Kong, such as architecture, theater, literature, cinema, and television, the deadline theme was prominent. In this sense, a new Hong Kong culture emerged through a process of "disappearance," not in terms of an absence or lack of presence but of representing a thing as something else, that is, replacement and substitution.[3]

The development of this culture of disappearance aimed at constructing meanings for the present (transitional time) by means of reconciling the relationship between the past (the colonial time of British rule) and the future (the national time of the HKSAR). Thus, the culture of disappearance had simultaneously to preserve the past and anticipate the future. This problem of synchronization was expressed in terms of the dialectic between "not-change" (*bubian*) and "change" (*bian*).[4] Many of Hong Kong's elites, such as business leaders and tycoons, actively participated in the process of drafting the Basic Law of the HKSAR. The Basic Law legally guaranteed the right of HKSAR to continue its own system, not only capitalism but also lifestyle, for fifty years.[5]

In addressing the dialectical relationship between anticipation of the future and preservation of the past, the culture of disappearance went far beyond legal and administrative arrangements. It was commonly expressed in three different ways. First, it entailed a displacement of Hong Kong through the increasing influence of the Chinese state.[6] As described in the previous chapter, Hong Kong-based corporations owned by the Chinese government, like China Travel Service (Hong Kong) Ltd., actively participated in the development of this culture of disappearance by inserting a time of the Chinese nation into the everyday life of Hong Kong residents. Meanwhile, the Hong Kong countdown clock at Tiananmen Square also became a public time-telling device in Hong Kong, where it was used by various print, electronic, and digital media.[7] It triggered a flourishing of historical narratives in Hong Kong. On October 1, 1996, for example, performers and entertainers (mainly from Hong Kong) held a show called the Entertainment Party to Celebrate the 47th Birthday of the People's Republic of China by Hong Kong Compatriots at Hong Kong Stadium. The official program read in part (in Chinese): "Warmly celebrating the 47th anniversary of the founding of the People's Republic of China. Happily greeting Hong Kong's return to the Motherland. The time remaining in the countdown: 273 days."[8] The Hong Kong-based scholar Li Siu-leung viewed the passing seconds of the countdown clock as a virtual clock time in Hong Kong:

> Look, in the north across thousands of kilometers, the white-colored-board and red-colored-character giant electronic countdown clock, looking down on Tiananmen Square, like a magnificent military gate that has lasted for a thousand years and could not be broken down, even by tens of thousands of soldiers. The neon numbers were transforming themselves incessantly, just as mercury falling onto the ground seeks every penetrating opportunity. [The clock's] gaze controls in the distance the progressive steps of Hong Kong history; nobody could possibly escape from it?![9]

Obviously, Beijing's countdown clock inevitably became a daily reality in Hong Kong, part of its culture of disappearance.

The second way the culture of disappearance addressed the relationship between the past and the future as a problem of the present was by displacing politics with the economy. Abbas wrote:

> Historical imagination, the citizens' belief that they might have a hand in shaping their own history, gets replaced by speculation on the property or stock market, or by an obsession with fashion or consumerism. If you cannot choose your political leaders, you can at least choose your own clothes. We find therefore not an atmosphere of doom and gloom, but the more paradoxical phenomenon of *doom and boom*: the more frustrated or blocked the aspirations to "democracy" are, the more the market booms.[10]

The domination of the market in everyday life contributed to Hong Kong's neoliberal system, which was reinforced by the Chinese government's "one country, two systems" policy (for a detailed discussion, see Conclusion, this volume).

The third expression of the culture of disappearance was a cultural transformation in Hong Kong, the focus of this chapter. During the transition period, cultural workers inside and outside Hong Kong—writers, columnists, singers, dramatists, and designers, as well as academics—identified an urgent need to develop a *Hongkong* cultural identity.[11] The art critic Oscar Ho said in 1993, "Time is running out: people in Hong Kong need to find their cultural heritage and to reassure their sense of identity, for in four years' time they might have lost it."[12] Historical representation emerged as an important site for identity development. The transition period witnessed a saturation of historical narratives, not only formal and institutional historical narratives, but also informal and biographical narratives of history (historical anecdotes or personal narratives of past experiences, *zhanggu*). Li Siu-leung warned this process was so prominent that Hong Kong history might become clichés and "historical consciousness" might lose its meaning.[13] At the same time, many scholars also critiqued misunderstandings and misrepresentations of Hong Kong's historical experience. Rey Chow, in warning against Chinese nationalist representations of Hong Kong's postcolonial experience, drew attention to a "unique" aspect of Hong Kong: an awareness of "an inbetweenness," or "impure origins," that allowed cultural production in Hong Kong to be a practice of negotiation. Esther M. K. Cheung, in critiquing the grand narrative of colonialism as a developmental project, argued for a mode of representation she calls a "historical bricolage," through which "the 'local' is subjected to constant flux amid an uneasy coexistence of localism (a complex mix of nationalism and traditionalism) and globalism (urbanization and modernization)."[14]

Museums and related institutions in Hong Kong played a crucial role in historical preservation projects and in the standardization of representations of Hong Kong's history. To illuminate how Hong Kong's historical representations in the transition period constructed a Hongkong identity under the condition of disappearance, in this chapter I focus on the development of "exhibition" as a governmental issue in Hong Kong, the important role of the Hong Kong Museum of History in historical representation, and the development of monuments and heritage education. From the early twentieth century, commodity exhibitions often used material objects and artifacts to express Hong Kong as a place. Then, from the late 1960s to the mid-1980s, the government developed cultural exhibitions as an important means for managing everyday life, particularly leisure and entertainment, as part of "public health." Between the early commodity and the later cultural exhibitions, the understanding of Hong Kong evolved from a "borrowed place, borrowed time" to a place that began to construct its own identity.[15]

During the transition period, museums emerged as an important site for representing Hong Kong's history and constructing a Hongkong identity. The Hong Kong Museum of History has been developed as a repository of official Hongkong history, particularly for building an archive of the historical time of Hongkong. The museum's permanent exhibition "The Story of Hong Kong" (opened in 1991), for example, constructed the notion of "Heunggong" ("Hong Kong" in Cantonese) as a natural category by means of negotiating between different historical narratives. The historical time of Hongkong was constructed as being the transformation of Heunggong from a fishing village to an international metropolis, in which the city was represented as the "essential" marker of Heunggong and the village merely its reflection (and its other). The village-to-city transformation was a common theme in historical representations in Hong Kong.

As the history museum displayed artifacts removed from the context of daily lives, the Monuments and Antiquities Office of the Hong Kong government preserved historical sites and buildings within everyday settings. By transforming ordinary buildings in everyday life into historic ones, the Hong Kong government constructed a "cultural heritage" of Hongkong, particularly for urban residents in search of a cultural identity. The development of the Pingshan Heritage Trail in the New Territories transformed Pingshan village into a heritage community. As I will discuss, however, different understandings of Pingshan in the historical context of Sino–British relations has led to different interpretations of the meaning of the trail.

Hong Kong in industrial and cultural exhibitions

Exhibition (telling-through-showing), the spatial arrangement and display of artifacts, can be an important means for registering a stretch of time as a historical time.[16] In public displays, the use of other times and places to measure Hong Kong's historical time has gradually shifted to the use of Hong Kong's own sense of place. Industrial fairs and commercial exhibitions organized by the Chinese Manufacturers' Union in the first half of the twentieth century linked the development of a historical time of Hong Kong (represented by its manufacturing industry) to the times of the Chinese nation state and the British Empire. From the late 1960s to the mid-1980s, cultural exhibitions and institutions began both to represent Hong Kong's own historical time and to regulate the leisure time of Hong Kong residents.

Industrial and commercial organizations played an important role in developing the consciousness of Hong Kong as a locality with a historical time. The Chinese Manufacturers' Union, formally established in 1933, began in 1937 to hold regular exhibitions of "Chinese products" manufactured in Hong Kong. These exhibitions linked the development of Hong Kong's historical time to both China and Britain and explicitly to China's industrial output. The 1939 exhibition, for example, was directly supported by the Nationalist government to promote "national products" (*guohuo*), as its published program stated:

> The number of products made by our Chinese increases day by day, and their quality is better and better. It is essential to introduce them more often and make us know more about them. How can we know completely about so many products? This is very difficult to do. Therefore, we organized this exhibition and displayed products from all over China in one place for the public. This is the best way of knowing about national products.[17]

The objective of this exhibition was to promote both products made by Huaren (Chinese) capitalists in Hong Kong and products made in China.[18] There was a clear consciousness of Hong Kong as a geographical location, but it was part of the Chinese nation.

The 1939 exhibition was divided into six sections entitled *minzu* (nationality), *minquan* (civil or human rights), *minsheng* (livelihood), *ziqiang* (self-strengthening), *ziyou* (freedom), and *zizhi* (self-ruling).[19] These titles were taken directly from the "Three Principles" (*sanminzhuyi*), core values advocated by the Chinese Nationalist government. Objects on display included silk and cotton products, electronics, toys, cosmetics, medicine, food, leather, rubber, glass, carvings, umbrellas, stationery, matches, toothbrushes, and soaps. These products were referred to as national products and thus became cultural artifacts of Chinese nationalism.[20] The exhibition also promoted the development of the manufacturing industry in Hong Kong. Yeh Lan-chuan, the director of the Chinese Manufacturers' Union, stated:

> Since the beginning of Hong Kong's history, Hong Kong has been an entrepôt and rarely manufactured products. Local prosperity was often threatened by the outside world. More and more factories are established, particularly by Huaren . . . If more factories are established, Hong Kong will change from an entrepôt to an industrial area. Under this situation, Hong Kong may maintain its prosperity. In addition, factories can manage a large number of people. It is good for the government.

> China is in the war against the Japanese. Large numbers of refugees came to Hong Kong and factories have accepted many refugees.[21]

His statement implies that the Hong Kong government did not really make an effort to develop a local manufacturing industry. Because of this situation, the exhibition had to claim its purpose, at least partially, as being to serve the need of the colonial government to control its residents, particularly managing the large number of war refugees from China.

Hong Kong's historical time was also represented by its link to the British Empire. As early as 1886, the British government requested that the Hong Kong colonial government participate in the Colonial and Indian Exhibition held in London, in order to represent Hong Kong as part of the empire.[22] Hong Kong also took part in the British Empire Exhibition at Wembley in 1924–1925, designed by the British government to show "a solid foundation for the Imperial Building."[23] Hong Kong's participation was based on the "patriotic desire to claim its place as a 'member of the family' " of the empire. Upon the closure of the exhibition in 1925, the Imperial Institute selected samples of Hong Kong exports as its collections.[24]

Local businessmen participating in British colonial exhibitions used these venues as opportunities to showcase products made in Hong Kong and to gather information for developing local industries. During the British Industries Fair in London in 1948, for example, the Hong Kong Fair Committee, mainly made up of members of the Chinese Manufacturers' Union, aimed to show "what the Colony was doing in the way of Industry, Banking, and the like, and in doing so, to offer . . . [Hong Kong's] products and services to overseas buyers," while also contacting industrialists in Britain and visiting factories in England. The four hundred-square-foot exhibition space was filled with "commodities of eminently practical utility," such as woven and knitted articles, hats, rubber goods, foodstuffs, preserved ginger, tobacco, flashlights, soap, and paint. Moreover, the exhibition was "educational" for Hong Kong representatives and gave them "a revised opinion on individual organization" and "a new outlook on industry, which is bound to affect their attitude towards local industry." Meanwhile, the committee also saw the British Industries Fair as "the centre of the Empire in which Hong Kong is an integral and essential unit, where the people who call Hong Kong their home are welcomed because they are members of a larger whole we call the Empire."[25]

As Hong Kong participated in colonial exhibitions in Britain in the late 1940s, exhibitions of industrial products held in Hong Kong stopped showing products manufactured in China. The consciousness of Hong Kong as a unique place closely associated with its own industries was quite clear in this period. At the opening of the seventh exhibition of Chinese products in 1949, for example, exhibition chairman Shum Choy Wah stated:

> From our experience at the British Industries Fair these two years, and from our experience in previous exhibitions, we have had many chances

> to study the manufacturing world at large and the marketing conditions for our products.
>
> We are here to show what we manufacture in Hong Kong and what progress we have made during the past year. In the next nineteen days we will present to the local public and to the world the goods we manufacture here in Hong Kong, and ask the local public and world at large to pass judgment on our products.
>
> In this world of keen competition we manufacturers in Hong Kong are always looking forward, hoping to open new markets. At the same time we are not unconscious of our own shortcomings, which we try continually to reduce. We are in an isolated [position] in the manufacturing world, and for this reason some of our factories are less well equipped than they might be, though we can boast that a number of them are comparable with the best in the world. We try continually to keep our technical ability abreast of that in the rest of the world, and to develop our management and manufacturing organizations to the best possible state. We try to see to the well-being of our labor [force], and to keep our workmen well trained—in other words, we try to be model employers.[26]

Although Shum mentioned the British Industries Fair, he clearly represented Hong Kong as a city of the world, rather than just a city of China or the British Empire. The uniqueness of Hong Kong as a place was identified by what was made in Hong Kong.

The Hong Kong government directly supported the 1949 exhibition by assisting with its preparation and site selection. The government's goal, as was clear from Governor Alexander Grantham's speech at the opening, was to maintain Hong Kong's status as a trading port:

> The English and Chinese peoples are great traders, and Hong Kong is one of the great centres of the world. Today even though war is raging in China with a blockade along the coast, trade still goes on. The Exhibition, of course, is concerned primarily with industrial products rather than trade. It shows what we can make in Hong Kong, from roofing tiles to nails, from ginger to cosmetics, from spinning yarn to making felt hats . . . [T]he Hong Kong market is a comparatively small one and we have to rely upon exports, and if we export, our prices and the quality of our goods must be able to compete with the products of other countries.[27]

Thus, the governor drew public attention to the crucial role of trade, even though he was speaking at an exhibition of manufacturing.

Manufacturers' exhibitions were held annually as the manufacturing industry developed rapidly in the 1950s and 1960s. In the 1950s the Chinese Manufacturers' Union launched a campaign to persuade Hong Kong's people to buy local products. According to an award-winning essay, "Hong Kong Residents Should Use Hong Kong Products" by Joseph Veiga, "If we do not

'Buy Hong Kong' as we should, the result will be less factories, less production, less employment, less prosperity for Hong Kong and therefore for you and me and all other residents."[28] Consuming products made in Hong Kong in a sense became a civilizing process by which Hong Kong residents were encouraged to accept the idea of Hong Kong as a place. That is, the culture of Hong Kong was experienced and expressed in terms of the practice of consumption, the development of a consumer culture. In this commercial popular culture, everyday time was measured as continuous change and repetition in ready-to-wear fashions; the values of flows (of people, capital, and information) were ensured by the rapid development of urban (residential and commercial) projects; and more important, the new historical time of Hong Kong was perceived not as static but as a continual negotiation of the problematic relationship between the traditional and the modern, or between "the East" and "the West."[29]

Until the 1960s, commercial and industrial exhibitions had linked the development of Hong Kong's own historical time to other times and places (China, Britain, and other countries). The exhibitions, on the one hand, supported a sense of Hong Kong's historical time as a borrowed time that was inseparable from China and Britain. On the other hand, they also promoted the development of local industries and contributed to the development of Hong Kong culture as consumer culture. The idea of "borrowed time" was most prevalent among individuals who stayed in Hong Kong temporarily, using Hong Kong as a springboard to other places.[30] For those who considered Hong Kong as their home, however, the idea of borrowed time led to the development of a socioeconomic time that focused on the present rather than on a predetermined destiny in the future.[31] The present-orientation of Hong Kong's historical time dovetailed with the development of commercial popular culture and the development of flexible accumulation as an important characteristic of Hong Kong's economy—manifested both in small-scale organization of labor and less concern with brand-making than with flexibility in production and marketing.[32]

In the late 1960s, cultural exhibitions responded to local social problems. The 1967 riot was sparked by social problems specific to the Hong Kong community, not the colonial government or the "Chinese motherland."[33] The Hong Kong government recognized this and began for the first time to address local problems rather than social problems that primarily originated from or were related to China (such as the Sino–French War in 1884–1885, the 1911 Revolution, the May Fourth Movement in 1919, the formation of the Guomingdang–Communist United Front for anti-imperialist national revolution in 1924, the Sino–Japanese War of 1937–1945, and the communist takeover of China in 1949).[34]

After the 1967 riot, the Hong Kong government was forced to deal with social issues such as employment and health care, and to put more effort into providing leisure activities for local residents. This change led to a series of government-sponsored and -managed recreational and entertainment activities, of which cultural exhibitions were part. The first Hong Kong Festival was held in 1969 and became an annual event thereafter. The Hong Kong Urban Council was also restructured in 1973 to administer the "public health" of Hong Kong residents in terms of environmental hygiene, leisure services, and "culture:" the council's mandate ranged from street cleaning, operation of crematoria, food inspection, and management of public markets to such recreational services as parks, swimming pools, sports stadiums, libraries, museums, theaters, and concert halls.[35]

Cultural exhibitions became a governmental tool for managing the daily lives of Hong Kong residents. The first Hong Kong Festival, December 6–15, 1969, included more than four hundred events, such as a parade, fashion shows, amusement fairs, sports, concerts, dancing parties, and exhibitions.[36] The 1969 festival was said to have proven one thing:

> The big and successful festival is a most effective means of uniting the conglomerate masses in Hong Kong into feeling a true attachment and pride for the place to which they now mostly belong. It speaks so very much for Hong Kong's future indeed. It shows and encourages the fine arts and culture. It promotes industry and the economy of Hong Kong's future.[37]

Media coverage of the festival was positive. The *Overseas Chinese Daily*'s editorial on the festival even emphasized Hong Kong as a shared community:

> Hong Kong is not a country but a modern society. Most of the Hong Kong people are really Chinese, but they are also residents of Hong Kong. Therefore, Hong Kong's status, cultural spirit, and customs are all closely related to China, or are inseparable from China. [However, a]s long as we carry on the spirit of traditional Chinese culture and Chinese morals, and regard Hong Kong as the second homeland, we surely will construct the spiritual civilization in Hong Kong gradually, improve the customs and habits in Hong Kong, and make Hong Kong's future bright. In other words, whoever lives and works in Hong Kong should love, take care of, and commit himself/herself to Hong Kong.[38]

The development of Hong Kong as a community was part of the government's plan of regulating everyday life through festivals. Governor Murray MacLehose (1971–1982), for example, treated the annual festival as an important opportunity to define the "right combination of hard work with leisure and fun" in order to show Hong Kong as a "happy and successful community." This characterization of Hong Kong as a community reflected the British government's policy of not treating Hong Kong as a political entity.[39]

Museums were also formally institutionalized in the 1960s, under the administration of the Urban Council,[40] to contribute to the regulation of the "public health" of Hong Kong residents, that is, of practices of everyday life outside the factory or workplace. The City Museum and Art Gallery was established in 1962 and was divided in 1975 into the Hong Kong Museum of History and the Hong Kong Museum of Art.[41] The mission of the Hong Kong Museum of History was to "record and reflect" Hong Kong's "historical, social and cultural changes which have molded modern Hong Kong."[42] The museum played an important role in preserving and exhibiting local history, collaborating with the Hong Kong Archaeological Society to excavate archaeological sites and increase knowledge of archaeological work. By 1982, it had assisted the Antiquities and Monuments Section of the Urban Services Department in recording more than four hundred important historical sites and buildings in Hong Kong.[43] From 1975 to the mid-1980s, the museum developed more than forty exhibitions and attracted on average 300,000 visitors a year.[44] Nevertheless, the Urban Council considered the museum's public displays of local history as a lower priority than the exhibitions of arts and sciences at the Hong Kong Museum of Art, the Space Museum, and the Science Museum. This situation began to change as Hong Kong entered the transition period in 1984.

The Story of Hong Kong: Historical representation in the countdown period

The use of historical representation to construct a historical time for Hongkong in the transition period entailed a rapid development of the Hong Kong Museum of History. Not only did the museum amass a collection of more than 50,000 items on local history in this period, but it also renovated its building at Kowloon Park in 1988 and moved into its first permanent building at Tsimshatsui East in 1998. The museum's gallery space expanded significantly from less than 700 square meters in 1975, to 1,520 square meters in 1989, and to 17,500 square meters in 1998.

Beginning in the mid-1980s, the museum conducted a series of local history projects. One of the first was to identify who the people of Hong Kong were. In 1987, for example, it launched a two-year oral history project entitled The Hongkongese and Their Lives, the first time the history of "common people" in Hong Kong was emphasized.[45] Researchers interviewed 136 people aged fifty-five to ninety-three. Through the project, museum staff gained new knowledge about life in the Japanese occupation period (1941–1945), various kinds of businesses, particularly those that had disappeared or were disappearing, and immigration of businesspeople from the Middle East and India. In the process, they also came to recognize the ethnic diversity of the Hongkongese and collected many new artifacts such as furniture, clothing, and documents, including identification cards, passports, leases, bills, and personal letters.

This effort led to a series of exhibitions on the history of Hong Kong. In 1991, the museum opened the Historical Materials for Hong Kong Studies exhibition to educate the public about various categories of historical materials, such as printed matter, documents, photographs, and paintings, all of which were used to illustrate different phases of local development. "Through case studies of a particular institute, person or event, the exhibition illustrated how government and non-government historical materials, together with oral sources, could re-construct the past."[46] By promoting the development of Hong Kong Studies as an academic discipline around the same time, the museum played its part in transforming knowledge of Hong Kong historiography into a public history.[47] It staged many important temporary thematic exhibitions exploring a range of topics in local Hongkong history. Some examples from 1986 to 1995 were Local Traditional Chinese Wedding; Postal History of Hong Kong (The War Years, 1941–1945); People and Life: Old Photos of Hong Kong; Puppet Theatres in Hong Kong; Made in Hong Kong: A History of Export Design in Hong Kong, 1900–1960; 150 Years of Postal Service in Hong Kong, 1841–1991; Education in Hong Kong: Past and Present; An Economic Miracle: The Success Story of Hong Kong; Of Hearts and Hands: Hong Kong's Traditional Trades and Crafts; and Life under the Japanese Occupation, 1941–1945.

In terms of local history, the most important project was the museum's permanent exhibition entitled The Story of Hong Kong (see Figure 6.1), which was designed by a Canadian exhibition-design firm, J. J. André Associates Ltd., based in Victoria, British Columbia.[48] The exhibition opened in 1991 and closed in 1998 before the museum moved into its new home at Tsimshatsui East. More than one million people had visited it by 1997.[49] According to the exhibition brochure, the exhibition's primary objective was to "stimulate public interest in local history as well as foster understanding of Hong Kong's unique past." The largest of its kind ever held in Hong Kong, this 1,302-square-meter exhibition depicted the political, economic, and social development of Heunggong from the Neolithic Age to the signing of the Sino–British Joint Declaration in 1984. Its nine sections followed the spatial order of The Natural Environment; The Early Settlers; The Village; The City—Cession and Early Development (1841–1851); The City—Growth of Society and Expansion of the Territory (1852–1862); The City—Development of Trade, Industry and Establishment of Social Organizations (1863–1893); The City—Revolution of Ideas and Lifestyles and New Perspectives on the City (1894–1941); Japanese Occupation (1941–1945); and Modern Hong Kong. Through the display of historical photographs, documents, farming implements, and models, and with the aid of audiovisual and multi-sensory devices, dioramas, and walk-through scenes, the exhibition traced the development of Heunggong "from a small fishing village to a metropolis."[50]

Within this grand narrative of Heunggong, the development of the "City" was the central theme, occupying more than one-third of the total gallery space and being treated as an essential marker of Heunggong. Heunggong's urbanization was narrated as a homogenous process, beginning with the arrival of the Europeans and their discovery of the "Village." The label "A Popular Watering Hole" explained the process of discovery as follows:

Figure 6.1 The brochure of the Story of Hong Kong (1991–1998) exhibition at the Hong Kong Museum of History, Kowloon Park, Hong Kong.

Foreign vessels sailing for Guangzhou, the only city where Sino–Western trade was allowed after 1757 and before the opening of the Treating Ports in 1840s, had to approach by the Pearl River via Lingding and the Bogue. Ships often called at Hong Kong to replenish their fresh water supply after a long voyage. A natural, well-sheltered site for this brief sojourn was the area surrounded by Lamma Island, Ap Lei Chau and Shek Pai Wan. Sailors obtained fresh water at a waterfall near the present Wan Fu Estate before continuing their voyage to Guangzhou. The very name of Hong Kong was derived from the stopping point: there was a Hong Kong Village in the vicinity and Westerners mistook it for the name of the whole island.

This narrative linked Hong Kong to a world history based on a homogeneous European time and space. Heunggong on display could not enter into world history without first being discovered by the Europeans, who did not merely find a watering hole, but also discovered indigenous people on the island. This was, of course, part of the marvellous "discovery" of China. When Heunggong was ceded to Britain after the first Opium War, it was then ready to become urbanized. Land sales, settlements of European trading companies, and migrations of populations from Europe and China were important events in the city's early development. The emergence of business in the city was represented by such companies as Jardine, Matheson & Co., Dent & Co., and Russell & Co. The City of Victoria (today's Central District) became the British residential area on the island. "Historical paintings" made by European artists and travelers were used as illustrations of Victoria. Clearly, the vision of the City was based exclusively on European perceptions.

The exhibition also used photographs taken by Europeans to re-create a streetscape of the City "to give the audience a rough idea of what Hong Kong looked like in the latter part of the 19th century" (exhibition label). This streetscape was represented as "a typical 19th-century street scene with Chinese shops on one side and European buildings on the other, serving as a comparison" (exhibition label). The European side of the street contained the main entrance of A. S. Watson & Co. and display windows of other influential companies, including Lammert Brothers, Hongkong & Kowloon Wharf & Godown Co. Ltd., Lane Crawford & Co. Department Store, Dodwell & Co. Ltd., and Hongkong & Shanghai Banking Corporation. The visitor could not only view artifacts in the display windows of these companies, but also might walk into each unit to explore more artifacts on display. This arrangement of gallery space offered the visitor relevant information about postal and telecommunications services, shipping, banking, electricity, land reclamation, reservoirs, and transportation.

By contrast, the full-size building facades on the Chinese side of the street included a teahouse, salted-fish shop, community office, gambling house, pawnshop, fortune-teller's booth, and Eurasian house, as well as a back alley. Various aspects of the daily lives of local people were shown, with prostitution and gambling highlighted as social problems. The viewer was unable to walk into any buildings, but could only look at the artifacts displayed in front of them while listening to the sounds of street vendors and gambling in the background.

To understand the streetscape exhibit as a mode of historical narration, I would like to compare it with Walter Benjamin's arcade project. In his "One-Way Street," Benjamin constructed an arcade, or sheltered streetscape, based on a juxtaposition of two kinds of artifacts. The first group of artifacts represented a particular kind of modern experience associated with the fragmentary, the spontaneous, and the forgotten, such as childhood pastimes (reading, collecting, playing, and hiding), antiques, travel souvenirs, and toys. The second group represented another kind of modern experience associated with technology and instrumental rationality; for example, a standard clock, the Ministry of the Interior, and a teaching aid.[51] Both Benjamin's and the museum's streetscapes juxtaposed two groups of artifacts, but they deployed exhibition for different purposes. For Benjamin, juxtaposing the two kinds of artifacts enabled him to highlight ambiguity as "the figurative appearance of the dialectic, the law of the dialectic at a standstill."[52] That is, the arcade was deployed as a material critique of the dialectical image of capitalism, of "the internal consciousness, or rather, the *un*conscious of the dreaming" bourgeoisie in late nineteenth-century Europe.[53]

In The Story of Hong Kong, the two groups of artifacts facing each other across a street obviously showed a contrast between a rich capitalist European culture and a basic but lively Chinese culture. Whereas Benjamin's arcade illustrated two kinds of modern experiences under commodity capitalism, the museum's streetscape highlighted cultural differences under British colonial rule. The development of the City of Victoria was historically inseparable from the practices of racial and class segregation. Ethnic Chinese elites were not allowed to live in the European residential areas because European settlers commonly believed that the practice of concubinage by Chinese elite families was harmful to the moral values of European families.[54] Meanwhile, racial and class segregation could not be separated from the practice of cultural representation. Because European historical photographs were used to portray the lives of the ethnic Chinese, the Chinese side of the streetscape remained superficial, in sharp contrast to the European side. This contrast resulted from its design:

> Two cultures were effectively represented by a street scene with opposing facades of shops and businesses—one side was entirely Chinese and was colorful, intense, and cramped, while the other side, British Colonial, was more prosperous—indicating the cultural differences of the two peoples. Continued sounds enlivened the tempo of the street. Some were visitor activated such as the tea house chatter, cries of the bamboo seller, the call of the scissors sharpening man, and the clatter of tram cars. The night scene inspired exciting light effects not possible had the street been flooded with artificial daylight.[55]

This design shaped visitors' perspective. Compared with the interactive and participatory experience of visiting the European side of the street, the experience of visiting the Chinese side was passive and impressionistic.[56] Visitors might situate themselves in the European environment but could not meaningfully position themselves in the Chinese environment.

In its juxtaposition of a rich description of the European side of the City and a superficial portrayal of the Chinese side, the streetscape constructed a built environment sheltering the interior space of the British expatriates and protecting the colonial memory from disappearance.[57] That is, the streetscape gave a spatial quality to the colonial past; it thickened and enacted the memory of the City's achievement as a colony. In walking down the streetscape, the visitor traveled through a spatially sheltered British colonial time.

Because it both promoted the representation of Heunggong as a miracle of colonialism and sheltered the memory of the City's colonial heritage, the exhibit could not possibly display any explicit conflicts and tensions caused by British colonial rule, as the museum's curators reminded me in 1995. The superficiality of the displayed Chinese lives in the context of the City illustrated one difficulty of displaying Hong Kong's history during the transition: in the politics of disappearance, British colonialism underlay all cultural and historical representations.[58]

If the City was primarily represented as a British achievement, with only superficial roles accorded to the ethnic Chinese, how was the Village—"the people and life of Hong Kong" beyond the metropolis—represented?[59] The representation of "the people" in the Village closely followed the "development of Hong Kong from a fishing village to an important metropolis" framework. Consequently, the Village was represented as the other in opposition to the City. First, the Village was linked to "the boat people" with artifacts portraying the role of junks, sea-god worship, and coastal lifestyles. The centerpiece was a boathouse, which the visitor could enter to view its interior and a female mannequin posed as if sewing a piece of clothing. A recording of song and the sound of the ocean played continuously, and eight large black-and-white photos showed boats and activities of the boat people.

The second part of the Village focused on the "means of livelihood and life pattern" of the people on the land, including agriculture, production of pearls and incense, clan organizations, rituals, and beliefs. According to the label "Life in the Village,"

> At the beginning of the 19th century, the New Territories were primarily an agricultural district consisting of a few broad valleys and many pockets of land among the hills with a few market towns here and there. There were two rice crops in summer and autumn. Visits to the market town, often at least half-a-day's journey away, had to be made on foot, the farmer frequently laden with produce and livestock to sell or exchange.
>
> Life followed a set pattern. Apart from the cultivation of rice, a series of village activities were held to meet the clan needs, among which was the proper observance of ancestral rites, the management of ancestral property including clan houses and land, as well as the needs of the family such as the education of the young, the care of the old, assisting with weddings and funerals, repairs to the ancestral temple and so on.

In the context of this introduction, a reconstructed "village house" "illustrate[d] village life in rural Hong Kong in the 19th century" (exhibition label).

"The people" on display in the Village belonged to four ethnic groups, differentiated by their clothing: the Punti, or the local people; Hakka, or the guest people; Tanka, or the boat people; and the Hoklo. In this exhibit, recorded songs were played to introduce each group: as the audio system played a song belonging to a particular group, that group's showcase was highlighted while the others remained in the dim background. As the visitor moved into the area of the next ethnic group, so did the media system and its spotlight. Thus, the multimedia system guided visitors by coordinating sounds, lights, and displayed artifacts. This coherent built environment was effective not only in representing the four different populations as the people of the Village, but also in shaping the experience of visitors.

The exhibition represented the Village as the other of the City by means of both narration and narrative. With respect to narration, the Village display was ordered before the City one, a chronological arrangement that framed the development of Heunggong from a fishing village to an international metropolis. This spatial ordering also shaped the experience of visitors, who had to view the Village section prior to entering the City. Yet in contrast to this apparently chronological arrangement, the exhibition's labels (narrative) represented the Village as synchronic with the City in the nineteenth century.

This discrepancy between the narration and the narrative arose from the Village's dual meanings in the context of the exhibition. First, the narrative referred to the Village as encompassing the rural areas of late nineteenth-century southern Guangdong, China. As quoted earlier, the "Life in the Villages" label referred to the nineteenth-century Village as synonymous with "the New Territories." This representation was problematic for historical reasons. The New Territories did not exist as part of Hong Kong until Britain leased part of southern Guangdong Province in 1898. Hence, the Hong Kong government did not control the large rural area of southern Guangdong until the end of the nineteenth century. Nineteenth-century southern Guangdong Province never existed as the nineteenth-century Village of Hong Kong. If it could ever exist, it could only be staged in a representation like the museum exhibition in the transition period. The artifacts exhibited—furniture, food vessels and wares, a bed, two mannequins (a mother and a child), clothes, agricultural implements, and basketry—were all used to construct this representation.

The second meaning of the Village appeared in the exhibition's Village-to-City narration: the Village was represented as having given rise to the City. Due to the default operation of the exhibition's built environment and its shaping of visitors' experience, the second meaning of the Village overruled the first; namely, nineteenth-century southern Guangdong Province served the purpose of giving rise to the development of the City. Thereby, the exhibition incorporated the historical time of China into the historical time of Heunggong through representing the Village as the other of the City.

In this representational opposition between Village and City, Heunggong was constructed as a natural category. It did not correspond to the present geopolitical space of Hong Kong. It could refer to Hong Kong Island alone, southern Guangdong Province prior to the formation of the New Territories, or the whole territory of Hong Kong (Hong Kong Island, Kowloon, and the

New Territories). Simultaneously, Heunggong also referred to a place that was not the same as Hong Kong, or the British crown colony. Heunggong's history went beyond that of a metropolis developed under British colonial rule. Although it was a fiction, the nineteenth-century Village of Hongkong nevertheless functioned to represent a local historical time prior to the history of British colonialism. In this way, the exhibition used the notion of Heunggong to negotiate between different modes of historical narratives.

How do we evaluate the exhibition in the scholarly debate over the problem of historical representations in Hong Kong? In an important analysis of historical narrations focusing on the meaning of the local in Hong Kong, Esther M. K. Cheung critiqued two modes of historical narration. The first mode, which she called "the epics of the imperial empire," was a monolithic discourse of modernity-as-progress: that is, colonialism as a developmental project. This lineal representation of Hong Kong history focused on Hong Kong's "capitalist success and the miraculous transformation of it from a remote fishing village to a world-class metropole." Cheung's second mode of historical representation was a kind of micro-history that went "beyond the metropolis" and supplemented the first mode of historical narration. It paid attention to "the tragic narratives of the resilient rural"—the amnesia of conflicts, tensions, and processes of domination and negotiation in the rural and everyday space of colonial Hong Kong.[60] The Story of Hong Kong exhibition basically followed the first mode of representation, while partially adopting the second mode in order to challenge Hong Kong's stereotypical image as a metropolis. However, because the exhibition could not address conflicts and tensions arising from British colonial rule, it might be viewed as an epistemological support for colonial governance.[61]

Nevertheless, this historical exhibition was part of the culture of disappearance developed in the context of the countdown in order to construct a historical time for Hongkong. The representation of the fictional nineteenth-century Village enabled the museum to negotiate between the grand narrative of Hong Kong as a successful international metropolis under British rule and the narrative of Xianggang as a purely Chinese community inseparable from the Chinese mainland. In the exhibition, Hongkong emerged as a cultural identity that was tied both to the (colonial) City and to the (Chinese) Village (the City's other).

Cultural heritage in the leased territory

The category of the village was used not only in museum exhibitions, but also in historical preservation, particularly the development of cultural "heritage." Whereas The Story of Hong Kong exhibition's notion of the village incorporated nineteenth-century Guangdong Province as part of Hong Kong's historical time without explicitly referencing China, the representation of the village in historical preservation focused on the ninety-nine years of the New Territories (1898–1997), during which the Hong Kong government transformed southern Guangdong into the rural area of Hong Kong while maintaining its ambiguous status as a territory leased from China.[62] I will address several questions: How did the Hong Kong government use the New Territories to develop a notion of "heritage" and construct a historical time for Hong Kong? What role did Hong Kong's heritage trails, especially the first heritage trail, the Pingshan Heritage Trail in the New Territories, play in historical preservation and education?[63] How did the historical interpretations constructed by local residents differ from the official ones? And how did everyday life shape the development of "heritage" as an ongoing process of negotiation?

The Antiquities and Monuments Office, a division of the Recreation and Cultural Branch of the Government Secretariat, was and is responsible for the development of Hong Kong's "heritage."[64] Its work included five aspects:

> (1) identifying, recording and researching buildings and items of historical interest; (2) organizing and coordinating surveys and excavations of areas of archaeological significance; (3) maintaining and developing archives of written and photographic material relating to these places and items; (4) organizing the protection, restoration and maintenance of monuments; and (5) fostering public awareness in Hong Kong's heritage through a series of education and publicity programs.[65]

In keeping with this mission, staff members of the office identified buildings and developed sites representative of daily life and used legislative means to register them as historic landmarks. From 1976 (when the Antiquities Office was established) to June 27, 1997 (immediately before the handover), the government declared a total of sixty-four monuments.[66]

There was a significant shift in what was designated as historic after Hong Kong entered the transition period. From 1976 to 1984, a total of twenty-nine monuments were declared: thirteen historic buildings and sixteen historic sites. In the countdown period (1985–1997), by comparison, thirty-five monuments were declared: thirty-three historic buildings but only two historic sites. This shift from sites to buildings was significant to the development of heritage. Many architectural symbols of colonialism in the Central District, such as Government House (the governor's mansion), Flagstaff House, and the Central Police Station Compound, were preserved in this period. Meanwhile, a significant number of historic buildings were located in the New Territories. Thus, in the practice of historic preservation, Hongkong's heritage included both colonial and Chinese elements. By the time the Chinese government resumed sovereignty over Hong Kong, the development of heritage had effectively preserved Hong Kong's British colonial heritage (especially in the urban context) and its ethnic Chinese heritage (in the New Territories not in China).

The official description of heritage during the transition period appeared to focus on the Chinese elements, however. According to *The Heritage of*

Hong Kong (1992), an official publication of the Antiquities and Monuments Office:

> Hong Kong's position as an international crossroads of culture, commerce and transport has given its citizens an understandable tendency to look outwards. This openness to new ideas and influences is a valuable part of our identity. But we sometimes overlook our own heritage. *The Heritage of Hong Kong* provides a flavour of the human story in the Hong Kong area. It explains how archaeologists have tried to piece together the lives of the earliest inhabitants from clues buried underground for thousands of years. It describes how the remains of Hong Hong's time as a rural backwater of imperial China can be found all over Hong Kong. And it records the reminders of Hong Kong's early beginnings as one of the most dynamic cities in Asia.[67]

From this description one might conclude that "the representation of Hong Kong as a fishing village turned modern metropolis has been replaced through the construction of a heritage with distinctive Chinese traditional characteristics."[68] This was however a misconception. In the politics of disappearance during the countdown period, neither did the declared monuments focus solely on ethnic Chinese culture, nor did the development of heritage replace the representation of Hong Kong's transformation from a fishing village to a modern city. Instead, the historical representation of Hong Kong's transformation from a village to a city always served as the background of heritage development. The quoted official description situated heritage in both colonial and Chinese history. Colonial heritage was regarded as the modernization of Hong Kong in the "international" (instead of "colonial") context. Colonialism was treated as an important heritage because it enabled the residents to develop a cultural identity of "openness to new ideas and influences." Whereas colonial heritage was represented as the default, the representation of ethnic Chinese heritage focused on the work of discovery: "people . . . want to know more about the way our ancestors lived"[69] through visiting "historic sites" and "historic buildings" in the New Territories, which used to be the "rural backwater of imperial China."

For the Hong Kong government, the development of a Hongkong heritage was critical to the (post-1997) future of Hong Kong. At the preview of the Hong Kong Heritage Painting exhibition (December 12, 1989–January 16, 1990), A. K. Chui, secretary of the Recreation and Culture Branch of the Antiquities Office, told his audience: "Our heritage is more than one of architectural relics, antiquities and the stuff of museums. It is enshrined in our very history, in our language, our arts and the customs to which we cling. We must be careful that our roots reach down through more than the insubstantial clay of memory and nostalgia. They must touch on the bedrock of what we can show and demonstrate to our children of the landmarks we have passed on our journey through time."[70] Thus, the development of Hongkong's heritage also had a pedagogical function, because historical buildings were regarded as "physical reminders of our history and our cultural heritage," that "undoubtedly help to cultivate a strong sense of belonging."[71]

The Antiquities and Monuments Office regularly organized conferences, exhibitions, and educational programs for local schools. In 1995, for example, the office collaborated with the Education Department of Hong Kong to launch a heritage education program. With the support of HK$200,000 from the Lord Wilson Heritage Trust (established in 1992), the office funded twenty projects submitted by thirteen schools to carry out extracurricular activities for learning local history. The objective of the education program was to "enhance students' interest in and concern for our cultural heritage."[72]

The office also collaborated with the Hong Kong Tourist Association (established in 1957) to develop heritage tourism. On December 12, 1993, Governor Christopher Patten officially inaugurated the Pingshan Heritage Trail, Hong Kong's first heritage trail, connecting a series of buildings owned by the Tang clan in Pingshan, the New Territories.[73] Restoration of the buildings was funded by the Royal Hong Kong Jockey Club and the Lord Wilson Heritage Trust, with support from the Tang clan. According to the Antiquities and Monuments Office, the trail "links up a number of traditional Chinese structures within easy walking distance, providing visitors with an opportunity to recapture aspects of life in the New Territories in the old days in a convenient half-day excursion."[74]

The Pingshan Heritage Trail created a theme environment showcasing Hongkong's heritage. Ordinary buildings in Pingshan were designated as historically significant to Hongkong—but only from the perspective of those living in urban Hongkong. The official operation of the trail ignored the meanings of these buildings in the local historical context. The historicized buildings included Tsui Shing Lau (Pagoda of Gathering Stars) as "Hong Kong's only historic pagoda," the Tang Ancestral Hall as "the largest ancestral hall in the territory," Sheung Cheung Wai as "a walled village," and the Kun Ting Study Hall as one "built for students preparing for the Imperial Civil Service Examination" (see Figure 6.2).[75] The spatial reorganization of ordinary buildings into a trail transformed their meaning from ordinary to markers of the heritage of Hongkong.

For example, the Kun Ting Study Hall, built around 1760, was owned by five families in the Tang clan. By the late 1980s, the building's façade was in good condition, but the interior was run down from lack of maintenance. Three of the owner families suggested tearing the building down and subdividing the land for new houses, whereas the other two wanted to keep it. They eventually agreed to restore the building with financial support from the Royal Hong Kong Jockey Club and the Lord Wilson Heritage Trust, funding contingent on the Hong Kong government receiving a degree of control over the building. In November 1986, the government classified the Kun Ting Study Hall as a "deemed monument." ("Declared monuments" are owned by the government, but deemed monuments are not.) Under the Antiquities and

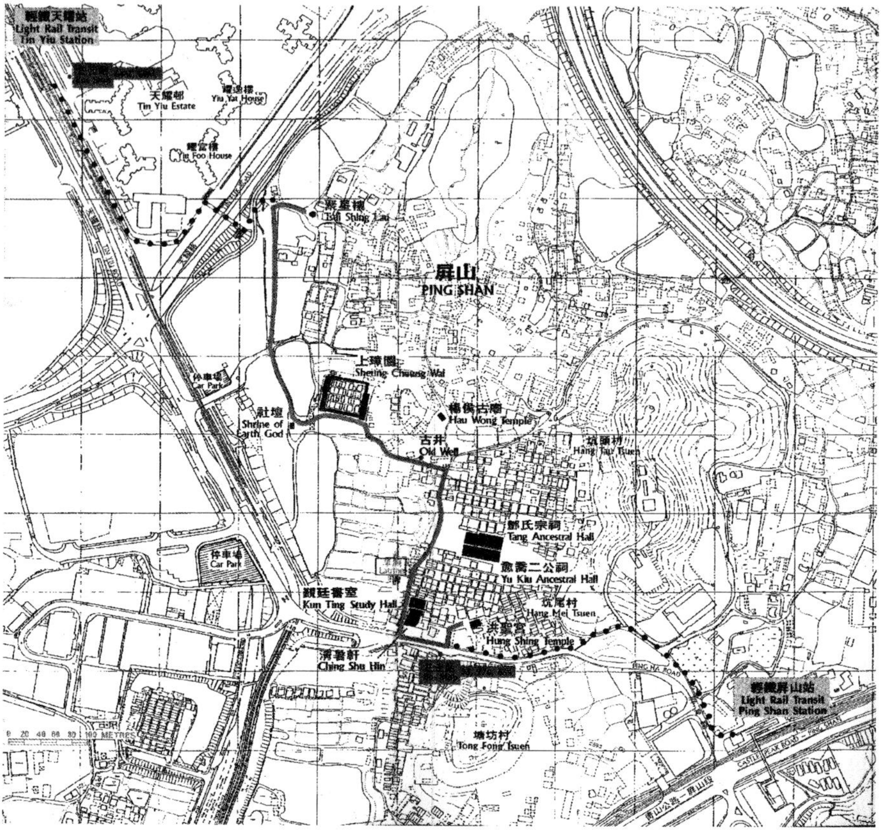

Figure 6.2 The Pingshan Heritage Trail, the New Territories, Hong Kong (from Heritage Resource Centre, Antiquities and Monuments Office, Hong Kong Government, 1993).

Monuments Ordinance, this designation meant the Tang families still owned the building but could not modify any part of it without government authorization.[76] Through the renovation and restoration of the building, completed in June 1991, the Tang families' preservation of the history and memory of the building was transformed into the development of heritage for Hongkong. By providing financial support for the restoration and preservation of old buildings, the government gained the authority to recontextualize local temples, residential buildings, ancestral halls, and study halls according to the theme of heritage, and in the process of recontextualization, it constructed a new time frame, a homogenous "monumental time" that "reduces social experience to collective predictability."[77]

The locations of the buildings structured the tour of the trail in the following order: Hung Shing Temple, Kun Ting Study Hall, Ching Shu Hin, Tang Ancestral Hall, Yu Kiu Ancestral Hall, Yeung Hau Temple, Old Well, Sheung

Cheung Wai, Shrine of the Earth God, and Tsui Shing Lau (see Figure 6.2). This ordered sequence shaped the experience of walking the trail as being thematically tied to the meaning of these buildings—at least for urban Hong Kong residents—as the heritage of Hongkong.

As a result of the development of the Pingshan Heritage Trail, Pingshan became a "heritage neighborhood," attracting tourists from both Hong Kong and other parts of the world. Tours for foreign visitors were primarily organized by the Hong Kong Tourist Association, which reports that from 1995 to 1997, an average of three thousand foreign visitors per year completed the tour. The Hong Kong tourists were primarily urban residents whose trips were organized by public housing estates, educational groups, social service institutions for the elderly and disabled, and other specialized voluntary associations. Local residents calculated that about five thousand Hong Kong visitors toured the trail every Sunday in early 1995.[78]

As a built theme environment, the heritage trail functioned as a space for sheltering or assuring a sense of self for urban residents. The urban Hong Kong residents were interested in discovering "the distinctive cultural differences between themselves, as Hongkongese (or *Heunggongyan* in Cantonese), and other Chinese people situated elsewhere."[79] As Sidney C. H. Cheung points out, "Going into the inner rural part of the New Territories is, for urban Hong Kong residents, a journey into their inner selves."[80] The search for a cultural heritage focused on "the local, rural, and pre-colonial"—exemplified by eating local food, enjoying rural scenery, and visiting villages or temples in the New Territories.[81] In the built environment of the heritage trail, urban visitors' sense of cultural heritage was reinforced not merely by the buildings themselves, but also by the information posted along the trail. A placard inside Tsui Shing Lau, for example, explained the transformation of Hong Kong as a process of urbanization: "Hong Kong's history in the past century has been one of material and social improvement: the expansion of cities and towns by cutting into demands of the growing population. The once well-planned and well-cultivated landscape of farms and villages in Pingshan has practically vanished due to the abandonment of farming and postwar development. Topographic change has been particularly rapid since the commencement of the Tin Shui Wai new town project." This information linked urban visitors' experience of living in the city to the transformation of the rural areas, thereby reassuring those who visited in search of a sense of self that they were part of the shared heritage of Hongkong.

The heritage trail's construction of a sense of belonging for urban residents was a production of history. It attempted to unify multiple sources of social time into a homogenous community time, to convert multiple types of social space into a particular place, and to group multiple kinds of people into "the people of Hongkong."[82] To ensure the smooth production of a particular kind of history, the official trail excluded anything that might embarrass the government. This was especially difficult in Pingshan, which was one of the main areas where local residents (mainly from the Tang clan) staged organized resistance to the British military takeover in 1899.[83] A placard from Pingshan at the time showed how local residents reacted to the British takeover:

> We hate the English barbarians who are about to enter our boundaries and take our land, and will cause us endless evil. Day and night we fear the approaching danger. Certainly people are dissatisfied at this and have determined to resist the barbarians. If our fire-arms are not good, we shall be unable to oppose the enemy. So we have appointed an exercise-ground and gathered all together as patriots to drill with fire-arms. To encourage proficiency rewards will be given. On the one hand we shall be helping the [Chinese] Government; on the other we shall be saving ourselves from future trouble. Let all our friends and relatives bring their fire-arms to the ground and do what they can to extirpate the traitors. Our ancestors will be pleased, and so will our neighbours. This is our sincere wish. Practice takes place every day.
>
> First prize: one gauze goat, a packet of 1,000 crackers.
>
> Second prize: one pair of brown gauze trousers, a packet of 500 crackers.
>
> Third prize: one straw hat.
>
> 17th Day 2nd Moon. 25th Year of Kwong-sui (28th March 1899).[84]

The organized resistance to the British takeover was an important chapter in the local history of Pingshan that was excluded from the official history constructed by the heritage trail. A building near the north end of the trail—the community office, used both as a base for resisting the British and as a temple for remembering those killed in the conflict—was omitted from the heritage trail. Although the building was flooded inside in 1995 (when I first visited the place), it was still in relatively good shape (see Figure 6.3). But as a symbol of resistance, it could not become part of the heritage of Hongkong. Some local residents reminded me that they still maintained an active memory of the building's function, which they shared with visitors who might be interested in an alternative history of the Pingshan Heritage Trail.

On the surface, the Tang clan's interest in preserving old buildings seemed to be a recent phenomenon stimulated by the government effort to develop a Hongkong's heritage. In practice, however, it had been part of an ongoing process of both maintaining and constructing the meaning of Pingshan as a harmonious space for the prosperity of the Tang clan. In fact, the clan was prepared to offer an interpretation of local history in opposition to the official interpretation of Hongkong's heritage. The government's development of heritage provided one means the clan could use to renovate certain old study halls, temples, and shrines. Yet, whenever possible, the clan tried to retain control over important buildings by using their own funds to restore them. For example, in 1991 the clan spent HK$4.3 million to renovate the Tang Ancestral Hall in order to maintain control over the key architectural element that determined the meaning of Pingshan.

Figure 6.3 The abandoned community office was used as a base for organizing resistance to the British takeover of Pingshan in early 1899 (photo by the author, December 1995).

With respect to the historical representation of Pingshan, on the one hand, the clan contributed to the official construction of Hongkong's heritage by cooperating fully with the Antiquities and Monuments Office to make their own properties available to the public. Local residents welcomed the heritage trail as an educational tool because the ancestors of the Tang clan had been dedicated to education, and they tolerated the inconvenience caused by inflows of visitors to the already crowded environment of Pingshan. Clan elder Tang Shing-sze told me in 1995 that sometimes he had to wait for tourists to pass along a narrow path in front of his house before opening his own front door.

On the other hand, however, the clan actively produced their own versions of local history and made them available to visitors. In 1993, the year the heritage trail opened, for example, Tang Shing-sze opened his father's and grandfather's house, in which he had been born, to visitors by appointment and without charge. This residential building was not part of the heritage trail, but was nearby. In opening his own property to the public, Tang hoped to teach them more about the Tang clan, and more important, to portray everyday family life, in contrast to the focus on the collective in the heritage trail. The well-preserved residence contained a central room, two side rooms, a room for unmarried girls, a bridal room, a grain-storage room, a grain-processing room, and a kitchen. It was built five generations, or about 160 years, ago. Tang removed some of the original furniture to other buildings he owned and rearranged the objects into an exhibition of a family's daily life.

The artifacts on display included foods, food-processing tools, clothes, furniture, an ancestral shrine, paintings, and family photos. The uses of most of the objects were explained in labels written in Chinese. He did not display everything in the house, as one label indicated: "Due to the lack of management staff, please excuse the owner for not displaying all artifacts" (my translation)—an implicit invitation for visitors to ask to see them. Sometimes, his relatives assisted with showing the house (Figure 6.4).

At his auto-ethnographic "museum," Tang Shing-sze showed the visitors all the rooms, let them walk around the house, and answered their questions. He also provided copies of a twenty-four-page Chinese-language booklet he had written on local history, titled *A Preliminary Study of Past Events in Pingshan*. It discussed the roots of the Tang clan in Pingshan, the history of

Figure 6.4 Joseph Lai Kam Tang (a relative of Tang Shing-sze) guiding a group of tourists on a tour organized by the Hong Kong Anthropological Society of old buildings owned by the Tang clan but not included in the official Pingshan Heritage Trail, December 17, 1995 (photo by the author).

immigration of Tang ancestors into the area, the reasons the clan chose to settle there, and stories about important buildings both on and off the heritage trail. In guiding visitors, Tang made sure they understood the local, historical, and political meanings of Pingshan.

On a December 17, 1995, tour, for example, Tang pointed to a painting in the central room, which portrayed the landscape of Pingshan seven hundred years ago, and explained Pingshan's meanings in terms of *fungshui* (literarily "wind and water"), or geomantic order of space.[85] The primary buildings of the heritage trail—including the Kun Ting Study Hall, Tang Ancestral Hall, Yu Kiu Ancestral Hall, Tsui Shing Lau, and Sheung Cheung Wai—were believed to form a spatial structure of self-defense and to bring protection and luck to the clan. Although constructed at different times, these architectural elements were designed to build up the energy of the physical environment of Pingshan. The whole space was organized by key built structures, including three walled villages, six non-walled villages, two ancestral halls, four temples, five shrines, and one pagoda. They were built to conform to the natural environment, which contained a large hill, two small hills, a river, and ponds. The placement of structures within the natural setting constructed Pingshan as a well-protected space. Two ancestral halls located at the center of the space were surrounded by the large hill to their back, two small hills to their right and left, and on the other sides three non-walled villages and one walled village. The natural environment formed a "Giant Crab Situation:" the major hill represented the body, and the two smaller hills symbolized its pincers. The clan believed that this space was webbed by the elements of the natural environment and the buildings intentionally arranged within it. Because of its well-balanced *fungshui*, the space brought tremendous good fortune to the clan, as shown by the many degree holders and officials to come from it. However, the *fungshui* meaning of Pingshan had been damaged by the British construction of buildings in inharmonious locations.

Whereas the official historical representation of Pingshan offered urban Hong Kong residents a "cultural heritage" that differentiated them from the people of China, Tang's interpretation explicitly referred to China.[86] A placard explained the meaning of the ancestral shrine in the central room:

> Clearly, Zhongguoren [people of China] sincerely respect their ancestors. Believing in gods and Buddhism, they always put an ancestral tablet in a supreme position . . . The most beautiful and most magnificently carved wooden sacred stool, ancestral tablet, and tin incense burner are situated most respectfully at the center of the central room. This arrangement, like anywhere else in our country, demonstrates the most important custom—the virtue of respect [my translation].

Tang used the word *Zhongguoren* (people of China) instead of *Huaren* (ethnic Chinese) or Heunggongyan, thereby linking the "culture" represented by the artifacts (the same types of artifacts used officially to represent Hongkong's heritage) to China as "our country," even though his concept of China was entirely based on the local historical condition in Pingshan. In addition to using such terms as "people of China" and "our country" at his museum, Tang also sometimes guided visitors to the abandoned community office used as a base for resisting the British in 1899 (Figure 6.3). For example, he gave a tour of the building to a famous writer from Beijing, who later published a story in which she described the building as "the most significant historical artifact" that testified to "the crime of the British—the killing of the people of China" (*Beijing Evening News*, December 6, 1996, p. 24).

Tang's interpretation of local history had implications for the operation of the heritage trail. On December 17, 1995, for example, while guiding a Hong Kong Anthropological Society organized tour, he commented on a local conflict that temporarily closed the heritage trail. Pointing to the ancestral shrine in the central room, he said in Putonghua (or Mandarin, the official language of China): "The shrine displayed here represents a kind of Chinese custom . . . Zhongguoren [people of China] sincerely respect their ancestors. The British dug out our ancestors, they maliciously insulted us . . . Because the British destroyed the collaborative foundation, we decided to close the heritage trail" (my translation). Tang's comment referred to an incident that was closely tied to the historical condition of Sino–British relations, namely, the removal of two two-hundred-year-old graves by the county government in Nimwan, Pingshan, on August 10, 1995. The graves were located in the site being developed as the West New Territories Landfill, which was supposed to meet Hong Kong's refuse disposal needs for the next twenty-five years. According to the government, excluding the gravesites from development would reduce the landfill's capacity by 30 percent, and it would cost an extra HK$1.2 billion to develop another site to make up for the lost capacity.[87]

Negotiations between the government and the clan started in 1991. In April 1995, the government offered them HK$1.7 million in compensation for the voluntary removal of the graves. The clan made a "*fungshui* exchange" counteroffer, asking the government instead to demolish the Pingshan Police Station and build a park on the site. This request had intense local significance because the clan believed that the construction of the police station on top of the large hill behind the ancestral halls was the element most damaging to the *fungshui* meaning of Pingshan. On March 28, 1898, when British Captain Superintendent of Police F. H. May had come to Pingshan to prepare for the construction of a police station on the hill, local residents had argued with him that the building would damage the *fungshui* of Pingshan. To protect Pingshan's *fungshui*, villagers rose in armed resistance over the following weeks, an act that, from the British perspective, reinforced their decision to build the police station. By April 20, Colonial Secretary Steward Lockhart informed the elders that the police station must be built "on whatever site is considered most suitable" by the British authorities.[88] Since losing this conflict more than one hundred years ago, the clan had been trying to restore the *fungshui* meaning of Pingshan. The request for the demolition of the police station was only one part of the long struggle to regain control over local *fungshui* meaning. Unfortunately, no agreement was reached.

The government ordered the clan to remove the graves by May 28, 1995, and later extended the deadline to June 30. In protest, the clan began to ban tourist groups, particularly those organized by the Hong Kong Tourist Association, from the trail. After the government unilaterally removed the ancestral tombs, the clan held a meeting on September 3, 1995, at which they decided to close the heritage trail. Tang Jun-fu, the head of the clan, made a statement regarding the closure of the trail on September 26, 1995, which was published in major newspapers on October 7, 1995. Tang argued that the government's "damaging of the ancient tombs by force maliciously destroys historical heritage, and insults the ancestors who created that historical heritage and those who fight to protect them at the present" (*Sing Tao Daily*, October 7, 1995). The clan also accused the government of breaking its promise to respect local customs of the indigenous people in the New Territories, including its intention not to remove any graves.[89] Furthermore, after consulting with China's Xinhua News Agency in Hong Kong, clan elders, including Tang Shing-sze, argued that the project should have been approved by the Chinese government before its initiation, because it would not be completed by July 1, 1997.[90]

The construction of the police station on the top of the hill behind the ancestral halls symbolized both the repression of British colonial rule and the damage to the *fungshui* meaning of Pingshan. By closing the heritage trail, the clan forced the official construction of Hongkong's heritage to address historical meanings embedded within the process of British colonization. In the context of historical production and practice before the Chinese government's resumption of sovereignty over Hong Kong, the clan's representation of the meaning of Pingshan exposed the limitations of the development of an artificial cultural heritage for urban Hong Kong residents, a project that both treated the rural areas of the New Territories as the other of the City and excluded any local histories that would embarrass the Hong Kong government.

Conclusion: Historical representations and public feelings about the future

Historical representations in Hong Kong in the transition period contributed to the development of both museums and a Hongkong culture. Early exhibitions in Hong Kong drew on both trade shows and the governance of everyday life. Hong Kong's manufacturing industry regularly used trade shows as an important means for promoting products and commodities made in Hong Kong. By the late 1960s, cultural exhibitions also became a regular part of Hong Kong residents' daily lives. In this context, the Hong Kong government institutionalized museums as a "public health" measure. During the transition period, museums began to play an important role in representing Hong

Kong's history. Not only were more museums established, but their capacity for representing history was also increased. The collections of the Hong Kong Museum of History were expanded significantly to preserve local historical materials, its gallery space was enlarged several times to fulfill the museum's role in educating the public about local history, and modern exhibition design techniques were also used to build exhibitions appropriate to Hong Kong's status as an international metropolis. All these developments were evident in the museum's development of the Story of Hong Kong, the territory's most important public display of Hong Kong's history. Meanwhile, historical preservation and education also played important roles. Through official designation, a significant number of ordinary buildings and sites were transformed into "historic buildings" and "historic sites." Furthermore, the Pingshan Heritage Trail, along with other heritage trails, linked selected historic buildings and sites in a walking trail for the purpose of telling a particular story about Hong Kong's cultural heritage.

Historical representations in the transitional period encoded Hong Kong's history in a particular way to construct a cultural identity of Hongkong. The encoding of Hongkong addressed three types of public feelings about China's resumption of sovereignty over Hong Kong. The first type related to the historical role of Britain in Hong Kong. Although the Basic Law legally ensured that Hong Kong would maintain its own system from 1997 to 2046, it did not specify whether that system would be the one developed under British rule. The Chinese government's resumption of sovereignty would definitely entail a process of decolonization in Hong Kong. For these reasons, the preservation of British influences was more than a matter of declaring buildings and sites associated with the colonial period to be historical monuments. It was also a process of representing the historical achievements of Hong Kong under British rule; namely, Hong Kong's evolution from a fishing village to an international metropolis. For example, the Story of Hong Kong exhibition highlighted Hong Kong's unique position in the global economy in the fields of finance, trade, telecommunications, and shipping, as well as the city's achievements in the areas of housing, reservoirs, land reclamation, recreation, education, telecommunications, transportation, reindustrialization, shipping, aviation, and political reforms. Thus, the representation of Hong Kong as a major international city in the global economy was inseparable from the representation of its people as having a successful way of life.

Moreover, the encoding of Hongkong as a culture had to address public feelings about the role of China in Hong Kong. Clearly, the Chinese state was always present in Hong Kong, and during the transition period, it became increasingly influential through organizations and companies connected to China, like China Travel Service (as discussed in the previous chapter). With respect to historical representations in the context of museums and historic preservation projects, China was represented as part of Hong Kong's historical present, but only as Hong Kong's "other." China's otherness meant that

China was not treated as a contemporary of Hong Kong; the two did not exist in the same temporal space.[91]

The village-to-city relationship was the foundation for the historical representation in the Story of Hong Kong exhibition. The portrayal of the village as the city's other via the chronological and spatial arrangement of exhibits was crucial to representing colonial Hong Kong's achievement as an international metropolis. Because the village's portrayal was based on the rural areas of southern Guangdong Province in nineteenth-century China, the representation of the village as the city's "other" incorporated the time of imperial China. Yet the village was never acknowledged as a representation of China. In this sense, the exhibition constructed a historical time of Hongkong by displacing a culture of China to Hong Kong.

In the Pingshan Heritage Trail, the New Territories were never acknowledged as a leased territory of China, but instead treated merely as a cultural reservoir for constructing a cultural heritage for the city. The representation of the New Territories (rural areas of Hong Kong) as the city's "other" in historical preservation affected everyday life in Pingshan. Heritage development used architecture as a kind of medium for storing historical memories. The linkage of ordinary buildings in Pingshan into a heritage trail transformed Pingshan into a built theme environment, where tourists experienced the buildings as the cultural heritage of Hongkong and residents negotiated the official meaning of the trail. The representation of the New Territories as the cultural heritage of urban residents excluded historical artifacts that, despite being important to the history of the place, might contradict the identity claims of urban residents or embarrass the government. This exclusion operated similarly to the treatment of nineteenth-century rural China in the Story of Hong Kong. The heritage trail also contributed to the construction of a historical time of Hongkong by incorporating a culture of China into Hong Kong, not as a contemporary but as a belated other.

Finally, the development of Hongkong as a culture had to confront public feelings of uncertainty about Hong Kong's future during the time of the Hong Kong Special Administrative Region from 1997 to 2046. One of the most common expressions during the transition period, "Hong Kong's future will be brighter," said nothing about its uncertain future. The concluding panel in the Story of Hong Kong exhibition reminded visitors of Hong Kong's uncertain status. This can be shown by a comparison of the English-language panel versus the Chinese one. According to the English text:

> With the signing of the Joint Declaration by China and the United Kingdom in 1984, China will resume sovereignty over Hong Kong on 1 July 1997. Hong Kong is now entering a new chapter in her history. *We believe that Hong Kong will become even more prosperous if all her citizens can maintain that dedicated and hardworking spirit*. (My emphasis)

And the Chinese version reads:

> With the signing of the Joint Declaration by China and the United Kingdom in 1984, China will resume sovereignty over Hong Kong on 1 July 1997. Hong Kong is now entering a new chapter in her history. *We believe that Hong Kong residents will overcome various difficulties to make Hong Kong more prosperous and stronger if they can maintain their dedicated and hardworking spirit.* (My translation and emphasis)

The Chinese version clearly indicates that China's resumption of sovereignty over Hong Kong could bring about a series of difficulties for the region.

Understandably, Hong Kong residents feared that the future HKSAR government would strip away their way of life. The Hong Kong way of life developed historically out of shared experiences of emigrating from China to escape political turmoil and natural disasters, to search for a better life, and to live in a capitalist society, but was also based on the formation of a bourgeois, middle-class identity supported by the rapid development of consumer culture since the late 1960s.[92] This Hong Kong way of life was reinforced through highlighting differences between the Hongkongese and the Mainlanders, between the Heunggongyan and the Dailuyan (Cantonese for Mainlanders), or simply between "we" and "they" in the everyday context of Hong Kong. In the transition period, the differences were often characterized in terms of two distinct lifestyles. The Heunggongyan way of life was associated with comfort, luxury, and style, and the Dailuyan way of life with poverty, hardship, and dullness.[93] In 1989, on witnessing live television broadcasts of the violent repression of the student demonstrations by the People's Liberation Army, Hong Kong residents further distrusted the Chinese government's willingness to accommodate their different lifestyle. Thus, the construction of a historical time of Hongkong through historical representations in museum exhibitions and historic preservation projects was part of the process of building up a cultural system that would allow the Hong Kong residents to preserve their middle-class lifestyle. In this context, the production of history became an important means for coping with an uncertain future by creating memories that would endure in post-1997 Hong Kong.

Conclusion

Is China truly neoliberal, or a state with neoliberal characteristics?

Since the late 1970s when the Chinese government began its economic reforms and initiated diplomatic negotiations with Britain to seek a resolution to the Hong Kong question, China has steadily become more neoliberal. Over the years, popular and official discourses inside and outside the country have referred to China as "socialist with Chinese characteristics," "communist China," or simply "changing China." None of these designations accurately characterizes China, especially in terms of its relations to the rest of the world, so in this book, I have chosen to refer to China as a "neoliberal state" to reflect on its past and future. Following and extending neoliberalism, an economic-political philosophy that has become dominant in capitalist globalization since the 1970s, and operating through the project of national reunification with Hong Kong beginning in the late 1970s, this Chinese state shows several major characteristics: the critical role of the state in normalizing neoliberalism, the constructivist practice of neoliberalism, and neoliberal citizenship. Governmental and social policies implement neoliberalism as a constructionist project by expanding the logic of economic rationales to politics, society, culture, and all aspects of human life. The practice of neoliberalism would not be possible without the state. By reinventing a new politics of the state to create and improve institutional frameworks appropriate to neoliberalism, the government intervenes and orchestrates the normalization of neoliberalism.

China's transformation into a neoliberal state has been expressed through two closely related processes. Through a series of governmental decisions (see the Introduction), the Chinese government completely rejected the political significance formerly attached to the Cultural Revolution, thereby shifting the Maoist (state) politics of socialism as a political system to the Dengist (state) politics of socialism as an administrative system. Over the years, this change has been justified by various discourses about "economic reforms," "modernizations," "development as an undisputable truth," "a relatively well-off society," and "synchronization with the world." The constitutions of both the Chinese Communist Party (now the Communist Party of China) and the People's Republic of China have been modified to treat socialism as only one of the legitimate administrative systems. Today, the political status of the Communist Party of China has shifted from being a "revolutionary party" (*geming dang*) in Maoist China or an "underground party" (*dixia dang*) in pre-1949 China and pre-1997 Hong Kong to becoming the "ruling party" (*zhizheng dang*) of China.[1] If the official term "socialism with Chinese characteristics" has any meaning in China today, it actually refers to Dengist socialism with neoliberal characteristics.

This reinvented politics of the state, that is, of the shift of socialism from a state political system to an administrative system, would have been impossible without the parallel process of national reunification, which began with the reunification with Hong Kong, one of the freest capitalist economies in the world. To achieve complete national unification or "full sovereignty" (*zhuquan wanzheng*) over lost geopolitical spaces such as Hong Kong, Macau, and Taiwan, the Chinese government strategically determined that the future of China was a country with two administrative systems (socialism and capitalism). Hong Kong's return to China became the important historical event that created a necessary condition for the realization of this new national state configuration. The Sino–British Joint Declaration in 1984 formalized the "one country, two systems" principle as an international agreement. Not only did it offer a road map for the Chinese government's resumption of sovereignty over Hong Kong in 1997, but it also has far-reaching long-term effects. Not unlike the treaties China signed with Western powers in the nineteenth century, including those regulating the historical formation of the Hong Kong territories, this agreement entails changes in sovereignty that make exception function as the norm. One fundamental change was the incorporation of capitalism, an exception to the Maoist socialist state, into the Chinese state, making capitalism a legitimate administrative system. This change was so decisive that it practically suspended socialism as the *only* legitimate administrative system. During Hong Kong's return process, the principle of "one country, two systems" was implemented as the governing logic for transforming China from a socialist to a neoliberal state. Thus, the cultural changes in China and Hong Kong discussed in the book are not just about the countdown to Hong Kong's return to China, but more important, about the countdown to the formation of a neoliberal Chinese state. By the time the Chinese government resumed sovereignty over Hong Kong, the Chinese state had transformed itself culturally, economically, and politically into a neoliberal state.

This appearance of the Chinese neoliberal state became accelerated through the development of an affective economy of the countdown. The establishment of the Hong Kong countdown clock at Tiananmen Square was incidental and not unprecedented.[2] Nevertheless, it was an immediate success, effectively functioning as the master timepiece that synchronized all the activities explicitly or implicitly concerning Hong Kong's return, not only in China but also in Hong Kong. In a significant departure from a traditional clock, which is a mechanical device with a linear temporal logic, the Hong Kong clock with its multimedia technology evoked a temporal logic of multiplicity. The multiplicity-based logic expanded beyond the countdown to facilitate the communication of public feelings about Hong Kong's return to China. In China, these feelings concerned the historical effects of the unequal treaties it had been forced to sign with Britain that had created the territory of Hong Kong in the nineteenth century. These public feelings were commonly characterized by the government as "national humiliations," "national pains," "national shames," and "national disasters." The clock's nonlinear, multiplicity-based temporal logic allowed both the general public and the government to talk about these feelings in new ways that situated them in the new context of "national revitalization" associated with China's current economic success and the recovery of Hong Kong. That is, at the level of public communication or the spectacle, the countdown clock's multiplicity-based time enabled a creative fix to the political memory of socialist China, which became problematic during Hong Kong's return. Meanwhile, for Hong Kong, the countdown's main problem during the transition period was to address public feelings regarding the uncertainty of the territory's post-1997 future. Although the Basic Law formally codified the principle of "one country, two systems", legally guaranteeing that Hong Kong's capitalist system would endure, it said nothing about whether the mainland would develop a compatible capitalist system. Part of the post-1997 uncertainty related to preservation of the people's civil liberties, but there was also anxiety about whether Hong Kong could maintain a distinct economic system and how that system would interface with the evolving system on the mainland.

Both Hong Kong and China engaged in cultural productions to effectively narrate how Hong Kong and China were historically unique, and thus manifested visions of the future "one country, two systems." Among the cultural and media products and symbols that proliferated during the transition period, cultural representations in museums and heritage preservation and development played critical roles. Exhibitions at the Hong Kong Museum of History and government-sponsored development of cultural heritage, for example, contributed to the representation of Hong Kong's way of life as distinct from the mainland's through a cultural politics of disappearance. Urban-based identities were privileged over rural-based ones because the former were associated with the development of Hong Kong as an international metropolis under British rule whereas the latter were associated with the mainland—not only as the "backward" past of the now-successful capitalist Hong Kong but also as the "other" of the future Hong Kong. Inside the mainland, exhibitions at the National Museum of Chinese Revolution, the leading institution for standardizing the history of modern China, represented Hong Kong's return as the end of the colonial period associated with the loss of Hong Kong to Britain in the nineteenth century, and as the incident that discursively helped the CCP to establish its legitimate rule of the country in the second half of the twentieth century. The disappearance of colonial time was celebrated neither because remnants of colonialism and imperialism were no longer present in China nor because patriotic education had stopped considering the impacts of colonialism and imperialism in China, as shown by the case of Yuanming Yuan. Rather, the representation of the idea of "one country, two systems" reconfigured China's historical time: The end of colonial/imperial time was no longer represented as a revolutionary struggle, the solution to the contradictions between socialism and capitalism, but as a success in terms of harmony, the peaceful reconciliation of all differences between the two systems. Therefore, during the transition period, cultural representations presented post-1997 China as two different spectacles: Hong Kong as a capitalist system with a culture and way of life radically different from the mainland's, and China as a nation state capable of accommodating all differences, including capitalist and socialist administrative systems.

In Hong Kong, cultural representations and political practices were situated in Hong Kong's neoliberal economy, often recognized as an outstanding model in contemporary global capitalism.[3] The Hong Kong Museum of History hired a Canadian firm to design its permanent exhibition, The Story of Hong Kong, the largest and most important exhibition of Hong Kong's history. In its storyline, colonial Hong Kong was understandably represented as having successfully developed its economy and economic activities. In the historic preservation and development arena, heritage became an important part of Hong Kong's tourist industry, playing a significant role in Hong Kong's continued economic development. In addition, the Hong Kong government's policies generally focused on the promotion and advancement of the neoliberal economy. The continuation of Hong Kong's economic development, that is, the maintenance of its economic prosperity, an imperative established in the Sino–British Joint Declaration, became one of the most important criteria for legitimizing governmental politics. Many attempts at governmental reforms and political struggles took place in response to the fears generated by the Chinese government's repressions of social movements in China in 1989. Christopher Patten, the last British governor of Hong Kong, tried to reverse Britain's longstanding policy of discouraging Hong Kong's development of a democratically elected representative government. His reforms failed not simply because they betrayed the Sino–British Joint Declaration but because they did not adequately address the fundamental problem of safeguarding the future of Hong Kong's neoliberal economy. By comparison, Hong Kong-based Chinese state-owned organizations were successful in showcasing the appearance of the Chinese state through their participation in shaping Hong Kong's public culture and everyday life. Chinese Travel Service's participation in the Hong Kong Dance Festival was just one example of the Chinese state's manifestation in pre-1997 Hong Kong through transnational practices of capitalism. Thus, it was within the context of the neoliberal transnational economy that two different entities, Hong Kong and China, could coexist in pre-1997 Hong Kong.

In China, the government itself was reorganized according to economic rationales rather than revolutionary ideals. Like the imperative to maintain Hong Kong's economy, the health and growth of the Chinese economy also became a legitimacy issue for the Chinese government. The impressive growth of China's gross domestic product and foreign direct investments during this period were merely indicators of the health of the Chinese economy. The close relationship between the economy and governance lay in the reorganization of state-owned organizations through "industrialization" (*chanyehua*) and "internationalization" (*guojihua*), two major trends that emerged during the transition period. The development of private property through such processes as the privatization of some state-owned enterprises, especially those that could not operate efficiently in the market economy, and the privatization of housing in cities has been well documented by scholars.[4] Cultural institutions such as museums and exhibition halls became "industrialized" to operate in the market economy. The theme park (or broadly speaking, the built theme environment) emerged as a new model by which museums could not only reform themselves from "cultural institutions" (*wenhua jigou*) to "cultural enterprises" (*wenhua chanye*), but also participate in a new communication-based economy. Yuanming Yuan, for example, was operated both as a site for moral education and as a built theme environment for tourist consumption. China Travel Service, a Hong Kong-based, Chinese state-owned transnational corporation, pioneered the establishment of theme parks as a model for producing capitalist spaces within China, such as the Overseas Chinese Town and the Shenzhen Special Economic Zone. Splendid China, China Folk Culture Villages, and Window on the World, theme parks in Shenzhen developed by China Travel Service, were business enterprises even though their focus was cultural representations, especially of ethnic minorities in China and foreign cultures around the world. These theme parks were created as capitalist spaces, staging multicultural spectacles for profit purposes. The business experiences and skills developed in the operation of these built theme environments have transferred to various real estate projects across the country, fueling real estate development to become one of the fastest growing and the most profitable sectors of the Chinese economy.[5]

In addition to transforming state-owned cultural institutions into economic enterprises, the neoliberal reconfiguration of the Chinese government has permitted some state-owned organizations to grow into super-firms that combine both the state's governmental power and the state's economical operations. Even the National Museum of Chinese Revolution has been reorganized as part of the new National Museum of China in a manner similar to a business conglomerate. Not only does this reorganization reflect the general process of reforming state-owned museums and similar institutions in China, but it also has dropped *revolution* from the museum's name, downgrading the relevance of "revolution" in the neoliberal age. Meanwhile, China Travel Service, a transnational corporation, acted as a super agent of the Chinese state in both Hong Kong and Shenzhen Special Economic Zone. Through its transnational business operations, the company effectively transgressed normative spaces to create sovereign spaces of exception that were not regulated by existing norms and rules: Socialist China was initiated as an exceptional space within British-ruled Hong Kong, and capitalist spaces modeled after Hong Kong were developed within socialist China. This spatial manifestation of the "one country, two systems" principle was modeled on the way the company created and operated its theme built environments.

With respect to citizenship, the normalization of neoliberalism through spectacles of the countdown also prompted individual citizens to conduct their lives according to such economic ideals as calculation, efficiency, and profit-oriented success. Both museum galleries and the built environments of theme parks and heritage communities were carefully designed and planned to construct particular narratives about Hong Kong's return. Whether at the National Museum of Chinese Revolution, the Ruins Park of Yuanming Yuan, or the built theme environments in Hong Kong and Shenzhen, cultural and historical representations were staged to frame Hong Kong's return as spectacles. Visitors developed individual understandings and expressions of Hong Kong's return through consuming these spectacles via various interactions, which were deliberately guided by the way these environments were structured. As shown by cases like a visitor's hawking of his patriotic T-shirts at the National Museum of Chinese Revolution, Hong Kong's return provided an average Chinese citizen with invaluable opportunities to interpret making money and being economically successful as an important virtue of citizenship. The T-shirt seller exemplifies the way a neoliberal citizen conducts his or her life: Rather than abiding by existing norms and/or rules, the neoliberal citizen calculates the costs and benefits of transgressing them to gain economic success, in the same way as a state-owned super firm like China Travel Service transgressed norms and rules.[6]

Moreover, the affective economy of the countdown normalized the practice of "do-it-yourself," or entrepreneurial, life-making and life-building. Chinese citizens used the Tiananmen countdown clock, or made their own clocks, to synchronize their lives with Hong Kong's return. Not only did they accept the countdown clock as a time-telling device, but they also treated the countdown as an everyday technology of the self in making and building their lives. Years after Hong Kong's return in 1997, many still use the countdown as an important register of their lives. Bloggers on the Internet commonly recall such personal events as graduating from high school, taking college entry exams, falling in love, getting married, giving birth to a child, starting a private business, or building their first website relative to the timing of the countdown.[7] For these bloggers, who are reasonably successful in managing their lives, the countdown to Hong Kong's return is much more than a "memory" (*jiyi*); it continues to be an important marker of taking personal responsibility for building one's life as an entrepreneurial individual.

In summary, the countdown to Hong Kong's return to China enabled the appearance of the Chinese neoliberal state. The multimedia countdown clock made multiplicity-based temporal logic workable. The practice of this temporally displaced linearity—where the temporal modality of the surface displaced that of the line, as Vilém Flusser would argue[8]—made it possible to recalculate the colonial, socialist, and capitalist periods of modern Chinese history. The coexistence of Hong Kong and China as separate entities under the sovereign imperative of national unification became the coexistence between capitalism and socialism precisely because of the use of multiplicity (rather than linearity) in configuring the new historical time of the nation.[9] Moreover, the affective economy of the countdown enabled expressions of public feelings about the past to be refocused on the successful experience of China's synchronization with neoliberal globalization since the 1970s. The national melancholy associated with Western colonialism and imperialism since the first Opium War in 1840 was substituted with consumer spectacles. This discursive shift took place via the transformation of state-owned cultural institutions into cultural enterprises in the spatial model of "one country, two systems." Finally, while reconfiguring the government according to economic rationales, the countdown also cultivated entrepreneurialism as the ideal model of citizenship for a future China. Hong Kong's return to China became actively managed as a significant deadline for building one's individual life. In this way of life, individualization—giving up the standard life path planned by the government under socialism in favor of choosing one's own life path—took the direction of individuals making strategic cost–benefit calculations, rather than abiding by the rules, with being economically competitive and successful as the ultimate goal.

Synchronization with neoliberal China: "One World, One Dream?"

The countdown as an effective technology of synchronization has continued to play a critical role in spectacles of economic development. The countdown to the Beijing Olympics in 2008 is the most recent example of the ongoing cultural practice of synchronization. It follows the same four trajectories established and normalized by the Hong Kong countdown. First, just like the Hong Kong countdown, the Olympics countdown is a communication-based public relations campaign aimed at promoting China's relation to the rest of the world in a particular way through spectacles. After the Olympics countdown clock was erected in Tiananmen Square (the same location where the Hong Kong countdown clock used to be) on September 21, 2004, the Olympics countdown gradually took on the full force of realizing what the Chinese government calls "China's century-long Olympic dream."[10] On June 26, 2006, the Chinese organizing committee, after carefully screening more than 200,000 messages from all over the world, unveiled the slogan for the Beijing Olympic and the Beijing Paralympic Games: "One World One Dream" (*tong yige shijie tong yige mengxiang*).[11] By the end of the countdown, on August 8, 2008, Zhang Yimou, one of the country's most celebrated film directors, put on a lavish opening ceremony in front of the global audience to showcase "China" through artifacts and performances. This is similar to the effective way in which the English businessman Danton, in the 1997 film

Opium War, which I discussed in the beginning of this book, uses bronze-ware, jade and porcelain vases to represent China before the British Parliament. Compared with the vulnerable and fragile image of China in *Opium War*, Zhang's creative deployment of cinema, architecture, and computer technology represents China as a magnificent *brand*, historically enduring, aesthetically creative, and economically successful.[12] All kinds of spectacles have been developed to communicate the theme through such media as newspaper, television, film, music, and the Internet.

Moreover, like Hong Kong's return to China, the Olympics countdown itself is an economic process in which advertising appropriates the established theme in various ways through innovative media spectacles. Major companies such as Coca-Cola, McDonald's, Lenovo, Johnson & Johnson, China Unicom (a major mobile phone network), and the Yili Group (China's largest dairy company), spend billions of dollars on Olympics-related advertising. China is on its way to replacing the United States in 2008 as the biggest source of growth in global advertising spending.[13] With respect to the event itself, the Chinese government spent more than $40 billion, a new record for a host country. This figure would be appropriately included in "Go World," the main advertising theme of Visa, the world's largest credit card processing company, during the Olympics.

Next, the use of the countdown clock means that the countdown itself offers a technology for managing time efficiently and at a seemingly accelerated speed through foregrounding the date of this important event. The government used the occasion of exactly two years remaining before the Olympics opening ceremonies to address to the importance of raising the *suzhi* (quality) of Beijing residents so that that they would be ready to show the best of the host country to the rest of the world.[14] The celebration of the one-year countdown on August 8, 2007, coincided with launching a campaign entitled "We Are Ready," addressing upgrades to the environment (e.g. air quality), transportation, facilities, and organization. To improve air quality, for example, the Beijing Municipal Government has regulated the number of cars allowed on the roads.[15] The countdown clock's emphasis on deadlines heightens temporal consciousness, often reminding its viewers of how fast time flies, not just in terms of the Olympics but also in everyday life (birthdays, graduations, vacations, and work).[16] During the opening ceremony, the countdown of the final seconds became incorporated into the performance of the spectacular China brand; it became a globally shared moment of the Olympics experience.

Finally, like the Hong Kong countdown, the Olympics countdown promotes the association of economic success and reward with competition. The term *Olympics* has become a floating signifier that has moved far beyond the meaning of physical competition in sports to encompass a range of competitions, from commerce to arts, from national rituals to everyday life. All these competitions are closely tied to the promotion of spectacles. Many contemporary Chinese artists, for example, compete in an "art Olympics" (*yishu de aulinpike*), meaning their goal in their artistic production is to garner the highest price on the international art market.[17] In advertising, Coca-Cola's campaign focuses on "*shuang* (literally, "cool"), a kind of "physical, emotional and spiritual refreshment;" Johnson & Johnson's campaign centers on "the spirit of winning . . . infused with the warmth" of its products; Lenovo promotes "responsibility" associated with "success;" and General Electric captures "imagination at work." The advertising slogan of Anta Sports Products is "forget yourself:" "from sweat, talent and hard work, glory emerges."[18] These campaigns link business to athletic competition to promote consumption as one of the rewards of competition.

Through these four interrelated strategies (communication-based public relations campaign, advertising-centered economy, use of countdown clocks, and competitive success), the Olympics countdown synchronizes activities around a shared theme to transcend differences and generate public feelings about the upcoming event. Where the Hong Kong countdown addressed the relationship between China and Hong Kong, the Olympics countdown deals with China's relationship with the rest of the world. The organizing committee states, " 'One World One Dream' fully reflects the essence and the universal values of the Olympic spirit—Unity, Friendship, Progress, Harmony, Participation and Dream. It expresses the common wishes of people all over the world, inspired by the Olympic ideals, to strive for a bright future for Mankind. In spite of the differences in colors, languages and races, we share the charm and joy of the Olympic Games, and together we seek for the ideal of Mankind at peace. We belong to the same world and we share the same aspirations and dreams."[19] As the whole world zoomed in on China during the Games, the "one world, one dream" slogan appeared in news media around the world. *The Arizona Daily Star*, an English-language newspaper in Tucson, Arizona, for example, printed the slogan both in English and Chinese in its sports section. At the closing ceremony, the Mayor of Beijing handed the Olympic flag over to the Mayor of London, the host city of the 2012 Olympics. One of the hosts of NBC, the television network that provided the only live broadcasting in the United States, was telling the audience that this resembled the Hong Kong handover ceremony in 1997. If this scene symbolizes a handover, what is its content? Speaking live from London, Michael Phelps, the American swimmer who won the record number of gold medals in Beijing, told his television audiences that his "dream" came true in Beijing and he looked forward to realizing the same dream in London in 2012.

Like Phelps, observers around the world are cautiously wondering: Will Britain synchronize itself with the world through the preparations of the next Olympics? Will the British host the Games in a way comparable with the expectations created by the Chinese?[20] As suggested by these questions, "one world, one dream" is clearly not merely the slogan of the 2008 Olympics but also a vision of the global future China wants the rest of the world to embrace. The fact that "one world, one dream" is being implemented following the countdown strategy established in the process of China's neoliberalization raises an important question: Does "one world, one dream" in fact mean one world with one neoliberal dream? If so, whose version of the neoliberal dream may capture the audiences around the globe?

In recent years, people around the world—from businesspeople to politicians, ordinary people to scholars—have begun to consider whether China's increasing international importance suggests a global future that might parallel China's development over the past three decades. Scholars speculate on China as a future model of the nation state. In the post-Cold War era, the world's future has been dominated by the hegemonic expansion of the American way of life in the name of liberty. The Washington Consensus became the concrete expression of the world's future, as countries in Latin America, Eastern Europe, and Asia were forced to adopt it as a condition of receiving international economic aid.[21] However, rising worldwide waves of resistance to American-led globalization have darkened the prospects for the American way as the world way of the future. Moreover, the Bush administration's unilateral decisions in the "war on terror" have systematically undermined the cultural foundation of the alliance the United States had built with Western Europe in the Cold War era.[22] As the world moves away from the version of liberty promised by the United States, it opens to other versions of the future.[23]

The successful formation and expansion of the European Union (EU) in the post-Cold War era suggests one alternative that some scholars have advocated following. According to U.S. futurist Jeremy Rifkin, the "European dream" has quietly eclipsed the "American dream" to lay out "a visionary road map to a new promised land, one dedicated to reaffirming the life instinct and the Earth's indivisibility."[24] As "[m]uch of the world is going dark, leaving many human beings without clear direction," he argues, "[t]he European Dream is a beacon of light in a troubled world. It beckons us to a new age of inclusivity, diversity, quality of life, deep play, sustainability, universal human rights, the rights of nature, and peace on Earth."[25] British diplomat Robert Cooper, a special adviser on security to former Prime Minister Tony Blair and later to Romano Prodi (former head of the European Commission), the EU's future is best characterized as "the postmodern state" operated as a "cooperative empire," in which a "voluntary movement of self-imposition" takes place because the empire offers "unilateral free-market access" to all of its members, just as the EU did, especially to those countries that did not have the "free market" system.[26] The expansion of this European dream, as Perry Anderson argues, is in fact itself a neoliberal process. In the expansion of the "free market" to Eastern Europe, transnational companies based in Western Europe have deployed cheaper labor in and from Eastern Europe, thereby strategically reducing labor costs in Western Europe (for example, through lower salaries, fewer benefits, and longer working hours).[27] In the neoliberal context, modeling the world's future after the EU means that a transnational market system will operate as a political super-system that displaces the democratic political systems of individual nation states. Members of the super system would voluntarily adopt policies of the sort that currently are debated in national legislatures but would in future be decided by those who control the political super-system.

China also emerges as an alternative for the global future. In 2004, the Foreign Policy Centre, a London-based think tank published a long essay entitled "The Beijing Consensus" written by Joshua Cooper Ramo, managing partner in the office of John L. Thornton, senior advisor to Goldman Sachs, professor at Tsinghua University, and the China analyst during NBC's live broadcasting of the Beijing Olympics. Ramo argues the "Beijing consensus" represents a new model for world development. It is based on innovation-led growth, the management of chaos (such as social disorder and environmental problems), and national self-determination. Ramo explains the significance of this model: "Rather than building a US-style power, bristling with arms and intolerant of other world views, China's emerging power is based on the example of their own model, the strength of their economic position and their rigid defense of the Westphalian system of national sovereignty."[28] Some Chinese scholars further argue that if the Washington Consensus creates the imperative of a systematic transition to the market economy, the "Chinese consensus" lays out a "practical road map" for that transition.[29]

This model of "globalization with Chinese characteristics"[30] has been highly praised by neoliberal theorists. In an interview with *New Perspectives Quarterly* in early 2006, Friedman argues that we now live in a "freer world" because of "the changes in China," a main contributor "to freedom in our time . . . Everyone, everywhere, now understands that the road to success for underdeveloped countries is free markets and globalization."[31] By "the changes in China," Friedman is referring to what Hong Kong has done for China: "The success of laissez-faire in Hong Kong was a major factor in encouraging China and other countries to move away from centralized control toward greater reliance on private enterprise and the free market . . . The ultimate fate of China depends . . . on whether it continues to move in Hong Kong's direction faster than Hong Kong moves in China's."[32] Thus, Friedman argues, for China to offer a viable vision of the global future, it must continue down the neoliberal path it embarked on during Hong Kong's return.

Despite taking Friedman's suggestions about economic reforms (see the introduction) and pursuing an efficient neoliberalization, the Chinese government does not use the term "neoliberalism" to characterize China's globalizing experience because it intentionally differentiates the Chinese model from the Washington Consensus, to which the term "neoliberalism" commonly refers. In 2009, to celebrate the sixtieth anniversary of the founding of the People's Republic of China, major government organizations such as the China Central Television (CCTV), the Xinhua News Agency, and *The People's Daily*, all of which are the *de facto* "properties" of the Communist Party of China,[33] launched a major media campaign to promote the idea of "China's model" (*zhongguo moshi*) of national development.[34] They advocated such terms as "China's road" (*zhongguo daolu*), "China's experience" (*zhongguo jingyan*), "China's miracle" (*zhongguo qiji*), and "China's time" (*zhongguo shijian*). These expressions acknowledged various warm and positive receptions of the Chinese model by foreign leaders and scholars. Quoting a "Harvard Business School professor" and "an expert on Chinese political economy," for example, a report claims that the American scholar argues that the practices based on "China's model" represent three major interventions in the understanding of the ways in which the economy operates: It "overthrows" (*dianfu*) "the conventional view that public owned enterprises are inefficient and ineffective," "the perception that a new rising superpower ought to become a war-loving aggressive state," and "the presumption that economic development ultimately leads to Western style democracy."[35] Within the context of celebrating the country's sixtieth anniversary, such a representation was part of the official media's public relations campaign to highlight the Communist Party's critical role in "representing the fundamental interests of the people," its capacity for deploying national resources to avoid economic crisis, and its "unique creation" (*duchuang*) of a "universal" (*pu shi de*) model of development.[36]

Strategically using such terms as "China's model," "China's road," and "China's time" to convey a sense of the global future closely associated with the Chinese state that has emerged as a global power in the past three decades, the media campaign avoided the term "neoliberalism" and instead emphasized China as exceptional. As I have argued in this book, the enactment of exception is critical to neoliberal sovereignty. Without deploying the sovereign power of exception in national reunification, the Chinese government could not possibly have legitimized the incorporation of capitalism into the Chinese state. The current media campaign to normalize China's status in the world raises many new questions about exception. For example, how will the normalization of this new Chinese exception become implemented around the globe during crises, especially those perceived as caused by the Washington Consensus model?[37] Since 1997, the Chinese state has taken advantage of international economic crises to establish, improve, or re-establish its relations to the people in China (the mainland, Hong Kong, and Macau), the people in Taiwan, overseas Chinese, as well as non-Chinese audiences around the world. The 1997 Asian financial crisis, for example, not only weakened Hong Kong's economy (falling stock and property prices, and a sharp rising unemployment rate) but also extended the sense of "crisis" associated with Hong Kong's return to China (lack of confidence in the newly established Hong Kong Special Administrative Region government). Confronting this situation, the Hong Kong and the Chinese governments reached new agreements to create closer economic ties between Hong Kong and the mainland. Consequently, as Stephen Chiu and Tai-Lok Lui argue, Hong Kong's "struggle for survival and recovery from the recession triggered by the Asian financial crisis has . . . brought it closer to China."[38] The territory has become "increasingly dependent on China's development" by participating in "China's grander national marketization and 'going global' projects"[39] such as raising international capital by listing Chinese state-owned companies in Hong Kong's stock market. The more Hong Kong depends on China economically, the closer it becomes to China politically.

Within the current context of the global financial crisis soon after the Beijing Olympics, China's neoliberal model, in a sharp contrast to the United States' one, remains a major hope and inspiration. To minimize the negative consequences of significant export retraction, to stimulate domestic economy, and to maintain economic growth, the Chinese government announced an impressive $586 billion economic stimulus plan, a very significant percentage of China's GDP.[40] An action like this leads to ongoing international debate about ways in which China might rescue the capitalist global economy and prevent the collapse of capitalism.[41] Whereas stock markets around the world warmly welcomed the Chinese stimulus package, they poured cold water on the $787 billion stimulus plan passed by the U.S. Congress. This seems to suggest that investors have more confidence in the Chinese government than in the American government. That is, they expect the Chinese state to continue its active role in managing the capitalist economy in the same way it has done in the past decades. By contrast, they remain skeptical about the American government's capacity for doing the same, in part due to the systematic development of a public culture of distrust in the American democratic-style government since the Regan administration.

With respect to the future of the modern nation state's political system, does the Chinese neoliberal state represent an alternative to the democratic political system, the very foundation of Western capitalism? In a recent article entitled "China's Valley of Tears," Slavoj Zizek argues that the Chinese model of development represents a movement toward "authoritarian capitalism" as the world's future. In Europe in the early modern period (for example, in the Netherlands during the seventeenth century), a brutal state dictatorship created and sustained the conditions of capitalism (for example, by legalizing violent expropriations of the common people by turning them into laborers). According to Zizek, China has clearly undergone a similar transformation. What is unclear is whether capitalist practices promise that China will eventually arrive at democracy. Therefore, China offers a very unsettling vision of the world's political future.[42] A critical understanding of what has happened in China since the late 1970s calls for rethinking the relationship between neoliberalism and democracy. Neoliberals such as Friedman believe that the private free market system eventually leads to political freedoms associated with democratic representation.[43] Instead of reaffirming that belief, China's development in fact shows the opposite effect. Doesn't the whole history of Hong Kong's return to China suggest that neoliberal globalization (its aspiration, its practice, and its future)—through which neoliberals declared capitalism's triumph over communism—finally breaks capitalism's alliance to democracy, reconfiguring our basic assumptions about the modern trajectory of capitalism?[44]

Notes

Preface

1 These items were first mentioned by John Williamson of the World Bank in April 1990. Gradually, they become popularly associated with the doctrine of free trade.
2 Blomgren, *Nyliberal Politisk Filosofi*, 224. Cited in Thorsen and Lie, "What is Neoliberalism," 12.
3 Harvey, *A Brief History of Neoliberalism*, 2.
4 Ibid.
5 Ong and Zhang, "Introduction," 9.
6 Ibid.
7 Ibid.
8 In *Neoliberalism as Exception*, Ong highlights exception as an important issue of neoliberalism in the cases of China and Southeast Asia, but she focuses on Asian governmental technologies as an issue of alternative modernity. She does not adequately address exception as a problem of sovereignty in neoliberalism.
9 The scholarship on the modern nation state has basically developed through addressing the relationship between the multiple and the one. Here, I draw primarily on the writings of scholars in France, Germany, and Italy, including Alain Badiou, Etinne Balibar, Michel Foucault, Carl Schmitt, Giorgio Agamben, Paolo Verno, and Antonio Negri.
10 Badiou, *Being and Event*, "Mediations" 8 and 9, pp. 93–111. His discussion focuses on the political ontology of counting the multiples.
11 Although the nation state is a common denominator of the historical state, it is not the same as the historical state. In a place like Hong Kong, the historical state always goes beyond the form of the nation (see Chapter 6).
12 Agamben, *Homo Sacer*, Chapter 1.
13 Schmitt, *Political Theology*, 27–28, quotation on p. 5.
14 Friedman, "Economic Freedom, Human Freedom, Political Freedom."
15 Becker mentions this example in his Nobel lecture to the memory of Alfred Nobel on December 9, 1992. See his "The Economic Way of Looking at Life."
16 See Thaler and Sunstein, *Nudge*; and Ariely, *Predictably Irrational*.
17 For media coverage, see *Times* magazine and *Wall Street Journal* in the first half of 2009.
18 While some become neoliberals while others do not. If one becomes disenfranchised, she or he can never pursue the dream of a positive life-extension. In this situation, individual sovereignty cannot possibly aim at improving liberty and well-being; rather it is merely conceived in practical terms such as pursuing bodily pleasures at least momentarily. It makes more sense to speak of practical sovereignty, as opposed to liberal or neoliberal sovereignty (Lauren Berlant, "Slow Death"). I have developed this point elsewhere (see Ren, "Living with Risks").

19 Deng Xiaoping, "Yige guojia, liangzhong zhidu (One Country, Two Systems)," 60–61.

20 Ibid.

21 I have benefited from the works of many scholars. Perry Anderson's "History and Lessons of Neoliberalism" analyzes neoliberalism's impacts on new left politics. David Harvey's *A Brief History of Neoliberalism* offers a clear explanation of the uneven development of neoliberalism in various parts of the world since the late 1970s. Wendy Brown's "Neo-Liberalism and the End of Liberal Democracy" examines the case of the United States. Noam Chomsky's *Profit over People* critically examines the impacts of Washington Consensus, especially in Latin America. Hai Ren's "Subculture as a Neo-Liberal Conduct of Life in Leisure and Consumption" investigates the link between neoliberalism and subculture. Lisa Duggen's *The Twilight of Equality?* explores how neoliberalism has affected American countercultural practices since the 1960s. As for scholarship related to China, Aihwa Ong's *Neoliberalism as Exception* offers more detailed analysis of China, especially neoliberal development in China's special economic zones. Katharyne Mitchell's *Crossing the Neoliberal Line* documents how the immigration of Hong Kong residents to Canada in the 1980s and 1990s affected the development of neoliberalism there.

Introduction: The role of reunification with Hong Kong in the neoliberalization of the Chinese state

1 The links between the museum space and a commercial space like a shopping mall, and between politics and commerce, are investigated in later chapters.

2 The information below is from *The Opium War*, DVD, directed by Xie Jin (1997; released by Star Trere Holdings Ltd in 2002).

3 The historical counterpart of this scene is Britain's first diplomatic mission to China to negotiate a formal trade agreement with Emperor Qianlong. It was headed by George, Viscount Macartney, with an entourage of guards, artists, and scientists. In an effort to please the emperor, Lord Macartney presented gifts such as clocks, chandeliers, and astronomical instruments. The emperor, however, interpreted the gift giving as an act of submission and completely rebuffed him. What Macartney did learn about was the Qing Dynasty's splendor and arrogance, very similar to what Danton describes here.

4 This synchronization is not about reducing modernity's belatedness as a way of catching up with the West and Japan, but about creating a culturally unique version of capitalism (see Karl, " 'Joining Tracks with the World' "). For this reason, synchronization is always closely tied to consideration of China's "nationally unique situations" (*guoqing*).

5 Guo Weicheng, *Chenlun yu juexing*, 148–149. All translations from Chinese are mine unless otherwise indicated.

6 Many economists of China, who have studied the process of China's economic transformation during the Deng Xiaoping era (1978–1997), argue that the transition to a market-oriented system is characterized as gradualism, a developmental process based on a series of experiments (for example, see Chris Bramall, *Chinese Economic Development*, Chapter 10). Missing in their studies is an understanding of the way in which national reunification in general, and Hong Kong's return to China in particular, become inseparable from economic transformation. This book fills that gap.

7 Since the late 1980s, many scholars have made explicit or implicit claims that Hong Kong's return to China has had remarkable impacts on China. The majority of scholars, however, focus on economic development through building social and cultural ties between Hong Kong and China (for example, Josephine Smart and

Alan Smart; Leslie Sklair; George C. S. Lin; Xiangming Chen; and Constance Lever-Tracy, David Ip and Noel Tracy). Some also examine the ways in which the business operations of Hong Kong firms exemplify a distinctive mode of transnational capitalism (Henry Wai-chung Yeung; You-tien Hsing; Michael J. Enright, Edith. E. Scott and David Dodwell; David R. Meyer; and Stephen Chiu and Tai-Lok Lui). Others show the influences of Hong Kong popular culture in China (Andrew Scobell, and Thomas Gold). Compared with these studies, my work focuses on the connections between Hong Kong's return and neoliberalism.

8 Hong Kong's economy has generally ranked very high by the four major international economic indexes of free-market practices and competitiveness, the *Economic Freedom Index* (jointly published by the Heritage Foundation and the Wall Street Journal), the *World Competitiveness Yearbook* (published by the International Institute for Management Development of Lausanne), the *Global Country Forecast* (published by the Economist Intelligence Unit of *The Economist*), and the *Global Competitiveness Report* (by the World Economic Forum based in Geneva). From 1996 to 2007 the *Economic Freedom Index* has consistently ranked Hong Kong as the world's freest economy. Milton Friedman, the world's leading neoliberal economist, argues that since the end of World War II Hong Kong has been the only world economy close to his ideal of a private free-market system ("The Hong Kong Experiment").

9 For critical analyses of the serious damage the Washington Consensus has caused in Latin America, see David Harvey, Perry Anderson, and Noam Chomsky's works. Also see Mao Zengyu, " 'Beijing gongshi' yu 'huashengdun gongshi' shi bijiao (A Comparison between 'Beijing Consensus' and Washington Consensus')," 394–395.

10 Lemke, " 'Birth of Bio-Politics,' " 192.

11 Anderson, "History and Lessons of Neo-liberalism."

12 Cohen, "Consumers' Republic," 58.

13 According to Lizabeth Cohen, the exhibition "explicitly encouraged the French to imagine a rosier future of shorter working hours and greater earnings that still made possible the ownership of new consumer durables. For example, displays proclaimed that one of six Americans owned a television, that 822 hours of work bought an American worker a car, and that there were three hundred cars per thousand inhabitants in the United States (in contrast to the 2,299 hours of labor required and only fifteen cars per thousand in the Soviet Union). It took 144 working hours for an American to earn the money for a washing machine, and so on down the shopping list to clothing and butter. Thanks to all these consumer opportunities, the exhibition concluded, 'the American worker knows that he receives an equitable part of the wealth he creates' " (see Cohen, "Consumers' Republic," 59).

14 Cohen, "Consumers' Republic," 47.

15 See, for example, Shunya Yoshimi, "Consuming America, Producing Japan," 73–75.

16 Kotz, "Globalization and Neoliberalism," 66.

17 Following Hayek and Friedman, University of Chicago economists won six more Nobel Prizes in 1979, 1991, 1992, 1995, 2000, and 2007.

18 See Anderson, "History and Lessons of Neoliberalism"; and Harvey, *Brief History of Neoliberalism*, Chapter 4.

19 Chile was a "laboratory" of neoliberal programs. See Anderson, "History and Lessons of Neoliberalism."

20 Neoliberal programs in these two countries have been well documented. See Anderson, "History and Lessons of Neoliberalism;" and Harvey, *Brief History of Neoliberalism*, Chapter 2.

21 Perry Anderson, "Xinziyouzhuyi de lishi he jiaoxun (History and Lessons of Neoliberalism)," 23.

22 An example is U.S. economic guru Jeffrey Sachs, who proposed a "shock treatment" experiment in Bolivia to Poland and Russia (see Anderson, "Xinziyouzhuyi de lishi he jiaoxun," 25).

23 See Li Qiqing, "Quanqiuhua beijing xia de xin ziyouzhuyi (Neoliberalism in the background of globalization)," 21–24.

24 Iain Pirie, *The Korean Developmental State*, 39. Also see Jesook Song, *South Koreans in Debt Crisis*.

25 Many of the debates are published as conference proceedings and research reports, for example, He Bingmeng, *Xinziyouzhuyi pingxi (Analyses of Neoliberalism)*; Wu Yifeng, Ding Bing, and Li Zhong, *Kaifangxia de hongguan jingji yu qiye lilun yanjiu (Macro Economy under Opening and Company Studies)* and *Jingji Quanjiuhua yu xinziyouzuyi sichao (Economic Globalization and Neoliberal Theories)*; and Wu Yifeng, *Makesizhuyi jingjixue he xinziyouzheyi jingjixue (Marxist Economics and Neoliberal Economics)*.

26 For example, see the report written by the research group on neoliberalism from the Chinese Academy of Social Science. Ketizhu, "Xinziyouzhuyi jiqi benzhi (Neoliberalism and Its Nature)."

27 See Li Qiqing, "Quanqiuhua beijing xia de xin ziyouzhuyi." Within the present political context of China as a risk society, their critical reflections on neoliberalism seem to make sense for formulating policies that may address the problems associated with neoliberalization, such as the privatization of state-owned companies.

28 Wang Hui, "Depoliticized Politics, From East to West," 31.

29 Wallerstein, "New Revolts against the System," 34; also see Badiou, "Cultural Revolution: The Last Revolution?" 481–514.

30 It would be reasonable to consider the way in which this event influenced the Soviet Union and Eastern European countries. However, such an analysis is beyond the scope of this book. Perhaps one way to examine this problem is to look at the normalization of the Sino–Soviet relationship. In the middle of student demonstrations at Tiananmen Square and in the wake of the fall of the Berlin Wall in 1989, for example, Soviet leader Mikhail Gorbachev met Deng Xiaoping in Beijing. How the two leaders viewed the future of socialism might be a research topic. In recent years, a number of scholars, such as Wang Hui, Alessandro Russo, Alain Badiou, and Christopher Connery, have clearly noted the current depoliticization of the political, with particular reference to the Cultural Revolution in China. Russo and Badiou point out that the current depoliticization of the political in China is not an isolated case. Similar depoliticization has happened to the French Revolution, the Russian October Revolution, and the events of 1968 (see Badiou and Russo, "International Center for the Study of the Cultural Revolution: Elements of a Project," 673–704). To extend their argument, I would like to add that unlike the other depoliticized events, the rejection of the Cultural Revolution is part of China's neoliberal process.

31 This is suggested by Wang Hui's "Depoliticized Politics."

32 Those who were active in the Cultural Revolution still disagree with the decision. In the summer of 2007, I interviewed a number of elderly, retired workers who consistently mentioned to me that they still "cannot think through" (*xiang bu tong*) this decision.

33 Wang Hui, "Depoliticized Politics," 34.

34 Steven N. S. Cheung (Zhang Wuchang) can be loosely considered a member of the Chicago School, because he was the first to introduce concepts from the Chicago School of Economics into China. He headed the Department of Economics at the University of Hong Kong and accompanied Friedman to China to meet Chinese government officials in 1988. Cheung, a faithful follower of neoliberalism, is known for his work on private property rights and transaction costs; he achieved fame with an economic analysis on China's open-door policy following the 1980s.

35 Steven N. S. Cheung, *Will China Go "Capitalist?"* 33.
36 For details, see Friedman and Friedman, *Two Lucky People: Memories*, app. C, pp. 607–609.
37 Cheung, "Datong yu xiaoyi (Great Similarity and Minor Difference)," 94–98.
38 See, for example, the work of Pun Ngai, Ching Kwan Lee, and Andrew Ross. Between 2002 and 2004, some authors began to discuss something called the "Beijing Consensus" as an alternative to the Washington Consensus (Joshua Looper Romo, "The Beijing Consensus," 13). Chinese economists have also picked up on this discussion [for example, Mao Zengyu, " 'Beijing gongshi' yu 'huashengdun gongshi' shi bijiao (A Comparison between 'Beijing Consensus' and Washington Consensus'), 390–398; and Yu Wenlie, " 'Beijing gongshi' yu siyouhua 'yiyi' ('Beijing Consensus' and Privatization 'Alternative Discussion'), 479–486]. On the eve of the sixtieth anniversary of the founding of the People's Republic in 2009, the Chinese government officially embraced the idea of the "Chinese experience" (*zhongguo jingyan*) as distinguishable from other experiences shaped by the Washington Consensus (see the conclusion).
39 I propose that there are four major models of state formation in neoliberal globalization. First is the transformation of the U.S. nation state in an American imperial empire through (a) the end of the Cold War, ending competition with the Soviet Union; (b) the deliberate use of the Washington Consensus as a political strategy to take advantage of foreign financial crises to weaken state sovereignty in developing countries, first in Latin America and then in Asia and Africa; and (c) the events since September 11, 2001, which have enabled the United States to implement a U.S. "national security" state to displace international or global security, under the George W. Bush administration. Underlying this is a major energy crisis comparable to the 1974 one. In the second model major European countries decided to formulate a transnational political structure through the European Union (EU). In this context, a model of the postmodern state emerges. In 2002, Robert Cooper, British Prime Minister Tony Blair's foreign policy guru, published an article called "The Post Modern State." In it, Cooper argues for a doctrine of "new liberal imperialism"—which contains such ideas as the designation of countries as "failed states," "modern states," and "postmodern states"—and makes statements such as, "The challenge to the postmodern world is to get used to the idea of double standards." The third model involves the disappearing or weakening of nation state sovereignty in Latin America and the Middle East. The fourth model is China.
40 Friedman and Friedman, *Two Lucky People*, 609.
41 Cheung, *Will China Go "Capitalist?"* 34.
42 Coase, "The Problem of Social Cost," 95–156. The article was originally published by the *Journal of Law and Economics* in 1960 and reprinted in his book *The Firm, the Market, and the Law*, which was translated into Chinese and published by a major press in Shanghai in 1990.
43 Cheung, *Will China Go "Capitalist"?* 39–40.
44 Ibid., p. 38.
45 For Coase, the state may exercise its governmental power by avoiding the market altogether, which an ordinary firm can never do (see Coase, "Problem of Social Cost," 117).
46 International media such as *The New York Times* have provided continuous coverage on food- and toy-related safety issues.
47 Michael Dutton points out that Mao's distinction between the enemy and the friend in Chinese revolutionary practices came from Lenin, who was originally influenced by Carl Schmitt's theory on the political (*Policing Chinese Politics*). That distinction was expressed as one between the capitalists and the proletariat. The link between the socialist state and its political representation of the proletariat was addressed in Lenin's book *The State and Revolution*.

48 The article can be accessed at www.marx2mao.com/Mao/PDD49.html (accessed January 19, 2008).

49 See *Renmin ribao (People's Daily)*, May 16, 2000, p. 1.

50 Aihwa Ong argues that special economic zones and their expansion have created a phenomenon called graduated sovereignty, meaning that in these zones, populations are governed by techniques and laws different from those used in non-special economic zones and their expanded areas. See her *Neoliberalism as Exception*, especially Chapters 3–4.

51 Hai Ren, Field notes dated August 1, 2007.

52 Yu Wenlie, "Jingji lujing de zhexue sikao (A Philosophical Thinking on the Direction of the Economy)," 20.

53 Hu's idea was first announced publicly in early 2005. For a detailed explanation, see *Xinhua News*, "Hu Jintao chanshi huxie shehui jibeng tezheng (Hu Jintao Elaborates the Basic Characteristics of Harmonious Society)."

54 This debate was clearly apparent in the seminar "How to Interpret the Idea of the Harmonious Society," organized by China's *Newsweek* on March 17, 2005. See http://news.sina.com.cn/c/2005-03-17/12246111762.shtml (accessed March 2007).

55 The issue of risk in Chinese society after Hong Kong's return to China is beyond this scope of the current book. I address it in a book-length study (*The Chinese Middle Class Society*).

56 My treatment of national attitudes as public feelings has benefited from the work of Ann Cvetkovich and Lauren Berlant. Cvetkovich suggests, "There is a need to critique liberal forms of affect and, moreover, to think about liberalism and neoliberalism in affective terms—to take on the vocabularies of tolerance, diversity, and multiculturalism as connected to certain affects or structures of feeling that are inadequate to, or that too conveniently package and manage, the messy legacies of history" ("Public Feelings," 10). I follow this suggestion to address the relationship among national affect, colonialism, and neoliberalization in this book.

57 In *Keywords*, Raymond Williams notes that "culture" has three meanings: culture as history ("civilization"); culture as aesthetic or intellectual culture ("the independent and abstract noun which describes the works and practices of intellectual and especially artistic activity"); and culture as ordinary or everyday culture ("a particular way of life, whether of a people, a period, or a group") (p. 80). Since this book's publication, scholars in humanities and social sciences have widely accepted Williams' explanation, while debating culture's specific meanings in the contemporary period (history, creative culture, and way of life). Williams' insight is useful to the discussion of the modification of *wenhua* ("culture" in the Chinese context). Related to the three dimensions is the issue of research methodology. In this book, which intends to address all three cultural aspects, I strategically adopt a multidisciplinary approach. Archival research offers a valuable understanding of historical change; textual analysis and interpretation provide fine tools for theorizing media rhetoric, cultural displays, and other forms of representation; participant observation and interviews are useful to the understanding of nuanced and situated experiences. Combining these methods strengthens my overall analysis.

58 The historical dimension includes the historical processes of both the reincorporation of Hong Kong into the Chinese state and the incorporation of the mainland into Hong Kong. Since the late 1980s, an abundance of historical narratives have been written about the historical event of Hong Kong's return to China. Some focus on everyday lives while others examine the problem of the Chinese nation. On the mainland, books on Hong Kong's history rarely take a critical approach toward the mainstream perspective of Chinese history. In Hong Kong, reunification has enabled a flourishing of Hong Kong studies. What is unique about my book is its focus on museums and historical representations closely associated with the problematic imagined community of the nation state.

59 Kirk Denton argues, "As China moved boldly into a market economy in the 1980s and 1990s . . . museums of modern history edged slowly away from standard narratives of class oppression and revolutionary struggle towards representations of the past that legitimize the contemporary ideology of commerce, entrepreneurship and market reform" ("Museums, Memorial Sites and Exhibitionary Culture in the People's Republic of China," 567). While agreeing with Denton's assessment, I suggest that Hong Kong's return was a key historical condition for this change.

60 Ye Junzhi, "Woguo bowuguan wenhua chanye kaifa wenti (Problems of Developing the Culture Industry in China's Museums)," 42.

61 Andrew Ross writes, "Labor laws and workplace regulations were nonexistent, and compradors could take advantage of an inexhaustible supply of rural laborers, many of them indentured, streaming into the shantytowns of Zhabei, Hongkou, and Pudong, or the sampan colonies along the Suzhou Creek. Though it had many other infamous competitors, Shanghai could claim some of the world's worst working conditions for the 200,000 workers who sweated their lives away inside the factories, while even more coolies worked the wharves, warehouses, and rickshaw circuits until they dropped. It was no coincidence that resistance to these conditions on the part of China's first proletariat helped give birth to the Chinese Communist Party in Shanghai in 1921, and fueled its rise through a series of large industrial strikes" (*Fast Boat to China*, 139). For a detailed study of the link between the Communist Party and the workers' movement in this period, see Ren Wuxiong, "Zhongguo gongchandang chuangjian shiqi makeshi zhuyi yu gongren yundong de jiehe (The Integration between Marxism and Workers' Movement in the Founding Period of the Chinese Communist Party)," 3–28.

62 Denton, "Museums, Memorial Sites and Exhibitionary Culture in the People's Republic of China," 586.

63 Ibid., 585–86.

64 Ni Xingxiang, "Shilun geming jinianguan kuojian zhong ying zhongshi de jige wenti (Preliminary Study of Several Problems in Expanding Revolutionary and Commemorative Museums)," 52.

65 It has become a textbook example of marketing. See Guo Huimin, *Zhongguo youxiu gongguan anli xuanping* (*Excellent Public Relations Cases*), 3–23, and Ouyang Guozhong, *Meiti huodong shizhan baogao* (*Campaign Reports of Media Practices*, 118–22).

66 For Althusser, the ideological state apparatuses include religion, education, the family, law, labor unions, political parties, the media, and the cultural sphere. For Gramsci, hegemony characterizes the way in which an ideological state apparatus wields its power. In this book, I extend the insights of both authors to the historical condition of neoliberalism.

67 For the philosopher Badiou, appearance refers to the localization of being or a situated exposition of being there. When the spectacle becomes a logic or principle of being's appearance, it regulates being's appearance (its order and its legislation). That is, the spectacle regulates the ordering of a multiple belonging to the world of appearance (as a world of relation and cohesion). In this way, however, the spectacle works against the presence of being, the ontological existence of the pure multiple, which has no ties with anything other than itself ("Being and Appearance," 171). The pure multiple comes into existence (that is, comes into being) through an eventful decision, an operation based on the enactment of the void. If the spectacle does appear to present something, it cannot present the appearance of being or the pure multiple at the ontological level. Rather, the thing manifested through the spectacle is a particular relation that has nothing to do with the ontological being. Therefore, the distinction between the ontological appearance or existence of being (the pure multiple) and the de-ontological appearance of the spectacle is crucial to understanding the way in which a subject

may approach truth. In contemporary neoliberal globalization, the spectacle's appearance is not a philosophical question but an economic problem, and thus, the subject of the spectacle is not a truthful but a neoliberal subject.

68 The idea of communication as the means of production in neoliberal capitalism was developed by Paolo Virno in his *A Grammar of the Multitude*. On the definition of informational economy, see Castells, *Rise of the Network Society*.

69 The changes in Chinese museums, especially their reforms to mesh with China's economic redevelopment, have been a major theme among the featured articles recently published in *Zhongguo bowuguan (Chinese Museum)*, the leading museum journal published by the State Bureau of Cultural Relics, a ministry-level branch of the State Council. Note that changes in Chinese museums are part of the broader transformation of the propaganda work of the Communist Party. For an excellent study of transformation in the area of journalism, see Yuezhi Zhao, *Media, Market, and Democracy in China*.

70 The discourse of the image works through the power of the sayable (significance and affect) associated with the image itself (see Rancière, *Future of the Image*, 11).

71 In "Socialism: A Life-Cycle," Régis Debray historicizes the history of media by distinguishing between three major media spheres: the logosphere (from the invention of writing to the coming of the printing press), the graphosphere (1448–1968, or from the Gutenberg revolution to the rise of television), and the videosphere (since 1968) (pp. 5, 26–28).

72 Paul Virilio argues that contemporary acceleration has reconfigured modernity from a positive to a negative development. He uses such terms as "disappearance" and "negative horizon" to characterize this new modernity. See his *The Aesthetics of Disappearance* and *Negative Horizon*. Ackbar Abbas has applied Virilio's work to the culture of Hong Kong; see his *Hong Kong*, 7–8.

73 Friedman, "The Hong Kong Experiment."

74 See the organization's website at http://www.heritage.org/.

75 The Economist Intelligence Unit (EIU), *Hong Kong: Country Profile 2006*, p. 10.

76 Friedman, "The Hong Kong Experiment."

77 Tsang, "Big Market, Small Government."

78 Scobell, "Hong Kong's Influence on China," 604.

79 Lee Yee, "Take to the Seas," 433.

80 Abbas, *Hong Kong*, 7–8.

81 Scobell, "Hong Kong's Influence on China," 604.

82 For a good review of administrative reforms, see Huque and Yep, "Globalization and Reunification."

83 Thus, citizenship development in the context of Hong Kong's return to China continued to focus on self-reliant and self-enterprising (Ku and Pun, "Introduction," 5–7).

84 For a detailed analysis, see Eric Kit-wai Ma, "Re-advertising Hong Kong: Nostalgia Industry and Popular History" (2004 version).

85 On Hong Kong popular culture see, for example, Sinn, *Culture and Society in Hong Kong*; and Abbas, *Hong Kong*. Regarding architecture, see Abbas, *Hong Kong*; and Cheng, "Resurgent Chinese Power in Postmodern Discourse." For cinema, see Abbas, *Hong Kong*; Marchetti, "Transnational Cinema, Hybrid Identities and the Films of Evans Chan;" and Williams, "Under 'Western Eyes.'" Kit-wai Ma, "Hong Kong Remembers," addresses television. Wong Wang-chi, Li Siu-leung, and Chan Ching-kiu Stephen, *Hong Kong Un-Imagined*, is a good resource on literature, and Lilley, *Staging Hong Kong*, on theater. See Kit-wai Ma, "Re-Advertising Hong Kong" on consumer culture.

86 See Wing-sang Law, "Northbound Colonialism," 201–33; Siu-keung Cheung, "Speaking Out," 235–62; and Chun, "Colonial 'Govern-mentality' in Transition," 430–61.

87 Abbas, *Hong Kong*, 24.
88 David Bordwell's characterization of the use of time in the films made by Wong Kar-wai as passive (*Planet Hong Kong*, p. 273) has missed the main point of the politics of time in these films. From the perspective of using time in martial arts, the "act of doing nothing" (*wuwei*) in Taoism is recognized as one of the greatest achievements in action.
89 I made several trips to mainland China and Hong Kong between 1994 and 2007 to conduct interviews, engage in participant observation, and collect relevant historical and mass media materials for this project.
90 Although Rancière focuses on the image, his insight applies to media more generally.
91 My discussion of history as a governmental problem draws on Wendy Brown's discussion of civilization as a governmental discourse (see her *Regulating Aversion*, Chapters 1, 7).
92 This chapter uses corporate materials such as newsletters and annual reports; participation observations of festivals sponsored by the company in Hong Kong from 1995 to 1997; and interviews with the company's employees in both Hong Kong and China.
93 During my field trips to Hong Kong between 1994 and 2000, I did archival research on the history of local commercial exhibitions, trade fairs, and museums in Hong Kong University Library's Special Collections, and studied the development of "The Story of Hong Kong" exhibition at the Hong Kong Museum of History and of the Pingshan Heritage Trail in the New Territories.

Chapter 1: The Hong Kong question: From sovereignty to government

1 See, for example, Liang Weiji and Zheng Zhemin, *Zhongguo jindai bupingdeng tiaoyue xuanbian yu jieshao* (*Introduction to Selected Unequal Treaties in Modern China*), 2, 9.
2 Macau was permanently settled by the Portuguese in 1557 but did not officially become a Portuguese colony until 1887.
3 For an overview of Chinese emigration, see Spence, *Search for Modern China*, 208–214.
4 See Hsu, *Dreaming of Gold, Dreaming of Home*, 10.
5 Jameson, "Modernism and Imperialism," 44.
6 Shih, *Lure of the Modern*, 33; see also Hevia, *English Lessons*.
7 Sun Yat-sen (Sun Zhongshan), *Sun Zhongshan xuanji* (*Sun Zhongshan Selections*), 951–954.
8 For a detailed account of China's efforts, see Qi Pengfei, *Richu riluo: Xianggang wenti yibai wushiliu nian, 1841–1997* (*Sun Rises, Sun Sets: The 156-Year Hong Kong Question, 1841–1997*), 235–268.
9 Note, however, that maintenance of the status quo is not the same as preservation of Hong Kong's capitalist system.
10 Zhou Enlai, "Guanyu Xianggang wenti (Regarding the Hong Kong Question)," 353–355. My translation.
11 Young, "Building Years," 132–133.
12 For detailed discussions of the Hong Kong government's immigration policies, see Agnes Ku, "Immigration Policies, Discourses and the Politics of Local Belonging in Hong Kong (1950–1980)," and Alan Smart and Josephine Smart, "Time–space Punctuation."
13 See Pei-kai Cheng and Michael Lestz with Jonathan D. Spence (eds.), *The Search for Modern China*, 439.
14 Hence, when Deng Xiaoping's government proposed the "one country, two systems" principle in the late 1970s with regard to the handover of Hong Kong, it

focused on that government's administrative functions while ignoring its legislative and juridical dimensions.

15 Qi Pengfei, *Richu riluo*, 346–349.

16 Ibid., 354.

17 Ibid., 352.

18 Ibid., 357.

19 Thatcher, *Downing Street Years*, 259, 493–494.

20 Deng Xiaoping, "Yige guojia, liangzhong zhidu (One Country, Two Systems)," 60–61.

21 Deng Xiaoping, *Deng Xiaoping wenxuan* (*Selections of Deng Xiaoping's Works*), 220.

22 The British government ruled Hong Kong as a colonial territory via a governor appointed by the Queen. In general, the governor consented automatically to legislation passed by the Legislative Council (Legco), and regularly consulted the Executive Council (Exco), over which he presided, before taking major decisions. Exco consisted of three *ex officio* members (the chief secretary, the financial secretary and the attorney-general) and twelve members of the local elite appointed by the governor. Exco met at least once a week, in camera, to advise the governor on policy and to propose legislation, which was then sent to Legco to be debated. Legco consisted of a total of sixty members, representing three groups—those directly elected by geographical constituencies, those appointed by the governor, and those indirectly elected to represent professional and other groups (functional constituencies). See Economist Intelligence Unit, *Hong Kong: Country Profile 1996–97*, 9.

23 Deng Xiaoping, *Deng Xiaoping wenxuan* (*Selections of Deng Xiaoping's Works*), 221.

24 In March 1984, the popular Hong Kong columnist Hah Gong used "rape" to characterize Hong Kong's victimization during the Sino–British negotiation. See his "A Hong Kong Absurdity."

25 Shu Kei, "Sunless Days," 434–435.

26 The immigration caused rapid development of the real estate market in Vancouver, as well as challenging fundamental presumptions about Canadian multiculturalism, which was based on British liberalism. For a detailed analysis, see Mitchell, *Crossing the Neoliberal Line.*

27 Ching, "Toward Colonial Sunset," 178.

28 Chan Ching-kiu, "Fighting Condition in Hong Kong Cinema," 77–78.

29 Ching, "Toward Colonial Sunset," 180–81.

30 Economist Intelligence Unit, *Hong Kong: Country Profile 1996–97*, 5–6, 9.

31 Quoted in Ewing, "Secret Hong Kong Story." No page number.

32 Economist Intelligence Unit, *Hong Kong: Country Profile 1996–97*, 11.

33 Ibid., 11, 13.

34 See *Jingbao Monthly* (Hong Kong), February 1993.

35 Before the finalization of the Basic Law on February 16, 1990, two drafts were published: the first in April 1988, and the second in February 1989 (see Ching, "Toward Colonial Sunset," 176).

36 This is the view Harvey takes in *A Brief History of Neoliberalism.*

Chapter 2: The affective economy of the Hong Kong countdown: Media convergence, public feelings, and neoliberal subjectivity

1 *Beijing Evening News*, July 10, 1997, 19.

2 In his work on the aesthetics of media, Rancière focuses on the concept of the image as a way of examining media. His insight is also relevant to my discussion of the countdown clock.

3 My study of media spectacle builds on the work by such important scholars as Guy Debord and Douglas Kellner. Debord focuses on the spectacle as the principal problem of consumer capitalism, while Kellner explicitly links the spectacle to media consumption. My work further addresses the consumption of media spectacle as a governmental problem of neoliberalism.
4 Cited in Hung Wu, "Hong Kong Clock," 341.
5 Ibid., 342.
6 Lien-sheng Yang, "Schedules of Work and Rest in Imperial China," 315.
7 Ibid.
8 Bedini, *Trail of Time*, 5; see also p. 7.
9 Bedini, "Oriental Concepts of the Measure of Time," 458; Needham, Ling, and Price, *Heavenly Clockwork*, 142.
10 Needham, Ling, and Price, *Heavenly Clockwork*, 152–153.
11 Greenberg, *British Trade and the Opening of China, 1800–42*, 22–23.
12 Needham, Ling, and Price, *Heavenly Clockwork*, 150–151.
13 Gallagher, *China in the Sixteenth Century*, 194, 201.
14 Bedini, "Oriental Concepts of the Measure of Time," 463.
15 In Needham *et al.*, *Heavenly Clockwork*, 165–166.
16 Landes, *Revolution in Time*, 40.
17 Bedini, "Oriental Concepts of the Measure of Time," 463. On the tasks assigned to Jesuits hired by Emperor Qianlong, see Catherine Jami, "Western Devices for Measuring Time and Space," 187–190.
18 The Nationalist government moved to Taiwan in 1949, where the two time systems remain in effect to this day.
19 Needham, Ling, and Price, *Heavenly Clockwork*, 173–178; Beijing Tianwenguan, *Zhongguo gudai tianwenxue chengjiu* (*The Achievements of Astrology in Ancient China*), 196–210.
20 Blaise, *Time Lord*, 194.
21 Chen Zungui, *Zhongguo tianwenxue shi* (*The History of Astronomy in China*), 4: 1991, 1983.
22 Ibid., 1953–1956.
23 Liu, *Radio Broadcasting in Communist China*, 19a.
24 Guojia Tongjiju, *Zhongguo tongji nianjian 1986* (*China Statistical Yearbook, 1986*), 669, 676.
25 Lull, *China Turned On*, 20–24.
26 Liu, *Radio Broadcasting in Communist China*, 37–47.
27 The figures are cited in Wang Peigeng's "What on Earth Can Advertising Do?"
28 Brownell, "Strong Women and Impotent Men," 210–213.
29 Virilio, "Indirect Light," 66.
30 Heidegger, *Being and Time*, 382; emphasis in the original.
31 Stiegler, "Time of Cinema/On the 'New World' and 'Cultural Exception,' " 84–90.
32 In his *Cinema 2: The Time-Image*, Gilles Deleuze has referred to a cinematic representation of time that focuses on discontinuity, contingency, and interruption as "the time-image." For excellent elaborations of Deleuze's work on cinema, see Rodowick, *Gilles Delleuze's Time Machine*, and *Reading the Figural, or, Philosophy after the New Media*; and Bogue, *Deleuze on Cinema*.
33 The sequence of numbers from 0 through 24 in the decimal and binary systems looks like this:

$0 = 0$ [$0 \times 2^0 = 0$] [read: 0 times of 2^0]

$1 = 1$ [$1 \times 2^0 = 1$]

$2 = 10$ [$1 \times 2^1 + 0 \times 2^0 = 2 + 0$]

$3 = 11$ [$1 \times 2^1 + 1 \times 2^0 = 2 + 1$]

$4 = 100\ [1 \times 2^2 + 0 \times 2^1 + 0 \times 2^0 = 4 + 0 + 0]$

$5 = 101\ [1 \times 2^2 + 0 \times 2^1 + 1 \times 2^0 = 4 + 0 + 1]$

$6 = 110\ [1 \times 2^2 + 1 \times 2^1 + 0 \times 2^0 = 4 + 2 + 0]$

$7 = 111\ [1 \times 2^2 + 1 \times 2^1 + 1 \times 2^0 = 4 + 2 + 1]$

$8 = 1000\ [1 \times 2^3 + 0 \times 2^2 + 0 \times 2^1 + 0 \times 2^0 = 8 + 0 + 0 + 0]$

$9 = 1001\ [1 \times 2^3 + 0 \times 2^2 + 0 \times 2^1 + 1 \times 2^0 = 8 + 0 + 0 + 1]$

$10 = 1010\ [1 \times 2^3 + 0 \times 2^2 + 1 \times 2^1 + 0 \times 2^0 = 8 + 0 + 2 + 0]$

$11 = 1011\ [1 \times 2^3 + 0 \times 2^2 + 1 \times 2^1 + 1 \times 2^0 = 8 + 0 + 2 + 1]$

$12 = 1100\ [1 \times 2^3 + 1 \times 2^2 + 0 \times 2^1 + 0 \times 2^0 = 8 + 4 + 0 + 0]$

$13 = 1101\ [1 \times 2^3 + 1 \times 2^2 + 0 \times 2^1 + 1 \times 2^0 = 8 + 4 + 0 + 1]$

$14 = 1110\ [1 \times 2^3 + 1 \times 2^2 + 1 \times 2^1 + 0 \times 2^0 = 8 + 4 + 2 + 0]$

$15 = 1111\ [1 \times 2^3 + 1 \times 2^2 + 1 \times 2^1 + 1 \times 2^0 = 8 + 4 + 2 + 1]$

$16 = 10000\ [1 \times 2^4 + 0 \times 2^3 + 0 \times 2^2 + 0 \times 2^1 + 0 \times 2^0 = 16 + 0 + 0 + 0 + 0]$

$17 = 10001\ [1 \times 2^4 + 0 \times 2^3 + 0 \times 2^2 + 0 \times 2^1 + 1 \times 2^0 = 16 + 0 + 0 + 0 + 1]$

$18 = 10010\ [1 \times 2^4 + 0 \times 2^3 + 0 \times 2^2 + 1 \times 2^1 + 0 \times 2^0 = 16 + 0 + 0 + 2 + 0]$

$19 = 10011\ [1 \times 2^4 + 0 \times 2^3 + 0 \times 2^2 + 1 \times 2^1 + 1 \times 2^0 = 16 + 0 + 0 + 2 + 1]$

$20 = 10100\ [1 \times 2^4 + 0 \times 2^3 + 1 \times 2^2 + 0 \times 2^1 + 0 \times 2^0 = 16 + 0 + 4 + 0 + 0]$

$21 = 10101\ [1 \times 2^4 + 0 \times 2^3 + 1 \times 2^2 + 0 \times 2^1 + 1 \times 2^0 = 16 + 0 + 4 + 0 + 1]$

$22 = 10110\ [1 \times 2^4 + 0 \times 2^3 + 1 \times 2^2 + 1 \times 2^1 + 0 \times 2^0 = 16 + 0 + 4 + 2 + 0]$

$23 = 10111\ [1 \times 2^4 + 0 \times 2^3 + 1 \times 2^2 + 1 \times 2^1 + 1 \times 2^0 = 16 + 0 + 4 + 2 + 1]$

$24 = 11000\ [1 \times 2^4 + 1 \times 2^3 + 0 \times 2^2 + 0 \times 2^1 + 0 \times 2^0 = 16 + 8 + 0 + 0 + 0]$

34 This was implied by Hung Wu's discussion of the clock in reference to Harvey's book *The Condition of Postmodernity*.
35 I draw on Jason Barker's discussion of Alain Badiou's mathematical ontology in *Alain Badiou*, 87.
36 *Zhongguo boweguan tongxun*, no. 1, 1995, pp. 20–21.
37 The informational economy, according to Jodi Dean, employs three general types of labor. Physical labor manufactures and distributes material goods such as infrastructure or equipment. Symbolic labor produces nonmaterial goods such as symbols and cultural products (texts and artifacts). Affective labor produces as its product feelings, such as attachment, affection, excitement, fear, contentment, or well-being (see Dean, "Networked Empire," 267–268).
38 *Beijing Youth Weekly*, no. 14, 1997.
39 Li Ren, Guo Jin, and Zhu Wei, "Wei le na yi tian: ji Tiananmen guangchang Xianggang 'daojishi' huodong (Preparing for the Day: Hong Kong Countdown Activities at Tiananmen Square)," 81.
40 Ibid., p. 335.
41 Ibid., 336; see also Hung Wu, "Tiananmen Square."
42 *Beijing Youth Weekly*, no. 14, 1997.
43 *China Top Brands*, August 1995, p. 53.
44 The designer initially considered the phase "Hong Kong's return to the motherland" (*Beijing Youth Weekly*, no. 14, 1997).
45 *Beijing Youth Daily*, July 2, 1996, p. 4.

46 See Heim, "Handover Tokens Take an Esoteric Twist," 2, 10.
47 Before becoming governor of Hong Kong, "Lugard was a romantic figure; campaigns in Afghanistan, the Sudan and Burma, [were] interrupted by big-game hunting (he bought his favorite rifle with his reward for shooting a man-eating tiger); explorations and fights against slavers in Africa had led him to work for Sir George Goldie, the founder of the United Africa Company, in opening up Nigeria" (Welsh, *A Borrowed Place*, p. 349). During his tenure as governor, Lugard had to deal with the fallout of the Chinese Revolution that brought down the Qing Dynasty on the mainland.
48 "Last Gasps of the Empire—You Can Buy It Canned in HK," Reuters News Agency, May 30, 1997.
49 See Stein, "Marketing Plans Using 1997 Theme in China May Go Up in Smoke," 1.
50 The Hong Kong-based *Wenhuibao* also published similar advertisements on July 1, 1996.
51 For more information, see the company's website: www.changhong.com.
52 The company also mentions this mission on its website, see www.changhong.com.
53 The information about the auction comes from *Ta Kung Daily*, July 2, 1996, p. A2.
54 See Wu Lijuan, "Qinchi' pinpai jingying linian sumiao" (A Sketch of the Operational Logic of the 'Qinchi' Brand)," 34.
55 See Feng Xuehui and Zhang Zhong, "Qinchi Liquor Factory," 1.
56 Wu Lijuan, " 'Qinchi' pinpai jingying linian sumiao" 34.
57 Ibid., 35.
58 *Wenhuibao*, July 2, 1996, p. B11.
59 *Beijing Evening News*, July 1, 1997, p. 12.
60 *Beijing Youth Daily*, July 2, 1997.
61 For a detailed discussion of the "small paper" phenomenon, see Yuezhi Zhao, "The Rich, the Laid-off, and the Criminal in Tabloid Tales: Read All about It!" 111–135.
62 The newspaper's articles about Hong Kong were primarily recycled pieces. Only the first was written for the paper, while the latter two (filling half the page) were originally published elsewhere.
63 The larger the size of the display panel is, the higher resolution it requires; the greater the number of colors, the higher the number of pixels the display panel needs. At a popular place like New York's Times Square, where there are hundreds of neon signs, the size of a sign and its resolution would have important implications for attracting the viewer's attention. The 55-foot by 55-foot "Discover" sign (containing a total of 1,140 sections) installed in the early 1990s, which used 77,000 six-watt incandescent light bulbs, was replaced in 2000 by light-emitting diodes capable of shooting out millions of colors (see Wilkes, "Guts of Times Square," 71). The information is also available at www.nytimes.com/library/magazine/home/20001022mag-timessquare.html
64 Cheng Sheng, "Dumiao Tiananmen: daojishipai beihou de gushi (Counting Down Seconds in Tiananmen: A Story behind the Countdown Clock)," 19.
65 The event was one of a series during the Hong Kong handover process. Other important activities included the official handover ceremony at the Hong Kong Convention Center, the entering of the People's Liberation Army into Hong Kong, and the demonstration led by Martin Lee in front of Hong Kong's Legislative Council building.
66 CCTV English Service, *Capturing the Moment: Reflections on CCTV-9's Live Coverage of Hong Kong's Return*.
67 Virilio, "Indirect Light," 65. There are no formal statistics on the exact number of journalists covering the handover events, but the *Beijing Youth Daily*, for example,

reported that more than eight thousand reporters from about seven hundred news agencies covered the official handover ceremony at the Hong Kong Convention Center (July 1, 1997). The news media I studied included newspapers, magazines, television programs, and online news groups such as the *People's Daily*, *Beijing Youth Daily*, *Beijing Evening News*, *Wen Hui Bao*, *Ming Bao*, *Apple Daily*, *Xingdao Ribao*, *Da Gong Bao*, *South China Morning Post*, the *Asian Wall Street Journal*, the *New York Times*, the *Seattle Times*, *Newsweek*, *Time*, *Far Eastern Economic Review*, *Asia Magazine*, *Business Week*, cnn.com, pbs.org, asia1.com, cctv.com, ClarisNews, ABC News, NBC News, CBS News, King-5 News (Seattle), ATV (Hong Kong), and TVB (Hong Kong).

68 Ho, "In Search of an Identity," 14. Also cited in Wu, "Hong Kong Clock," 352.
69 Li Siu-leung, "zhimin de lishi xiangxiang (Historical Imaginary of Colonialism)," 137.
70 Wu, "Hong Kong Clock," 348.
71 The meaning of everyday life is structured by the dialectical relationship between the modern (the significant) and the ordinary (the insignificant). The significant becomes mundane as a result of its normalization in repetitive daily practices (see Lefebvre, *Everyday Life in the Modern World*).
72 *South China Morning Post*, July 5, 1996, p.21.
73 The same journalist commented on this situation: "Despite its unmistakable presence, the passing of the seconds until July 1, 1997, does not give many of the passing cyclists and drivers much pause for thought" (*South China Morning Post*, July 5, 1996, p. 21).
74 My idea of the organization of everyday life as a time-sharing practice that works through flows draws on Manuel Castells' concept of "the space of flows," by which he means "the material organization of time-sharing social practices that work through flows" (Castells, *Rise of the Network Society*, 442).
75 *Beijing Youth Daily*, May 22, 1997.
76 *Beijing Youth Daily*, July 2, 1997, p. 8.
77 *Beijing Youth Daily*, June 30, 1997, p. 1.
78 My discussion draws on information published by *Beijing Youth Daily* on June 30, 1997.
79 The information is from http://club.lywww.com/Announce/announce2.asp?BoardID=118&ID=20503 (accessed January 2006).
80 This information is from http://blogs.xmu.edu.cn/ocean/ (accessed June 10, 2004).
81 The concept of neoliberal time derives from Aihwa Ong's concept of neoliberal space as a space of exception in her book *Neoliberalism as Exception*.
82 My discussion of future uncertainty draws on the book *Histories of the Future* (edited by Daniel Rosenberg and Susan Harding), especially its introduction and the chapter "Trauma Time" (by Kathleen Stewart).
83 My understanding of the link between time and its embodiment draws on the philosophical work of Heidegger and Badiou.
84 The normative situation derives from Badiou's discussion of the ways an individual relates to the counting of a state in *Being and Event*. The concept of sovereign is from Carl Schmitt's *Political Theology*.

Chapter 3: History as a governmental discourse

1 All translations are my own unless otherwise indicated.
2 Yan Fan, "Quanmian jianzheng xianggang lishi xianzhuang (Complete Witness to Hong Kong's Past and Present)," p. A3.
3 Other museums that shared similar status were the National Museum of Chinese History, the Palace Museum, and the National Military Museum of the Chinese People's Revolution.

4 See Wenhuabu Wenwuju, *Zhongguo bowuguanxue gailun (Introduction to Chinese Museology)*, 40.
5 Ibid., 40, 42–48. Also see Lu Jimin, "Zhongguo bowuguan de texing ji gongzhuo guifan (The Characteristics and Principles of the Museums in China)," 38–40.
6 The notion of linear history used in museums derives from intellectual discussions of Chinese history in the early twentieth century. For a detailed analysis, see Presenjit Duara, *Rescuing History from the Nation*, 33–48.
7 Lu Jimin, "Zhongguo bowuguan de texing ji gongzhuo guifan," 39. Lu, a former director of the State Bureau of Cultural Relics, is a well-known scholar of the history of China's museums.
8 Dirks, "History as a Sign of the Modern," 25–31.
9 Luo Ge has written in detail about the process. See "Nanwang de suiyue, nanwang de huiyi: xian gei zhongguo geming bowuguan sishi zhounian (Unforgettable Years, Unforgettable Memory: Dedicating to the Fortieth Anniversary of the National Museum of Chinese Revolution)," 59–82. Local museums in that period were forced to send the best elements of their collections to the three national museums to demonstrate the greatness of the nation. After local museums complained, the national museums sent them replicas of their artifacts.
10 Lu Jimin, "Wenwu gongzhuo gaishuo (Introduction to the Work of Cultural Relics)," 196.
11 Ibid., 196, 200.
12 Shen Qinglin, "Tan geming wenwu de shouji gongzhuo (On the Work of Collecting Revolutionary Artifacts)," 171–173; quotation on pp. 171–172.
13 In terms of the historiography of Chinese revolution, the museum systematically displays important figures in Chinese revolutions, such as heroes, leaders, and martyrs, in a large number of paintings (see Denton, "Visual Memory and the Construction of a Revolutionary Past," 203–235).
14 Lu Jimin, "Zhongguo bowuguan de texing ji gongzhuo guifan," 39.
15 Lu Jimin, "Zhou Enlai yu bowuguan (Zhou Enlai and Museums)," 2–3.
16 Hu Jun, "Shehuizhuyi xin shiqi woguo bowuguan shiye de huigu, 1976–1988 (A Review of the Museum Enterprise of Our Country in the New Era of Socialism, 1976–1988)," 3–4.
17 *Zhongguo wenwu bao* (Beijing), June 23, 1996, p. 1.
18 Ibid.
19 Lin (1785–1850) was a scholar and government official who founded a movement to revive and strengthen traditional Chinese institutions; widely recognized in China for his moral standards, he vehemently opposed Britain's importation of opium into China.
20 The label was written both in Chinese and English. My quotation is from the English text.
21 Visitors, however, might have different perspectives on the meaning of this exhibit. When I visited the exhibition in 1996, for example, I overheard a mother telling her daughter: "Look, *laobaixing* [ordinary folks] lived a backward life, while the palace lived in by the emperor was so luxurious!" Clearly, the woman had incorporated her everyday life experience into this reading.
22 Wenhuabu, *Zhongguo bowuguanxue gailun*, 147–148.
23 The use of *duibi* in exhibitions dates back to the Yan'an period (see Luo Ge, "Dali jiaqian chenlie yu zhanlan zhong de shixiangxing he zhandouxing: tan duibi yuanze de tedian ji zhuoyong (Reinforcing the Ideology and the Power of Exhibitions: On the Characteristics and Functions of the Principle of Contrast)," 388–393. Another important article on the use of *duibi* in Chinese museums is Su Donghai's "Jian lun wenwu zhuhe (Preliminary Study on the Combination of Artifacts)" 139–143.
24 This is Ernesto Laclau's interpretation of Marx. See his *New Reflections on the Revolution of Our Time*, 17. Emphasis in original.

25 Mao agues that a contradiction includes both "mutual dependence" (*huxian yilai*) and "struggle" (*douzheng*) or "opposition" (*duikang*). In a contradictory situation, the existence of one side always depends on the existence of the other. This relationship is however conditional and thus changes. In contrast, a contradiction always entails struggle or opposition. Despite being unconditional, struggle or opposition may or may not appear, or become obvious (see Mao Zedong, "Maodunlun (On Contradiction)," sections 5–6).

26 Ibid.

27 Hai Ren, field notes dated July 1, 1996.

28 *Ming Bao* (Hong Kong), January 21, 1997, p. A11.

29 The same practice was used in the Story of Hong Kong permanent exhibition at the Hong Kong Museum of History (see Chapter 6), but the two uses pointed to different meanings, as I discuss in the conclusion.

30 Shen Qinglin, "Zhonggong dangshi chenlie guilu tanshuo (An Inquiry into the Law of Displaying the History of the Chinese Communist Party)," 105.

31 *Wen Hui Bao* (Hong Kong), June 29, 1996, p. A3.

32 Nu Jizheng, "Lue tan bowuguanxue de zucheng bufen: chenliexue (A Brief Discussion of the Science of Exhibition, an Essential Part of Museology)," 42–44.

33 See Hang and Ching, "MacLehose–Youde Years," 150–151.

34 Reproduction shapes and shifts the aura of an original object (see Benjamin, "Work of Art in the Age of Mechanical Reproduction").

35 I use *dissemiNation* to highlight the idea that the representation of the nation involves an active circulation of the idea of the nation (see Bhabha, "DissemiNation")

36 Our conversation ended when the museum staff member who allowed me to use a phone in his office indicated that he was ready to leave for lunch.

37 Wang Tieya, *Zhongwai jiuyue zhang hui bian* (*Collections of the Sino–Foreign Treaties*), 1: 30–33. The same text published in Wang's book also appears in Liang Weiji and Zheng Zhemin's edited book *Zhongguo jindai bupingdeng tiaoyue xuanbian yu jieshao* (*Introduction to Selected Unequal Treaties in Modern China*), 19.

38 For the principles of the "traveling exhibition" (*liudong zhanlan*) in Chinese museology, see Wenhuabu, *Zhongguo bowuguanxue gailun*, 178–179.

39 For a range of types of T-shirts available in China in the 1990s, see Barmé, "Consuming T-shirts in Beijing," Chapter 6 of his book *In the Red* (pp. 145–78).

40 My idea of history as a governmental problem of ordering draws on Wendy Brown's discussion of "civilization" as a governmental discourse in *Regulating Aversion*, 178–199.

41 Denton, "Museums, Memorial Sites and Exhibitionary Culture in the People's Republic of China," 567.

Chapter 4: Morality and pleasure in the synchronization with the world

1 For a brief description of the festival, see *Beijing wanbao*, June 21, 1997.

2 See Young-Tsu Wong, *A Paradise Lost*, 128.

3 Yuanming Yuan may be one of the earliest prototypes of the modern theme park, dating at least one hundred years earlier than the Scandinavian "folk museum" model developed between 1870 and 1905 (see Sandberg, "Effigy and Narrative," 320).

4 In "The Dialectics of Ruins in Yuanmingyuan," Haiyan Lee has examined this situation through a detailed study of the debate between two groups of Chinese intellectuals over the future of Yuanming Yuan. One group focuses on preserving its ruins and the other argues for rebuilding it.

5 See Malone, *History of the Peking Summer Palaces*, 96–97.

6 Lee's "The Dialectics of Ruins in Yuanmingyuan" also engaged in a critique of

this discourse. Whereas she addresses the debates over the restoration of Yuanming Yuan, my critique focuses on the use of the site as a material encoding of history and for shaping the moral character of Chinese citizens.

7 The map was destroyed in the fire of 1860. For an English description of the forty "scenes," see Malone, *History of the Peking Summer Palaces*, 72–96, 98–101.

8 For an English description, see Malone, *History of the Peking Summer Palaces*, 98–101.

9 These engravings were in circulation by 1786. See Zhang Enyin, *Yuanming Yuan yuanshi jieshao* (*An Introduction to the History of Yuanming Yuan*). Also see Osvald Sirén, *The Imperial Palaces of Peking*, 1:47. For a detailed description of them, see Malone, *History of the Peking Summer Palaces*, 141–160. A series of photographs of the ruined buildings, taken by Europeans since the 1870s, also provide important visual images of Xiyang Lou (see Thiriez, *Barbarian Lens*).

10 The importance of the ruins of the European Buildings was highlighted in the 1985 plan of the park. See Han Li, "Yuanming Yuan yizhi gongyuan zongti guihua tigang (The Planning Outline of the Ruin Park of Yuanming Yuan)," 136–139.

11 Zhang, *Yuanming Yuan yuanshi jieshao*, 9.

12 Jean-Denis Attiret's letter describing Yuanming Yuan was published in France in 1749 and in England in 1765. This letter, along with other Jesuits' accounts of their China experiences, contributed to the flourishing of the Chinoiseries in eighteenth-century Europe (see Thiriez, *Barbarian Lens*, 52). For some English translations of his account, see Malone, *History of the Peking Summer Palaces*, 134–137.

13 At the park's exhibition hall is a section regarding Chinese, including Zhang Deyi, Xue Fucheng, Kang Youwei, Liang Qichao, and Shi Shuqing, who traveled overseas and saw artifacts looted from Yuanming Yuan. None of them saw Yuanming Yuan prior to its destruction.

14 Zhang, *Yuanming Yuan yuanshi jieshao*, p. 11.

15 In the case of the ruins park, I agree with James Hevia that in the context of China's historical relationship to Western colonialism and imperialism, Chinese modernity is constructed through a complicated interaction with and participation in coding and decoding the colonial process; for example, mimicking, manipulating, translating, imbricating, and struggling. The production of modernity has been "shaped by and through continual dialogue with transnational forces and formations" (see Hevia, *English Lessons*, 348).

16 For a description of the looting and destruction, see Malone, *History of the Peking Summer Palaces*, 177–191.

17 See Wang Mingzhen, "Beijing tushuguan fen'guan de Yuanming Yuan yiwu (Remains from Yuanming Yuan at a Branch of the Beijing Library)," 154–155.

18 The book *Yuanming Yuan xueshu lunwenji* describes the history of destruction.

19 Zhao Guanghua, "Yuanming Yuan 'yizhi gongyuan' de beiju meixue yuanzhe he zhengxiu de guodu xingshi (The Aesthetic Principle of Tragedy at the 'Ruins Park' of Yuanming Yuan and its Transitional Form in Restoration)," 107; also see 106–109.

20 Zhang, *Yuanming Yuan yuanshi jieshao*, p. 11.

21 Ibid., 16.

22 In 1997, the walls surrounding the Great Fountains were torn down and the whole site of Xiyang Lou became one park again.

23 Lee, "Dialectics of Ruins in Yuanmingyuan."

24 On the miniature as a technology of representation, see Stewart, *On Longing*; Bachelard, *Poetics of Space*; Anagnost, *National Past-Times* (particularly Chapter 7); and Ren, "Displacement and Museum Representation of Aboriginal Cultures in Taiwan."

25 See Stewart's discussion of the dollhouse in *On Longing* (61–65).

26 In the first years following the official opening of the park (June 1988–October 1994), more than ten million people visited Yuanming Yuan. Costumes are available for rent at the site. Dressing up as a form of play in the Xiyang Lou garden goes back to Qianglong's time, when court ladies dressed up in Western-style clothing (see Thiriez, *Barbarian Lens*, 52).

27 For a detailed analysis of this phenomenon, see Zeitlin, "Disappearing Verses."

28 For an excellent study of graffiti in New York City, see Austin, *Taking the Train*. Jean-Luc Nancy, in *The Sense of the World*, 116, discusses graffiti's production of meaning as a form of "wandering." When scholars fix the meaning of graffiti writing according to a particular mode of understanding, they betray its producer.

29 I take this quotation from Malone's *History of the Peking Summer Palaces*, 192. The original words, written by Marquis Tseng, were quoted by Charles Denby in his message to Mr. Bayard dated March 8, 1887 (see United States Department of State, *Executive Documents of the House of Representatives for the First Session of the Fiftieth Congress, 1887–'88*, 198).

30 See Masataka Banno, *China and the West, 1858–1861*.

31 Liu, "Legislating the Universal," 127–164, and "Desire for the Sovereign," 150–177.

32 See Thiriez, *Barbarian Lens*, 145–146.

33 This quotation is from Malone, *History of the Peking Summer Palaces*, 192.

34 See Young-Tsu Wong, *Paradise Lost*, 157.

35 Hevia, *English Lessons*, 334.

36 Lee, "Dialectics of Ruins in Yuanmingyuan."

37 For a description of the Garden of Long Spring and its relation to the Garden of Perfect Brightness, see Malone, *History of the Peking Summer Palaces*, 98–101.

38 For a description of these buildings, see Mu Jingyuan, Chen Wen, Fang Hanlu, and Zong Tianliang, *Yuanming Yuan fengyun lu (A Changing History of Yuanming Yuan)*," 33.

39 Stewart, *On Longing*, 65.

40 The miniature and the gigantic form a dialectical relationship. According to Stewart (*On Longing*, 70): "Whereas the miniature represents closure, interiority, the domestic, and the overly cultural, the gigantic represents infinity, exteriority, the public, and the overly natural." Stewart does not discuss a transformation of the miniature to the gigantic.

41 The theme of wandering first emerged as part of the panoramic literature on daily life in Paris during the July Monarchy (1830–1848) (Cohen, "Panoramic Literature and the Invention of Everyday Genres," 239). The flâneur, a wandering figure captured by Charles Baudelaire, became famous when he was treated as an object of analysis in Walter Benjamin's critique of commodity capitalism ("On Some Motifs in Baudelaire," 155–200). The general implications of the flâneur are discussed by the contributors to the book *The Flâneur* (edited by Keith Tester). In contemporary cultural studies, Michel de Certeau (*Practice of Everyday Life*) takes up the subject in relating movement in a major city like New York to trajectories of power. In this chapter, I treat wandering as a governmental problem of shaping the agency of the consumer-subject through spatial narratives.

42 Interview with Mr. Wang Shuming, a park manager, in July 1996.

43 Qiu also designed another popular theme park called the Primitive Tribe Park (*Yuanshi buluo yuan*) in Huairou County, Beijing.

44 The issue of employing ethnic minorities to represent "primitive peoples" outside China will be further examined in the next chapter.

45 The idea of instrumental discipline draws on the work of Clifford D. Shearing and Philip C. Stenning ("From the Panopticon to Disney World," 335–349).

46 This kind of juxtaposition may be traced back to the world's fairs and expositions.

For example, at the Columbia Exposition in Chicago in 1893, the White City was separated from and juxtaposed with Midway. The former represented a space of civilization while the latter represented the primitive world of underdevelopment.

47 Roth, preface to *Irresistible Decay*, xi.
48 Wang Zhili, "Yuanming Yuan yu Yuanming Yuan yizhi (Yuanming Yuan and the Ruins of Yuanming Yuan)," 262–265.
49 Chen Zhihua, "Liu yi fang yizhi feixue, Yuanming Yuan gai fou chongjian (Preserving the Ruins Site, Should Yuanming Yuan be Rebuilt?)," 724.
50 Ye Tingfang "Yuanming Yuan yizhi qian de tanxi (A Sigh in Front of the Ruins of Yuanming Yuan)," 2.
51 Ji Yuemu, "Yuanming Yuan jiujing shi shui shao de? (Who Burned Yuanming Yuan, After All?)," 2.
52 Ibid.
53 *Beijing wanbao*, June 21, 1997, p. 2.
54 Both Paul Cohen and James Hevia argue that the mass phenomenon of "remembering" the "national humiliation" in the past decade reflects the rise of nationalism in China. Whereas Hevia (in *English Lessons*) regards the phenomenon as part of the historical process of constructing Chinese modernity affected by Western imperialism, Cohen argues that the phenomenon reflects the government's need for a "new legitimating ideology" after 1989 ("Remembering and Forgetting National Humiliation in Twentieth-Century China," 167). Thus, the historical meaning of "national humiliation" consists of both past and present aspects. As a key national historical site, Yuanming Yuan connects to both temporal dimensions of "national humiliation." A new commemorative structure, the Never Forget National Humiliation Wall, was built at the site during the Hong Kong countdown in 1997. While the ruins tell stories about the past, the new structure focuses on the present. Both, however, could not be understood without reference to the operation of Yuanming Yuan as a series of theme parks based on the logic of mass consumption.

Chapter 5: The super-firm in spatial representations of socialism and capitalism

1 See Ren, "Landscape of Power;" Anagnost, *National Past-Times*.
2 Studies of the development of the Shenzhen Special Economic Zone have addressed a variety of issues such as China's development strategy (Sklair, "Problems of Socialist Development"), gendered labor regimes and class formations (Pun, *Made in China*), and Hong Kong's investment (Smart and Smart, "Personal Relations and Divergent Economies"). Compared with these studies, my work focuses on the effects of Hong Kong's return to China and the roles played by Chinese state-owned companies like the CTS in China's neoliberal practices.
3 In this chapter, I focus on the period up to 1997 when China resumed sovereignty over Hong Kong.
4 United Nations Conference on Trade and Development, *World Investment Report, 1996*, 34–35; and *World Investment Report, 1995*, 56.
5 By comparison, South Korea's foreign direct investment outflows averaged about US$2.4 billion annually in the same period (United Nations Conference on Trade and Development, *World Investment Reports* for 1996 and 2000–2002).
6 United Nations Conference on Trade and Development, *World Investment Report, 1995*, 57.
7 Some of the essays were published in Zhonggong Zhongyang Zuzhibu Ganbu Jiaoyuju *et al.*'s *Xianggang sichang jingji jiejian yu shikao* (*Thoughts on Learning from Hong Kong's Market Economy*).
8 *Wenhuibao* May 22, 1995.
9 In addition to performances by professional dancers from Hong Kong, Taiwan,

and China's Shanghai, Beijing and Lanzhou Provinces, the festival included an exhibition, China's Ethnic Minority Dance Costumes, and the Dance and the Audience international conference.

10 Four regular troupes perform at Splendid China theme park: Performance Troupe of Ethnic Songs and Dances, Ethnic Fashion Performance Troupe, Performance Troupe of Native and Folk Songs and Dances, and Chinese Acrobatics Troupe. Ethnic minority employees are selected from these troupes to perform overseas under one of the two names: Ethnic Minority Arts Troupe or Ethnic Arts Troupe (author interview with park employees, 1995).
11 Hsieh Shih-Chung, "From *Shanbao* to *Yuanzhumin*," 404–419.
12 At the Chinese Ethnic Culture Park in Beijing, for example, as well as at CTS theme parks in Shenzhen.
13 For a general discussion of the narration of nation, see Bhabha, "DissemiNation," 291–322.
14 The multiplicity of an image or picture leads us to read it in multiple ways (see Mitchell, *Iconology*, 67).
15 For an excellent work on translation as a translingual practice, see Liu, *Translingual Practice*.
16 United Nations Conference on Trade and Development, *World Investment Report, 1995*, 59.
17 Gao Xinglie, Wang Maoliang, and Hou Jun, "Huaqiao cheng fazhan guan (The Concept of Developing the Overseas Chinese Town)," 28–30.
18 China Travel International Investment Annual Report, 1997.
19 China Travel International Investment Annual Reports, 1992–1998.
20 Ma Chi-man decided to build this "miniature scenic spot" after his visit to the Netherlands' Madurodam "Lilliputian Land" in 1985. In designing it, Ma solicited suggestions from experts, professors, engineers, and technicians throughout China.
21 Anagnost, *National Past-Times*, 163–164.
22 Ma Chi-man (Ma Zhimin), "Renzhao jingguan de shijian yu tiyan (Practice of Artificial Scenery and Experience Thereof)," 87.
23 These twenty-one groups were the Mongolian, Korean, Uygur, Tibetan, Kazak, Tujia, Li, Jingpo, Wa, Hani, Bai, Gaoshan, Mosuo, Naxi, Dong, Miao, Yao, Yi, Bouyei, Zhuang, and Dai.
24 I collected the brochure in 1995.
25 Interview conducted in November 1995; my translation.
26 For a detailed discussion of the historical development of the concept of the folk in the context of official popular culture in China, see Liu, "Metamorphosis of a Folksong Immortal."
27 The general manager of the Chinese Ethnic Culture Park in Beijing, for example, worked with Ma Chi-man before she started her own theme park.
28 Interview in November 1995.
29 In *The Special Economic Zones of China and Their Impact on Its Economic Development*, Jung-Dong Park demonstrates that contracting workers for one to three years has become standard practice for all enterprises in China's SEZs.
30 See Ren, " 'Zhonghua minzuzhuyi' de huayu yu qi duili huayu."
31 The majority of this "fieldwork" took place in the late 1950s and the early 1960s so that ethnic groups could be classified by the government.
32 For a detailed discussion, see Ren, "Landscape of Power."
33 The subjects filmed by the Lumières included the demolition of a wall, a snowball fight, workers leaving the factory, the arrival of a train, and children clam digging and jumping off a pier into the sea. (Many of these films are collected in the DVD *Landmarks of Early Film* [1994, Distributed by Image Entertainment]). In "Cinema of Attractions" Tom Gunning calls this kind of film "cinema of attractions."
34 Early cinema created certain psychological problems with regard to how to

understand reality, for example, the portrayal of a person who had passed away. Without a narrative to structure time, a cinematic presentation of the life of a dead person threatened the present reality of the viewer (see Doane, *Emergence of Cinematic Time*).

35 For a historical discussion, see Crary, *Suspensions of Perception*.

Chapter 6: Memories of the future in Hong Kong

1 Erni, "Like a Postcolonial Culture," 389.

2 For a discussion of this phenomenon, see Wong Wang-chi, Li Siu-leung, and Chan Ching-kiu Stephen, *Fouxiang Xianggang: lishi, wenhua, weilai* (*Hong Kong Un-Imagined: History, Culture and the Future*), 16–17, n. 5.

3 The notion of disappearance has been commonly used by scholars, for example, Ackbar Abbas, Li Siu-leung, Lui Tai-lok, and Oscar Ho. According to Ackbar Abbas, disappearance in Hong Kong was shaped by three factors: abstraction (by means of concrete forms such as images), the ephemeral (what is no longer or not yet there), and speeding up (distortion of the real and indiscernibility); see Abbas, *Hong Kong*, 7–10.

4 The countdown in Hong Kong, according to the Hong Kong-based sociologist Lui Tai-lok, constituted a "situation containing changes within minimum changes" (*yige jinliang bubian de bianju*), a flexible situation in which changes are kept under control. See Lui, *Wugai, maidan! yige shehuixuejia de xianggang biji* (*Check, please! A Sociologist's Notes on Hong Kong*), 127.

5 The Chinese government appointed the Basic Law Drafting Committee in June 1985. Of its fifty-nine members, thirty-six were from the mainland and twenty-three from Hong Kong. The first task of the Hong Kong members was to set up a Basic Law Consultative Committee, consisting of 180 members from Hong Kong, to advise the drafting committee. The first draft of the Basic Law was published in April 1988, and the second draft in February 1989. It was finalized and adopted on February 16, 1990 (see Ching, "Toward Colonial Sunset," 176, 180–181).

6 Lui, *Wugai, maidan!* 128.

7 For examples of radio and television programs, as well as fiction, using the countdown clock, see Li Siu-leung, "zhimin de lishi xiangxiang (Historical Imaginary of Colonialism)," 131–261.

8 Cited in Li Siu-leung, "zhimin de lishi xiangxiang," 137.

9 Ibid.

10 Abbas, *Hong Kong*, 5. Rey Chow criticized this "gloom-doom-boom" situation as a libidinal economy based on a "binary opposition between lack and compensation:" "the more Hong Kong excels in its materialistic accomplishments, the more this excellence must be taken to be a sign of its deficiency, degeneracy, abnormality, and hence basic inferiority" (*Ethics after Idealism*, 171). While I understand Chow's position and agree with her caution about the implications of Abbas' argument, I would not dismiss the question of displacement simply as "a libidinal economy based on a binary opposition between lack and compensation." As Abbas himself argues, this displacement is about decadence under colonial conditions: "It is decadent not in the sense of decline (because we see what looks like progress everywhere) but in the sense of a one-dimensional development in a closed field. It is such decadence that has made it difficult to recognize the existence of a Hong Kong culture" (*Hong Kong*, 5).

11 I use *Hongkong* to refer to Hong Kong/Heunggong as a cultural construction in transition. Currently, three terms—*Hong Kong* (English), *Xianggang* (Putonghua), and *Heunggong* (Cantonese)—are commonly used to designate Hong Kong. Each carries a specific set of cultural and historical meanings. *Heunggong* is closely associated with Heunggongyan ("Hong Kong people" in Cantonese), a term used

by ethnic Chinese in Hong Kong. It draws our attention to a cultural specificity but excludes those who are not ethnic Chinese. The two other terms, *Hong Kong* and *Xianggang*, have the same problem of cultural specificity. For this reason, I use *Hongkong* to highlight the multiplicity of peoples in Hong Kong.

12 Ho, "In Search of an Identity," 14. Cited in Hung Wu, "Hong Kong Clock," 352.

13 Li Siu-leung, "zhimin de lishi xiangxiang," 131–261.

14 See Chow, *Ethics after Idealism*, 157; Cheung, "Hi/Stories of Hong Kong," 571.

15 The description of Hong Kong as a "borrowed place, borrowed time" is from Richard Hughes' book of the same name. According to Hughes, the phrase came originally from an article written by the Chinese writer Han Suyin and published in *Life* in 1959.

16 A time period cannot be eventful, and therefore historical, without first being displayed in public, which requires material support or measures (see Bachelard, "Instant," 81).

17 Chinese Manufacturers' Union in Hong Kong, *Pictorial Record of the Exhibition of Chinese Products, 1939*, 20.

18 Ibid., 19.

19 Ibid.

20 For a detailed study of "national products" exhibitions in China, see Gerth, *China Made*.

21 Chinese Manufacturers' Union in Hong Kong, *Pictorial Record of the Exhibition of Chinese Products, 1939*, 17.

22 Many scholars have examined the historical link between international exhibitions and the economies of colonial empires; see, for example, Mitchell, *Colonising Egypt*; and Mattelart, *Invention of Communication*.

23 Hong Kong Legislative Council, "British Empire Exhibition, Wembley, 1924 and 1925," 3.

24 Ibid., 6.

25 See the British Industries Fair Committee, "Report on Hong Kong's Participation in the British Industries Fair, 1948," 26, 28, 29.

26 Chinese Manufacturers' Union, *Seventh Exhibition of Chinese Products, Hong Kong*, 5.

27 Ibid., 5.

28 Cited in Turner, "Hong Kong Sixties/Nineties," 33, n. 28.

29 For an excellent discussion of the relation of Hong Kong's identity to consumer culture, see Turner and Ngan, *Hong Kong Sixties*, particularly Turner's chapter "Hong Kong Sixties/Nineties" (pp. 13–34).

30 See Wong, Li and Chan, *Fouxiang Xianggang*.

31 Lui Tai-lok argues that because of the sense of borrowed time, Hong Kong lacked political time as an independent community. Therefore, an economic time was developed to focus on the present, disconnected from the future (see Lui, *Wugai, maidan!* 115–116). I argue that Hong Kong, despite its lack of a unified political time, did not and does not lack political time at the mundane level of the everyday.

32 For a detailed discussion of flexible accumulation, see Harvey's *Condition of Postmodernity*. Amy K. Glasmeier's work on the history of Hong Kong's watch manufacturing industry shows the importance of flexible accumulation in Hong Kong, noting that the average size of a watch manufacturing firm in 1970s to 1990s Hong Kong was twelve to forty-five employees (see her *Manufacturing Time*, 216–241).

33 The "riot" started as a clash between laid-off workers and police on May 6, 1967. The tempo of violence steadily increased afterwards. A series of bombings took place from August to December 1967 (for a detailed discussion, see Young "Building Years," especially p. 140). For alternative perspectives on the 1967 riot and its links to the 1966 Star Ferry riots, see Robert Bickers and Ray Yep, *May*

Days in Hong Kong, and Wai-man Lam, *Understanding the Political Culture of Hong Kong*. The closure of the border between Hong Kong and China in this period also fostered a Hong Kong identity (Agnes Ku, "Immigration Policies, Discourses and the Politics of Local Belonging in Hong Kong (1950–1980)").

34 See Ming K. Chan, *Precarious Balance*.

35 The development of the council is a historical process. In fact, the Urban Council had existed since 1935, replacing the former Sanitary Board (1887–1935), but it had been controlled by the Legislative Council rather than the colonial government. Throughout its history, the council has been tied to sanitation, the most important issue for the government. The Committee of Public Health was instituted as early as 1843, two years after Britain occupied Hong Kong Island. Osbert Chadwick, a former military engineer, carried out a full-scale survey of sanitary conditions in the early 1880s, after which the government set up the Sanitary Board and formulated the Public Health Ordinance (1887). Gradually, the government institutionalized its control over sanitation. (For a detailed discussion of the relationship between the history of the Urban Council and institutionalization of public health, see Lewis, "Health of a Great City," in *Hong Kong Urban Council Annual Report*, 1992–1993.)

36 For a list of events, see Universal News Agency, *Festival of Hong Kong Commemoration Magazine, 1969*, 23–24.

37 Foreword to *Festival of Hong Kong Commemoration Magazine, 1969*, 2.

38 Editorial in *Huaqiao Ribao* (*Overseas Chinese Daily*), December 13, 1969. Quoted in Universal News Agency, *Festival of Hong Kong Commemoration Magazine, 1969*, 41.

39 For MacLehose's speech at the 1971 Hong Kong Festival, see his "Right Combination of Work and Play," 9. On the role of the government in the development of recreation and culture in Hong Kong, see To Kwai-mui, *Government's Role in the Development of Recreation and Culture in Hong Kong*. The British government's position on Hong Kong's status is documented in *Hong Kong: Long Term Study* (see Ewing, "Secret Hong Kong Story").

40 After the Regional Council was established in 1985, the Urban Council's responsibility shifted from administering all museums in Hong Kong to those in Hong Kong Island and Kowloon.

41 Note that the former museum's English name was the Hong Kong Museum of History, whereas its Chinese name translated to the Hong Kong Museum (*Xianggang bowuguan*). It was not until 1998 that the Chinese name was also formally changed to the Hong Kong Museum of History (*Xianggang lishi bowuguan*).

42 Ching-Hin Ho, "Hong Kong Museum of History," 141.

43 Hong Kong Urban Council, *Urban Council Annual Report*, 1982, 87.

44 Ho, "Hong Kong Museum of History," 143. Also see Hong Kong Urban Council, *Urban Council Annual Reports*, 1975–1985.

45 See Ting, "Xianggang bowuguan koushu lishi jihua jianjie, 1987–89 (The Oral History Project by the Hong Kong Museum of History, 1987–89)," 59–62.

46 See Hong Kong Urban Council: *Urban Council Annual Report*, 1991, 127.

47 One of the first events in the development of Hong Kong Studies was the Hong Kong Culture and Society conference held at the University of Hong Kong Centre of Asian Studies in December 1991. The conference papers were collected in Sinn, *Culture and Society in Hong Kong*. For the development of Hong Kong cultural studies, see the special issue of *Cultural Studies* (vol. 15, nos. 3–4, 2001), particularly John Nguyet Erni's "Like a Postcolonial Culture."

48 The head of the firm, Jean Jacques André, was director of exhibits for the British Columbia Provincial Museum (now the Royal British Columbia Museum) from 1970 to 1982, when he formed his own company. In addition to The Story of Hong Kong exhibitions (both the original version that opened from 1991 to 1998 and the

new version that opened in the summer of 2001), the firm has also designed and installed exhibitions for many other museums. For more information about the company and its completed projects, see its website: www.aaid.ca/beta.

49 See Urban Services Department, *The Five-Year Plan of the Provisional Urban Council's Museums Select Committee (Consultation Paper)*, September 1997, Annex IV.

50 Hong Kong Urban Council, *Urban Council Annual Report*, 1991–1992, 102.

51 Benjamin, "One-Way Street," 444–488.

52 Benjamin, *Charles Baudelaire*, 171.

53 Benjamin's articulation of the external physical experience to the internal, mental experience of memory was a critique of "all of the errors of bourgeois consciousness"—"commodity fetishism, reification, the world as 'inwardness,' " and "all of its utopian dreams" such as "in fashion, prostitution, gambling." See Susan Buck-Morss, *The Dialectics of Seeing*, 39.

54 Chinese concubines and their "golden lily" feet became a favored stereotype among European and American writers. Among famous Chinese elites, Robert Ho Tung, who worked for Jardine, Matheson and Co., was often singled out as a typical example of a Chinese elite that practiced concubinage and evoked in nostalgic narratives about colonial Hong Kong (see, for example, Wiltshire, *Old Hong Kong*, 11). David Tang, the owner of the famous Shanghai Tang and the son and grandson of concubines, talked about the experience of living on the Peak as that of "the embourgeoisement of the Hong Kong Chinese:" "For years we Chinese didn't really live with or even near the British expatriates who more or less ran the colony. It wasn't until as recently as the early 1970s that the more prosperous Chinese (most of them having ridden high out of the shaky property market following the riots) started living up the hill on the island, and even on the Peak, which had been an almost exclusively white enclave. Such ascendancy was more than merely symbolic" (*Old Hong Kong*, viii, the companion book to the documentary film of the same title made by the Film Business Ltd, Hong Kong, produced by Elaine Forsgate Marden and directed by Libby Halliday). The ostracism of Chinese families based on the practice of concubinage had much broader implications around the world. For example, the U.S. government's implementation of the Page Law of 1875 often identified Chinese females seeking to enter the United States as concubines and prostitutes, and excluded them accordingly (see Luibhéid, *Entry Denied*, particularly Chapter 2).

55 See André & Knowlton Associates Ltd., "The Story of Hong Kong, Hong Kong Museum of History," www.andreknowlton.com/Pages/Complete/hkmh1.html (accessed December 16, 2002).

56 Lu Weiluan wrote about her experience of visiting the street exhibit, particularly her comparison of the experience of listening to the sounds versus experiencing them in real life. See *Xianggang gushi: geren huiyi yu wenxue shikao* (*The Story of Hong Kong: Personal Memories and Literary Thinking*), 6–7.

57 Space shelters time. This is the point Gaston Bachelard makes in *The Poetics of Space*.

58 I expect that the politics of disappearance is expressed differently in post-1997 Hong Kong, as I discuss briefly in the conclusion.

59 For historical discussions of Hong Kong moving beyond the metropolis, see the volume *Beyond the Metropolis* (edited by Hase and Sinn).

60 Cheung, "Hi/Stories of Hong Kong," 565, 567–568, 564. Cheung's examples of "the epics of the imperial empire," mode of representation include Nigel Cameron's *An Illustrated History of Hong Kong*, Alan Birch's *The Colony That Never Was*, and Frank Welsh's *A History of Hong Kong*. Her examples for the second metropolis include *From Village to City* (edited by David Faure *et al.*) and *Beyond the Metropolis*.

61 For discussions of the relationship between the politics of colonialism and the academy, see Chiu, "Politics and the Body Social in Colonial Hong Kong," 185–215; and Erni, "Like a Postcolonial Culture."
62 For an excellent study of the colonial transformation of the New Territories, see Chun, "Colonial 'Govern-mentality' in Transition," 430–461.
63 This discussion is a significant expansion of my article "Kan de bianzheng: zhanlangui zhong de xianggang (The Dialectics of Seeing: *Hongkong* in Showcases)," 106–120. (Reprinted in Liu Qingfeng *et al.*, *Zhuanhua zhong de xianggang*, 195–219.)
64 This office, due to its being part of the Government Secretariat, had more administrative authority than the Hong Kong Museum of History, which was under the administration of the museum section of the Urban Council.
65 Antiquities and Monuments Office, *Report of the Antiquities Advisory Board*, 1992 & 1993, 6.
66 By June 29, 2007, the total declared monuments had reached eighty-two, according to information provided by the Antiquities and Monuments Office.
67 Antiquities and Monuments Office, Recreation and Culture Branch, *The Heritage of Hong Kong*, 5.
68 This quotation is from Sidney C. H. Cheung's discussion of Hong Kong's "heritage" in "The Meanings of a Heritage Trail in Hong Kong," 573.
69 Antiquities and Monuments Office, *Heritage of Hong Kong*, 59.
70 Government press release, December 8, 1989.
71 Ng, "Role of Architects in Conservation."
72 Advisory Inspectorate Division, Education Department, Hong Kong, *Heritage-Related Activities in Schools*, 11.
73 Currently, Hong Kong has three heritage trails launched by the Antiquities and Monuments Office. In addition to the Pingshan Heritage Trail, there is the Lung Yeuk Tau Heritage Trail, inaugurated on December 4, 1999, and the Central and Western Heritage Trail, with three sections: the Central Route (launched October 1997), the Sheung Wan Route (July 1999), and the Peak Route (December 2000).
74 See the booklet *Pingshan Heritage Trail*, n.p.
75 Ibid.
76 See "Antiquities and Monuments Ordinance," in Antiquities and Monuments Office, Recreation and Culture Branch, *Report of the Antiquities Advisory Board*, 1988 and 1989, 14–27.
77 Michael Herzfeld has differentiated two types of time in the context of historical preservation: social and monumental time. "Social time is the grist of everyday experience . . . It is the time that gives events their reality . . . Monumental time, in contrast, is reductive and generic. It . . . reduces social experience to collective predictability. Its main focus is on the past—a past constituted by categories and stereotypes. In its extreme forms, it is the time frame of the nation state" (*A Place in History*, 10).
78 Statistics cited in Cheung, "Meanings of a Heritage Trail in Hong Kong," 578.
79 Ibid.
80 Cheung, "Meanings of a Heritage Trail in Hong Kong," 579.
81 See Watson and Watson, "From Hall of Worship to Tourist Center," 33–35.
82 Writing history involves the active production of history. As Michel de Certeau points out, writing history "constantly mends the rents in the fabric that joins past and present. It assures a 'meaning,' which surmounts the violence and the division of time. It creates a theater of references and of common values, which guarantee a sense of unity and a 'symbolic' communicability to the group. . . . [I]t reunite(s) all sorts of separated things and people into the semblance of a unity and a presence that constitutes representation itself" ("History: Science and Fiction," 205).

83 Pingshan's relation to the history of Hong Kong includes the military takeover of the New Territories by the British as well as local resistance to the British in 1899. For a balanced discussion of this colonial history, see Allen Chun, "Colonial 'Govern-mentality' in Transition."

84 Cited in Hong Kong Legislative Council, "Despatches and Other Papers Relating to the Extending of the Colony of Hongkong," 6.

85 I acknowledge that many anthropologists such as Maurice Freedman, James Hayes, Allen Chun, and Jack Potter have written on *fungshui* politics in the New Territories.

86 While mentioning the former aspect, Sidney Cheung's discussion in "The Meanings of a Heritage Trail in Hong Kong" (574) completely ignores the latter aspect. Given that any knowledge production is also a social production, I understand why he did so: he explicitly described himself as an urban Hong Kong resident in search of a Hongkong cultural heritage. However, it is vital not to ignore the local historical construction of the space of Pingshan, even though the Tang clan's historical narratives might contradict the Hongkong heritage.

87 Ng Kang-chung, "Trail Closed in Grave Row," 3.

88 See written statement of Ng K'i-ch'eng, dated April 21, 1899, and Colonial Secretary's minutes, dated April 20, 1899, in Hong Kong Legislative Council, "Despatches and Other Papers Relating to the Extension of the Colony of Hong-kong," pp. 45 and 40, respectively.

89 In an April 4, 1899, proclamation issued by Tam, viceroy of Two Kwong Provinces and Luk, governor of Kwong-tung Province, the residents of the newly leased territory were informed:

> Whereas Kowloon has been leased under the instructions of the Emperor and the boundary has been defined in accordance with the original map forwarded by the Tsung-li Yamen, the following agreement has been come to with the foreign officials:
>
> 1 The people are to be treated with exceptional kindness.
> 2 There can be no forced sale of houses and lands.
> 3 The graves in the leased territory are never to be removed.
> 4 Local customs and habits are to remain unchanged according to the wishes of the inhabitants.
>
> In these respects, therefore, the villages and market towns in the leased territory will not differ from those within Chinese territory. Wherefore this notification is issued to let all know that whatever occurs in the villages and market towns of China has now nothing to do with you (who live in the leased territory). No one must under any pretext excite or mislead the minds of the people. You who live in the villages and market towns of the leased territory should follow your occupations and abide by the law as heretofore.
>
> If in disobedience to the Imperial decree you dare to create strife or avail yourselves of any pretext to stir up trouble, there is now a large military force in the territory which will arrest and deal with the guilty without mercy.

This notice was laid before the Legislative Council by command of H. A. Blake, governor of Hong Kong, and published in Hong Kong Legislative Council, *Hong Kong Legislative Council Sessional Papers, 1899*. After the New Territories were officially leased to Britain in 1898, major clans in the area organized local residents against the British troops. The Chinese government sent this proclamation to the residents at the British government's request. Hence, it appears that the British government agreed to the terms in the proclamation, even if it did not issue the notice directly. Moreover, the issuance of this notice by the Chinese government showed the ambiguity of the territory's status as land "leased" from China, for both China and Britain. The New Territories as a leased territory was a newly constructed category in colonial situations in East Asia in 1898. Its status and effect on international law had not been carefully worked out. The British were intent on ensuring that the leased territory be transferred to Britain in the same manner as Kowloon and Hong Kong Island. The Chinese, meanwhile, insisted on maintaining a military garrison and customshouse there, and retaining sovereignty over the land and people of the leased territory. See Wesley-Smith, *Unequal Treaty 1898–1997*, 90; and Chun, "Colonial 'Govern-Mentality' in Transition," 446–447.

90 The Chinese and the British governments had agreed that any major projects that would not be completed by July 1, 1997 should receive the consent of the Chinese government prior to implementation.

91 On the relationship between the other and cultural representation, see Fabian, *Time and the Other*. Haun Saussy further examines the problem of temporal representation in Chinese studies, see his "No Time Like the Present," 91–117.

92 Several authors have examined the issue of consumer culture in Hong Kong. See Turner, "Hong Kong Sixties/Nineties;" Ma, "Consuming Satellite Modernities," 444–63; and Mathews and Lui, *Consuming Hong Kong*.

93 For some examples of this distinction, see Mathews, "What in the World Is Chinese?" 148–149. For a critical discussion of this difference, see Xiaoying Wang, "Hong Kong, China, and the Question of Postcoloniality," 95.

Conclusion: Is China truly neoliberal, or a state with neoliberal characteristics?

1 It is reported that this narrative of the party's status is championed by China's Vice President Xi Jingpin, who is widely tipped to succeed President Hu Jingtao (Wu Zhong, " 'Red Capitalists' Unravel the Party Line").

2 Elsewhere, I have examined various other countdown phenomena in "The Merit of Time."

3 In addition to claims by Friedman and the U.S.-based Heritage Foundation that Hong Kong has the freest economy in the world, many other studies have examined Hong Kong's distinctive mode of capitalism. Gary Hamilton's *Cosmopolitan Capitalists* presents a series of examples of the cultural practices of Hong Kong-based capitalists. Henry Wai-chung Yeung's *Transnational Corporations and Business Networks* links network-based Hong Kong capitalism to the rise of transnational capitalism in Southeast Asia. Stephen Chiu's and Tai-Lok Lui's *Hong Kong* analyzes Hong Kong's capitalism as a transition to a global city.

4 On housing development as an important dimension of consumption in China, see Davis, "Urban Consumer Culture," 692–709, and "Urban Chinese Homeowners as Citizen–Consumers," 281–299.

5 Real estate is one of the key operations of the Overseas Chinese Town group. It has developed projects in such major cities as Shenzhen, Beijing, Shanghai, and Chengdu. For information, see the company's website: www.chinaoct.com/home.aspx. In addition, housing is increasingly the area where Chinese consumers spend their savings (see Deborah Davis' publications).

6 That neoliberal individuals and organizations transgress rules and norms might explain the widespread corruption in China.

7 This list of events was generated in September 2007 through a search for the phrase "countdown to Hong Kong's return" on Baidu.com, a Chinese Internet search engine similar to Google.com in the United States.

8 Flusser distinguishes between "line thought" (a linear mode of thought dealing with objective codes, consciously learned conventions, and clearly conceptualized

facts) and "surface thought" (a mode of thought characterized by subjective codes and fully represented facts) in his "Line and Surface" (1973) in his *Writings*, 21–34.

9 Such coexistence would be unthinkable under the linear mode of historical time. See Duara, *Rescuing History from the Nation*; and Saussy, "No Time Like the Present," 103.

10 "The countdown clock for the Beijing 2008 will be a new sight in the city symbolizing the concept of People's Olympics, and it will also serve as a window to showcase Beijing," said BOCOG Vice President Jiang Xiaoyu at the unveiling ceremony, "The clock will witness the realization of China's century-long Olympic dream and will add fresh impetus to the preparations for the Olympic Games" (http://en.olympic.cn/08beijing/bocog/2004-09–22/326030.html, accessed on January 9, 2008).

11 From http://baike.baidu.com/view/174409.htm#4 and http://en.beijing2008.cn/spirit/beijing2008/graphic/n214068253.shtml (both accessed January 9, 2008).

12 Branding China has become an important strategy for the Chinese government in recent years. See Yuezhi Zhao, *Communication in China*; and Jing Wang, *Brand New China*.

13 Pfanner, "For 2008 Olympics Campaigns, the Starter's Gun Went Off This Month."

14 See the editorial "The Two-Year countdown to the Olympics: Glory and Responsibility" (Auyun daojishi liang zhounian: guangrong yu zheren) in the *People's Daily*, one of the most important official newspapers, on August 8, 2006. Available online at http://sports.sina.com.cn/r/2006-08-08/16222385391.shtml (accessed January 9, 2008).

15 For example, cars with even license plate numbers and cars with odd numbers were permitted to drive on alternate days (from my fieldwork in Beijing in August 2008).

16 This is shown by comments on the Internet. For a good example, see the web forum on the launching of the Olympics countdown clock at www.hoolee8.com/forum-7-1.html (accessed January 9, 2008).

17 Zhang Peili, "Chinese Artists in a Chinese Spectacle."

18 See Pfanner, "For 2008 Olympics Campaigns, the Starter's Gun Went Off This Month;" and Elliott, "For Olympics, China's Marketers Are Showing Their Pride."

19 From http://en.beijing2008.cn/spirit/beijing2008/graphic/n214068253.shtml (accessed January 9, 2008).

20 For example, Cox and Silva, "Keeping Up With Beijing," C13.

21 For an insider's critique of the global implications of the Washington Consensus, see Stiglitz, *Globalization and Its Discontents*.

22 Recently, U.S. scholars in international relations have called for the rebuilding of this alliance. See Ikenberry, "Rise of China and the Future of the West," 23–37.

23 For example, the former editor of *Newsweek International* Fareed Zakaria titles his recent book *The Post-American World* to characterize the growth of other countries such as China, India, Brazil, and Russia.

24 Rifkin, *European Dream*, 382.

25 Ibid., 385.

26 Cooper, "Post-Modern State," April 7, 2002. Available online through the website of the Foreign Policy Centre, a major think-tank based in London, at http://fpc.org.uk/articles/169 (accessed May 10, 2008).

27 Anderson, "European Hypocrisies," 18.

28 Ramo, "Beijing Consensus," 37.

29 Mao Zengyu, " 'Beijing gongshi' yu 'huashengdun gongshi' zhi bijiao" (A Comparison between the "Beijing Consensus" and the "Washington Consensus"), 396.

30 Ramo, "Beijing Consensus," 33.

31 Friedman, "Free Markets and the End of History."

32 Friedman, "Hong Kong Wrong."
33 Zhao, *Communication in China*, 101–105.
34 For example, http://www.news.cn/politics/2009jrht51/, http://www.xinhuanet.com/politics/60zn/mlzg.htm, and http://www.xinhuanet.com/politics/60zn/zgqs.htm (accessed October 1, 2009).
35 From http://news.xinhuanet.com/world/2009-05/08/content_11334668.htm (accessed September 28, 2009).
36 See http://news.xinhuanet.com/theory/2008-11/18/content_10373496.htm (accessed September 28, 2009).
37 Foucault refers to strategy as a positive manipulation of power in a mutually supporting relationship to certain type of knowledge. A governmental strategy is formed to respond to an urgency developed at a given historical moment. It may be expressed in a number of ways: developing power relations in a particular direction, or blocking them, stabilizing them, and utilizing them (*Knowledge/Power*, 194–196).
38 Chiu and Lui, *Hong Kong*, 130.
39 Ibid.
40 Barboza, "China Unveils $586 Billion Economic Stimulus Plan."
41 From November 2008 on, for example, *The Wall Street Journal* has published many opinion articles that consider China a key player in fighting global economic crisis.
42 Zizek, "China's Valley of Tears." Harvey argues that although China may have one of the world's fastest-growing economies, it has also become one of the most unequal societies (*Brief History of Neoliberalism*, 142). The Gini coefficient, a measure of income differentials, has risen from 2.281 in 1981 to 0.51 in 2002, the fastest increase in any country (see Hu Angang, "Equity and Efficiency," 222).
43 Friedman (in "Economic Freedom, Human Freedom, Political Freedom") argues that economic freedom (established by free private markets) facilitates political freedom (democracy).
44 According to Carl Schmitt (*Concept of the Political*, 74–75), since the eighteenth century, modern capitalism has been based on the historical logic of progress and has developed through an alliance between the economy and the democratic political system. Modern capitalism could not have evolved without any of its three pillars, namely, a democratic (rather than authoritarian) political system, the economy (including industry and technology), and liberalism (freedom, progress and reason).

Bibliography

Abbas, Ackbar. 1997. *Hong Kong: Culture and the Politics of Disappearance*. Minneapolis: University of Minnesota Press.

Advisory Inspectorate Division, Education Department, Hong Kong. 1996. *Heritage-Related Activities in Schools*. Hong Kong: Advisory Inspectorate Division, Education Department, Hong Kong.

Agamben, Giorgio. 1998. *Homo Sacer: Sovereign Power and Bare Life*, translation Daniel Heller-Roazen. Stanford. CA: Stanford University Press. (Originally published 1995.)

Althusser, Louis. 1994 [1969–1970]. "Ideology and Ideological State Apparatuses (Notes Towards an Investigation)." In Slavoj Zizek, ed., *Mapping Ideology*, pp. 100–140. London: Verso.

Anagnost, Ann. 1997. *National Past-Times: Narrative, Representation, and Power in Modern China*. Durham, NC: Duke University Press.

Anderson, Perry. 2007. "European Hypocrisies." *London Review of Books*, Vol. 29, No. 18, September 20, 2007, pp. 13–21.

——. 2007. "History and Lessons of Neoliberalism." Online document at http://www.religion-online.org/showchapter.asp?title=1562&C=1404. Accessed September 7, 2007.

——. 2003. "Xinziyouzhuyi de lishi he jiaoxun (History and Lessons of Neoliberalism)." In *Quanqiuhua yu xinziyoushuyi* (*Globalization and Neoliberalism*), eds Li Qiqing and Liu Yuanqi. Guilin: Guangxi Shifan Daxue Chubanshe.

André & Knowlton Associates Ltd. n.d. "The Story of Hong Kong, Hong Kong Museum of History," at http://www.andreknowlton.com/Pages/Complete/hkmh1.html.

——. n.d. "The Hong Kong Museum of History," at http://www..andreknowlton.com/.

Antiquities and Monuments Office, Recreation and Culture Branch. 1993. *Report of the Antiquities Advisory Board 1992 & 1993*. Hong Kong: Antiquities and Monuments Office.

——. 1992. *The Heritage of Hong Kong*, (ed. P. D. W. Burton) Hong Kong: Government Printer.

——. 1989. "Antiquities and Monuments Ordinance." In *Report of the Antiquities Advisory Board, 1988 and 1989*. Hong Kong: Antiquities and Monuments Office, Recreation and Culture Branch.

——. n.d. *Pingshan Heritage Trail*. Hong Kong: Antiquities and Monuments Office.

Arendt, Hannah. 1958. *The Human Condition*. Chicago: University of Chicago Press.

Ariely, Dan. 2008. *Predictably Irrational: The Hidden Forces That Shape Our Decisions*. New York: HarperCollins.

Austin, Joe. 2001. *Taking the Train: How Graffiti Art Became an Urban Crisis in New York City*. New York: Columbia University Press.

Bachelard, Gaston. 2001. "The Instant," translation Mary McAllester Jones. In *Time & the Instant: Essays in the Physics and Philosophy of Time*, ed. Robin Durie. Manchester: Clinamen Press.

——. 2000. *The Dialectic of Duration*, translation Mary McAllester Jones. Manchester, UK: Clinamen Press.

——. 1969. *The Poetics of Space*, translation Maria Jolas. Boston: Beacon Press.

Badiou, Alain. 2005. "The Cultural Revolution: The Last Revolution?" *positions: east asia cultures critique*, Vol. 13, no. 3 (Winter, 2005).

——. 2005. *Being and Event*, translation Oliver Feltham. London: Continuum. (Originally published 1988.)

——. 2004. "Being and Appearance." In his *Theoretical Writings*, eds. and translation Ray Brassier and Alberto Toscano, pp. 163–175, 249–250. London: Continuum.

——. 2003. *Saint Paul: The Foundation of Universalism*, translation Ray Brassier. Stanford, CA: Stanford University Press. (Originally published 1997.)

——. 2001. *Ethics: An Essay on the Understanding of Evil*, translation Peter Hallward. London: Verso. (Originally published 1998.)

——. 2000. *Deleuze: The Clamor of Being*, translation Louise Burchill. Minneapolis: University of Minnesota Press. (Originally published 1997.)

——. 1999. *Manifesto for Philosophy*, translation Norman Madarasz. Albany, NY: State University of New York Press. (Originally published 1989.)

Badiou, Alain and Alessandro Russo. 2006. "International Center for the Study of the Cultural Revolution: Elements of a Project." *Inter-Asia Cultural Studies*, Vol. 7, No. 4.

Balibar, Étienne. 2004. "Citizenship without Community?" In his *We, the People of Europe?: Reflections on Transnational Citizenship*, translation James Swenson. Princeton, NJ: Princeton University Press. (Originally published 2001.)

——. 1992. *Les frontières de la démocratie*. Paris: La Découvete.

——. 1991. "The Nation Form: History and Ideology." In *Race, Nation, Class: Ambiguous Identities*, by Etienne Balibar and Immanuel Wallerstein. London: Verso. (Originally published 1988.)

Banno, Masataka. 1964. *China and the West, 1858–1861: The Origins of the Tsungli Yamen*. Cambridge, MA: Harvard University Press.

Barboza, David. 2008. "China Unveils $586 Billion Economic Stimulus Plan." *New York Times*. November 9, 2008.

Barker, Jason. 2002. *Alain Badiou: A Critical Introduction*. London: Pluto Press.

Barmé, Geremie R. 1999. *In the Red: On Contemporary Chinese Culture*. New York: Columbia University Press.

Baudrillard, Jean. 1998. "In the Shadow of the Millennium (Or the Suspense of the Year 2000)" (Originally published September 23, 1998). Online document: http://www.ctheory.net/articles.aspx?id=104. Accessed March 2010.

——. 1998. "The End of the Millennium or The Countdown." *Theory, Culture & Society*, 1998, Vol. 15, no. 1, 1–9.

——. 1994. *The Illusion of the End*, translation Chris Turner. Stanford, CA: Stanford University Press. (Originally written in 1992.)

——. 1994. "The Precession of Simulacra," in his *Simulacra and Simulation*, translation Sheila Faria Glaser. Ann Arbor: University of Michigan Press. (Originally published 1981.)

——. 1988. "For a Critique of the Political Economy of the Sign." In his *Jean Baudrillard: Selected Writings*, ed. Mark Poster. Stanford, CA: Stanford University Press. (Originally published 1981.)

——. 1988. "Simulacra and Simulations." In his *Jean Baudrillard: Selected Writings*, ed. Mark Poster. Stanford, CA: Stanford University Press.

Becker, Gary S. 1992. "The Economic Way of Looking at Life." Online document. http://www.nobel.se/economics/laureates/1992/becker-lecture.html, accessed July 11, 2007.

Bedini, Silvio A. 1994. *The Trail of Time: Time Measurement with Incense in East Asia*. Cambridge, UK: Cambridge University Press.

——. 1975. "Oriental Concepts of the Measure of Time." In *The Study of Time*. Vol. 2, eds J. T. Fraser and N. Lawrence. New York: Springer-Verlag.

Beijing Tianwenguan. 1987. *Zhongguo gudai tianwenxue chengjiu (The Achievements of Astrology in Ancient China)*. Beijing: Beijing Kexue Jishu Chubanshe.

Benjamin, Walter. 1999. *The Arcades Project*, translation Howard Eiland and Kevin McLaughlin, Cambridge, MA: The Belknap Press of Harvard University Press.

——. 1996. "One-Way Street." In his *Selected Writings. Volume 1, 1913–1926*, eds Marcus Bullock and Michael W. Jennings. Cambridge, MA: Belknap Press of Harvard University Press.

——. 1973. *Charles Baudelaire: A Lyric Poet in the Era of High Capitalism*. translation Harry Zohn. London: NLB.

——. 1968. "On Some Motifs in Baudelaire." In his *Illuminations*, ed. Hannah Arendt. translation Harry Zohn. New York: Schocken.

——. 1968. "Theses on the Philosophy of History" in his *Illuminations*, ed. Hannah Arendt, translation Harry Zohn, New York: Schocken.

——. 1968. "The Work of Art in the Age of Mechanical Reproduction." In his *Illuminations*, ed. Hannah Arendt, translation Harry Zohn. New York: Schocken. (Originally published 1936.)

Bergson, Henri. 1990. *Matter and Memory*, translation W. S. Palmer and N. M. Paul. New York: Zone Books. (Originally written in 1896.)

Berlant, Lauren. 2007. "Slow Death (Sovereignty, Obesity, Lateral Agency)." *Critical Inquiry*, Vol. 33, No.4, 754–780.

Bhabha, Homi K. 1994. *The Location of Culture*. New York: Routledge.

——. 1990. "DissemiNation: Time, Narrative, and the Margins of the Modern Nation," in *Nation and Narration*, ed. Homi K. Bhabha. London: Routledge.

Bickers, Robert and Ray Yep, ed. 2009. *May Days in Hong Kong: Riot and Emergency in 1967*. Hong Kong: Hong Kong University Press.

Birch, Alan. 1991. *The Colony That Never Was*. Hong Kong: Twin Age.

Blaise, Clark. 2000. *Time Lord: Sir Sandford Fleming and the Creation of Standard Time*. New York: Pantheon Books.

Blomgren, Anna-Maria. 1997. *Nyliberal Politisk Filosofi: En Kritisk Analys av Milton Friedman, Robert Nozick och F. A. Hayek*. Nora: Bokförlaget Nya Doxa.

Bogue, Ronald. 2003. *Deleuze on Cinema*. New York: Routledge.

Bordwell, David. 2000. *Planet Hong Kong: Popular Cinema and the Art of Entertainment*. Cambridge, MA: Harvard University Press.

Bramall, Chris. 2009. *Chinese Economic Development*. London: Routledge.

British Industries Fair Committee. 1949. "Report on Hong Kong's Participation in the British Industries Fair, 1948." *Hong Kong Legislative Council Sessional Paper 1948 Part II*. Hong Kong: Noronha & Co., Ltd.

Brown, Wendy. 2006. *Regulating Aversion: Tolerance in the Age of Identity and Empire*. Princeton, NJ: Princeton University Press.

——. 2003. "Neo-Liberalism and the End of Liberal Democracy." *Theory and Event* vol. 7, no. 1 2003.

Brownell, Susan. 1999. "Strong Women and Impotent Men: Sports, Gender, and Nationalism in Chinese Public Culture." In *Spaces of Their Own: Women's Public Sphere in Transnational China*, ed. Mayfair Mei-hui Yang. Minneapolis: University of Minnesota Press.

Buck-Morss, Susan. 1989. *The Dialectics of Seeing: Walter Benjamin and the Arcades Project*. Cambridge, MA: MIT Press.

Cameron, Nigel. 1991. *An Illustrated History of Hong Kong*. Hong Kong: Oxford University Press.

Castells, Manuel. 2000. *The Rise of the Network Society* (2nd edition). Malden, MA: Blackwell.

Castoiadis, Cornelius. 1991. "Time and Creation." In *Chronotypes: The Construction of Time*, eds John Bender and David E. Wellbery. Stanford, CA: Stanford University Press.

CCTV English Service. 1998. *Capturing the Moment: Reflections on CCTV-9's Live Coverage of Hong Kong's Return*. Beijing: Central Compilation and Translation Press.

Chan, Ming K. ed. 1994. *Precarious Balance: Hong Kong Between China and Britain, 1842–1992*. Hong Kong: M.E. Sharpe, Inc.

Chan, Stephen Ching-kiu. 2006. "The Fighting Condition in Hong Kong Cinema: Local Icons and Cultural Antidotes for the Global Popular." In *Hong Kong Connections: Transnational Imagination in Action Cinema*, eds Meaghan Morris, Siu Leung Li and Stephen Chan Ching-kiu. Durham, NC: Duke University Press.

——. 2001. "Figures of Hope and the Filmic Imaginary of Jianghu in Contemporary Hong Kong Cinema." *Cultural Studies* vol. 15, no. 3/4 (2001), 486–514.

Charney, Leo and Vanesse K. Schwartz, eds. 1995. *Cinema and the Invention of Modern Life*. Berkeley, CA: University of California Press.

Chen, Kathy and Lan Johnson. 1997. "Chinese Celebrates With Patriotism, Pomp." *The Asian Wall Street Journal*, July 1, 1997, 2.

Chen Xiangming. 2000. "Both Glue and Lubricant: Transnational Ethnic Social Capital as a Source of Asia-Pacific Subregionalism." *Policy Sciences* vol. 33, 269–287.

Chen Zhihua. 1999. "Liu yi fang yizhi feixue, Yuanming Yuan gai fou chongjian (Preserving the Ruins Site, Should Yuanming Yuan be Rebuilt?)" In *Yuanming Yuan: lishi, xianzhuang, lunzheng* (*Yuanming Yuan: the Past, the Present, and Debates*) (vol. 2), eds Wang Daocheng and Fang Yuping, pp. 718–727. Beijing: Beijing Chubanshe.

Chen, Zungui. 1989. *Zhongguo tianwenxue shi* (*The History of Astronomy in China*), Volume 4. Shanghai: Shanghai Renmin Chubanshe.

Cheng, Christina Miu Bing. 1997. "Resurgent Chinese Power in Postmodern Discourse: The New Bank of China Buildings in Hong Kong and Macau." In *Hong Kong: The Anthropology of a Chinese Metropolis*, ed Grant Evans and Maria Tam. Honolulu: University of Hawai'i Press.

Cheng, Pei-kai and Michael Lestz with Jonathan D. Spence (eds). 1999. *The Search for Modern China: A Documentary Collection*. New York: W. W. Norton & Company.

Cheng, Sheng. 1997. "Dumiao Tiananmen: daojishipai beihou de gushi (Counting Down Seconds in Tiananmen: A Story behind the Countdown Clock)." *Beijing wanbao*, July 10, 1997, 19.

Cheung, Esther M. K. 2001. "The Hi/Stories of Hong Kong." *Cultural Studies* Vol. 15, no. 3/4 (2001).

Cheung, Sidney C. H. 1999. "The Meanings of A Heritage Trail in Hong Kong." *Annals of Tourism Research*, vol. 26, no. 3, 1999.

Cheung, Siu-keung. 2000. "Speaking Out: Days in the Lives of Three Hong Kong Cage Dwellers." *positions* Vol. 8, No., 1, Spring 2000, 235–262.

Cheung, Steven N. S. 1989. "Datong yu xiaoyi (Great Similarity and Minor Difference)." In his *Chunwang zhijiu* (*Between Life and Death*). Xianggang: Xianggang Jingji Ribao.

——. 1982. *Will China Go "Capitalist?"* London: Institute of Economic Affairs.

China Travel International Investment Hong Kong Limited (CTII). 1992–1998. *Annual Reports*, Hong Kong: CTII.

Chinese Manufacturers' Union in Hong Kong. 1949. *The Seventh Exhibition of Chinese Products, Hong Kong*. Hong Kong: the Chinese Manufacturers' Union.

——. 1939. *Pictorial Record of the Exhibition of Chinese Products, 1939*. Hong Kong: the Central Press.

Ching, Frank. 1994. "Toward Colonial Sunset: The Wilson Regime, 1987–92." In *Precarious Balance: Hong Kong Between China and Britain, 1842–1992*, ed. Ming K. Chan. Hong Kong: M. E. Sharpe.

Chiu, Fred Y. L. 1996. "Politics and the Body Social in Colonial Hong Kong." *positions*, Vol. 4, no. 2, Fall 1996, 185–215.

Chiu, Stephen and Tai-Lok Lui. 2009. *Hong Kong: Becoming a Chinese Global City*. London: Routledge.

Chomsky, Noam. 1999. *Profit over People: Neoliberalism and Global Order*. New York: Seven Stories Press.

Chow, Rey. 1998. *Ethics After Idealism: Theory-Culture-Ethnicity-Reading*. Bloomington: Indiana University Press.

Chun, Allen. 2002. *Unstructuring Chinese Society: The Fictions of Colonial Practice and the Changing Realities of "Land" in the New Territories of Hong Kong*. London: Routledge. (Originally published 2000.)

——. 2000. "Colonial 'Govern-mentality' in Transition: Hong Kong as Imperial Object and Subject." *Cultural Studies*, Vol. 14, No. 3/4, 2000, 430–461.

ClarisNews. 1997. "China Holds Marathon Party for Hong Kong Hanover," Monday, June 30, 1997, 13:01:23 PDT, newsgroup "clari.world.asia.china," from AFPC-afp@clari.net.

Coase, Ronald H. 1988. "The Problem of Social Cost." In his *The Firm, the Market, and the Law*. Chicago: University of Chicago Press. (Originally published by *Journal of Law and Economics*, 1960).

Cohen, Lizabeth. 2006. "The Consumers' Republic: An American Model for the World?" In *The Ambivalent Consumer: Questioning Consumption in East Asia And the West*, eds Sheldon Garon and Patricia L. Maclachlan. Ithaca, NY: Cornell University Press.

Cohen, Margaret. 1995. "Panoramic Literature and the Invention of Everyday Genres." In *Cinema and the Invention of Modern Life*, eds Leo Charney and Vanesse R. Schwartz. Berkeley, CA: University of California Press.

Cohen, Paul A. 2003. "Remembering and Forgetting National Humiliation in

Twentieth-Century China." In his *China Unbound: Evolving Perspectives on the Chinese Past*. New York: Routledge Curzon.

Connery, Christopher. 2006. "The Asian Sixties: An Unfinished Project." *Inter-Asia Cultural Studies*, Vol. 7, No. 4, 545–553.

Cooper, Robert. 2002. "The Post Modern State." London: the Foreign Policy Centre, online document: http://fpc.org.uk/articles/169. Accessed September 13, 2007.

Cox, Rob and Lauren Silva. 2008. "Keeping Up With Beijing." *Wall Street Journal*, August 26, 2008, p. c13.

Crary, Jonathan. 1999. *Suspensions of Perception: Attention, Spectacle, and Modern Culture*. Cambridge, MA: MIT Press.

Cvetkovich, Ann. n.d. "Public Feelings." Unpublished manuscript.

Davis, Deborah. 2006. "Urban Chinese Homeowners as Citizen–Consumers." In *The Ambivalent Consumer: Questioning Consumption in East Asia and the West*, eds Sheldon Garon and Patricia L. Maclachlan. Ithaca, NY: Cornell University Press.

——. 2005. "Urban Consumer Culture." *China Quarterly*, September 2005, Issue 183.

de Certeau, Michel. 1986. "History: Science and Fiction." In his *Heterologies: Discourse On the Other*, translation Brian Massumi. Minneapolis: University of Minnesota Press.

——. 1984. *The Practice of Everyday Life*, translation Steven Rendall. Berkeley, CA: University of California Press. (Originally published 1980.)

de Certeau, Michel, Luce Giard, and Pierre Mayol. 1998. *The Practice of Everyday Life: Vol. 2: Living and Cooking*, translation Timothy J. Tomasik. Minneapolis: University of Minnesota Press.

Dean, Jodi. 2004. "The Networked Empire: Communicative Capitalism and the Hope for Politics." In *Empire's New Clothes: Reading Hardt and Negri*, eds Paul A. Passavant and Jodi Dean. New York: Routledge.

Dean, Mitchell. 2002. "Liberal Government and Authoritarianism." *Economy and Society* Vol. 31, no. 1, 2002, 37–61.

Debord, Guy. 1995. *The Society of the Spectacle*, translation Donald Nicholson-Smith. New York: Zone Books. (Originally published 1967.)

Debray, Régis. 2007. "Socialism: A Life-Cycle." *New Left Review*, Vol. 46, July–August 2007.

——. 1996. *Media Manifestos: On the Technological Transmission of Cultural Forms*, translation Eric Rauth. London: Verso.

Deleuze, Gilles. 1989. *Cinema 2: The Time-Image*, translation Hugh Tomlinson and Robert Galeta. Minneapolis: University of Minnesota Press. (Originally published 1985.)

——. 1986. *Cinema 1: The Movement-Image*, translation Hugh Tomlinson and Barbara Habberjam. Minneapolis: University of Minnesota Press. (Originally published 1983.)

Deleuze, Gilles and Félix Guatttari. 1987. *A Thousand Plateaus: Capitalism and Schizophrenia*. translation Brian Massumi. Minnesota: University of Minnesota Press. (Originally published 1980.)

——. 1983. *Anti-Oedipus: Capitalism and Schizophrenia*. Minnesota: University of Minnesota Press.

Deng Xiaoping. 1993. "Yige guojia, liangzhong zhidu (One Country, Two Systems)." In *Deng Xiaoping wenxuan* (*Selections of Deng Xiaoping Works*). Volume 3. Beijing: Renmin Chubanshe.

——. 1993. *Deng Xiaoping wenxuan* (*Selections of Deng Xiaoping Works*). Volume 3. Beijing: Renmin Chubanshe.

Denton, Kirk A. 2005. "Museums, Memorial Sites and Exhibitionary Culture in the People's Republic of China." *China Quarterly* 183 (September).

——. 2000. "Visual Memory and the Construction of a Revolutionary Past: Paintings From the Museum of the Chinese Revolution." *Modern Chinese Literature and Culture*, Vol. 12, no. 2 (Fall 2000).

Derrida, Jacques. 1996. *Archive Fever: A Freudian Impression*. translation Eric Prenowitz. Chicago: University of Chicago Press. (Originally published 1994.)

——. 1994. *Specters of Marx: The State of the Debt, the Work of Mourning, and the New International*. translation Peggy Kamuf. New York: Routledge. (Originally published 1993.)

——. 1986. "Différance" in *Deconstruction in Context: Literature and Philosophy*, ed. Mark C. Taylor. Chicago: University of Chicago Press. (Originally published 1982.)

——. 1978. "Freud and the Scene of Writing." In his *Writing and Difference*, translation Alan Bass. Chicago: University of Chicago Press.

Derrida, Jacques and Bernard Stiegler. 2002. *Echographies of Television: Filmed Interviews*, translation Jennifer Bajorek. Cambridge, UK: Polity. (Originally published 1996.)

Dickson, Glen. 2000. "CBS Goes Virtual for Millennium." *Broadcasting & Cable*, January 3, 2000, p. 64.

Dirks, Nicholas B. 1990. "History as a Sign of the Modern." *Public Culture*, Vol. 2, no. 2 (Spring 1990), pp. 25–31.

Dirlik, Arif. 2007. *Global Modernity: Modernity in the Age of Global Capitalism*. Boulder, CO: Paradigm Publishers.

Doane, Mary Ann. 2002. *The Emergence of Cinematic Time: Modernity, Contingency, the Archive*. Cambridge, MA: Harvard University Press.

Duara, Prasenjit. 1995. *Rescuing History from the Nation: Questing Narratives of Modern China*. Chicago: University of Chicago Press.

Duggen, Lisa. 2003. *The Twilight of Equality?* Boston: Beacon Press.

Dung, Kai-cheung. 1998. *Visible Cities (V-cheng-fan-sheng-lu)*. Hong Kong: Hong Kong Arts Centre.

Durie, Robin, ed. 2000. *Time & the Instant: Essays in the Physics and Philosophy of Time*. Manchester: Clinamen Press.

Dussel, Enrique. 1998. "Beyond Eurocentrism: The World-System and the Limits of Modernity." In *The Cultures of Globalization*, eds Fredric Jameson and Masao Miyoshi. Durham, NC: Duke University Press.

Dutton, Michael. 2005. *Policing Chinese Politics: A History*. Durham, NC: Duke University Press.

Economist, Intelligence Unit. 1997. *Hong Kong: Country Profile 1996–97*. London: Economist Intelligence Unit.

Elliott, Stuart. 2007. "For Olympics, China's Marketers Are Showing Their Pride." *New York Times*, November 14, 2007. Online document: http://www.nytimes.com/2007/11/14/business/media/14adco.html. Accessed December 30, 2007.

——. 1999. "Real or Virtual? You Call It." *New York Times*, October 1, 1999.

Enright, Michael J., Edith. E. Scott, and David Dodwell. 1997. *The Hong Kong Advantage*. Hong Kong: Oxford University Press.

Erni, John Nguyet. 2001. "Like A Postcolonial Culture: Hong Kong Re-Imagined." *Cultural Studies*, Vol. 15, no. 3/4, 2001, 389.

Ewing, Kent. 2006. "The Secret Hong Kong Story." *Asia Times Online*, November 28, 2006. Web: http://www.atimes.com/atimes/China/HK28Ad01.html. Accessed November 28, 2006.

Fabian, Johannes. 1983. *Time and the Other: How Anthropology Makes Its Object*. New York: New York University Press.

Faure, David, James Hayes, and Alan Birch, eds. 1984. *From Village to City: Studies in the Traditional Roots of Hong Kong Society*. Hong Kong: Hong Kong University Press.

Feng Xuehui and Zhang Zhong. 1966. "The Qinchi Liquor Factory: Spent All on Advertisements. Making Money or not?" (in Chinese) *Zhongguo jingying bao* (*China Business*), July 2, 1996, p. 1.

Flusser, Vilém. 2002. "Line and Surface." In his *Writings*, ed. Andreas Ströhl, translation Erik Eisel. Minneapolis: University of Minnesota Press. (Originally written in 1973.)

Foucault, Michel. 1991. "Governmentality." In *The Foucault Effect: Studies in Governmentality*, eds. Graham Burchell, Colin Gordon, and Peter Miller. Chicago: University of Chicago Press. (Originally published 1978.)

——. 1990. *The History of Sexuality, Volume 2, The Use of Pleasure*, translation Robert Hurley. New York: Vintage Books. (Originally published 1984.)

——. 1988 "Technologies of the Self." In *Technologies of the Self: A Seminar with Michael Foucault*, ed. Luther H. Martin, Huck Gutman, and Patrick H. Hutton. Amherst, MA: University of Massachusetts Press.

——. 1986. "Of Other Spaces." *Diacritics*, Vol. 16, 1986, 22–27.

——. 1980. *Knowledge/Power: Selected Interviews and Other Writings, 1972–1977*, ed. C. Gordon. New York: Pantheon Books.

——. 1984. "Nietzsche, Genealogy, History" in *The Foucault Reader*, ed. Paul Rabinow. New York: Pantheon Books.

——. 1978. *The History of Sexuality, An Introduction, Volume 1*, translation Robert Hurley. New York: Vintage Books. (Originally published 1976.)

——. 1977. *Discipline and Punish: The Birth of the Prison*. translation Alan Sheridan. New York: Vintage Books. (Originally published 1975.)

Fraser, J. T. 1975. *Of Time, Passion, and Knowledge: Reflections on the Strategy of Existence*. New York: George Braziller.

Fraser, J. T., T., N. Lawrence, and F. C. Haber, eds. 1986. *Time, Science, and Society in China and the West*. Amherst, MA: University of Massachusetts Press.

Friedman, Milton. 2006. "Free Markets and the End of History." Online document: http://www.digitalnpq.org/archive/2006_winter/friedman.html. Accessed October 10, 2006.

——. 2006. "Hong Kong Wrong." Originally published by *Wall Street Journal* on October 6, 2006. Online document: http://online.wsj.com/article/SB116009800068684505.html. Accessed January 11, 2008.

——. 1998. "The Hong Kong Experiment." *Hoover Digest*, 1998, No. 3. Online document: http://www.hoover.org/publications/digest/3532186.html. Accessed October 10, 2006. (First published in *National Review*, December 31, 1997.)

——. 1991. "Economic Freedom, Human Freedom, Political Freedom." Lecture given November 1, 1991. Online document: http://www.cbe.csueastbay.edu/~sbesc/frlect.html. Accessed October 10, 2006.

Friedman, Milton and Friedman, Rose D. 1998. *Two Lucky People: Memories*. Chicago: University of Chicago Press.

Fukuyama, Francis. 1992. *The End of History and the Last Man*. New York: Free Press.

Gallagher, Louis J. 1953. *China in the Sixteenth Century: The Journals of Matthew Ricci: 1583–1610*. New York: Random House.

Gao, Xinglie, Wang Maoliang and Hou Jun. 1995. "Huaqiao cheng fazhan guan (The Concept of Developing the Overseas Chinese Town)." *Liaowan zhoukan* (overseas edition) (Beijing), 1995, nos 10, 28–30.

Ge, Luo. 1993. "Nanwang de suiyue, nanwang de huiyi: xian gei zhongguo geming bowuguan sishi zhounian (Unforgettable Years, Unforgettable Memory: Dedicating to the Fortieth Anniversary of the National Museum of Chinese Revolution)." In his *Bowuguan gongzhuo sishi nian* (*Forty Years of Museum Work*). Beijing: Hongqi Chubanshe.

Gerth, Karl. 2004. *China Made: Consumer Culture and the Creation of the Nation*. Cambridge, MA: Harvard University Asia Center.

Glasmeier, Amy K. 2000. *Manufacturing Time: Global Competition in the Watch Industry, 1795–2000*. New York: Guilford Press.

Gold, Thomas. 1993. "Go with Your Feelings: Hong Kong and Taiwan Popular Culture in Greater China." *China Quarterly*, Vol. 136, 907–925.

Gonzalez, Michael. 2006. "Informal Finance: Encouraging the Entrepreneurial Spirit in Post-Mao China." *The 2006 Index of Economic Freedom*. Washington, D.C.: Heritage Foundation and *Wall Street Journal*.

Gordon, Colin. 1991. "Governmental Rationality: An Introduction." In *The Foucault Effect: Studies in Governmentality*, eds. Graham Burchell, Colin Gordon, and Peter Miller. Chicago: University of Chicago Press.

——. 1987. "The Soul of the Citizen: Max Weber and Michel Foucault on Rationality and Government." In *Max Weber, Rationality and Modernity*, eds. Scott Lash and Sam Whimster. London: Allen & Unwin.

Gramsci, Antonio. 1971. *Selections from the Prison Notebooks of Antonio Gramsci*, eds. and translation Quintin Hoare and Geoffrey N. Smith. New York: International Publishers.

Greenberg, Michael. 1951. *British Trade and the Opening of China, 1800–42*. Cambridge, UK: Cambridge University Press.

Guldin, Gregory Eliyu. 1995. "Toward a Greater Guangdong: Hong Kong's Sociocultural Impact on the Pearl River Delta and Beyond." In *The Hong Kong-Guangdong Link: Partnership in Flux*, ed. R. Yin-Wang Kwok and A. Y. So. Hong Kong: Hong Kong University Press.

Gunning, Tom. 1990. "The Cinema of Attractions: Early Film, Its Spectator and the Avant-Garde." In *Early Cinema: Space, Frame, Narrative*, ed. Thomas Elsaesser. London: British Film Institute.

Guo Huimin (ed.). 1999. *Zhongguo youxiu gongguan anli xuanping* (*Excellent Public Relations Cases*). (Vol. 3) Shanghai: Fudan University Press.

Guo Weicheng. 1997. *Chenlun yu juexing: cong yapian zhanzheng dao "yapian zhanzheng"* (*Sinkage and wakening: from the Opium War to The Opium War*). Shanghai: Shanghai Wenyi Chubanshe.

Guojia Tongjiju. 1986. *Zhongguo tongji nianjian 1986* (*China Statistical Yearbook, 1986*). Beijing: Zhongguo Tongji Chubanshe.

Hacking, Ian. 1990. *The Taming of Chance*. Cambridge, UK: Cambridge University Press.

Hah Gong. 1992. "A Hong Kong Absurdity." In *New Ghosts, Old Dreams: Chinese*

Rebel Voices, eds Geremie Barme and Linda Jaivin, pp. 429–431. New York: Times Books.

Hallward, Peter. 2003. *Badiou: A Subject to Truth*. Minneapolis, MN: University of Minnesota Press.

Hamilton, Gary G. ed. 1999. *Cosmopolitan Capitalists: Hong Kong and the Chinese Diaspora at the End of the 20th Century*. Seattle: University of Washington Press.

Han Li. 1992. "Yuanming Yuan yizhi gongyuan zongti guihua tigang (The Planning Outline of the Ruin Park of Yuanming Yuan)." In *Yuanming Yuan xueshu lunwenji* (*A Collection of Essays on Yuanming Yuan*), Volume 5, ed Zhongguo Yuanming Yuan xuehui. Beijing: Zhongguo Jianzhu Gongye Chubanshe.

Hang, James T. H. and Frank Ching. 1994. "The MacLehose-Youde Years: Balancing the 'Three-Legged Stool,' 1971–86." In *Precarious Balance: Hong Kong Between China and Britain, 1842–1992*, ed. Ming K. Chan. Hong Kong: M.E. Sharpe, Inc.

Hardt, Michael, and Antonio Negri. 2000. *Emoire*. Cambridge, MA: Harvard University Press.

Harvey, David. 2005. *A Brief History of Neoliberalism*. New York: Oxford University Press.

——. 1990. *The Condition of Postmodernity*. Cambridge, MA: Blackwell.

Hase, Patrick and Elizabeth Sinn, eds. 1995. *Beyond the Metropolis: Villages in Hong Kong*. Hong Kong: Joint Publishing.

Hayes, James. 1996. *Friends and Teachers: Hong Kong and its People, 1953–87*. Hong Kong: Hong Kong University Press.

He Bingmeng, ed. 2004. *Xinziyouzhuyi pingxi* (*Analyses of Neoliberalism*). Beijing: Shehui Kexue Wenxian Chubanshe.

Heidegger, Martin. 1996. *Being and Time*, translation Joan Stambaugh. Albany: State University of New York Press. (Originally published 1953.)

Heim, Kristi. 1997. "Handover Tokens Take an Esoteric Twist." *Asian Wall Street Journal*, April 7, 1997, pp. 2, 10.

Herzfeld, Michael. 1991. *A Place in History: Social and Monumental Time in A Cretan Town*. Princeton, NJ: Princeton University Press.

Hevia, James L. 2003. *English Lessons: The Pedagogy of Imperialism in Nineteenth-Century China*. Durham, NC: Duke University Press.

Ho, Ching-Hin. 1988. "The Hong Kong Museum of History: A Challenge in A Fast-Changing City." *Museum* (Paris), Vol. XL, 1988, No. 3.

Ho, Oscar. 1993. "In Search of an Identity." *Art AsiaPacific*, 1, 1 (1993), 14.

Holm, David. 1991. *Art and Ideology in Revolutionary China*. Oxford: Clarendon Press.

Hong Kong Legislative Council. 1928. "British Empire Exhibition, Wembley, 1924 and 1925." In *Hong Kong Legislative Council Sessional Papers 1928*. Hong Kong: Noronha & Co. (Government Printers).

——. 1900. "Despatches and Other Papers Relating to the Extension of the Colony of Hongkong." In *Hong Kong Legislative Council Sessional Papers 1899*. Hong Kong: Noronha & Co. (Government Printers).

Hong Kong Urban Council. 1975–1992. *Urban Council Annual Reports*. Hong Kong: Public Information Unit, Urban Services Department.

Hsieh, Shih-Chung. 1994. "From *Shanbao* to *Yuanzhumin*: Taiwan Aborigines in Transition." In *The Other Taiwan: 1945 to the Present*, ed. Murray A. Rubinstein. Armonk, NY: M.E. Sharpe.

Hsing, You-tien. 1998. *Making Capitalism in China: The Taiwan Connection*. Oxford, UK: Oxford University Press.

Hsu, Madeline Y. 2002. *Dreaming of Gold, Dreaming of Home: Transnationalism and Migration Between the United States and South China, 1882–1943*. Stanford, CA: Stanford University Press.

Hu Angang. 2005. "Equity and Efficiency." In *One China, Many Paths*, ed. Chaohua Wang, pp. 219–233. London: Verso.

Hu Jun. 1991. "Shehuizhuyi xin shiqi woguo bowuguan shiye de huigu, 1976–1988 (A Review of the Museum Enterprise of Our Country in the New Era of Socialism, 1976–1988). *Zhongguo bowuguan* (*Chinese museum*), no. 4, 1991.

Huang, Chun-Chieh and Erick Zürcher, eds. 1995. *Time and Space in Chinese Culture*. Leiden: E. J. Brill.

Huanqiao Ribao. 1969. "Editorial." *Huaqiao Ribao* (*Overseas Chinese Daily*), December 13, 1969 (in *Festival of Hong Kong Commemoration Magazine 1969*, Universal News Agency. Hong Kong: Universal News Agency).

Hughes, Richard. 1968. *Borrowed Place, Borrowed Time: Hong Kong and Its Many Faces*. London: André Deutsch.

Huque, Ahmed Shafiqul and Ray Yep. 2003. "Globalization and Reunification: Administrative Reforms and the China–Hong Kong Convergence Challenge." *Public Administration Review*, Vol. 63, No. 2 (March/April 2003): 141–152.

Ikenberry, G. John. 2008. "The Rise of China and the Future of the West." *Foreign Affairs*, Jan/Feb 2008, Vol. 87, Issue 1.

Jameson, Fredric. 2003 "The End of Temporality" *Critical Inquiry* 29 (4).

——. 2002. *A Singular Modernity: Essay on the Ontology of the Present*. New York: Verso.

——. 1991. *Postmodernism, or the Cultural Logic of Late Capitalism*. Durham, NC: Duke University Press.

——. 1990. "Modernism and Imperialism." In *Nationalism, Colonialism, and Literature*, eds. Fredric Jameson, Edward Said, and Terry Eagleton. Minneapolis: University of Minnesota Press.

Jami, Catherine. 1995. "Western Devices for Measuring Time and Space: Clocks and Euclidian Geometry in Late Ming and Ch'ing China." In *Time and Space in Chinese Culture*, eds. Chun-chieh Huang and Erick Zürcher. Leiden: E.J. Brill.

Ji Yuemu. 1996. "Yuanming Yuan jiujing shi shui shao de? (Who Burned Yuanming Yuan, After All?)." *Beijing guangbo dianshi bao* (*Beijing Broadcasting and Television*) (weekly newspaper published in Beijing), July 16, 1996.

Karl, Rebecca E. 2005. " 'Joining Tracks with the World:' The Impossibility of Politics in China." *Radical Philosophy*, no. 131 (May/June 2005).

——. 2002. *Staging the World: Chinese Nationalism at the Turn of the Twentieth Century*. Durham, NC: Duke University Press.

Kellner, Douglas. 2003. *Media Spectacle*. London: Routledge.

Kern, Stephen. 1983. *The Culture of Time and Space, 1880–1918*. Cambridge, MA: Harvard University Press.

Ketizhu. 2004. "Xinziyouzhuyi jiqi benzhi (Neoliberalism and Its Nature)." In *Xinziyouzhuyi pingxi* (*Analyses of Neoliberalism*), ed. He Bingmeng. Beijing: Shehui Kexue Wenxian Chubanshe.

Kittler, Fredrich A. 1999. *Gramophone, Film, Typewriter*. translation Geoffrey Winthrop-Yong and Michael Wutz. Stanford, CA: Stanford University Press. (Originally published 1986.)

——. 1990. *Discourse Networks 1800/1900*. translation Michael Metteer and Chris Cullens. Stanford, CA: Stanford University Press. (Originally published 1985.)

Klein, Kerwin Lee. 2000. "On the Emergence of *Memory* in Historical Discourse." *Representations* No. 69 (Winter 2000), 127–150.
Knight, Alan and Diane Stormont. 1999. "The Tourist of History." In *Reporting Hong Kong: Foreign Media and the Handover*, eds. Alan Knight and Yoshiko Nakano. New York: St. Martin's Press.
Koselleck, Reinhart. 2002. "Time and History" In his *The Practice of Conceptual History: Timing History, Spacing Concepts*, translation Todd Samuel Presner and others. Stanford, CA: Stanford University Press.
——. 1985. *Futures Past: On the Semantics of Historical Time*, translation Keith Tribe. Cambridge, MA: MIT Press. (Originally published 1979.)
Kotz, David M. 2002. "Globalization and Neoliberalism." *Rethinking Marxism*, Vol. 14, No. 2 (Summer 2002).
Ku, Agnes. 2004. "Immigration Policies, Discourses and the Politics of Local Belonging in Hong Kong (1950–1980)." *Modern China* Vol. 30, No. 3: 326–360.
Ku, Agnes and Ngai Pun. 2004. "Introduction." In *Remaking Citizenship in Hong Kong: Community, Nation and the Global City*, eds. Agnes S. Ku and Ngai Pun, pp. 15. London: RoutledgeCurzon.
Laclau, Ernesto. 1990. *New Reflections on the Revolution of Our Time*. London and New York: Verso.
Lam, Wai-man. 2004. *Understanding the Political Culture of Hong Kong: The Paradox of Activism and Depoliticization*. Armonk, NY: M.E. Sharpe.
Landes, David L. 2000. *Revolution in Time: Clocks and the Making of the Modern World*. Cambridge, MA: Harvard University Press.
Lash, Scott and John Urry. 1994. *Economies of Signs and Spaces*. London: SAGE.
Laurie, Jim and Alan Knight. 1999. "Whiter Hong Kong?—In the Minds of Many Americans, So What." In *Reporting Hong Kong: Foreign Media and the Handover*, eds. Alan Knight and Yoshiko Nakano. New York: St. Martin's Press.
Law, Wing-sang. 2000. "Northbound Colonialism: A Politics of Post-PC Hong Kong." *positions* Vol. 8, No. 1, Spring 2000, 201–233.
Lee, Ching Kwan. 2007. *Against the Law: Labor Protests in China's Rustbelt and Sunbelt*. Berkeley, CA: University of California Press.
Lee, Haiyan. n.d. "The Dialectics of Ruins in Yuanmingyuan." Unpublished manuscript.
Lee Yee, 1992. "Take to the Seas." In *New Ghosts, Old Dreams: Chinese Rebel Voices*, eds. Geremie Barme and Linda Jaivin, p. 433. New York: Times Books. (Originally published in *The Asian Wall Street Journal*, May 31, 1990).
Lefebvre, Henri. 1984. *Everyday Life in the Modern World*, translation Sacha Rabinovitch. New Brunswick, NJ: Transaction Publishers. (Originally published 1971.)
Lemke, Thomas. 2001. " 'The Birth of Bio-Politics': Michel Foucault's Lecture at the Collège de France on Neo-Liberal Governmentality." *Economy and Society*, Vol. 30, No. 2, 2001.
Lenin, V. I. 1992. *The State and Revolution*. New York: Penguin Books (written 1917, published 1919).
Lever-Tracy, Constance, David Ip, and Noel Tracy. 1996. *The Chinese Diaspora and Mainland China: An Emerging Economic Synergy*. Houndmills: Macmillan Press.
Lewis, D. K. 1993. "The Health of A Great City: Hong Kong and Its Urban Council." In *Hong Kong Urban Council Annual Report*" 1992–1993. Hong Kong: The Public Information Unit, Urban Services Department.
Li, Siu-leung. 1997. "zhimin de lishi xiangxiang (Historical Imaginary of Colonial-

ism)." In *Fouxiang Xianggang: lishi, wenhua, weilai (Hong Kong Un-Imagined: History, Culture and the Future)*, eds. Wong Wang-chi, Li Siu-leung and Chan Ching-kiu Stephen. Taipei: Rye Field.

Li Ling. 1996. "Zou xiang zui jia zhuangtai: ziwo shixian (Towards the Optimum State: Self-realization)." *Zhongguo qingniao bao (China Youth Daily)*, October 25, 1996, p. 5.

Li Qiqing. 2003. "Quanqiuhua beijing xia de xin ziyouzhuyi (Neoliberalism in the Background of Globalization)." In *Quanqiuhua yu xinziyouzhuyi (Globalization and Neoliberalism)*, eds. Li Qiqing and Liu Yuanqi. Guilin: Guanxi Shifan Daxue Chubanshe.

Li Ren, Guo Jin, and Zhu Wei. 1995. "Wei le na yi tian: ji tiananmen guangchang xianggang 'daojishi' huodong (Preparing for the Day: Hong Kong Countdown Activities at Tiananmen Square)." *Zhongguo mingpai (China Brand-names)*, January issue.

Liang Weiji and Zheng Zhemin, ed. 1993. *Zhongguo jindai bupingdeng tiaoyue xuanbian yu jieshao (Introduction to Selected Unequal Treaties in Modern China)*. Beijing: Zhongguo Guangbo Dianshi Chubanshe.

Lilley, Rozanna. 1998. *Staging Hong Kong: Gender and Performance in Transition*. Honolulu: University of Hawai'i Press.

Lin, George C. S. 1997. *Red Capitalism in South China: Growth and Development of the Pearl River Delta*. Vancouver: University of British Columbia Press.

Liu, Alan P. L. 1964. *Radio Broadcasting in Communist China*. Cambridge, MA: Research Program on Problems of International Communication and Security, Center for International Studies, Massachusetts Institute of Technology.

Liu, Lydia H. 2003. "The Metamorphosis of a Folksong Immortal: Understanding official Popular Culture in Twentieth-Century China." In *Writing and Materiality in China*, eds. Judith T. Zeitlin and Lydia H. Liu. Cambridge, MA: Asia Center, Harvard University.

——. 1999. "The Desire for the Sovereign and the Logic of Reciprocity in the Family of Nations." *Diacritics* Vol. 29, no. 4 (Winter 1999), 150–177.

——. 1999. "Legislating the Universal: The Circulation of International Law in the Nineteenth Century." In *Tokens of Exchange: The Problem of Translation in Global Circulation*, ed. Lydia H. Liu. Durham, NC: Duke University Press.

——. 1995. *Translingual Practice: Literature, National Culture, and Translated Modernity—China, 1900–1937*. Stanford: Stanford University Press.

Liu Qingfeng and Kwan Siu-chun, eds. 1998. *Zhuanhua zhong de xianggang: shenfen yu zhixu de zai xunqiu* (*Hong Kong in Transition: the Continued Search for Identity and Order*). Hong Kong: Chinese University Press.

Liu, Xin. 2002. *The Otherness of Self: A Genealogy of the Self in Contemporary China*. Ann Arbor, MI: University of Michigan Press.

Lu Jimin. 1998. "Zhou Enlai yu bowuguan (Zhou Enlai and Museums)." *Zhouguo bowuguan*, no. 1, 1998.

——. 1992 "Wenwu gongzuo gaishuo (Introduction to the Work of Cultural Relics)." In his *Bowuguan ji wenwu gongzhuo luncong (Essays on Museums and the Work of Cultural Relics)*.

——. 1992. "Zhongguo bowuguan de texing ji gongzhuo guifan (The Characteristics and Principles of the Museums in China)." In his *Bowuguan ji wenwu gongzhuo luncong (Essays on Museums and the Work of Cultural Relics.)* Beijing: Wenwu Chubanshe.

Lu Weiluan. 1996. *Xianggang gushi: geren huiyi yu wenxue shikao* (*The Story of Hong Kong: Personal Memories and Literary Thinking*). Hong Kong: Oxford University Press.

Lui, Tai-lok. 1997. *Wugai, maidan! yige shehuixuejia de xianggang biji (Check, Please! A Sociologist's Notes on Hong Kong)*. Hong Kong: Xianrenhang.

Luibhéid, Eithne. 2002. *Entry Denied: Controlling Sexuality at the Border*. Minneapolis: University of Minnesota Press.

Lull, James. 1991. *China Turned on: Television, Reform, and Resistance*. London: Routledge.

Luo Ge. 1993 "Nanwang de suiyue, nanwang de huiyi: xian gei zhongguo geming bowuguan sishi zhounian (Unforgettable Years, Unforgettable Memory: Dedicating to the Fortieth Anniversary of the National Museum of Chinese Revolution)." In his *Bowuguan gongzhuo sishi nian (Forty Years of Museum Work)*. Beijing: Hongqi Chubanshe.

——. 1993 "Dali jiaqian chenlie yu zhanlan zhong de shixiangxing he zhandouxing: tan duibi yuanze de tedian ji zhuoyong (Reinforcing the Ideology and the Power of Exhibitions: On the Characteristics and Functions of the Principle of Contrast)." In his *Bowuguan gongzhuo sishi nian (Forty Years of Museum Work)*.

Lyotard, Jean-François. 1984. *The Postmodern Condition: A Report on Knowledge*, translation Geoff Bennington and Brian Massumi. Minneapolis: University of Minneapolis Press. (Originally published 1979.)

Ma Chi-man (Ma Zhimin). 1995. "Renzhao jingguan de shijian yu tiyan (Practice of Artificial Scenery and Experience Thereof)." *Journal of Shenzhen University (Humanities and Social Sciences)* 1995, Vol. 12, Nos 4, 87.

Ma, Eric Kit-wai. 2004 "Re-advertising Hong Kong: Nostalgia Industry and Popular History." In *Asian Media Studies: Politics of Subjectivities*, ed. John Nguyet Erni and Siew Keng Chua. Oxford, UK: Blackwell.

——. 2001. "Consuming Satellite Modernitites." *Cultural Studies*, Vol. 15, no. 3/4.

——. 2001. "Re-Advertising Hong Kong: Nostalgia Industry and Popular History." *positions* Vol. 9, No. 1, Spring 2001, 131–159.

——. 1999. "Hong Kong Remembers: A Thick Description of Electronic Memory." *Social Text* 58, Vol. 17, No. 1, Spring 1999, 75–91.

MacLehose, Murray. 1971. "Right Combination of Work and Play." In the Universal News Agency, *Festival of Hong Kong Commemoration Magazine 1971*. Hong Kong: Universal News Agency.

Malone, Carroll Brown. 1934. *History of the Peking Summer Palaces under the Ch'ing Dynasty*. Urbana: University of Illinois Press.

Mao Zedong. 1937. "Maodunlun (On Contradiction)." Online document: http://www.people.com.cn/GB/channel1/10/20000529/80822.html. Accessed October 19, 2007.

Mao Zedong. 1949. "On the People's Democratic Dictatorship." Online document: www.marx2mao.com/Mao/PDD49.html. Accessed January 19, 2008.

Mao Zengyu. 2004. " 'Beijing gongshi' yu 'huashengdun gongshi' shi bijiao (A Comparison between 'Beijing Consensus' and 'Washington Consensus')." In *Kaifangxia de hongguan jingji yu qiye lilun yanjiu (Macro Economy under Opening and Company Studies)*, ed. Wu Yifeng, Ding Bing, and Li Zhong. Beijing: Zhongguo Jingji Chubanshe.

Marchetti, Gina. 1998. "Transnational Cinema, Hybrid Identities and the Films of Evans Chan." *Postmodern Culture* Vol. 8, no. 2, 1998.

Marx, Karl. 1973. *Grundrisse: Foundations of the Critique of Political Economy*, translation Martin Nicolaus. New York: Random House. (Originally published 1939.)

Marx, Karl and Friedrich Engels. 1994. "The Communist Manifesto." In *Selected Writings*, ed. Lawrence H. Simon. Indianapolis, IN: Hackett Publishing Company. (Originally published 1848.)

Mathews, Gordon. 2000. "What in the World is Chinese?: On the Cultural Identities of Hong Kong Intellectuals in the Shadow and Wake of 1 July 1997." In his *Global Culture/Individual Identity: Searching for Home in the Cultural Supermarket*. London: Routledge.

Mathews, Gordon and Tai-lok Lui, eds. 2001. *Consuming Hong Kong*. Hong Kong: Hong Kong University Press.

Matterlart, Armand. 1996. *The Invention of Communication*, translation Susan Emanuel. Minneapolis: University of Minnesota Press. (Originally published 1994.)

McLuhan, Marshall. 1994. *Understanding Media: The Extensions of Man*. Cambridge, MA: MIT Press. (Originally published 1964.)

Meyer, David R. 2000. *Hong Kong as a Global Metropolis*. Cambridge, UK: Cambridge University Press.

Mitchell, Katharyne. 2004. *Crossing the Neoliberal Line: Pacific Rim Migration and the Metropolis*. Philadelphia: Temple University Press.

Mitchell, Timothy. 1991 *Colonising Egypt*. Berkeley: University of California Press. (Originally published 1988.)

Mitchell, W. J. T. 1986. *Iconology: Image, Text, Ideology*. Chicago: University of Chicago Press.

Mu, Jingyuan, Chen Wen, Fang Hanlu, and Zong Tianliang. 1998. *Yuanming Yuan fengyun lu (A Changing History of Yuanming Yuan)*. Shenyang: Liaoning Daxue Chubanshe.

Nancy, Jean-Luc. 1997. *The Sense of the World*, translation Jeffrey S. Librett. Minneapolis: University of Minnesota Press. (Originally published 1993.)

Needham, Joseph, Wang Ling and Derek J. de Solla Price. 1960. *Heavenly Clockwork: The Great Astronomical Clocks of Medieval China*. Cambridge, UK: Cambridge University Press.

Negri, Antonio. 2003. *Time for Revolution*, translation Matteo Mandarini. London: Continuum.

Ng, Anthony. 1991 "The Role of Architects in Conservation," paper represented at "The Future of Hong Kong's Past—A Conference on Development and Heritage Conservation," organized by the Recreation and Culture Branch, the Hong Kong Institute of Architects and the Hong Kong Institute of Planners, and held in Hong Kong Convention and Exhibition Centre, October 10–11, 1991.

Ng, Kang-chung. 1995. "Trail Closed in Grave Row." *South China Morning Post* (Hong Kong), May 19, 1995, p.3.

Ni Xingxiang. 2001. "Shilun geming jinianguan kuojian zhong ying zhongshi de jige wenti (Preliminary Study of Several Problems in Expanding Revolutionary and Commemorative Museums)." *Zhongguo bowuguan (Chinese Museum)*, no. 3.

Nowotny, Helga. 1994. *Time: The Modern and Postmodern Experience*, translation Neville Plaice. London: Polity Press. (Originally published in German, 1989)

Nu Jizheng. 1983. "Lue tan bowuguanxue de zucheng bufen: chenliexue (A Brief Discussion of the Science of Exhibition, An Essential Part of Museology)." In

Bowuguanxue lunji (Essays of Museology), ed. Zhongguo Bowuguan Xuehui, vol. 1. Beijing: Wenwu Chubanshe.

O'Donnell, Mary Ann. 2001. "Becoming Hong Kong, Razing Baoan, Preserving Xin'an: An Ethnographic account of Urbanization in the Shenzhen Special Economic Zone." *Cultural Studies* Vol. 15, no. 3/4, 2001, 419–443.

Ong, Aihwa. 2006. *Neoliberalism as Exception: Mutations in Citizenship and Sovereignty*. Durham, NC: Duke University Press.

Ong, Aiwha and Li Zhang. 2008. "Introduction." In *Privatizing China: Socialism from Afar*, eds. Li Zhang and Aihwa Ong, pp. 1–19. Ithaca, NY: Cornell University Press.

Osborne, Peter. 1995. *The Politics of Time: Modernity and Avant-Garde*. London: Verso.

Ouyang Guozhong. 2005. *Meiti huodong shizhan baogao (Campaign Reports of Media Practices)*. Guangzhou: Nan Fang Daily Press.

Park, Jung-Dong. 1997. *The Special Economic Zones of China and Their Impact on Its Economic Development*. Westport, Connecticut: PRAEGER.

Pfanner, Eric. 2007. "For 2008 Olympics Campaigns, the Starter's Gun Went Off This Month." *New York Times*, August 23, 2007. Online document: http://www.nytimes.com/2007/08/23/business/media/23adco.html. Accessed December 30, 2007.

Pirie, Iain. 2008. *The Korean Developmental State: From Dirigisme to Neo-Liberalism*. London: Routledge.

Potter, Jack M. 1968. *Capitalism and the Chinese Peasant: Social and Economic Change in a Hong Kong Village*. Berkeley and Los Angeles: University of California Press.

Povinelli, Elizabeth A. 2001. "Radical Worlds: The Anthropology of Incommensurability and Inconceivability" *Annual Review of Anthropology*, Vol. 30, pp. 319–334.

Pun Ngai. 2005. *Made in China: Women Factory Workers in a Global Workplace*. Durham, NC: Duke University Press.

Qi Pengfei. 1997. *Richu riluo: Xianggang wenti yibai wushiliu nian, 1841–1997 (Sun Rises, Sun Sets: The 156-Year Hong Kong Question, 1841-1997)*. Beijing: Xinhua Chubanshe.

Ramo, Joshua Cooper. 2004. "The Beijing Consensus." London: the Foreign Policy Centre. Available at http://fpc.org.uk/publications/123.

Rancière, Jacques. 2007. *The Future of the Image*, translation Gregory Elliott. London: Verso.

Ren, Hai. n.d. *The Chinese Middle Class Society: Risk Governance and Life-Extension in Neoliberal China*. Unpublished book manuscript.

——. 2009. "Living with Risks: The Question of the 'Middle Class' in Neoliberal China." Paper presented at the Advanced Seminar on "The Middle Classes: A Global Perspective," the School for Advanced Research, Santa Fe, NM, March 28–April 3, 2009.

——. 2007. "The Landscape of Power: Imagineering Consumer Behavior at China's Theme Parks." In *The Themed Space: Locating Culture, Nation, and Self*, ed. Scott A. Lukas. Lanham, MD: Lexington Books.

——. 2006. "The Merit of Time: A Genealogy of the Countdown" in *The End that Does: Art, Science, and Millennial Accomplishment*, ed. Cathy Gutierrez and Hillel Scwartz. London: Equinox Publishers.

——. 2005. "Subculture as a Neo-Liberal Conduct of Life in Leisure and Consumption." *Rhizomes: Cultural Studies in Emerging Knowledge*. Issue 10. Spring 2005.

——. 1998. "The Displacement and Museum Representation of Aboriginal Cultures in Taiwan." *positions*, Vol. 6, No. 2, 1998.

——. 1997. "Kan de bianzheng: zhanlangui zhong de xianggang (The Dialectics of Seeing: *Hongkong* in Showcases." *The Twenty-first Century* (Hong Kong), no.41 (June 1997), 106–120.

——. 1997. "Xianggang yu zhongguo dalu zhijian de kuaguo zibenzhuyi (Transnational Capitalism between China and Hong Kong)." In *Wenhua xiangxiang yu yishi xingtai* (*Cultural Imaginary and Ideology*), ed. Stephen C. K. Chan. Hong Kong: Oxford University Press.

——. 1994. " 'Zhonghua minzuzhuyi' de huayu yu qi duili huayu (The Discourse of the 'Chinese Nation' and Its Counter-discourses)." *Tangtai (Con-temporary)*, Taipei, No.96, 1994.

Ren Wuxiong. 1991. "Zhongguo gongchandang chuangjian shiqi makeshi zhuyi yu gongren yundong de jiehe (The Integration between Marxism and Workers' Movement in the Founding Period of the Chinese Communist Party)." In *Shanghai geminshi yanjiu ziliao (Research Materials on Shanghai's Revolutionary History)*, ed., Shanghai Gemin Lishi Bowuguan. Shanghai: Shanghai Sanlian Shudian.

Reuters News. 1997. "Last Gasps of the Empire—You can Buy It Canned in HK." May 30. At *Turkish Daily News*' website: http://www.turkishdailynews.com/old_editions/05_30_97/for3.htm.

Ricoeur, Paul. 1988. *Time and Narrative, volume 3*. Translation Kathleen Blamey and David Pellauer. Chicago: University of Chicago Press. (Originally published 1985.)

Rifkin, Jeremy. 2004. *The European Dream: How Europe's Version of the Future Is Quietly Eclipsing the American Dream*. London: Polity.

Rodowick, D. N. 2001. *Reading the Figural, or, Philosophy after the New Media*. Durham, NC: Duke University Press.

——. 1997. *Gilles Delleuze's Time Machine*. Durham, NC: Duke University Press.

Rofel, Lisa. 1999. *Other Modernities: Gender Yearnings in China after Socialism*. Berkeley, CA: University of California Press.

Romo, Joshua Looper. 2004. "The Beijing Consensus." *Financial Times* (London), May 7, 2004.

Rose, Nikolas. 1999. *Powers of Freedom: Reframing Political Thought*. Cambridge, UK: Cambridge University Press.

——. 1999. *Governing the Soul: The Shaping of the Private Self*. Second Edition. London: Free Association Books.

Rosenberg, Daniel and Susan Harding (eds.) 2005. *Histories of the Future*. Durham, NC: Duke University Press.

Ross, Andrew. 2006. *Fast Boat to China: Corporate Flight and the Consequences of Free Trade; Lessons from Shanghai*. New York: Pantheon Books.

Rossum, Dohrn-van. 1996. *History of the Hour: Clocks and Modern Temporal Orders*. translation Thomas Dunlap. Chicago: University of Chicago Press. (Originally published 1992.)

Roth, Michael S. 1997. "Preface." In *Irresistible Decay: Ruins Reclaimed*, eds. Michael S. Roth, Claire Lyons and Charles Merewether. Los Angeles: the Getty Research Institute for the History of Art and the Humanities.

Sandberg, Mark B. 1995. "Effigy and Narrative: Looking into the Nineteenth-Century Folk Museum." In *Cinema and the Invention of Modern Life*, eds. Leo Charney and Vanesse K. Schwartz. Berkeley, CA: University of California Press.

Sassen, Saskia. 1991. *The Global City; New York, London, Tokyo*. Princeton, NJ: Princeton University Press.

Saussy, Haun. 2001 "No Time Like the Present: The Category of Contemporaneity in Chinese Studies." In his *Great Walls of Discourse and Other Adventures in Cultural China*. Cambridge, MA: Harvard University Asia Center.

Schipper, Kristofer. 1993. *The Taoist Body*, translation Karen C. Duval. Berkeley, CA: University of California Press. (Originally published 1982.)

Schipper, Kristofer and Wang Hsiu-huei. 1986. "Progressive and Regressive Time Cycles in Taoist Ritual." In *Time, Science, and Society in China and the West*, eds. T. J. Fraser, N. Lawrence, and F. C. Haber. Amherst MA: University of Massachusetts Press.

Schmitt, Carl. 2005. *Political Theology: Four Chapters on the Concept of Sovereignty*, translation George Schwab. Chicago: University of Chicago Press. (Originally published 1922.)

——. 1996[1932]. *The Concept of the Political*, translation George Schwab. Chicago: University of Chicago Press.

Schumpeter, Joseph A. 1950. *Capitalism, Socialism, and Democracy* (Third Edition). New York: Harper.

Scobell, Andrew. 1988. "Hong Kong's Influence on China: The Tail That Wags the Dog?" *Asian Survey* Vol., 28, no. 6 (June 1988), 599–612.

Seife, Charles. 2000. *Zero: The Biography of a Dangerous Idea*. New York: Penguin Books.

Shearing, Clifford D. and Philip C. Stenning. 1985. "From the Panopticon to Disney World: The Development of Discipline." In *Perspectives in Criminal Law*, eds. Anthony N. Doob and Edward L. Greenspan. Aurora, Ontario: Canada Law Book.

Shen Qinglin. 1986. "Tan geming wenwu de shouji gongzhuo (On the Work of Collecting Revolutionary Artifacts)." In Zhongguo Bowuguan Xuehui (ed.) *Zhongguo bowuguan xuehui di er chi nianhui lunwen ji (Essays of the Second Annual Meetings of the Chinese Museum Association)*. Beijing: Wenwu Chubanshe.

——. 1983. "Zhonggong dangshi chenlie guilu tanshuo (An Inquiry into the Law of Displaying the History of the Chinese Communist Party)," in Zhongguo Bowuguan Xuehui (ed.) *Bowuguanxue lunji (Essays of Museology)*, Vol. 1. Beijing: Wenwu Chubanshe.

Shih, Shu-mei. 2001. *The Lure of the Modern: Writing Modernism in Semicolonial China, 1917–1937*. Berkeley, CA: University of California Press.

Shu Kei. 1992. "Sunless Days." In *New Ghosts, Old Dreams: Chinese Rebel Voices*, eds. Geremie Barme and Linda Jaivin, pp. 434–435. New York: Times Books.

Sinn, Elizabeth, ed. 1995. *Culture and Society in Hong Kong*. Hong Kong: Center of Asian Studies, University of Hong Kong.

Sirén, Osvald. 1926. *The Imperial Palaces of Peking*, Volume 1. Paris and Brussels: G. Van Oest.

Siu, Helen F. 1999. "Hong Kong: Cultural Kaleidoscope on a World Landscape." In *Cosmopolitan Capitalists: Hong Kong and the Chinese Diaspora at the End of the 20th Century*, ed. Gary G. Hamilton. Seattle: University of Washington Press.

Sklair, Leslie. 1991. "Problems of Socialist Development: The Significance of Shenzhen Special Economic Zone for China's Open Door Development Strategy." *International Journal of Urban and Regional Research* Vol. 15, No. 2: 197–215.

Smart, Alan and George C. S. Lin, 2004. "Border Management and Growth

Coalitions in the Hong Kong Transborder Region." *Identities: Global Studies in Culture and Power*. Vol. 11: 377–396.

Smart, Alan and Josephine Smart. 2008. "Time–space Punctuation: Hong Kong's Border Regime and Limits on Mobility." *Pacific Affairs* Vol. 81, No. 2 (Summer 2008): 175–193.

Smart, Josephine and Alan Smart. 1991. "Personal Relations and Divergent Economies: A Case Study of Hong Kong Investment in China." *International Journal of Urban and Regional Research*, Vol. 15, No. 2: 216–233.

Solinger, Dorothy J. 1999. *Contesting Citizenship in Urban China: Peasant Migrants, the State, and the Logic of the Market*. Berkeley: University of California Press.

Song, Jesook. 2009. *South Koreans in Debt Crisis: The Creation of a Neoliberal Welfare Society*. Durham, NC: Duke University Press.

Spence, Jonathan D. 1999. *The Search for Modern China* (2nd edition). New York: W.W. Norton.

Spivak, Gayatri C. 1991. "Time and Timing: Law and History." In *Chronotypes: The Construction of Time*, eds. John Bender and David E. Wellbery. Stanford: Stanford University Press.

Stein, Peter. 1995. "Marketing Plans Using 1997 Theme in China May Go Up in Smoke." *Asian Wall Street Journal*, December 20, 1995, p. 1.

Stewart, Kathleen. 2005. "Trauma Time: A Still Life." In *Histories of the Future*, eds., Rosenberg, Daniel and Susan Harding. Durham, NC: Duke University Press.

Stewart, Susan. 1993. *On Longing: Narratives of the Miniature, the Gigantic, the Souvenir, the Collection*. Durham: Duke University Press.

Stiegler, Bernard. 1998. "The Time of Cinema/On the 'New World' and 'Cultural Exception.' " *Tekhnema*, No. 4, Spring 1998, 84–90.

——. 1998. *Techics and Time 1: The Fault of Epimetheus*, translation Richard Beardsworth and George Collins. Stanford CA: Stanford University Press. (Originally published 1994.)

Stiglitz, Joseph. 2002. *Globalization and Its Discontents*. New York: W.W. Norton & Company.

Strozier, Charles B. and Michael Flynn, eds. 1997. *The Year 2000: Essays on the End*. New York: New York University Press.

Su Donghai. 1986. "Jian lun wenwu zhuhe (Preliminary Study on the Combination of Artifacts)." In Wenhuabu wenwuju jiaoyuchu and Nankai daxue lishixi, eds., *Bowuguanxue chankao ziliao (Reference Materials of Museology)*, Volume 2, 1986.

Sun Yat-sen (Sun Zhongshan). 1981. *Sun Zhongshan xuanji (Sun Zhongshan Selections)*. Beijing: Renmin Chubanshe.

Sung, Yun-wing. 1995. "Economic Integration of Hong Kong and Guangdong in the 1990s." In *The Hong Kong–Guangdong Link: Partnership in Flux*, eds. R. Yin-Wang Kwok and A. Y. So. Hong Kong: Hong Kong University Press.

Tang, David. 1997. "Preface." In *The Hong Kong Story*, eds. Caroline Courtauld and May Holdsworth. Hong Kong: Oxford University Press.

Tester, Keith, ed. 1994. *The Flâneur*. London: Routledge.

Thaler, Richard H. and Cass R. Sunstein. 2008. *Nudge: Improving Decisions about Health, Wealth, and Happiness*. Revised and expanded edition. New York: Penguin Books.

Thatcher, Margaret. 1993. *The Downing Street Years*. London: Harper Collins.

Thiriez, Régine. 1998. *Barbarian Lens: Western Photographers of the Qianlong Emperor's European Palaces*. Amsterdam: Gordon and Breach Publishers.

Thompson, E. P. 1991. "Time, Work-Discipline and Industrial Capitalism." In his *Customs in Common*. New York: New Press.

Thorsen, Dag Einar and Amund Lie. n.d. "What is Neoliberalism?" (unpublished manuscript). Online at: http://folk.uio.no/daget/neoliberalism.pdf. Accessed December 30, 2009.

Ting, Joseph S. P. 1994. "Xianggang bowuguan koushu lishi jihua jianjie, 1987–89 (Oral History Project by Hong Kong Museum of History, 1987–89)." *Wenshi Tungxun (Bulletin on Chinese and Chinese History Studies)* (Hong Kong), 1994, no.1, pp. 59–62.

To, Kwai-mui. 1984. *Government's Role in the Development of Recreation and Culture in Hong Kong* (MA thesis). Hong Kong: University of Hong Kong.

Tsang, Donald. 2006. "Big Market, Small Government." Press Release of the Chief Executive Office of the Hong Kong Government. September 19, 2006. Online at: http://www.news.gov.hk/en/category/ontherecord/060919/html/ ;060919en11001.htm.

Turner, Mathew. 1995. "Hong Kong Sixties/Nineties: Dissolving the People." In *Hong Kong Sixties: Designing Identity*, eds. Mathew Turner and Irene Ngan. Hong Kong: Hong Kong Arts Centre.

Turner, Mattew Turner and Irene Ngan, eds. 1995. *Hong Kong Sixties: Designing Identity*. Hong Kong: Hong Kong Arts Centre.

Tyler, Patrick E. 1997. "At Tiananmen Square, Exuberance Is Reined In." *New York Times*, July 1, 1997, A8.

United Nations Conference on Trade and Development. 1995–2002. *World Investment Report*, New York: United Nations.

United States Department of State. 1887–1888. *The Executive Documents of the House of Representatives for the First Session of the Fiftieth Congress. 1887–'88*. Washington, D.C.: U.S. Government Printing Office. Online at http://digital.library.wisc.edu/1711.dl/FRUS.FRUS1887–88. Accessed April 30, 2008.

Universal News Agency. 1969. *Festival of Hong Kong Commemoration Magazine 1969*. Hong Kong: Universal News Agency.

Urban Services Department. 1997. *The Five-Year Plan of the Provisional Urban Council's Museums Select Committee (Consultation Paper)*, September 1997. Hong Kong: Urban Services Department.

Virilio, Paul. 2005. *Negative Horizon: A Essay in Dromoscopy*. London: Continuum.

——. 2000. "Indirect Light." In *Paul Virilio: From Modernism to Hypermodernism and Beyond*, ed. John Armitage. London: SAGE.

——. 1991. *The Aesthetics of Disappearance*. translation Philip Beitchman. New York: Semiotext(e).

——. 1991. "Perspectives of Real Time." In *Metropolis: International Art Exhibition Berlin 1991*, eds. Christos M. Joachimides and Norman Rosenthal. New York: Rizzoli, 1991.

Virno, Paolo. 2004. *A Grammar of the Multitude: For an Analysis of Contemporary Forms of Life*, translation Isabella Bertoletti, James Cascaito and Andrea Casson. New York: Semiotext[e].

Wallerstein, Immanuel. 2002. "New Revolts Against the System." *New Left Review*, Vol. 18 (November–December 2002).

Wang, Hui. 2006. "Depoliticized Politics, From East to West." *New Left Review*, Vol. 41 (September–October 2006).

Wang, Jing. 2008. *Brand New China: Advertising, Media, and Commercial Culture*. Cambridge, MA: Harvard University Press.

Wang Mingzhen. 1996. "Beijing Tushuguan fen'guan de Yuanming Yuan yiwu (Remains from Yuanming Yuan at a Branch of the Beijing Library). In *Yandu shuogu (Old Stories of Beijing)*, ed. Hu Yuyuan. Beijing: Beijing Yanshan Chubanshe.

Wang Peigeng. 1999. "What on Earth Can Advertising Do?" (in Chinese), *Modern Advertising*. Beijing, No. 6, 1999, 16–17.

Wang Tieya, ed. 1957. *Zhongwai jiuyue zhang hui bian (Collections of the Sino-foreign Treaties)* (Vol. 1) Beijing: Shenghuo, Dushu, Xinzhi Shanlian Shudian.

Wang, Xiaoying. 2000. "Hong Kong, China, and the Question of Postcoloniality." In *Postmodernism & China*, eds. Arif Dirlik and Xudong Zhang. Durham, NC: Duke University Press.

Wang Zhili. 1992. "Yuanming Yuan yu Yuanming Yuan yizhi (Yuanming Yuan and the Ruins of Yuanming Yuan)." In *Yuanming Yuan xueshu lunwenji*, ed. Zhongguo Yuanming Yuan Xuehui. Beijing: Zhongguo Jiangsu Gongye Chubanshe.

Watson, James and Rubie Watson. 1997. "From Hall of Worship to Tourist Center: An Ancestor Hall in Hong Kong's New Territories." *Cultural Survival Quarterly* Vol. 21, no. 1, 1997, 33–35.

Weber, Max. 1964. *The Theory of Social and Economic Organization*, translation A. M. Henderson and Talcott Parsons. New York: Free Press. (Originally published 1947.)

——. 1958. *The Protestant Ethic and the Spirit of Capitalism*, translation Talcott Parsons. New York: Charles Scribner's Sons.

Welsh, Frank. 1997. *A History of Hong Kong*. London: Harper Collins.

——. 1993. *A Borrowed Place: The History of Hong Kong*. New York: Kodansha International.

Wenhuabu Wenwuju. 1985. *Zhongguo bowuguanxue gailun (Introduction to Chinese Museology)*. Beijing: Wenwu Chubanshe.

Wesley-Smith, Peter. 1980. *Unequal Treaty 1898–1997: China, Great Britain and Hong Kong's New Territories*. Hong Kong: Oxford University Press.

Wilkes, Stephen. 2000. "The Guts of Times Square." *New York Times Magazine*. October 22, 2000, 71.

Williams, Raymond. 1976. *Keywords: A Vocabulary of Culture and Society*. Oxford: Oxford University Press.

Williams, Tony. 2000. "Under 'Western Eyes': The Personal Odyssey of Huang Fei-Hong in *Once upon a Time in China*." *Cinema Journal* 40, No.1, Fall 2000, 3–24.

Wiltshire, Trea. 1991. *Old Hong Kong*. Hong Kong: FormAsia.

Wong, Wang-chi, Li Siu-leung and Chan Ching-kiu Stephen. 1997. *Fouxiang Xianggang: lishi, wenhua, weilai (Hong Kong Un-Imagined: History, Culture and the Future)*. Taipei: Rye Field.

Wong, Young-Tsu. 2001. *A Paradise Lost: The Imperial Garden Yuanming Yuan*. Honolulu: University of Hawaii Press.

Wood, David. 1989. *The Deconstruction of Time*. Evanston, IL: Northwestern University Press.

Wu, Hung. 1997. "The Hong Kong Clock: Public Time-Telling and Political Time/Space." *Public Cultusre* 9, 3 (Spring 1997), 329–354.

——. 1991. "Tiananmen Square: A Political History of Monuments." *Representations* 35, Summer 1991.

Wu Lijuan. 1997. " 'Qinchi' pinpai jingying linian sumiao (A Sketch of the Operational Logic of the 'Qinchi' Brand)." *Zhongguo mingpai (China Brand-names)*, 1997, no. 2, p. 34.

Wu Yifeng. 2006. *Makesizhuyi jingjixue he xinziyouzheyi jingjixue (Marxist Economics and Neoliberal Economics)*. Beijing: Zhongguo Jingjin Chubanshe.

Wu Yifeng, Ding Bing, and Li Zhong (eds.). 2005. *Jingji Quanjiuhua yu xinziyouzuyi sichao (Economic Globalization and Neoliberal Theories)*. Beijing: Zhongguo Jingji Chubanshe.

——. 2004. *Kaifangxia de hongguan jingji yu qiye lilun yanjiu (Macro Economy under Opening and Company Studies)*. Beijing: Zhongguo Jingji Chubanshe.

Wu Zhong. 2008. " 'Red Capitalists' Unravel the Party Line." *Asia Times Online*, October 17, 2008. Electronic document: http://www.atimes.com/atimes/China/JJ17Ad01.html. Accessed December 2009.

Xi Xi. 1996. *Fei Zhan (Flying Carpet: A Tale of Fertilla)*. Hong Kong: Sue Yeh.

Xie Jin. 1997. *The Opium War*. DVD. Released by Star Trere Holdings Ltd, 2002.

Xinhua News. 2006. "Hu Jintao chanshi huxie shehui jibeng tezheng (Hu Jintao Elaborates the Basic Characteristics of Harmonious Society)." *Harbin ribao*, February 20, 2005. Online at: http://www.sina.com.cn. Accessed March 6, 2006.

Yan Fan. 1996. "Quanmian jianzheng xianggang lishi xianzhuang (Complete Witness to Hong Kong's Past and Present)." *Wen Hui Bao* (Hong Kong), June 29, 1996.

Yang, Lien-sheng. 1955. "Schedules of Work and Rest in Imperial China." *Harvard Journal of Asiatic Studies*, Vol. 18, No. 3/4, 1955.

Ye Junzhi. 2003. "Woguo bowuguan wenhua chanye kaifa wenti (Problems of Developing the Culture Industry in China's Museums)." *Zhongguo bowuguan (Chinese Museum)*, no. 4.

Ye Tingfang. 1995. "Yuanming Yuan yizhi qian de tanxi (A Sigh in Front of the Ruins of Yuanming Yuan)." *Zhongguo wenwu bao (China's Cultural Relics)* (weekly newspaper published Beijing), November 12, 1995.

Yeung, Henry Wai-chung. 1998. *Transnational Corporations and Business Networks: Hong Kong Firms in the ASEAN Region*. London: Routledge.

Yoshimi, Shunya. 2006. "Consuming America, Producing Japan." In *The Ambivalent Consumer: Questioning Consumption in East Asia And the West*, eds. Sheldon Garon and Patricia L. Maclachlan. Ithaca, NY: Cornell University Press.

Young, John D. 1994. "The Building Years: Maintaining a China-Hong Kong- Britain Equilibrium, 1950–71." In *Precarious Balance: Hong Kong Between China and Britain, 1842–1992*, ed. Ming K. Chan. Hong Kong: M.E. Sharpe, Inc.

Yu Wenlie. 2005. " 'Beijing gongshi' yu siyouhua 'yiyi' ('Beijing Consensus' and Privatization 'Alternative Discussion')." In *Jingji Quanjiuhua yu xinziyouzuyi sichao (Economic Globalization and Neoliberal Theories)*, eds. Wu Yifeng, Ding Bing, and Li Zhong. Beijing: Zhongguo Jingji Chubanshe.

——. 2004. "Jingji lujing de zhexue sikao (A Philosophical Thinking on the Direction of the Economy)." In *Kaifangxia de hongguan jingji yu qiye lilun yanjiu (Macro Economy under Opening and Company Studies)*, eds. Wu Yifeng, Ding Bing, and Li Zhong. Beijing: Zhongguo Jingjin Chubanshe.

Zakaria, Fareed. 2008 *The Post-American World*. New York: W.W. Norton & Company.

Zeitlin, Judith T. 2003. "Disappearing Verses: Writing on Walls and Anxieties of Loss." In *Writing and Materiality in China: Essays in Honor of Patrick Hanan*, eds.

Judith T. Zeitlin and Lydia H. Liu. Cambridge, MA: Asia Center, Harvard University.

Zhang, Enyin. 1994. *Yuanming Yuan yuanshi jieshao (An Introduction to the History of Yuanming Yuan)*. Beijing: Yuanming Yuan Guanlichu.

Zhang, Li and Aihwa Ong. 2008. *Privatizing China: Socialism from Afar*. Ithaca, NY: Cornell University Press.

Zhang Peili. 2007. "Chinese Artists in a Chinese Spectacle." Paper presented at the international symposium on "China on Display: Past and Present Practices of Selecting, Exhibiting and Viewing Chinese Visual and Material Culture," Leiden University, December 6–8, 2007.

Zhang Yan. 1995. *Tutengzhi yu yuanshi wenhua (Totemism and the Primitive Culture)*. Shanghai: Shanghai Wenyi Chubanshe.

Zhao Guanghua. 1992. "Yuanming Yuan 'yizhi gongyuan' de beiju meixue yuanzhe he zhengxiu de guodu xingshi (The Aesthetic Principle of Tragedy at the 'Ruins Park' of Yuanming Yuan and Its Transitional Form in Restoration)." In *Yuanming Yuan xueshu lunwenji (A Collection of Essays on Yuanming Yuan)*, Volume 5, ed. Zhongguo Yuanming Yuan xuehui. Beijing: Zhongguo Jianzhu Gongye Chubanshe.

Zhao, Yuezhi. 2008. *Communication in China: Political Economy, Power, and Conflict*. Lanham, CO: Rowman & Littlefield.

——. 2002. "The Rich, the Laid-off, and the Criminal in Tabloid Tales: Read All about It!" In *Popular Culture: Unofficial Culture in a Globalizing Society*, eds. Perry Link, Richard P. Madsen, and Paul G. Pickowicz. Lanham, CO: Rowman & Littlefield.

——. 1998. *Media, Market, and Democracy in China: Between the Party Line and the Bottom Line*. Champaign, IL: University of Illinois Press.

Zhonggong Zhongyang Zuzhibu Ganbu Jiaoyuju *et al.* 1995. *Xianggang shichang jingji jiejian yu shikao (Thoughts on Learning from Hong Kong's Market Economy)*. Beijing: Zhongguo Jingji Chubanshe and Jingji Daobaoshe.

Zhou Enlai. 1984. "Guanyu Xianggang wenti (Regarding the Hong Kong Question)." In *Zhou Enlai tongyi zhanxian wenxuan (Zhou Enlai's Articles on the United Front)*. Beijing: Renmin Chubanshe.

Zizek, Slavoj. 2007. "China's Valley of Tears." Published on December 3, 2007. Online at: http://www.inthesetimes.com/article/3425/chinas_valley_of_tears. Accessed December 22, 2007.

——. 1997. "Multiculturalism, Or, the Cultural Logic of Multinational Capitalism" *New Left Review*, No. 225 (September/October 1997), pp. 28–51.

Index